Diversity, Culture and Counselling

A Canadian Perspective

Honoré France
María del Carmen Rodríguez
Geoffrey Hett

DETSELIG
ENTERPRISES LTD

Diversity, Culture and Counselling

© 2004 Detselig Enterprises Ltd.

National Library of Canada Cataloguing in Publication Data

Diversity, culture and counselling : a Canadian perspective / Honoré France, Maria del Carmen Rodriguez and Geoffrey Hett, editors.

ISBN 1-55059-260-2

1. Minority students -- Counseling of -- Canada. 2. Educational counseling -- Canada. 3. Cross-cultural counseling -- Canada. I. France, Honoré II. Rodriguez, Maria del Carmen III. Hett, Geoffrey

LB1027.5.D58 2004   371.4'089'00971   C2004-900285-6

DETSELIG
ENTERPRISES LTD

210-1220 Kensington Rd. N.W., Calgary, AB T2N 3P5

Telephone: (403) 283-0900/Fax: (403) 283-6947

E-mail: temeron@telusplanet.net

www.temerondetselig.com

We acknowledge the financial support of the Government of Canada through the Book Publishing Industry Development Program (BPIDP) for our publishing activities.

We also acknowledge the support of the Alberta Foundation for the Arts for our publishing program.

COMMITTED TO THE DEVELOPMENT OF CULTURE AND THE ARTS

ISBN 1-55059-260-2

SAN 115-0324

Printed in Canada

Contents

PART III: Application and Practical Approaches

Preface

Our rationale for developing this book was to bring Canadian content to our course on diversity, culture and counselling. For years, most students taking courses at Canadian universities have had to use American textbooks in an area where much of the materials were mostly irrelevant from a Canadian perspective. Also, it was important for us to give voice to the people multicultural counsellors work with – the various cultural groups that make up Canadian society. Therefore, we have a myriad of professional counsellors, from those of African-Canadian descent talking about counselling in their communities to counsellors who are Muslim and Sihk talking about dealing with specific aspects of counselling related to their faiths. In addition, because we have included chapters on various culturally related approaches, we have First Nations people talking about the use of traditional helping and healing methods as well as counsellors who advocate the use of nature to assist in the helping relationship. For us, such scope is one of the best features of this book, giving it more authenticity than it mightotherwise have.

Finally, because we believe in diversity and the importance of culture, we believe that multicultural counselling offers an approach to working with people from different ethnic, racial, religious backgrounds and sexual orientations, thus moving the profession to another dimension of effectiveness where racism and prejudice are major areas of concern in every society that need to be addressed. Understanding the causes and costs of stereotypes and biases is vital if counsellors are to bridge the ethnic and racial divide. There are important factors that can help or hinder effective counselling across cultures and differences; consequently, knowing how to enhance communication becomes not only vital but also necessary. Therefore, being secure in one's own identity, culturally and racially, can only help to ensure that people accept and respect individual and collective differences. Multicultural-oriented counsellors must remember that, as helpers, they are not just working with individuals but with groups of people with collective orientations.

We also recognized that as we completed each of the chapters that there was more we would have liked to say or include, but alas, we had to let go of our desire to be totally complete or perfect and send our manuscript to the publisher. We are grateful to Detselig Enterprises Ltd. for accepting our idea and promoting the book. We want to always remind ourselves of the words of Geronimo: "let us put our heads together and do what is best for our children...."

M. Honoré France, María del Carmen Rodríguez, Geoffrey Hett

January 15, 2004

Part I
Issues in Diversity, Culture and Counselling

A true multicultural society includes all ethnic and racial groups, including the original founders of the Canadian state – English and French immigrants. While these two formally dominant groups have made way for new groups of immigrants, such as the growing population of Asian Canadians, the English and French languages will continue to dominate. The term multiculturalism was first introduced to the Canadian public in 1971 by Prime Minister Pierre Trudeau, but did not become government policy until the mid-80s. The original idea behind the multicultural policy was to deal with the tensions between the English and French, which resulted in a number of strategies to unite these two communities, while at the same time changing the "racist" immigration policy. However, the term multicultural still has the stigma of political policy that is exclusive and for some people is unacceptable (e.g., First Nations). However, in the counselling literature, the word multicultural has been adopted to refer to culturally sensitive counselling. We have used this term, although we are really talking about how diversity, culture and counselling merge. Thus in using this word, multicultural, we include all people, not only visible minorities but the majority groups too. Therefore, multicultural is used to address the issue of culture, oppression and a host of other factors that influence the counselling process.

The focus of the chapters in Part I of this book is on celebrating cultural differences, exploring worldviews and developing culturally sensitive counselling skills. As counsellors, we believe in the need to embrace and encourage cultural diversity as being enriching and protective. As a human condition, people around the world and most importantly, in a society like Canada, possess the tendency to be distrustful of people who are different. However, the truth is that, regardless of one's language, race or culture, communities are interdependent. We profoundly believe that when a community discriminates and marginalizes people for being different, instability occurs and everyone suffers. The changing trends in Canadian immigration are having a major impact on how counselling services are offered. The multicultural reality in Canada is changing and necessitates a shift from the dominant Eurocentric counselling theories and practice that favor the white, middle class population to an approach that emphasizes diversity and a new world perspective. As counsellors, we need to recognize the importance of language and communication in counselling diverse groups of people. We believe that multicultural experiences can enhance a counsellor's personal growth and overall communication skills. When working with diverse groups our behavior and language greatly influence the communication process and counselling outcome. Further, we live in a time that warns us that our survival may depend on our ability to communicate effectively on a multicultural level. Counsellors are in a unique position to model the behavior and language that is culturally sensitive and help challenge the issues of discrimination and racism as part of counselling practice. Frequent contact with different cultures is particularly important in achieving this end.

The cornerstone of counselling with diverse clients is an understanding of worldview and how it relates to developing multicultural skills. No matter where one lives in the world, we modify our perception of the world by understanding, experiencing and making meaning of an array of customs dissimilar to our own, unique in their own right and indispensable while interacting with others in a culturally diverse setting. This need to modify our worldview goes beyond cultural legacies (i.e., folklore, customs, traditions and rituals) allowing us to pursue an understanding of the value, beliefs, attitudes and affective perceptions that constitute the life of a population and its members. In addition to these aspects, normative standards of subsistence, communication, technology and political ideas also come to form part of our new worldview.

As Canada has evolved, immigration has affected the population of the country, making it one of the most diverse in the world. The impact of this shift in immigration is significant for counsellors. The multicultural reality of Canadian society is a reality that will challenge counsellors in a time when universities are slow in providing multicultural training for the helping professions. As most Canadian counselling theories and practices originate from European models, counsellors are at a disadvantage when providing services to people who hold a different worldview. We encourage counsellors to seek out experiences, training and competencies necessary to support people who hold different worldviews and cultural values. Gaining multicultural counselling skills is not only necessary, but to do so is the only ethical way to proceed if we are to move beyond a Eurocentric position and empower all of our clients regardless of their culture, race, sexual orientation and religious beliefs.

Chapter 1
Counselling Across Cultures:
Identity, Race and Communication

M. Honoré France

"How have Torontonians gone from around 3% visible minorities in the early 1960s to more than 50% now without any major disruption, while the people of Los Angeles, experiencing about the same degree of change over the same period, felt the need to burn down parts of their city not once but twice?" Gwynne Dyer (2001, p. 45).

Nega Mezlekia's (2000) novel *Notes from the Hyena's Belly*, which won the Governor General's Literary Award, begins with the metaphor of a donkey and a hyena. In this story, a lion, leopard, hyena and donkey come together to discuss why their land is in such poor state. Each shares that the responsibility of the turmoil is because of the sin that has displeased God. Each of the animals, except the donkey, tell the story of attacking another animal and eating it, but each are told that eating an animal is their nature, so it is not wrong. When it is the donkey's turn, he relates that while his human master was busy talking with another man, he, the donkey, went off the trail and ate some grass. The other animals become enraged and tell the donkey that he is the one who has caused the problems by going off the path and eating the grass, so they attack the donkey, kill him and eat him. Mezlekia goes on to say that "we children lived like the donkey, careful not to wander off the beaten trail and end up in the hyena's belly" (p. 7).

Moving away from one's routines and traditions has a price; dangers are always present and change is a constant. There is a subtle warning too in the metaphor: being different, like the "donkey", can be dangerous. Yet Mezlekia's metaphor is very apt as a warning not to take risks, while at the same time showing that undertaking new challenges is a part of being human. So despite all the "best laid" plans, there are dangers in the world and "down the street." The challenge for counsellors in the world since the terrorist bombings on New York City and the "fallout" from the war in Iraq is that new tension and new alliances abound. For counsellors, these challenges are working with the new reality of a multicultural, multiethnic and multilingual society that is Canada today.

The rapid changes need to be addressed in a realistic, yet positive manner in which differences are not homogenized, but celebrated because diversity is beautiful and strengthening. Being accepting and open to differences is often elusive. But why is this so? According to Baron, Kerr and Miller (1992) it is "…the human tendency to disparage, distrust and dislike groups other than our own" (p. 134). One of the aspects about societies in general is how people exclude others who are different. In fact, it is not uncommon for people from the majority cultural and racial group to see someone different as being a stranger in their midst. Diller (1999) relates the story of someone of Asian extraction whose family has been living in North America for over a hundred years being taken as a foreign visitor because the country is seen as a country of European immigrants. People who are different "…are deeply disturbed by their second-class citizenry" (Diller, 1999, p. 26). In Canada, people of color who are not from the original founders of the Canadian state are called visible minorities, including the original inhabitants – First Nations people. It is a distinctive Canadian term that is often used as a substitute for racial minorities, who are "…non-white, with physical characteristics that distinguish them from Canada's mainstream" (Fleras & Elliot, 1991, p. 319).

The changing nature of society makes the argument for or against multiculturalism moot, but if society is to avoid cultural and racial misunderstanding, then the institutions of society need to adapt to the new realities. For counsellors, this may mean adopting a frame of reference in which counselling can be described as a "working alliance." In other words, the counsellor creates a common ground with clients by establishing an avenue to resolution rather than first building on the idea of a trusting relationship. Because of one's race or ethnic background, trust may not exist nor can it be established in the traditional manner that theoreticians like Carl Rogers suggested. So, how does one establish a trusting relationship? Going back to the idea of a working alliance, counsellors and clients work in a collaborative way to accomplish clients' goals. Furthermore, consider that perhaps all counselling is multicultural in one way or another, because it always deals with a variety of variables that are sometimes contradictory from situation to situation. Sciarra (1999) provides the following example: "the personalismo of the Latino culture can require a less formal and more affective counselor, whereas these same counselor characteristics may be alienating to some Asian clients" (p. 10). Therefore adapting the process to suit the situation is fundamental because there will always be cultural differences between clients and counsellors.

Rationale for Diversity and Multicultural Counselling

The rationale for multicultural counselling is in part the growing multicultural factor in everyday life and the increasing smaller world brought about by more efficient communication and transportation systems. In early 2003, as the war in Iraq began, the differences in spiritual practices between the Christians and Muslims and between the developed and non-developed world highlight the cultural differences that divide people. Thus waging war when differences are greater becomes easier and more acceptable. In counselling, the challenge is to understand the differences and enhance communication across cultures. More importantly, cultural differences are not just between one group of people in the West and another group in the Middle East, but within the borders of Canada. Therefore, Canadians have no choice but to face the challenge of diversity issues and the changing mosaic of the Canadian nation.

Do societies that have a variety of ethnic backgrounds experience more ethnic conflict than those that are more homogeneous? Certainly; cultural differences in a counselling group are usually an issue in how the members communicate with each other. Even in the recent political environment of "9-11", which has dominated television news, the issues of culture and religious values have been important factors in how terrorism and the invasion of Iraq have been dealt with in the media and everyday life. North American society cannot close its eyes to the issue of culture, race and language. Finally, in a world where most people are not Westerners, Caucasian or Christian and in a world that is growing smaller, to become multicultural is not only enriching, but also protective. All people must be aware that society, as a community, has the power to destroy our world through nuclear war and pollution. War has its genesis in society's disrespect for people who are different. People not only have to learn how to control their willingness to control those who have different customs and views, but also learn how to live in harmony with others and the environment.

Regardless of one's language, race or culture, every community is interdependent with another. Therefore, when society discriminates, marginalizes and ostracizes a person or people because they are different, then everyone suffers. Society has come a long way in being more accepting of different people, yet it has a long way to go in creating a society that respects diversity. According to Pedersen (1994), when cultural aspects are added to the counselling process, the following points have to be considered in order to be sensitive to different people:

1. A tolerance for logical inconsistency and paradox suggests a subjective definition of knowledge to supplement the more familiar rules of objective, rational logic;

2. The primary importance of relationships and collectivism contrasts with the more familiar bias toward individualism;

3. The implicit or explicit differentiation between modernization and westernization ignores the possibility that other cultures may have good solutions to our problems;

4. The implicit assumption that change and progress are good is challenged by clients having to deal with change as both good and bad at the same time;

5. The metaphor of a natural ecological setting reminds us of the many unknown and perhaps unknowable mysteries of relationship among people and their environments;

6. The absolute categories of problem and solution and success and failure are brought into question as inadequate;

7. The need to apply familiar counselling concepts to the less familiar multicultural settings is emphasized;

8. The need for new conceptual and methodological approaches to deal with the complexities of culture is apparent; and

9. The need for a grounded theory of multicultural counselling is essential to all counsellors and is not an exotic or specialized perspective (p. 23).

The world is changing very swiftly, and ethnic boundaries are changing. In the past, European cultural groups comprised the vast majority of new immigrants in North America, whereas today Asian groups top the list. According to the Canadian Census Bureau (2001), out of the total immigrant population during the 1990s, Asians comprise 58%; 20% were born in Europe; 11% in the Caribbean and Central and South America; 8% in Africa; and 3% in the United States. In addition, the aboriginal population increased by 3.4% during the period between 1996 and 2001. If current trends continue, Aboriginal people "may well be heading to majority status in many cities within the next 25 to 50 years" from Saskatchewan to northwestern Ontario (Dyer, 2001, p. 49). It has also been estimated by the Census Bureau that by the year 2030, the province of British Columbia's majority population will be non-white. Already many urban areas of Canada are largely comprised of racial minorities. However, what is making a remarkable impact is the large number of immigrants settling in North American cities. This trend can already be seen in cities like Vancouver, Toronto and Montreal where more than 70% of immigrants settled. The multicultural reality is evident in North American schools where large numbers of students do not come from the "founding" ethnic groups. However, it goes much deeper than accommodating the new multicultural fact, but necessitates changing the structures of our schools that were initially designed for a homogeneous population. The multicultural reality in effect has changed the nature of a Eurocentric counselling theory and practice that fits a homogeneous population to a system that emphasizes diversity and a world perspective. Lorde (cited in Siccone, 1995) said "…it is a waste of time hating a mirror or its reflection instead of stopping the hand that makes glass with distortions" (p. xvi).

The Cost of Racism

It is hard to understand a culture that justifies the killing of millions in past wars and is at this very moment preparing bombs to kill even greater numbers. It is hard for me to understand a culture that spends more on wars and weapons to kill, than it does on education and welfare to help and develop. It is hard for me to understand a culture that not only hates and fights his brothers but also even attacks nature and abuses her (George, 1994, p. 38).

The pain and sorrow in Chief Dan George's words in describing the cultural misunderstandings between First Nations people and "white" people typifies like nothing else the nature of prejudice and racism. Diller (1999) suggests that helpers need to understand important elements of racism in order to help people work together in a multicultural society. First, racism is a universal phenomenon that exists in all societies around the world among all races. Secondly, most people are uncomfortable talking about racism and even deny that it exists. There is a difference between prejudice and racism. Prejudice is an unfair and negative belief about the inferiority of a group of people, which is often based of faulty knowledge and a generalized view of others who are different. While racism "…involves the total social structure where one group has conferred advantage through institutional polices…it is a social construction based on sociopolitical attitudes that demean specific racial characteristics" (Robinson & Howard-Hamilton, 2000; p. 58). It is not a natural response, but a learned one from societal norms; observations from parents, friends and neighbors. Not surprisingly, prejudice does not result from constant negative experience with someone who is different, but through occasional contacts and reinforcers, such as a negative experience in a bar or an ethnic joke. "In Canada, minorities have been subjected to three forms of discrimination: individual racism, institutional racism and cultural racism" (Ramcharan in Alladdin, 1996, p. 12). The most obvious forms of individual racism are expressions that one race is superior to another, while institutional racism is conformed by established practices that perpetuate inequities and cultural racism is the belief of the inferiority of one culture over another. The government of Canada established the residential school system in order to "help" aboriginals assimilate into majority society; however, the result was very different and demonstrates the cost of racism on individuals and communities:

> *Social maladjustment, abuse of self and others and family breakdown are some of the symptoms prevalent among First Nation "baby boomers". The "graduates" of the "St. Anne's Residential School" era are now trying and often failing to come to grips with life as adults after being raised as children in an atmosphere of fear, loneliness and loathing. Fear of caretakers. Loneliness, knowing that elders and family were far away. Loathing from learning to hate oneself, because of repeated physical, verbal or sexual abuse suffered at the hands of various adult caretakers. This is only a small part of the story (Milloy, 2001, pp. 295-96).*

The reason for discriminating against others is not really complex. Consider that when people are faced with evidence of prejudice, they tend to reject it; "I'm not prejudiced against Indians, but most of them just want to live on government assistance." There is of course some cognitive dissonance going on, because it is difficult to admit. It is easy for a society to judge situations in other nations as racist or oppressive, such as Apartheid in South Africa or the practices of the Israeli occupation forces on the West Bank. Some might respond and say "It's their fault that their culture has disintegrated." That is not an uncommon response, but it is a curious one, because it blames the victim for being victimized. Aboriginals are penalized for being culturally different, because of a system that neither allowed them citizenship nor allowed them to practice their language and culture. Chief Dan George (de Montigny, 1972) said:

> *Do you know what it is like to have your race belittled...? You don't know for you have never*

tasted its bitterness...It is like not caring about tomorrow for what does tomorrow matter? It is having a reserve that looks like a junk yard because the beauty in the soul is dead...Why should the soul express an external beauty that does not match it? It is like getting drunk for a few brief moments, an escape from the ugly reality and feeling a sense of importance. It is most of all like awaking next morning to the guilt of betrayal. For the alcohol did not fill the emptiness but only dug it deeper (pp. 162-163).

The dehumanization of "enemies" can clearly be observed when examining the emotional demonstrations of Arabs shouting "Down with America" or the indifference of American leaders to the welfare of civilians during the first and second Gulf wars. In the war against Iraq, American President George W. Bush constantly compared the Iraqi President, Saddam Hussein, with Stalin and other despots, ignoring the fact that millions of people in the Middle East regarded him as a hero, a symbol of defiance, for standing up against the firepower of the U.S. military. In war, the "enemy" has to be dehumanized in order to sustain hate and it occurs in all wars. Such an image certainly helps to alleviate any guilt one nation may feel for waging war against another. In the same way, accepting stereotypes about a people, such as voiced by Chief Dan George, can justify actions such as war, colonization and the establishment of residential schools. These rationalizations are really a façade for an attitude that which allows one to treat the in-group different than the out-group. Conversely, co-operative activities can reduce racial tension if both work in a "strategic alliance." According to Baron, Kerr and Miller (1992) "cooperation may break down group boundary lines (the "us versus them" mentality) to some degree" (p. 150).

Ethnic stereotypes create a problem when they are inaccurate and produce a negative evaluation of other people. In a multicultural society, this brings a sense of exclusiveness that can result in a strong feeling of superiority. Interestingly, the research evidence suggests that individuals need to maintain a sense of group distinctiveness (Berry, Poortinga, Segall and Dasen, 2002). Sometimes people refer to this as "group pride," but why does pride hinge on a feeling of superiority? Pride in doing things well or in a feeling of solidarity with one's ethnic group is beneficial, but when it evolves into superiority it is destructive. There also seems to be a relationship between people who have a disposition towards authoritarian and prejudicial attitudes. People who seem to be more prone to prejudice are overly submissive, feel inadequate or are overly suspicious. While these examples demonstrate how racism is used to deprive foreigners of their human qualities, the process is the same in sexism, ageism, religious bigotry and homophobia. The kind of prejudice experienced by ethnic and racial minorities, intentional or unintentional, is the essence of the challenge of an open society. The scope of the issue is associated with integrating the culturally different into society in which "younger Canadians going to school feel that a great deal of racism exists in Canada (Decima Report in Alladin, 1996, p. 173). These results are not comforting, but the insidious aspect of racism is the manner in which it is reinforced by society's institutions. In addition, people ought to be cognizant of the effect of prejudice on others.

The Causes of Conflict and Prejudice

There has been a good deal of research examining what creates conflict and gives birth to prejudice. Is it a part of the human experience? Are people born feeling prejudice? Consider that when people compete for scarce resources, they will form groups to help them get ahead. Often, these groups are based on similarities within the group, which become the "in-group." Those who are different, become the "out-group." Differences could be based on a number of factors including group norms, language, race, religion or even goals. On a smaller scale, even people who are very similar, but who have different goals become frustrated with others whose goals are different. However, according to Baron, Kerr and Miller (1992), people become less aggressive and thus, more cooperative, reducing prejudice, if goals are mutual. In fact, friendships develop and differences of color or race are minimized when goals are mutual. Generally, people from one group are more generous or overcompensate for those in their group, while conversely, undercompensate for those from another group. In other words, people from one cultural group will be more forgiving for those in their group, while being less forgiving for those from another group. For some reason, there is a tendency to exaggerate similarities within group, while exaggerating differences with other groups. People react to each other based on their group membership. Since they do not know the other people, viewing the others as "faceless" and interchangeable is common. It is easy to not see the others in the same light as themselves and so differences become exaggerated (e.g., they don't value human life).

Is it human nature to try and simplify the environment, despite the fact that most day-to-day interactions among people are positive? A good question. One bias is that members of one group will "naturally" see themselves as acting responsibly, but see the other group and its members as being irresponsible. That is, according to Baron, Kerr and Miller (1992), a factor of the human experience. Also, for whatever reason, there is a tendency to promote negative views about others who are distinct and different. Thus, the bias is reinforced with each "negative" experience one has. In the end, one's attitude becomes more rigid, ideological and becomes part of one's cultural norm. This means, for example, that if one has attitudes that are negative towards the police, one will see examples that reinforce this bias more often than if one didn't have the bias. There is also the "reciprocity" rule or the "tit for tat" idea, in which if one "wrong" is done, one retaliates, causing a series of behaviors that reinforce one's beliefs. Social comparison is also a factor in creating a sense of anger, prejudice and aggression. And finally, if there is a "triggering" event, people react on the basis of emotion and do something that has a chain of events that can last for decades. Consider the Kosovo situation in which Serbs are fighting Albanians. Historical "wrongs" were enmeshed within the differing groups' attitudes about each other. The Turkish invasion during the 16th century is played out in the 21st century. People adapted to these attitudes and made them part of their behavior, thus creating another myth that reinforces prejudice.

Cultural Influences

Culture is a human necessity, a way of life, because it is the way people establish and maintain a relationship with their environment. As people of understanding interact with those who are culturally different, they must explore the socialization forces that affect behavior, values and language. For example, notice the dichotomy between the ways of understanding the relationship of people with nature: control and good/bad versus harmony and good. The stress of control over nature produces a feeling of seeing other people in terms of good and bad, which corresponds exactly with how humanity ought to be treated. If people are not good or consistent with societal norms, then they need to be controlled. Taken one step further, people with this attitude also have to control the urges they feel within themselves. Even in a relatively homogeneous population, there are cultural differences that are easier to be aware of in others than in self. According to many social scientists, culture is both a critical aspect of a person's lifestyle and an essential element of human behavior. While the clothes people wear and the attitudes they voice may reflect the dominant culture they are in, it is their cultural background that shapes their thinking and feelings, such as reflected in the analogy, "blood is thicker than water." There are strong indicators that cultural conditioning reflects how people communicate with others (Pedersen, Draguns, Lonner, & Trimble, 2002).

The biological force is the most universal, because no matter who people are or where they are from, they are human beings. Some biological differences include age, shape, size, color and gender. With the exception of a few cases, these differences are not going to change nor can they be manipulated. In all societies these biological differences have reflected attitudes relating to behavior and how people will interact with others. For example, someone large is viewed as powerful and possibly aggressive; as a result, more deference is shown towards that person. A big and muscular person may be seen as a brute, or a lean and slight person as effeminate, or someone with rough features as unrefined. The cultural norms that dictate reactions to biological differences are infinite, with each group having its own interpretation about the meaning of physical and biological characteristics; for example, plumpness is healthy in some groups.

All cultures are affected psychologically by various influences on the group. People in the group are continuously subjected to pressures to conform to the norms of the group. In this respect the personality to a large extent is formed through these group norms. The family, as a primary socializing agent, is responsible for the basic values that people exhibit. This is particularly true in Asian cultural values of respect for authority, traditions and learning

(France, 2001). In addition, exposure to significant others, relatives, friends, teachers and peers enhances the repertoire for the inculcation of the social mores and behaviors of the entire culture. This is obvious when a comparison is made between the ways people feel, think and act in different cultures. For example, Berry, Poortinga, Segall and Dasen (2002) postulate that people from different places in the world have a different construct of self:

> *The Western Concept of Self is of an individual who is separate, autonomous and atomized (made up of a set of discrete traits, abilities, values and motives, seeking separateness and independence from others). In contrast, in Eastern cultures relatedness, connectedness and interdependence are sought, rooted in a concept of the self not as a discrete entity, but as inherently linked to others. The person is only made "whole" when situated in his or her place in a social unit (p. 101).*

Behavior may also be affected by ideology or the characteristic manner of thinking (e.g., assertions, theories or aims). The ideological foundation of an individual's culture will, to a large degree, have impact on their behavior. It is from such foundations that people derive religious, social and political beliefs that direct and govern their behavior. Being born in a certain culture occasions the display of certain characteristics that are behaviorally right for that culture. In other words, people have a cultural or national way of thinking and seeing the world, which is reflected in their language, values and beliefs, norms, socio-political history and the like. The ideological differences can be observed in the behavior of group members who come from different ethnic groups.

The ideology of a nation dictates to people certain attitudes, beliefs and ways of thinking that frame their existence. Their beliefs about life, death and marriage determine the behavior between others. People tend to respond to their environment in consistent manners that are dictated by the attitudes in their society. Minorities have partially adopted the ideology of the dominant culture in order to survive, but the adoption may or may never be fully ingrained in their personality. Consider, that even after three generations of living in the United States, some Mexican-American adolescents modified their basic cultural characteristics in only a few small ways (cited in France, 2001). Yet these minorities are not totally similar to the cultures of their origin. For example, African-Canadians or Arab-Canadians will have more in common with each other than they would with people in Ethiopia or Jordan. This creates a strain for visible minorities who can feel that they are "neither here nor there." It is also true that some beliefs and values are more affected by gender than cultural differences (e.g., men have more freedom of choice regardless of culture). Finally, ecological forces refer to how the environment has influenced culture and behavior. Someone born on an isolated island may develop a different view of the world than someone born on a large continent. Climate, prosperity and population density, like terrain, can also play a role in developing a distinct cultural norm. People born in a highly populated area may have to be more assertive because that is the only way to survive, while someone born in a non-dense area can be more relaxed and quiet.

Class, Language and Diversity

As a primary form of communication, language is of great importance to people in groups. Language patterns are reflective of people's culture or subculture (Berry, Poortinga, Segall & Dasen, 2002). Even when people are speaking the same language there is a great deal of misunderstanding because of individual differences. Therefore, it becomes easy to understand or imagine why people who do not have the same cultural and linguistic background misunderstand each other. An inaccurate picture of another person's issue formed on verbal responses, or in some cases, formed on what is not said, produces real conflict. There are certain phrases in a language that are either un-interpretable, or if translated literally, do not convey the many dimensions the phrase encompasses.

Some words, phrases or the way(s) in which words are used might have negative meanings, which are acceptable to some people from one cultural group, but not to others. For example, many high school and professional sports teams have names and logos like the "Braves", "Indians" or "Redskins" and so on. First Nations communities have protested on the basis that this reinforces negative stereotypes, uses their images and icons in a disrespectful manner and trivializes their ethnic background. A recent incident in greater Vancouver created controversy when the Musqueam name, Spull'u'kwuks, was proposed. The problem was that authorities felt that the name, meaning "place of bubbling waters", could be used in a negative way because there was the potential for rhyming using the "F word" or "sucks" or so on. The response from the Musqueam First Nation was "...it was their language...and...it should be celebrated, not made the subject of humor" (France, 2001).

Even non-verbal gestures are relatively different from culture to culture. According to Matsumoto (2000) "...being unaware of these differences can definitely cause problems" (p. 352). Eye contact and personal space also differ from culture to culture. In North America people are taught that eye contact communicates closeness and attention, while lack of eye contact communicates dislike, disinterest, or disrespect. Arabic societies gaze even longer than do North Americans (Matsumoto, 2000), but the degrees of eye contact might have different implications for different cultures. According to Sue (cited in France, 2001), white middle class people, when speaking to others, look away (eye avoidance) approximately 50% of the time. When Whites listen, however, they make eye contact with the speaker over 80% of the time. But Blacks make more eye contact when speaking and infrequent eye contact when listening. This reinforces the idea that we should be careful when we try to attribute reasons for the amount of eye contact encountered. The amount of eye contact is not necessarily related to aggressiveness, shyness, or inattentiveness but rather it depends on cultural patterns. Each culture seems to develop a unique pattern of communicating messages.

Physical distance is another cultural variable that is different from culture to culture and language to language. Francophones touch more in conversation and kiss those they feel close to, while Anglophones touch far less and rarely kiss both cheeks in greeting. Matsumoto (2000) describes the differences between Latinos and Europeans in regards to distance and space as very different, with Latinos as feeling more comfortable in closer proximity than those of European ancestry. The following types of relationships identified by Matsumoto in North American society in regards to space illustrate the acceptable distance of space to the type of relationship:

—   Intimate relationships [0-1.5 feet];

—   Personal relationships [1.5-4 feet;

—   Social consultative relationships [4-8 feet]; and

—   Public relationships [10 feet].

According to Pedersen and Carey (2003), socio-economic factors affect the way people communicate and interact. For example, groups with members from lower economic and educational levels appear to prefer more concrete and structured activities. These people may actually want direct advice or at least, a chance to talk in terms of concreteness and tangibles. In general, those in the lower socio-economic spheres report that counselling activities are "all talk and no action." In addition, people from different cultures may be unfamiliar with the dynamics of groups, which may be incongruent with what they expect. This inexperience may, in turn, block their progress in counselling groups. As counsellors, it is therefore essential to be aware of and be able to identify the values of differing people that one will work with. All people have a tendency to project their cultural values in their behavior, verbal expressions and emotional expressions. Obviously, these differences may create distances between people. Some cultural groups have reluctance to self-disclose their feelings, which means their culture places a high priority on restraint of expressing feelings and thoughts, particularly to strangers. If one misinterprets the reasons behind the reluctance to self-disclose, the results may be a block of communication, severe anxiety and extreme discomfort.

Another important culture-bound value is the family relationship. People of European ancestry and those acculturated by these same values tend to center on personal responsibility and decisions are made based on the good of the individual. If someone makes a personal decision from a culture that emphasizes family involvement in decision-making, the family might block attempts to achieve individual goals. For example one Asian-Canadian client stated: "…whenever I disagreed with my mother, it seemed to her that I was questioning her character" (France, 2001; p. 220). In her family, the authority of the parents is paramount and not to be questioned by the child. When she made a decision without consulting anyone, her mother felt hurt and angry. She loved her mother, but felt a desire to assert her individuality and this produced a great deal of conflicting feelings. There are also positive aspects of family cultural values in which adult children only make important choices after consulting with their parents. Consider the following example from a Brazilian woman, aged 30, who said that she and her husband felt it was necessary to ask her parents whether their decision to buy a particular apartment was a good one. A Canadian male responded upon hearing her, that if he asked his parents what they thought, the response would be "you're an adult now, please decide what you think is best."

Cross-Cultural Communication Difficulties

When people encounter cultural differences as a sojourner they find "...that adjustment problems were greatest at the beginning and decreased over time" (Berry, Poortinga, Segall & Dasen, 2001, p. 409). Interestingly, there is a "honeymoon period" in adjustment in which the sojourner is enthusiastic; this is followed by anxiety, frustration and adjustment difficulties. However, these change as new coping mechanisms are developed. This experience is sometimes referred to as the **U** or **W shaped curve**, as cultural adjustment occurs. But what are some of the blocks that challenge people in cross-cultural communication? To be sensitive and aware of another person's frame of reference is elementary, but it is particularly significant with those of diverse cultural backgrounds. In some ways the following list of stumbling blocks applies to almost any group, but they are especially intense in cross-cultural groups (France, 2001).

Language: Vocabulary, syntax, idioms, slang and dialects can create problems of understanding. The problem is the tenacity with which people cling to "the" meaning of a word or phrase in the new language, regardless of the connotation or the context.

Nonverbal Areas: People from different cultures employ different nonverbal sensory words. They see, hear, feel and smell only that which has some meaning or importance for them. They extract whatever fits into their personal world of recognition and then they interpret it through the frame of reference of their own culture.

Tendency to Evaluate: Some people from different cultures need to approve or disapprove the statements and actions of others, rather than to try and completely comprehend the thoughts and feelings expressed. This bias prevents the open-minded attention needed to look at the attitudes and behavior patterns from the others' frame of reference. This is heightened when feelings and emotions are deeply involved. Yet this is the time when listening with understanding is most needed. As counsellors, we especially need to examine values that are negatively evaluative towards those who are different.

High Anxiety: This stumbling block is not distinct but underlies and compounds the others. Its presence is very common because of uncertainties present when people function in a foreign language where the normal flow of verbal and nonverbal interaction cannot be sustained. There is a sense of threat by the unknown knowledge, experience and evaluation of others, therefore bringing the potential for scrutiny and rejection by the self. There is also the added tension of having to cope with the differing pace, climate and culture. Self-esteem is often intolerably undermined unless people employ defenses such as withdrawal into their reference group or into themselves thus screening out or misperceiving stimuli, rationalizing, overcompensating or even showing hostility (p. 219).

Cross-Cultural Communication

Multicultural experiences can enhance a counsellor's personal power and improve overall communication skills not only with culturally different clients, but clients in general. What counsellors say and do can either promote or reduce their credibility and effectiveness with others. The style of self-disclosure, the perceived trustworthiness and the counselling style emphasize just a few of the variables. In this regard, the cultural background of counsellors is not as important in how effective they really are, but in how their credibility, attractiveness and trustworthiness are perceived by clients. However, in other studies on evaluating the effects of counsellors' race and ethnic background on perceived effectiveness in communication, people were affected by the person's race and ethnic background either in a negative or positive way (cited in France, 2001). In counselling situations, the evidence suggests that, for culturally different people, the issue of expertise is raised more often than whether the person has a similar cultural or racial background (Pedersen & Carey, 2003). This suggests that group members will have to be more sensitive and develop strategies that will attenuate or, perhaps, eliminate this effect, particularly if the effect is negative. In other words, using appropriate communication skills and strategies that are congruent with a person's values is more important than race or ethnic background. There seems to be no particular communication strategy which proves to be more successful with specific populations. Yet the approach used by group members from the majority culture must be consistent with those from other cultures' life-styles, along with flexibility for individual differences within a culture; not all people with a similar cultural background behave in the same way. On the other hand, equal treatment in communication may be discriminatory treatment. If group members proceed on the basis that everyone is the same without recognizing differences, this may have a negative effect. If all people could be more aware and appreciate their different parts, perhaps they would be more accepting of cultural differences in others.

The Process of Cultural Adjustment

The process of adaptation is a universal phenomenon that everyone experiences as they grow from infancy to adulthood within their cultural milieu. According to Sciarra (1999) "...counselors working with clients from non-dominant cultural backgrounds need to assess their acculturative levels and the amount of stress resulting from living in a different environment" (p. 25). Okun, Fried and Okun (1999) emphasize that cultural adaptation and

"...development can be considered as a series of fluctuations between agency or the ability to carry out one's purpose or function and communion or the ability to connect with another" (p. 24). That is the challenge of being one's self, while being able to connect with others who may be different. Depending on how this is done it can determine how safe one feels in any different cultural situation. However, there are three categories of processes of adaptation that have been identified as follows:

—   Unidirectional or adapting to one culture and away from another;

—   Bidirectional or adapting by moving back and forth between two cultures while feeling at home in both;

—   Multidirectional or adapting to other cultures, but feeling positively grounded in one's own culture.

At the present time there is much talk of the evil of terrorism and somehow Islam is the root cause of the terror. Terms like "regime change" convey the idea that somehow the invasion of Iraq is a positive endeavor and it dehumanizes the "other side." Dyer (1996) argues that each nation invents the myths of nationhood just as each country decides what is "good" or "bad." In effect, reasons behind various national policies are subjective. But reality is very subjective, because it looks different from an Arab perspective compared to an American perspective. Each side views the other as either an **"Axis of Evil"** or the **"Big Satan,"** when, in fact, both sides are human beings who love their children. Many of the issues that divide people are still unchanged, except now the Russians are like us, while the other side, whether it be Arabs or Muslims, are seen very differently. Over time the enemy changes, but the process of dehumanizing stays the same. Despite openness to new ideas, people in North America are quite ignorant of other world literature, customs and languages. The more people foster the notion that there are more explanations or sides to an issue, the less the chance that there will be fear of the unknown and ignorance. Fear, after all, is the culprit behind racism.

Encouragement of Cultural Identity:

All people want acceptance from others, yet regardless of how they adapt to new cultural situations, their cultural roots bind them and this, in turn, affects how they feel about themselves and are perceived by others. Sciarra (1999) stresses that "attitudes and behaviors are the result of complex cognitive and emotional processes around the relationship people have to their own cultural group" (p. 47).

People who have strong cultural identities seem to have a greater sense of control about their lives. Sue and Sue (1990) suggest that counsellors' cultural identity can adversely affect how they interact with clients by reinforcing negative self-esteem if the client is having some dissonance about their cultural development. Racial-ethnic identity development may be defined as pride in one's racial, ethnic and cultural heritage. Helms (1995) proposes two models of identity development to describe how minorities form their identity compared to the majority group. There are six stages in the Majority Racial Identity Development Model:

1. **Lack of Awareness:** A person has no sense that there are any differences in cultures simply because there is no contact;

2. **Contact:** the person has contact with someone who is different. This stage is characterized by curiosity and the recognition that there is a difference in people – color, race, language, etc.

3. **Conflict:** once differences occur, there is a great chance for conflict. Differences become exaggerated and "war" is inevitable. People become frustrated and differences create fear and so they become defensive and sometimes aggressive.

4. **Pro-Minority Stance:** once people understand that conflict is not a positive option, they begin to realize that something has to happen and so they reach out to others. But in their desire to connect, they embrace minority characteristics and values (e.g., language, dress, etc.). However, this strategy is bound to fail because they can never be a minority. They cannot change their complexion or culture and so they bury themselves in the "clock" of the other.

5. **Pro-Majority Stance:** this stage occurs when the pro-minority stance is not accepted. They then embrace an attitude that is not diverse or accepting of others (e.g., they only support their own).

6. **Internalization:** at this stage, people accept themselves. They are from a certain ethnic group and accept others in the same way. They have a good sense of their own boundaries and those of others, but they recognize that their ethnic identity is a part of themselves, but it is built on a positive foundation. They accept others who are different and value others based on their behaviors and not on their color.

In the Minority Identity Development Model, Helms (1995) suggested that if counsellors are to understand minority people they must understand that person's identity development. If there are problems, perhaps it might have something to do with where a person is at, so understanding this is vital. The model consists of 5 stages:

1. **Conformity:** the acceptance of majority standards and values at the deficit of one's own ethnic identity;

2. **Dissonance:** this occurs when the person perceives a difference between what they feel and what they experience.

3. **Resistance:** based on their sense of dissonance, they revolt. A sense of power and even exclusiveness takes place (e.g., "black power");

4. **Introspection:** based on the sense that resistance doesn't always get what one wants, there is a desire to look for reasons, for the why's and how's. What happens is an examination of everything.

5. **Synergetic Articulation & Awareness:** this occurs when there is acceptance of oneself.

What about mixed race people? The National Film Board (1990) video, **Domino**, relates stories of growing up bi-cultural. Biracial identity development, however, is a much more complex and undefined process. Poston (in France, 2002) developed the Biracial Identity Development Model to address the inherent weakness of the previously mentioned models and to recognize the increasing numbers of biracial youth. Admittedly, this progressive, developmental model is tentative and based on the scant amount of research on biracial individuals and information from support groups. Nevertheless, the following five-stage model does have implications for personal identity constructs (e.g., self-esteem) for biracial youth:

1. **Personal Identity.** Biracial children tend to display identification problems when they internalize outside prejudices and values. Young children's reference group observation attitudes are not yet developed, so their identity is primarily based on personal identity factors such as self-esteem and feelings of self-worth within their primary reference group.

2. **Choice of Group Categorization.** Youth at this stage are pushed to choose an identity, usually of one ethnic group. Numerous factors can influence the individual's identity choice (e.g., status, social support, personal). It would be unusual for an individual to choose a multiethnic identity, because this requires a level of knowledge of multiple ethnicities, races and cultures and a level of cognitive development beyond that which is characteristic of this age group.

3. **Enmeshment/Denial.** This stage is characterized by confusion and guilt at having to choose one identity that is not fully expressive of one's background. Biracial youth may experience alienation at the Choice stage and make a choice even if they are uncomfortable with it

4. **Appreciation.** Individuals at this stage begin to appreciate their multiple identity and broaden their reference group orientation. They might begin to learn about their racial-ethnic-cultural heritage, but they still tend to identify with one group.

5. **Integration.** Individuals at this stage experience wholeness and integration. They tend to recognize and value all of their racial and ethnic identities. At this level, biracial youth develop a secure, integrated identity.

This model is similar to the previously mentioned models in that it integrates a life-span focus. Yet, this model is different in that it underscores the uniqueness of biracial identity development. In addition, it recognizes that the most difficult time of adjustment and identification confusion is during the Choice stage and the Enmeshment-Denial stage. The implication is that helping professionals who understand and accept these five stages will be better prepared to assist biracial youth in their identity development.

The important role for the practitioner is to be in synch with the client and to facilitate movement toward the client's goals (Axelson, 1998). The practitioner's goal should be helping clients to develop functional environmental mastery behaviors that lead to personal adjustment and optimal mental health with the operational therapeutic objective of helping these clients to empower themselves for environmental mastery and competence. Many helping professionals, however, assume that all people from a specific ethnic or cultural group are the same and that one theoretical orientation is universally applicable in any intervention effort. This assumption is just as harmful for biracial youth as it is for specific ethnic youth. Professionals with this perspective may approach clients not as distinct human beings with individual experiences, but rather merely as cultural stereotypes.

Social ostracism and racism continue to direct stressors on many interracial couplings even though most legal barriers to interracial marriage and coupling have been abolished. A greater acceptance of interracial unions exists today than even 15 to 20 years ago (Matsumoto, 2000). This increase in acceptance is reflected in the steady growth in the number of interracial couples and their offspring. Therefore, helping professionals need to be cognizant of and prepared to address this increasing population in their professions. Matsumoto (2000) goes on to say that studies of intercultural marriages have:

> ...shown that conflicts arise in several major areas, including the expression of love and intimacy, the nature of commitment and attitudes towards the marriage itself and approaches to child rearing when couples have children. Other potential sources of conflict include differences in perceptions of male-female roles, differences in domestic money management, differences in perceptions of relationships with extended family and defenses in the definition of marriage itself (p. 419).

Interestingly, "anecdotal evidence suggests intercultural marriages are not necessarily associated with higher divorce rates than intracultural marriages" (Matsumoto, 2000, p. 421). Thus, the factors that contribute to a successful intercultural marriage are the same ingredients that make for successful multicultural counselling. That is, the ability to flexibly compromise and commit to the relationship, as well as the ability to negotiate differences existing within the relationship, the willingness to make compromises and the desire to stay together regardless of the challenges.

Conclusion

"At the time of the first Gulf War, I was amazed when then US president George Bush told my husband, speaking of Saddam Hussein: 'I will not allow this little dictator to control 25% of the civilized world's oil.' The key words here, for the Jordanians who would later describe this meeting as quite a raw experience, were of course, 'civilized world.'" (Queen Noor, 2003, p. 74)

For Arabs, this statement is both dismissive and stereotypical and reinforces how they are perceived by people in other parts of the world, particularly in North America. It is possible that there was a cultural misunderstanding, thus emphasizing the importance of meaning and language in communication. All counsellors working with people who are different need to realize how certain behaviors or words influence the communication process. In essence, people, like nations, have a tendency to look at the outside world from their own perspective. This is natural and perhaps, necessary, for all people are "prisoners" of a particular space and time. A global view of the group is that everyone is a stranger, just as everyone is a neighbor. In fact, at one time all of us were foreigners, outsiders and perhaps even outcasts. In essence, the challenge for counsellors is to be more culturally sensitive, yet maintain a sense of their own cultural identity.

According to Berry, Poortinga, Segall and Dasen (2001) "...a common core to psychotherapeutic practices may exist, but with different historical and cultural roots and with highly varied cultural expression" (p. 441). In other words, while there may be some universals in regards to counselling, the way in which they are perceived and used is definitely influenced by culture. A multicultural orientation has tremendous implications for counselling practice because being knowledgeable and sensitive to cultural diversity makes all the difference between success and failure. Multicultural counselling is concerned with the usual developmental issues, but with the added element of cultural differences. We live in a society in which the world is represented in our major cities that demand that we become engaged in intercultural communication for our survival. If the interaction is to be significant and if cross-cultural communication and multiculturalism are to foster increased understanding and cooperation, then counsellors must be aware of the factors that may affect how we relate to others. Counsellors must not only avoid actions that hinder effective communication, but must be actively engaged in helping others deal with diversity issues. It is axiomatic to suggest that the success of cross-cultural communication may well depend on the attitudes and philosophies people adopt. The way in which people in a group relate to each other is often a reflection of their philosophy towards life and themselves.

Counsellors must be models for promoting the acceptance of diversity and for encouraging others to not only be culturally sensitive, but also fight discrimination and racism. All people are capable of change from day to day and from situation to situation, but counsellors who work with people from different cultures have a unique opportunity to act as agents of change. "Every bigot was once a child free of prejudice" (Siccone, 1995, p. 133); therefore, celebrating diversity must begin early. Many attitudes and behaviors are deeply ingrained in people's psyche and many of them are subject to ethnocentrism. The challenge for counsellors is to help people become grounded in their cultural identity, develop an appreciation for others who are culturally different and look for ways of reaching out to others who are different. The changes required of people are not simple nor are they easy. They require that people possess a willingness to communicate; empathy toward foreign and alien cultures; tolerance of views that differ from their own; and that they develop a more open approach to communication with others from different cultural groups. In order to increase acceptance of people who are different, more contact with minorities is particularly important (Berry, Poortinga, Segall and Dasen, 2002). If people have the resolve to adapt their behaviors and attitudes with the desire to overcome ethnocentrism, they may begin to know the feelings of exhilaration that come when they have made contact with those from other cultures far removed from their own sphere of experience. This willingness to realize interdependency is voiced eloquently by McGaa (1990):

> *Our survival is dependent on the realization that Mother Earth is a truly holy being, that all things in this world are holy and must not be violated and that we must share and be generous with one another...think of your fellow men and women as holy people who were put here by the Great Spirit. Think of being related to all things (p. 208).*

References

Alladin, M.I. (1996). *Racism in Canadian schools*. Toronto, ON: Harcourt Brace.

Axelson, J. (1998). *Counseling and Development in a Multicultural Society*, 3nd Edition. Pacific Grove, CA: Brooks/Cole.

Baron, R. S., Kerr, N.L. & Miller, N. (1992). *Group Process, Group Decision, Group Action*. Pacific Grove, CA: Brooks/Cole.

Berry, J., Poortinga, H., Segall, M. & Dasen, P. (2002). *Cross-cultural psychology*, 2nd Edition. London, UK: Oxford Press.

de Montigny, L. (1972). Racism and Indian cultural adaptations. In Waubageshig (Editor), *The Only Good Indian* (pp. 97-111). Toronto, ON: New Press.

Diller, J. (1999). *Cultural Diversity: A Primer for Human Services*. Pacific Grove, CA: Brook/Cole.

Dyer, G. (2001). Visible majorities. *Canadian Geographic*, *121*(1), pp. 44-55.

Fleras, A. & Elliot, J.L. (1991). *The Challenge of Diversity: Multiculturalism in Canada*. Toronto, ON: Nelson.

France, M.H. (2001). *Nexus: Transpersonal Approach to Groups*. Calgary, AB: Detselig Enterprises.

George, D. (1994). *My Heart Soars*. Surrey, BC: Hancock House Publishers.

Helms, J.E. (1995). An update of Helms' white and people of color racial identity modes. In J.G. Ponterotto, J.M. Casas, L.A. Suzuki & C.M. Alexander (Eds.), *Handbook of Multicultural Counseling* (pp. 181-198). Thousand Oaks, CA: Sage.

Matsumoto, D. (2000). *Culture and Psychology: People Around the World*, 2nd Edition, Belmont, CA: Wadsworth.

McGaa, E. (1990). *Mother Earth Spirituality: Native American Paths to Healing Ourselves and the World*. San Francisco, CA: Harper.

Mezlekia, N. (2000). *Notes from the Hyena's Belly*. Toronto, ON: Penguin Books.

Pedersen, P. (1994). *Handbook of Multicultural Counselling,* 2nd Edition. Alexandria, VA: ACA Press.

Noor, Queen. (2003). *Leap of Faith: Memoirs of an Unexpected Life.* New York: Warner Books.

Okun, B., Fried, J. & Okun, M. (1999). *Understanding Diversity: A Learning-as-Practice Primer.* Pacific Grove, CA: Brooks/Cole.

Pedersen, P., Draguns, J., Lonner, W. & Trimble, J. (2002). *Counseling Across Cultures,* 5th Ed. Thousand Oaks, CA: Sage.

Pedersen, P. & Carey, J. (2003). *Multicultural Counseling in Schools,* 2nd Edition. Boston, MA: Allyn & Bacon.

Milloy, J. (1999). *A National Crime: The Canadian Government and the Residential School System.* Winnipeg, MB: The University of Manitoba Press.

Robinson, T.L. & Howard-Hamilton, M.F. (2000). *The Convergence of Race, Ethnicity and Gender.* Upper Saddle River, NJ: Merrill.

Sciarra, D.T. (1999). *Multiculturalism in Counseling.* Itasca, IL: P.F. Peacock Publishers.

Siccone, F. (1995),. *Celebrating Diversity: Building Self-esteem in Today's Multicultural Classrooms.* Boston, MA: Allyn and Bacon.

Chapter 2
Exploring Worldview

María del Carmen Rodríguez

"What we make of people and what we see in the mirror when we look at ourselves, depends on what we know of the world, what we believe to be possible, what memories we have and whether our loyalties are to the past, the present or the future." Theodore Zeldin

Worldview Foundations

The notion of worldview deals with a culture's orientation and relationship to ideas such as man, nature, spiritual beliefs, the universe and other philosophical issues that are concerned with the concept of being. Our worldview helps us locate our place and rank in the universe and it influences our beliefs, values, attitudes, uses of time and other aspects of culture. This construct is ample and complex since it deals with the condition of being human and thus, comprises more than just philosophical foundations but it also involves the understanding of socio-cultural components, anthropological conceptions and even psychological behaviors.

Historical Roots

The use of worldview has often been co-opted from one specific perspective. For example, Scofield (1991), states that the "Old World" (meaning Europe) was more advanced than the "New World " in terms of the fusion of cultural values and complex social structures into what is called civilization. This is a Eurocentric perspective since the inhabitants of the Americas also held social structures and cultural values as well as knowledge in regards to the ways in which the cosmos and thus, life was perceived, understood and lived. "Cosmovisión" (Spanish word that means vision of the cosmos) describes life encircling indigenous folklore, myths, legends, philosophy and sky-knowledge. According to Malinowski (cited in Erdoes & Ortiz, 1984) "…myth in its living, primitive form is not merely a story told but a reality lived" (p. xv). Therefore, myths favour the portrayal of diverse social functions in that they "…are magic lenses through which we can glimpse social orders and daily life: how families were organized, how political structures operated… how religious ceremonies felt to the people who took part, how power was divided between men and women… how honour in war was celebrated " (Erdoes & Ortiz, 1984). Sky-knowledge was fundamental to farming and owning the knowledge of weather patterns and seasonal changes was crucial for survival. However, there is more to a culture's cosmic understanding (or Worldview) than just sky-knowledge, folklore, myths and legends. Cosmovisión also embraces the wisdom, the learnings and the emblems of a culture, giving concrete form to a set of beliefs and traditions that link people living today to ancestors from centuries past. While some of these connections might prevail, other views and perceptions of the world develop and unfold as the result of an ever-changing existence. A culture's normative modes of subsistence, political ideas, ways of life, values, attitudes, affective perceptions, modes of communication and even technological advancement give origin to new worldviews.

Every culture around the world has its own view that reflects the nature of its world (e.g., African, Chinese, Indian, European, Amerindians and so forth). North American educational practices are rich in the philosophical schemes of worldview that stem from Egyptian, Greek, Roman and European traditions; in the latter, the notion of truth or *aletheia*, as Heidegger (1967) calls it, is understood as an active process of unveiling reality through the sharing of personal interpretations and the resulting fusion of individual horizons. Disregarding that Asian, African and Indigenous views were not included in Heidegger's notion, his ideas are rich in describing worldview. Historically, worldview translates from the German word: *Weltanschauung*. Heidegger (1988) explained *Weltanschauung* as a word derived from German roots and ingrained in a philosophical tradition which always includes a view of life. He argues that it is a way of being that requires conviction if the worldview is to guide the person in times of pressure.

Philosophical perspectives

A worldview originates out of a natural standpoint of the world, out of a range of conceptions and personal understandings, as the result of the possession of a particular horizon and it expands as one becomes more knowledgeable of the world and experiences life in all its dimensions in a unique way. The concept of worldview is complex and broad as it encompasses much more than personal reflections and understandings about one's values, beliefs, assumptions, behaviors, rules for interactions and so forth. Worldview also consists of what people make with such understandings, how they interact and behave with/in the world. According to Hans-George Gadamer (1986), when we come into the world we arrive in a physical place and in a tradition that is being lived by our family members and their friends. Those around us live in a particular context at a particular moment in history; they speak a particular language, express religious and philosophical beliefs and have preferred ways of acting socially and ethically. In learning the "patterns" of tradition of the significant others in our lives during our formative years, we lay the founding grounds for interpreting future experiences. Gadamer (1986) says that tradition is not learned; but rather, it is an experience that occurs as the result of social interaction; it is a particular style of carrying oneself in life, a unique way of possessing and interpreting one's being-in-the-world. Furthermore, worldview is defined by Montgomery, Fine and Myers (1990) as "…a structure of philosophical assumptions, values and principles upon which a way of perceiving the world is based" (p. 38).

Socio-cultural definition

Worldview refers to the outlook or image we have concerning the nature of the universe, the nature of humankind, the relationship between humanity and the universe and other philosophical issues or orientations that help us define the cosmos and our place in it. These orientations are tied directly to the ideological, historical, philosophical and religious dimensions of a culture. Culture has been defined as a set of implicit norms, values and beliefs that influences the attitudes, behaviors and customs of a group of individuals (Gushue, 1993). The culture of a family, for example, affects individual behaviors, child-rearing practices, discipline and the importance of achievement and education. Such sets of norms often determine its form and functioning, including the type of family, its size and shape (McGill, 1983; McGoldrick, Giordano & Pearce, 1996) and culture defines boundaries, rules for interaction and communication patterns between family members and within the community (Falicov & Brudner-White, 1983; McGill, 1983; McGoldrick et al., 1996; Preli & Bernard, 1993). The roles of family members and the ways of defining problems and outlining specific coping skills are defined by culture (Schwartzman, 1983). Falicov (1995) defined culture as a set of shared worldviews, meanings and adaptive behaviors derived from simultaneous membership and participation in a variety of contexts including language, age, gender, race, ethnicity, religion, socio-economic status, education and sexual orientation. Both definitions of culture indicate that cultural values define behaviors and therefore establish norms for attitudes and behaviors within families and in the larger cultural groups (e.g., religious affiliation, academic community and so forth). Families serve as the primary agent for transmitting cultural values and worldview to their children and parents and extended family help children to learn, internalize and develop understanding of culture through both covert and overt means (Preli & Bernard, 1993). Through cultural socialization, families must teach both positive and negative messages of their particular cultural group as well as those of other cultures (Preli & Bernard, 1993).

Every particular worldview is determined by cultural environment: folkways, lore, system, race, class and stage of culture (i.e. family history and specific culture, social expectations, working habits and so forth). Through the interaction of these countless events, culture provides people with a view of themselves, the rest of the world, the universe and their relationship of them.

Worldview manifests itself in the psychological, sociological and technical aspects of a society influencing its social organization, the use of tools and instruments, situational behavior and even language. Worldview as conceptualized provides a mechanism to understand how ethnicity, culture, socio-political history and life-style affect people's life choices and decision-making ability. This is the mediating variable that makes knowledge of a specific cultural group and knowledge of culture-consistent and culture-specific techniques meaningful. Without the worldview as a mediating variable, such knowledges can be misapplied, leading to ethical violation and cultural oppression particularly, within a multicultural setting (Ibrahim, 1991).

Sire (1976) stated that our worldview consists of the presuppositions and assumptions that we hold about the world while Horner and Vandersluis (1981) maintained that because worldviews are culturally based variables, they influence the relationship between two people and the way in which they interact. Our worldview directly affects and mediates our belief system, assumptions, modes of problem solving, decision-making and conflict resolution (Ibrahim, 1991). Seltzer, Frazier and Ricks (1995), in their review of multiculturalism, race and the educational system, indicate that knowledge of differences in worldviews can enhance one's ability to effectively manipulate an environment inclusive of others from diverse cultures.

Anthropological Contexts

Within anthropology, these general views of the world have been described by a number of terms, including patterns, themes, ethos and value orientations (Agar, 1996; Kearney, 1984). Also termed cultural models, folk models and schema, these specific views of the world encompass a multitude of more circumscribed domains related to various aspects of living. Because of the multiplicity of specific domains, anthropologists have not specified a single set of dimensions; instead, to investigate specific views, they have selected those that are salient within a particular area of interest. According to Kearney (1984), worldview systems consist of dynamic, interrelated views. For example, within the general domain of interpersonal relationships (Clyde Kluckhohn, 1951, 1956), specific views might include understandings about marriage, commitment, companionship, emotions and interpersonal conflict (D'Andrea, 1992; Quinn, 1985; White, 1983). Traditionally, worldview has been viewed solely as encompassing the broad, general understandings of the world. Within contemporary anthropology however, culture is viewed as intricately related to all aspects of personal experience, within both general (shared experiences) and specific domains of life activity (unique experiences) thus, recent work may more accurately reflect the nature of culture and the individual (Schwartz, 1992).

Cross-cultural foundations

Hall (1976) states that, in the past, individuals did not need to be aware of the structure of their behavioral system because their interactions occurred in limited settings with people who possessed similar outlooks on life. However, more recently, because of broader interactions and expansion, it has become necessary for individuals to transcend their own culture by making explicit the rules by which it operates. Interactions across cultures can enhance and/or lessen the perceptions one has of one self and others as the result of the fusion of the values, beliefs and traditions inherited from our parent culture. Value orientations and worldview are so much a part of what we perceive to be "the real life" that the philosophical division between existential postulates and normative acceptances becomes blurred. Therefore, it would be too ambitious to attempt to scrutinize the value orientations of other cultural groups without first beginning to accept one's own. In a multicultural society, cross-cultural encounters are inevitable and they require the understanding of, or at least the ability to conceptualize, cultural variables in order to hinder prejudice. Since multiculturalism is rooted in philosophical views of human nature and peoples' place in the universe (Atkinson, Maruyama & Matsui, 1978), worldview is a significant contribution to multicultural counselling.

Defined as our basic perceptions and understandings of the world (Howard & McKim, 1983; Kearney, 1984), this construct was first introduced into the literature on cross-cultural affairs by Sue (1978) who highlighted the importance of worldview in multicultural encounters. Sue (1978) defined worldview as an individual's perception of his or her relationship with the world (i.e. nature, things, institutions and people) and asserted that the knowledge of an individual's sociopolitical history, racial, cultural and ethnic background can be helpful in identifying the ways in which the world is perceived by him/her, therefore providing insight for a counselling approach based on such perceptions.

A rationale for using worldview assessment

According to Lonner and Ibrahim (1996), when two people from different cultures communicate, both of their worldviews need to be understood in order to establish trust and rapport. To understand culturally diverse clients, Ibrahim (1984, 1985) acknowledged the relevance of the construct of worldview in cross-cultural counselling and proposed a broader conceptualization in order to clarify basic human concerns that are pancultural. The theory uses worldview and cultural identity as mediational forces in an individual's life (Ibrahim, 1985a; Ibrahim & Schroeder, 1987). Ibrahim suggests the inclusion of an analysis of the cultural identities of the parties: ethnicity, culture, gender, age, life stage, beliefs, values and assumptions in order to establish effective communication. The worldviews, once clarified, must be placed within a socio-political context, history of migration, acculturation level (comfort within the mainstream assumptions and values) and languages spoken. Even though the Scale for Assessing World View (SAWV), developed by Ibrahim was primarily developed as a counselling tool for initial assessment and to understand of the client's worldview and cultural identity, we have found it to be a useful resource in a variety of situations. For example, in helping people from different cultures work together more effectively, having an understanding of the other's worldview enhances communication and cooperation.

In higher education, where students from different countries study in a second country (i.e., a foreign student) learning about differing worldviews can assist in cultural adjustment. It can also be utilized in higher education to facilitate the development of appropriate processes and goals based on a student's cultural assumptions. Without the worldview as a mediating variable, knowledge of specific cultures and culture-specific techniques can be misapplied, leading to miscommunication. For example, worldview provides a mechanism for those in government, education and counselling to understand how ethnicity, culture, socio-political history and life-style affect one's life choices and decision-making ability.

Ibrahim (1984, 1985a), Ibrahim and Schroeder (1987, 1990) and Sue (1978) have offered three major suggestions to ease the process of multicultural counselling. Such recommendations include an understanding of worldview, the knowledge of specific cultures and the knowledge of culture-specific verbal and non-verbal skills to facilitate such encounters. At the general level, worldview dimensions that are helpful in cross-cultural counselling meet three criteria: a) the dimensions are comprehensive (they capture a broad range of human experience); b) they are applicable across cultural groups; and c) they are relevant to encounters across cultures. The Scale to Assess Worldview (SAWV) developed by Ibrahim and Kahn (1984, 1987) taps the same five existential categories found in the Kluckhohn-Strodbeck (1961) research model. According to Ibrahim and Kahn (1987), the use of the SAWV helps those working with culturally diverse individuals to accomplish an understanding of specific worldviews, beliefs, values and assumptions (given that an individual's worldview is in direct relationship with their cognitive, emotional and social perceptions and interactions with the world). Furthermore, it helps in clarifying an individual's worldview as compared with his or her primary cultural group (Ibrahim, 1985; Ibrahim & Schroeder, 1990).

Interestingly, as multiculturalism has become government policy around the world, there are few assessment measures that can help clarify cultural identity and worldview. With additional information regarding one's socio-political history (i.e., groups that the student identifies with, history of migration, impact of gender from a minority or majority cultural perspective), personal experiences (i.e., family life/cycle history, religion) and primary and secondary identification with another culture (i.e., acculturation level, language[s] spoken), one can develop a clearer comprehension of the concerns of someone from a different culture.

Principles

Results from anthropological studies can be used to demonstrate that the cultures of the world can be arranged into two contrasting ways or categories in which the self is defined, conceptualized and articulated (Bateson & Mead, 1942; Brown & Lundrum-Brown, 1995; Gaines & Reed, 1995; Geertz, 1983; Shweder, 1991). The categories are (a) *relational* or *high-context cultures* (Triandis, 1994; Matsumoto, 1996) and (b) *analytical* (Geertz, 1983;

Shweder, 1991) or *low-context cultures* (Triandis, 1994; Matsumoto, 1996). Each category has a different outlook on constructs such as self, autonomy, concept of time, personal control, understanding of mind and body and construction of morality among others (see Table 1). However, these classifications should not be interpreted as opposing or definitive. Rather, it is my belief that they may exist in a continuum, as cyclical, within each other or even "in fragments." In a continuum, it could be proposed that, as cultures change, high-context cultures could become low-context ones (as paradoxical as it might seem). As cyclical, the latter description would apply, followed by a "return" to the original state or mode of being. Existing within each other would imply that a high-context culture could exist within a low-context culture and vice-versa. Let's take the example of a poor area in a developing country in contrast with an area (in the same country) where technology, health services, jobs and education opportunities are available for most people. This is highly possible particularly in developing countries where economy (the main condition to access education, health services and the like) is unequally distributed; value preference and value orientation might differ. High-context and low-context cultures can also exist as "fragments"; this means that a particular cultural group might exhibit a "mixture" or a combination of preferences that will vary depending on changing variables according to circumstances. Therefore, characteristics of both categories (high/low-context cultures) will be present in some specific populations. Such an interpretation could give shape to an extensive combination or amalgamation of possibilities in the way people understand the world. Some perceptions could be considered more central to a person's worldview. These perceptions involve abstract, core understandings of the world, including broad domains of life such as human nature, interpersonal relationships, nature, time and activity as proposed by Kluckhohn and Strodtbeck in 1961. Their research framework takes the following philosophical and psychological dimensions of existence into account:

1. What is man's assessment of innate human nature? (Perception of self and others). There are three dimensions in which this category can be viewed: (a) human nature is good; (b) human nature is a combination of good and bad parts; (c) human nature is bad. The need to understand how the self and others are viewed provides insight into understanding the quality of one's own life and the meaningfulness of relationships or how much a person might experience alienation from the self and others which might, in turn, engender negative attitudes. The understanding of this ontological dimension can also be representative of the objective-materialist or subjective-spiritual realms. Contrary to the dominant American orientation that humankind has an essentially evil but perfectible nature, may non-Western cultures assume human nature to be essentially good or a mixture of good and evil. Two of the forces present in the universe are good and evil. Since humanity is part of the universe, these forces are also naturally present in humankind. The view of the good and evil in humanity extends to the position that people cannot eliminate evil because it is a natural and necessary part of the universe.

2. What is man's relation to Nature? This category addresses a person's relationship to nature; some cultures emphasize living in harmony with nature; others highlight subjugating and controlling it while others recognize the power of nature and the frailty of humans. When the relationship between man and nature is ignored, people fall prey to oversimplification. It is necessary to understand the meaning that the environment has for individuals. The nature of such relationship can be a harmonious one where individuals are an integral part of surrounding nature, utilizing it only for survival purposes. In a world where man, as the supreme life form on earth, controls and exploits the natural environment for personal profit and for the benefit of society, the relationship to nature is one of domination. In this frame of thought, all natural phenomena have a logical or scientific explanation. Another type of relationship is that of subjugation, where people are helpless and at the mercy of nature. This view is found primarily among less developed cultures where everyday life is an on-going struggle to merely survive. Extreme climatic conditions, scarcity of food and water and a limited level of technological development situates them at the mercy of nature. Hence, nature is seen as active, often capricious, force beyond human control that must be appeased. Such views lead to volcano worship, worship of the sun and the like. The cooperative view is perceived as a working relationship where people live in harmony with nature; closely tied to the respect for the environment. Many cultures consider nature as a divine creation in which the spirit of God resides. Nature and all living things are sacred and no one has the right to destroy or be the master of nature.

3. What is the temporal focus of life? (time orientation). This category is discussed in terms of the perception and the value(s) that time has for people. Hall (1976) divides time into polychronic and monochronic. In the former, people are engaged in several activities at a time and are more spontaneous; the emphasis is on people and not schedules. In the latter, people experience time as a continuum fixed in nature, linear and as something tangible. Metaphorically, it is said that time "is lost, crawling, made up, accelerated, invested, slowed down, or running out." Different cultures perceive and understand the concept of time in different ways, focusing on the past (tradition-bound), the present (situational) or the future (goal-oriented). According to Ibrahim (1993) "…the capacity to relate to time is a uniquely human characteristic" (p.33).

4. What is the group's principal mode of activity? (forms of activity). The way in which individuals describe their existence in the world is basically in terms of: *doing* or *being-in-becoming*; the latter is a preference that underscores activities where the goal is the spontaneous development of all aspects of the self as an integrated being including the spiritual dimension. This is a more passive, process-determined and focused orientation, contrary to *doing*, a preference for initiating activity in pursuit of a specific goal. It is related to societies where reward and status are given on the basis of productivity and accomplishment. This approach takes universal concerns into account before moving into the specifics of understanding a person as a cultural entity (Ibrahim, 1993). The way in which different views towards work

and activity manifest themselves in different cultures is reflected in the following anecdote from Sitaram and Codgell (1976):

if you ask a Hindu why he got only ten bags of corn from his land while nearby farmers got much more, he would say it was the wish of God. An American farmer's answer to the same question would be: "Because I did not work hard enough" (p. 51).

5. What is the modality of the group's relationship to others? (Social relations). This classification pertains to people's relationship to other people; it can be described as (a) *collateral-mutual*, in which primacy is given to the goals and welfare of lateral extended groups and the self is enhanced through mutual relationships; and (b) *individualistic*, in which the individual's own goals are primary to the fulfillment of those of the family, a group or society. Additionally, this classification refers to the patterns of social relationships in a society, its organization and to the hierarchical system of a society or social group. Although Western cultures have well-defined hierarchies, there is a prevailing belief (sustained by occasional examples of accomplishment) that through industry and hard work, one can move freely to higher levels upon one's own merit. This creates greater mobility between social levels and the idea that anyone can attain high status. On the other hand, social status in Eastern cultures is more static with birth position tending to predict status; static cultures tend to have greater respect for persons of high status because of the limited social movement. Another aspect of social organization is affiliation to groups; Americans tend to be joiners, to be members of many groups based on form of activity. However, the depth of commitment to these groups and their members is very weak and the memberships and people move freely from group to group. In most Eastern cultures, people belong to only a few groups and it is virtually a lifetime commitment.

Additional to these outlooks, researchers have described other dimensions that focus on the ways of knowing, thinking and the concept of self (Brown and Lundrum-Brown, 1995; Oyserman, Coon & Kemmelmeier, 2002). In terms of the ways in which individuals grasp meaning (epistemology), the realms are cognitive/affective; the ways of thinking (logic) are linear/circular; and the self is defined as individual/extended (see Table 1). In the epistemological realm, it could be affirmed that there is a philosophy behind the way of life of every individual and of every relatively homogeneous group at any given point in their histories. This gives, with varying degrees of explicitness or implicitness, some sense of coherence or unity to living both in cognitive and affective dimensions. Each personality gives to the philosophy an idiosyncratic coloring and creative individuals will markedly reshape it. However, the main outlines of the fundamental values, existential assumptions and basic abstractions have only exceptionally been created out of unique biological heredity and peculiar life experiences. Almost every cultural group agrees in that their culture follows natural processes and that human nature, if not essentially rational, possesses rational dimension. However, the image or concept of what is rational is subject to cultural variation. The term refers to reaching logical and valid conclusions from the information at hand and from the metaphysical assumptions prevalent in the culture. To understand the rationality in any culture, we must understand the premises upon which it is based. American and European cultures tend to follow a system of logic based upon Aristotelian principles. Other cultures follow such principles as Yin and Yang (balance). Awareness of the principles, the premises and assumptions manifested in other cultures enables us to understand different lines of reasoning and logic processes.

The dimension of self is partially defined as culturally bound by individualistic and/or extended associations. All cultures reflect a dominant pattern that specifies the cultural location of self within this dimension. Oyserman et al. (2002) found that collectivism is related to a sense of self based on socially-oriented variables, sensitivity to rejection, the need for affiliation and a sense of self-worth based on family life. In most Western societies, the self is defined in relationship to the individual him/herself and there is little or no association with the members of any other group (i.e., family, neighbors, colleagues); conversely, in most non-Western cultures the group is the primary social entity and the ultimate goal is its well-being (Kearney, 1984; Schwartz, 1992; Samovar & Porter, 1995; Oyserman et al., 2002). Under this doctrine, individuals have significance within the context of the group, which provides them with the necessities of life in return for certain obligations that are undertaken to assist in the support and maintenance of the group. Moreover, in some cultures the importance of the self is never emphasized so that the ego does not impose upon others nor interferes with an individual's pursuit of life. According to Ibrahim, Roysircar-Sodowsky & Ohnishi (2001), a person's orientation towards individualism and/or collectivism has an effect on the way the helping relationship is viewed, the dilemmas are faced, as well as the means by which psychological relief can be achieved. It is these perspectives that have formed the basis of much of the work to date on worldview in cross-cultural counselling. Therefore, the discernment of these existential dimensions about a persons' worldview are essential in understanding those who are different within a given mainstream.

Applications for Multicultural Counselling

The Kluckhohn and Strodtbeck (1961) model of existential dimensions is based on the perception and orientation that individuals have of their world and it offers the possibility for exploring personal assumptions and understandings of one's worldview. Given that an individual's worldview is in direct relationship with their cognitive, emotional and social perceptions and interactions with the world, the framework is a significant contribution to multicultural counselling as it is rooted in philosophical and sociological views of human nature and peoples' place in the universe. Since value orientations and worldview are a substantial part of what we perceive to be "the real life," it is easy to overlook other people's perspectives particularly in cross-cultural encounters, which require the understanding of (or at least the ability to conceptualize) cultural variables in order to hinder prejudice. This framework,

Table 1
WORLDVIEW PERSPECTIVES
Culture Classification

Value Preference	Analytical/ Low context	Relational/ High context
Activity (psychological/behavioral)	Doing	Being
Relation to Nature	Mastery/ Domination	Harmony/ Communion
Time	Monochronic	Polychronic
Social Interaction/ Autonomy (ethos)	Independent/ Individual	Interdependent/ Collective
Human Nature (ontology)	Objective/ Materialistic	Subjective/ Spiritual
Concept of Self	Individualistic / referential	Interdependent/ extended
Logic (ways of thinking)	Linear	Circular
Epistemology (ways of knowing)	Cognitive	Affective
Axiology (social values)	Competition	Cooperation

(Adapted from Brown & Lundrum-Brown, 1995; Geertz, 1983; Kluckhohn & Strodtbeck, 1961; Matsumoto, 1996; Shweder, 1991; Triandis, 1994)

then, becomes a standpoint from which the world may be seen and interpreted from a location determined by a particular time in history, a particular time in culture and the orientation toward reality. While the framework is presented (see Table 1) as an apparent dichotomy (either/or) of the ways in which one perceives the world, it is important to remember that these categories can co-exist within individuals, communities and the world at large. Within multicultural counselling, the use of the worldview framework could help counsellors, clients and those in helping professions learn about themselves, expand their cultural visions, appreciate the relativity of their own reality and acknowledge the validity of other frames of reference and standpoints. Additionally, it is useful as a foundation to analyze one's own values, beliefs and assumptions as well as a tool to inquire about the construction and validity of diverse types of knowledge (i.e., cultural, social, political, historical and so forth). It is the awareness and the examination of personal perceptions and understandings that allows for constant organization or re-patterning of one's worldview, thus leading to an openness in the interactions with one another. Therefore, the use of worldview framework, which examines five existential dimensions and value orientations, might assist in eliminating: a) the risk of oppression due to cultural misconceptions and misunderstandings; b) concerns regarding the potential stereotyping that occurs when intergroup differences are generalized to all members of a particular group (Myers, Speight, Cox, Highlen & Reynolds, 1991); and c) the perpetuation of cultural myths when applying culture-specific information, knowledge and skills while interacting with others. The recognition of multiple causes of influence (e.g., ethnicity, gender, social class, religion) on the development of worldview as well as the examination, assessment and understanding of individual and group worldviews will greatly enhance inquiry in multicultural counselling, not only as a means to have a more in-depth understanding about individual differences, but also as a crucial variable to facilitate these processes.

The framework of value orientations developed by Kluckhohn and Strodtbeck in 1961 has been adapted and adopted across disciplines, proving its strength as a research approach that calls forth the need to examine, analyze and ponder personal standpoints in relationship to an individual's worldview. While other investigators (Ibrahim 1984; Ibrahim & Schroeder, 1997; Sue & Sue, 1999; Mikaylo, 1991; Ibrahim & Kahn, 1994; Kohls, 1994) have modified the original research scheme, the five initial existential dimensions or categories continue to be the foundation for the perspectives that have evolved throughout the years. However, the framework, as consistent and employed as it has been, does not escape scrutiny. In its original format, the questions posed only refer to the dichotomized nature of values as conceptualized by Kluckhohn and Strodtbeck (1961). The outcomes revealed the preferences from people with regards to the existential dimensions, but what was absent were the underlying principles or at least the clarification about such choices. The subjective nature of experience that enriches qualitative studies was not present. Therefore, the data from their study is raw and reflects only partial realities. The foundations and the variations of this framework offer a perspective that was developed 40 years ago and yet has expanded and evolved into different schemes that are being employed to this date. Some benefits that the framework offers can be summarized as follows:

– Is rooted in philosophical and sociological views of human nature where cultural values constitute cultural knowledge.

– Encourages the development of awareness through the exploration of values, assumptions, traditions, beliefs and the ways of knowing, behaving and thinking across cultures, thus promoting and facilitating the understanding of differing worldviews.

– Provides an understanding of worldview and its impact on identity, philosophy, modes of interaction with the world (problem solving, conflict resolution and decision making ability).

– Promotes the examination of individual worldview construction, deconstruction and reconstruction by determining how one's own cultural values, beliefs, perspectives and frames of reference influence personal development and transformation.

Conclusion

The way in which one perceives, experiences and makes meaning of life's driving forces varies from individual to individual over a life span. My father always reminds me that everything in this world of existence is relative and circumstantial and the more I learn about myself and others, the more I am inclined to believe this is true. Since the early 1950s until more recently, researchers (Kluckhohn, 1951; Sue, 1978; Ibrahim, 1981, 1984; Ibrahim & Kahn, 1984; Brown & Lundrum-Brown, 1995; Axelson, 1999; Diller, 1999; Okun, Fried & Okun, 1999) have extensively designed and defined cultural paradigms to describe the dimensions along which cultural groups can differ. Yet it seems that the assumptions, traditions, attitudes, values, beliefs and the ways of knowing, behaving and thinking, all of which comprise a worldview, have more in common across cultures than one would presume. However, it is undeniable that there is no substitute for direct, meaningful and comprehensive lived experience; nor can these be identical for any two human beings. The meaning and the insight gained when one chooses, decides, ventures and risks to experience the world thus, becoming vulnerable by opening to others, is irreplaceable and priceless. It is only directly that we may experience the everyday world with all its changes and accommodations; with all its revolutions and evolutions. Today, because of broader interactions and expansion, it has become necessary for people to transcend their own culture by making explicit the rules by which it operates; interactions across cultures can enhance and/or lessen the perceptions one has of one self. Such perceptions are the result of the fusion of the values, beliefs and traditions inherited from the parent culture. The construct of worldview is as ancient as the history of humankind. Plato and Socrates, like Parmenides and Heraclito, evaluated their own lives by constantly reviewing the way in which they saw themselves and thus, interacted with/in the world. Socrates' axiom "An unexamined life is not worth living" teaches about the importance of self-evaluation and self-discovery in everyday life and is perhaps the prelude to Tomas Mann's affirmation that "No one ever remains the same after they have seen themselves."

This chapter has examined the construct of worldview from various perspectives, seeking to bring forth some insight about the ways in which people perceive, experience and make meaning of the world. Philosophically, a worldview originates out of a natural standpoint of the world, out of a range of conceptions and personal understandings that arise out of life experiences and the experience of developing a conceptual system about the world. It is a conscious way of apprehending a universe of things and so it always includes a view of life. A worldview grows out of an "all inclusive reflection on the world... and this happens in different ways, explicitly and consciously in individuals or by appropriating an already prevalent Worldview" (Heidegger, 1988; p. 3). The mode in which worldview is constructed involves the ongoing development and maturation of diverse understandings: understanding of the world, of others and of self. It is a standpoint given by a person's experience from which the world may be seen and interpreted from a location determined by a particular time in history, a particular time in culture and a person's individual orientation toward reality. Sociologically, every individual's worldview is determined by cultural environment: folkways, lore, system, race, class and stage of culture (i.e., family history and specific culture, social expectations, working habits and so forth). Through the interaction of these countless events, culture provides people with a view of themselves, the rest of the world, the universe and their relationship of them. Within anthropology, these general views of the world have been described by a number of terms, including patterns, themes, ethos, value orientations, cultural or folk models and schema (Agar, 1996; Kearney, 1984) and they encompass a multitude of more circumscribed domains related to various aspects of living. Distinct cultural groups have developed particular modal patterns for understanding the world; as a result, there are multiple sources of variation within cultures that influence the formation of a given individual's worldview. Cross-culturally, Sue (1978) defined worldview as an individual's perception of his or her relationship with the world (i.e., nature, things, institutions and people) and asserted that the knowledge of an individual's socio-political history, racial, cultural and ethnic background can be helpful in identifying the ways in which the world is perceived.

However, worldview research needs yet to be unearthed for there is much to be discovered not in terms of cultural differences but, more importantly, in terms of perspectives, understandings and tolerance of one another. An important area for additional investigation involves instrumentation. Some instruments to assess worldview have been extensively developed but not tested across cultures, whereas others have been investigated cross-culturally but are still in need of additional development and improvement. Thus, it is apparent that continued work is needed to amount the worldview notion in cross-cultural situations, for not only does it appear to be a viable unifying construct for understanding change within cross-cultural education, psychology and counselling, but it also provides a powerful way for understanding others. In a multicultural society, cross-cultural encounters are inevitable and they require the understanding of, or at least the ability to conceptualize, other people's worldview in order to hinder prejudice and promote acceptance and inclusion. Wurzel (1988) complements these ideas by stating: "...the multicultural person questions the arbitrary nature of his or her own culture and accepts the proposition that others who are culturally different can enrich their experience" (p.10).

References

Agar, M. (1996). *Language Shock: Understanding the Culture of Conversation*. New York: Morrow

Atkinson, D.R., Maruyama, M. & Matsui, S. (1978). The effects of counsellor race and counselling approach on Asian American's perceptions of counsellor credibility and utility. *Journal of Counselling Psychology, 25*, 76-83.

Axelson, J. (1999). *Counselling and Development in a Multicultural Society* (3rd ed.). Pacific Grove, CA: Brook/Cole.

Bateson, G. & Mead, M. (1942). *Balinese Character: A Photographic Analysis*. New York: New York Academy of Sciences.

Brown, M.T. & Lundrum-Brown, J. (1995). Counsellor supervision: Cross-cultural perspectives. In J.P. Ponterotto, J.M. Casas, L.A. Suzuki & C.M. Alexander (Eds.). *Handbook of Multicultural Counselling* (pp. 263-287). Thousand Oaks, CA: Sage

D'Andrea, M. (1992). The violence of our silence. *Guidepost, 35,* (4), 31.

Diller, J. (1999). *Cultural Diversity: A Primer for Human Services*. Pacific Grove, CA: Brook/Cole.

Erdoes, R. & Ortiz, A. (1984). *American Indian Myths and Legends*. New York: Pantheon Books.

Falicov, C.J. (1995). Training to think culturally: A multidimensional comparative framework. *Family Process, 34*, 373-388.

Falicov, C.J. & Brudner-White, L. (1983). Shifting the family triangle: The issue of cultural and contextual relativity. In J.C. Hansen & C.J. Falicov (Eds.), *Cultural Perspectives in Family Therapy: The Family Therapy Collections* (pp. 51-67). Rockville, MD: Aspen.

Gadamer, H. (1986). *Truth and Method*. New York: Crossroad Publishing Company.

Gaines, S.O., Jr. & Reed, E. (1995). Prejudice. *American Psychologist, 50*, 96-103

Geertz, C. (1983). *Local Knowledge*. New York: Basic Books.

Gushue, G.V. (1993). Cultural-identity development and family assessment: An interaction model. *The Counselling Psychologist, 21*, 487-513.

Hall, E.T. (1976). *Beyond Culture*. New York: Anchor/Doubleday.

Heidegger, M. (1967). *Being and Time*. New York: Harper & Row.

Heidegger, M. (1988). *The Basic Problems of Phenomenology*. Bloomington: Indiana University Press.

Horner, D. & Vandersluis, P. (1981). Cross-cultural counselling. In G. Althen (Ed.), *Learning Across Cultures*. Washington, DC: National Association for Foreign Student Affairs.

Howard, M.C. & McKim, P.C. (1983). *Contemporary Cultural Anthropology*. Boston: Little, Brown.

Ibrahim, F. (1984). Cross-cultural counselling and psychotherapy: An existential-psychological perspective. *International Journal for the Advancement of Counselling, 7,* pp. 559-569.

Ibrahim, F. (1985). Cross-cultural counselling training. In McFadden, J. (Ed.). *Transcultural Counselling: Bilateral and International Perspectives* (pp. 23-58). Alexandria, VA: American Counselling Association Press.

Ibrahim, F. (1985a). Effective cross-cultural counselling and psychotherapy: A framework. *The Counselling Psychologist, 13,* 625-638.

Ibrahim, F. (1991). Contribution of cultural worldview to generic counselling and development. *Journal of Counselling and Development.* Vol. 70, p. 13-19.

Ibrahim, F. (1993). Existential worldview theory: Transcultural applications. In J. McFadden (Ed.). *Transcultural Counselling: Bilateral and International Perspectives* (pp. 23-58). Alexandria, VA: American Counselling Association Press.

Ibrahim, F. & Kahn, H. (1984). *Scale to Assess Worldview (SAWV).* Rockview, CT: Schroeder Associates.

Ibrahim, F. & Kahn, H. (1987). Assessment of worldviews. *Psychological Reports, 60,* pp. 163-176.

Ibrahim, F.A., Roysircar-Sodowsky, G. & Ohnishi, H. (2001). Worldview: Recent developments and needed directions. In J. G. Ponterotto, J.M. Casas, L.A. Suzuki & C.M. Alexander (Eds.), *Handbook of Multicultural Counseling* (pp. 425-456). Thousand Oaks, CA: Sage.

Ibrahim, F. & Schroeder, D.G. (1987). Effective communication with multicultural families. In J. McFadden (Ed.). *Transcultural Counselling: Bilateral and International Perspectives* (pp. 23-58). Alexandria, VA: American Counselling Association Press.

Kearney, M. (1984). *World view.* Novato, CA: Chandler & Sharp.

Kluckhohn, C. (1951). Values and value orientations in the theory of action. In T. Parsons & E. Shiles (Eds.). *Towards a General Theory of Action.* Cambridge, MA: Harvard University Press.

Kluckhohn, C. (1956). Towards a comparison of value-emphasis in different cultures. In L.D. White (Ed.). *The State of Social Sciences.* Chicago: University of Chicago Press.

Kluckhohn, F. & Strodtbeck, F. (1961). *Variations in Value Orientations.* Evanston, IL: Row Paterson.

Kohls, R. (1994). *Developing Intercultural Awareness: A Cross-cultural Training Book.* Yarmouth, MN: Intercultural Press.

Matsumoto, D. (1996). *Culture and Psychology.* Pacific Grove, CA: Brooks/Cole.

McGill, D.W. (1983). Cultural concepts for family therapy. In J.C. Hansen & C.J. Falicov (Eds.). *Cultural Perspectives in Family Therapy: The Family Therapy Collections* (pp. 108-121). Rockville, MD: Aspen.

McGoldrick, M., Giordano, J. & Pearce, J.K. (1996). *Ethnicity and Family Therapy* (2nd ed.). New York: Guilford.

Montgomery, D.E., Fine, M.A. & James-Myers, L. (1990). The development and validation of an instrument to assess an optimal Afrocentric worldview. *Journal of Black Psychology, 17,* 37-54.

Myers, L.J., Spreight, S.L., Highlen, P.S., Cox, C.I., Reynolds, A.L., Adams, E.M. & Henley, C.P. (1991). Identity development and worldview: Toward an optimal conceptualization. *Journal of Counselling and Development, 70,* 54-63.

Mykailo, M. (1991). Cross-cultural awareness in the foreign language class: The Kluckhohn model. *The Modern Language Journal, 75,* iv

Lonner, W. & Ibrahim, F. (l996). Research about effectiveness. In P. Pedersen, J. Draguns, W. Lonner, & J. Trimble, *Counselling across Cultures,* 4th edition, Thousand Oaks, CA: Sage Publications, pp. 323-352

Okun, B., Fried, J. & Okun, M. (1999). *Understanding Diversity: A Learning-as-Practice Primer.* Pacific Grove, CA: Brook/Cole.

Oyserman, D., Coon H.M. & Kemmelmeier, M. (2002). Re-thinking individualism and collectivism: Evaluation of theoretical assumptions and meta-analysis. *Psychological Bulletin, 128,* 3-72.

Preli, R. & Bernard, J.M. (1993). Making multiculturalism relevant for majority culture graduate students. *Journal of Marital and Family Therapy, 19*(1), 5-16.

Quinn, N. (1985). "Commitment" in American marriage: A cultural analysis. In J.W.D. Dougherty (Ed.). *Directions in Cognitive Anthropology* (pp. 291-320). Urbana: University of Illinois Press.

Samovar, L.A. & Porter, R.E. (1995). *Communication Between Cultures.* Belmont, CA: Wadsworth.

Schwartz, T. (1992). Anthropology and psychology: An unrequited relationship. In T. Schwartz, G.M. White & C.A. Lutz (Eds.), *New Directions in Psychological Anthropology* (pp. 324-349). Cambridge, England: Cambridge University Press.

Schwartzman, J. (1983). Family ethnography: A tool for clinicians. In J.C. Hansen & C.J. Falicov (Eds.), *Cultural Perspectives in Family Therapy: The Family Therapy Collections* (pp. 122-135). Rockville, MD: Aspen.

Scofield, B. (1991). *Day-Signs: Native American Astrology from Ancient Mexico.* Amherst, MA: One Reed Publication.

Seltzer, R., Frazier, M. & Ricks, I. (1995). Multiculturalism, race and education. *Journal of Negro Education, 64,* 124-140.

Sire, J.W. (1976). *The Universe Next Door.* Downers Grove, IL: Intervarsity.

Sitaram, K.S. & Codgell, R.T. (1976) *Foundations of Intercultural Communication.* Columbus, OH: Charles E. Merril.

Shweder, R. (1991). *Thinking Though Cultures.* Cambridge, MA: Harvard University Press.

Sue, D.W. (1978). Eliminating cultural oppression in counselling: Toward a general theory. *Journal of Counselling Psychology, 25,* 419-428.

Sue, D.W. & Sue, D. (1999). *Counselling the Culturally Different: Theory and Practice.* (Third Edition). New York: John Wiley and Sons.

Triandis, H.C. (1994). *Culture and Social Behavior.* New York: Mc Graw-Hill.

White, A. (1983). A factor analysis of the Counselling Orientation Preference Scale (COS). *Counsellor Education and Supervision, 23,* 142-148.

Wurzel, J. (1988). *Toward Multiculturalism: A Reader in Multicultural Education.* Yarmouth, MN: Intercultural Press Inc.

Chapter 3
Developing Culturally Sensitive
Counselling Skills

*M. Honoré France, Geoffrey Hett and
María del Carmen Rodríguez*

*"Others envisage Canada as a cultural and linguistic pressure cooker. A political entity con-
structed around the principle of consultation and compromise, Canada is depicted as a pot-
pourri of two unequal charter groups, coupled with a vanquished but increasingly assertive
aboriginal population and an ever-expanding racial and ethnic minority sector equally
intent on staking claims" (Fleras & Elliott, 1992, p. 1).*

The cultural reality of Canada and North America has changed drastically in the last 50
years, not only in the numbers of minorities, but in the attitude of the general population.
It isn't that Canada is less racist, but as the make-up of the world population changes,
national boundaries are not ordered in clear ethnic boundaries, but have become so
enmeshed that a generalized view of what a Canadian is has changed. In the past, European
cultural groups comprised the vast majority of new immigrants in North America, whereas
today Asian groups top the list of new immigrant groups, particularly in British Columbia
and Ontario. According to Statistics Canada (2002), the minority population of Canada
presents a picture of a growing visible minority group (Table 1). What is more significant is
the clustering of visible minorities in the north, where the majority or significant minority
are First Nations people. Also, the large cities of Canada, such as Toronto, Vancouver and
Montreal, are comprised of large groups of visible minorities. However, the new face of
Canada can be seen in provinces such as British Columbia; including First Nations people,
21.7 % of the population of British Columbia are visible minorities. And the vast majority
of the minority people in BC, other than First Nations people, live in the lower mainland.
That means that the chances of meeting a minority person in BC are more than 1 in 5 [see
table 2]. Consider the following joke making the rounds in British Columbia: "Do you
know what separates China and India?" asks my friend, in the precisely modulated English
spoken by graduates of New Delhi's elite private schools. "The Himalayas," I venture. "It's
the Fraser River. Surrey is all Punjabi. Richmond is all Chinese" (Das, August 28, 2000, p.
A6). What is significant in these numbers is the large number of people with Asian ancestry, 421 160, which makes them the largest minority in BC.

Table 1: Minority Populations in Canada					
Group	Population	Percentage	Group	Population	Percentage
Chinese	860 150	3.02%	South Asian	670 590	2.35%
Black	573 860	2.01%	Arab/West Asian	244 665	0.86%
Filipino	234 195	0.82%	Southeast Asian	172 765	0.61%
Japanese	68 135	0.24%	Latin American	176 970	0.62%
Korean	64 835	0.23%	Aboriginals	799 005	2.8%
Total Canada	28 528,125	100.00%	Total Visible Minorities	3 197 480	11.21%

Source: Citizenship and Immigration Canada, 2002

However, what is making a remarkable impact is the large numbers of immigrants settling in BC from non-European countries. This trend can already be seen in urban settings like the Greater Vancouver Area where many households are not native-born. The multicultural reality is evident in British Columbia's schools, where large numbers of students do not come from the Canadian nation previously dominated by European ethnic groups such as English and French. In addition, in the northern areas of BC, more First Nations groups are becoming a significant minority and are often the majority in the communities where they reside.

Table 2: Population by Visible Minority Population in British Columbia			
Chinese	299 860	Filipino	47 080
Japanese	29 815	Southeast Asian	25 355
Korean	19 050	South Asian	158 430
Aboriginal (Status only)	139 655	Latin American	17 655
Black	23 275	Arab/West Asian	20 090
Multiple visible minorities	19 924 [includes Pacific Islanders]		
Total population of British Columbia		3 689 755	
Total visible minority population (2)	800 195	[21.7%]	

Source: Citizenship and Immigration Canada, 2002

The significance for counsellors is that developing and maintaining multicultural counselling skills is imperative if counsellors are to provide adequate assistance to the clients they are charged with serving. The multicultural reality of Canadian society is a reality that challenges counsellors in a time when universities are just beginning to recognize the importance of multicultural instruction. Generally, out of a program of nine to twelve graduate courses, one or two focus on multicultural topics. Most of the course work in counselling graduate programs is still very much Eurocentric, using training interventions that are European in origin. Counsellors and counsellor educators "...need to be aware [of] and recognize their cultural encapsulation and work to overcome it" (Vinson & Neimeyer, 2000, p. 177). The purpose of this chapter is to outline the counselling outcomes of the model proposed by Helms and Cooks (1999) and to summarize the multicultural competencies as proposed by Sue, Arrendondo and McDavis (l992).

Fundamental Assumptions of Multicultural Counselling

The current literature illustrates how contemporary service delivery is still failing not only [First Nations people] but other ethnic groups as well…Most providers are trained only in delivering services to the majority/dominant population. Usually [counsellors] are unaware of the life experiences of the ethnic minority patient (Duran & Duran, 1995, p8).

In fact, the very nature of counselling, that is the theories and practice, is based on values and worldviews that are European models. These dominant theories are the basis of counsellor training and practice, include all of the major assessment tools, according to Duran and Duran (l995), perpetuating colonialism and the domination of people with different worldviews. However, there is a growing awareness of the changing realities of differing ethnic groups represented in Canada and of more holistic and non-eurocentric counselling approaches that are finding acceptance by practitioners. While there is "increased attention to diversity and multiculturalism in the counselling profession" (Walden, Herlihy & Ashton, 2003, p. 109), there is still much to be done to move counselling towards a "postcolonial" approach. In other words, moving the counselling profession towards more openness to diversity and a greater acceptance of other worldviews and culturally different counselling practices.

Helms and Cook (1999) state that ultimately, the outcomes of the counselling process are the result of what both counsellor and client bring to interaction, which to a large extent is influenced by racial or cultural factors. Helms and Cook (1999) outline four main components:

— The input of psychological, race, cultural and distal reactions of clients and therapists;

— The social role involving therapist skills and theoretical orientation and client reactions, preferences and expectations;

— Process variables including racial matching and identity levels; and

— The outcome phase, which is marked by distal and psychological factors such as attrition, service utilization, symptom remission, racial development and cultural congruence (p. 66).

Much has been written in regards to what makes a multiculturally sensitive counsellor and one of the most comprehensive models are the cross-cultural Competencies Model proposed by Sue, Arrendondo & McDavis (l993). This model is multidimensional, divided into three domains: attitudes/beliefs, knowledge and skills. It is based on the counsellor's awareness of his/her personal cultural values and biases and the client's worldview in order to develop culturally appropriate intervention strategies.

Counsellor Awareness of Assumptions, Biases and Values

Attitudes and Beliefs

The starting point of multicultural counselling is within the counsellor, in that to be effective in working with people who come from different cultures, one must become aware of one's values, biases and beliefs. "Know thyself"; this Delphic slogan is at the heart of being aware and sensitive to one's cultural heritage. That means recognizing that differences exist and that if one is to operate within cultures, it is important to value and respect such differences. Along with one's cultural background, there are experiences that are colored by attitudes from the majority community, reflecting not only values, but also biases that have influenced one's psychological processes.

Knowing that psychological processes are determined to a great degree by culture, counsellors need to identify how cultural experiences limit counselling competencies. Most minority clients, particularly visible minorities, have experienced racism; thus, they recognize that differences between themselves and majority society exist. Therefore, the counsellor needs to be comfortable with acknowledging and discussing cultural, ethnic and racial differences. Corollary to this is that there may exist significant differences in terms of beliefs between themselves and their clients (e.g., collective versus individual orientations).

Knowledge

Among the many characteristics that counsellors must have in order to be competent, three attributes top the list: 1) It is fundamental that counsellors have specific knowledge about their own racial and cultural heritage and recognize how this can personally and professionally affect their personal and professional definitions and biases of normality-abnormality and the process of counselling. 2) Counsellors must have knowledge about an understanding of how oppression, racism, discrimination and stereotyping affect them personally and professionally. 3) Competent counsellors must be able to acknowledge their own racist attitudes, beliefs and feelings. This applies to all counsellors, but for whites it may mean a better understanding of "white privilege." Counsellors should possess knowledge and be aware of their social impact upon others. This means knowing how their communication style may clash or facilitate the counselling process with minority clients. Part of this is being able to anticipate how one's communication style impacts others.

Skills

One fundamental commitment from counsellors should be the constant pursuit to understand themselves as racial and cultural beings and actively seek a non-racist identity. This means that counsellors should be able to recognize the limits of their competencies and seek consultation, training and references from more qualified individuals and/or resources. They should seek out educational, consultative and training experiences to enhance their understanding and effectiveness in working with culturally different populations. Duran and Duran (1995) go further and emphasize that the counsellor should not only learn appropriate strategies, but also "believe and practice these beliefs in his/her personal life if the intervention is to benefit the client" (p. 87).

Personal encounters with racism are not part of most counsellors' experiences; therefore, most counsellors do not know how debilitating this can be on one's view of the world and personality. There is considerable documentation that the effects of racism have negative impact on one's health and psychological well-being. Therefore, counsellors need to be aware of the negative emotional reactions caused by prejudice and stereotyping. This means knowing the political and social aspects of a specific situation and how it relates to visible minority groups. One attitude that enhances not only multicultural competency, but also communication, is openness to other ideas, cultures and experiences. This requires taking a non-judgemental position.

Counsellor Awareness of Client's Worldview

Attitudes and beliefs

According to Samovar, Rorter and Jain (1981), worldview "…refers to the outlook or image…. concerning the nature of the universe, the nature of humankind, the relationship between humanity and the universe and other philosophical or orientations that help us define the cosmos and our place in it" (p. 21). Worldview is an aspect of cultural value preferences that frame one's outlook. Therefore, culturally competent counsellors need to acquire specific knowledge of their clients' worldview, style and cultural identity development levels. Some clients may have had horrific experiences in regards to poverty and racism – which might have reinforced their sense of powerlessness. Counsellors should be aware of how their own preconceived notions about certain cultural groups influence the client-helper interaction in different ways.

Knowledge

It is fundamental that counsellors possess knowledge about the group of people they are working with and familiarize themselves with some of the historical, social and cultural background of their clients. Additionally, counsellors should be aware of how ethnicity, culture and tradition influence decision-making processes, vocational choices, specific behaviors (e.g., bullying at school) and integration. Recognizing how negative experiences impact client development is imperative in the counselling process. According to Aboud and Rabiau (2002) "…the prevalence and impacts of racial/ethnic discrimination … may affect [the] individual's health" (p. 304).

Skills

Counsellors should become involved with activities and functions outside of the counselling setting. They can act as advocates and advisors in order to get a different perspective and see the client interact in his/her "natural" setting. Participating in community events, social gatherings, traditional celebrations and other relevant happenings could assist them in broadening and fostering their knowledge, understanding and utilization of cross-cultural skills. One effective way of maintaining and enhancing good counselling skills is to read professional journals and to keep abreast of the latest research and theoretical findings on cross-cultural work. An important aspect of understanding changes in one's profession as a helper is to seek the appropriate professional development that will ensure that competencies are maintained.

Culturally Appropriate Approaches

Recognizing that clients bring with them different religious and spiritual beliefs may mean that they will have values that will affect counselling outcomes. In fact, these differences may even affect how they express emotional distress. Clients may see emotions as not being separate from the body or spirit. Because of these differences, counsellors can increase their effectiveness by incorporating indigenous helping practices and the natural helping networks in the minority community. Another important variable in counselling is the relationship between culture and language. Therefore, the counsellor needs to see that bilingualism is an asset and not a liability.

By and large, counselling training has followed the Eurocentric tradition in counselling theory and practice. These practices conflict with cultural values of other traditions (e.g., the reliance of self-disclosure in the Client-Centred approach may go against allegiance to the family). While most counsellors are aware that assessment instruments and techniques may be culturally biased, they need to be aware that in most cases, institutional barriers have been created based on assessment instruments. Diagnostic techniques fit majority culture, but do not necessarily reflect cultural minorities' values. Traditional counselling methods have emphasized the importance of helping the individual, thus going against the influence of the family and community structures. Knowing when and how to integrate the family and community into counselling practice will empower culturally different clients and help them seek a collective solution rather than an individual one. Counsellors need to understand that racism and oppression are a part of the minority experience; thus, goals need to reflect the reality of combating and dealing with this. However, helpers need to understand that racism is very complex and dynamic and people of color have developed the strategies of buffering and code switching to deal with it (Cross, Smith & Payne, 2002). Buffering is the process of developing "thick skin," of letting hurtful things "bounce off" while accomplishing an immediate task or goal (e.g., learning a skill from a racist teacher). Code switching is utilizing an alternative manner of interaction in order to get by (e.g., dealing with an aggressive white police officer).

A Culturally Sensitive Perspective

When working with minority clients, trust is a major issue that needs to be resolved, particularly since those with power have been the instruments of oppression. The most effective way of building trust is to ensure that verbal and non-verbal messages are not only congruent, but also accurate and appropriate. Minority clients have problems that are external in origin but that have roots in biases and racism. Therefore, counsellors need to take on an advocacy role to help clients with these external factors by utilizing institutional interventions. In addition, counsellors should have a working knowledge of the traditional healers and spiritual leaders in their areas and how they work. The "secret" is knowing when it is culturally appropriate to bring these "helpers" into the process. Part of this will be recognizing one's linguistic and assisting limitations.

The culturally competent counsellor also needs to be involved in educational intervention and combating oppression in their community. Not only should racism be the number one priority, but also the idea of "white privilege" needs to be addressed. Similarly the ethical lines established by organizations like the Canadian Counselling Association or the Canadian Psychology Association must be examined from a cultural perspective, because dealing with multiculturalism is such a new issue that these organizations need reform so that they do not perpetuate racism. The role of counsellors today is empowering clients and this may mean educating them about their personal and legal rights. It may also mean challenging the status quo and the counselling associations to deal with their institutional racism. As it exists now, counselling, in a post-colonial context, operates on a racist and Eurocentric manner!

Establishing Cultural Empathy

Chung and Bemak (2002) explored empathy and its importance in counselling people from other cultures. Empathy, as a core skill in counselling, is a reflection of the Client-Centered approach, thus a Eurocentric counselling practice and considered in a multicultural context to be of value in certain situations and circumstances. It is a useful skill that needs to be used in a context that reflects culture. A number of guidelines have been established in using empathy [reflection of feeling] that reflect the cultural situation of the clients being counselled. The following six guidelines compiled by Chung and Bemak (2002) are considered fundamental:

1. Many cultures are collective in nature; therefore, counsellors need to accept and understand the client's family and the community context;

2. Indigenous healing practices reflect beliefs and values that can easily be incorporated into the counselling environment, by working ccoperatively with healers;

3. Many clients come to counselling experiencing transgenerational trauma. Counsellors need to be knowledgeable about clients' historical and socio-political backgrounds;

4. Counsellors need to be aware and knowledgeable about psychosocial development and its effect on clients who move from one environment to another, whether it is from a rural area to an urban area or to another country;

5. People of color often experience oppression, discrimination and racism on a daily basis. As a result, counsellors need to accept and be aware of how it negatively affects their clients' well-being;

6. Counsellors need to provide support, resources and practices that can empower clients, including the promotion of social justice.

Conclusion

Many Western therapies are merely methods of colonizing the lifeworld of the…client. The end result of many Western therapies is the ongoing cultural hegemony of the client seeking help. Even though the efficacy of the therapeutic arena seems doubtful when the analysis places it in a colonialist paradigm, there are some integrated approaches that have been found to be effective (Duran & Duran, 1995, p. 87).

Gaining multicultural counselling competencies can ensure that counsellors are actively involved in combating racism that robs people of their self-respect and of their sense of dignity. It is a means of ensuring a more peaceful and prosperous society in which all people are equal. The kind of prejudice experienced by ethnic and racial minorities, intentional or unintentional, is the essence of the challenge of an open society.

Culture is a human necessity, a way of life. It is the way people establish and maintain a relationship with their environment. As people of understanding interact with those who are culturally different, they must explore the socialization forces that affect behavior, values and language. Therefore, it is good ethical practice to be multiculturally competent. Arrendondo and D'Andrea (2003) suggest that culturally skilled counsellors need to:

– Recognize the sources of discomfort and differences that exist between themselves and clients in terms of race, ethnicity, culture and religion;

– Identify at least five specific features of culture of origin and explain how those features affect the relationship with culturally different clients;

– Provide a reasonably specific definition of racism, prejudice and discrimination and how these adversely impact individuals identified with "terrorist" groups;

– Be aware of their negative and positive emotional reactions toward other racial and ethnic groups that may prove detrimental to the counselling relationship;

– Recognize the heterogeneity within all ethnic, religious and cultural groups;

– Explain the relationship between culture and power;

– Recognize among a variety of religious and spiritual communities the recognized forms of leadership and how these may differ from one's experience;

– Value bilingualism;

– Be aware of discriminatory practices at the social and community level that may affect the psychological welfare of individuals who are identified with the terrorist groups;

– Be aware of the effects of family separation on children with parents in the military;

– Recognize that fear, anxiety and vulnerability may be masked with silence or other ways of "coping";

– Recognize that differing worldviews require perspective-taking rather than an immediate judgment; and

– Recognize the limits of their multicultural competency.

The transformation from ignorance to multicultural competence is neither simple nor easy. The challenges require that we develop a more open approach to communication with others from different cultural groups, possess a willingness to understand, develop empathy toward foreign and alien cultures and be tolerant of views that differ from our own. If we have the determination to adapt our behaviors and attitudes with the desire to overcome ethnocentrism, we may begin to know the feelings of exhilaration that come when we have made contact with those from other cultures far removed from our own sphere of experience. This willingness to reach out, risk, learn and experience others is a challenge for everyone.

References

Aboud, F. & Rabiau, M. (2002). Health psychology in multiethnic perspectives. In P. Pedersen, J. Draguns, W. Lonner & J. Trimble (Eds.), *Counseling Across Cultures,* 5th Edition. Thousand Oaks, CA: Sage.

Arrendondo, P. & D'Andrea, M. (2003). The cultural universality of anxiety, vulnerability and fears. *Counselling Today*, April, pp. 26, 28.

Chung, R.C.-Y. & Bemak, F. (2002). The relationship between culture and empathy in cross-cultural counseling. In Pedersen, P., Draguns, J., Lonner, W. & Trimble, J. (Eds.). *Counseling Across Cultures*, 5th Edition. Thousand Oaks, CA: Sage.

Cross, W., Smith, L. & Payne, Y. (2002). Black identity: A repertoire of daily enactments. In P. Pedersen, J. Draguns, W. Lonner & J. Trimble (Eds.), *Counseling Across Cultures*, 5th Edition. Thousand Oaks, CA: Sage.

Das, S. (2000). Our new "two solitudes." *Victoria Times-Colonist*, Monday, August 28, p. A6.

Duran, E. & Duran, B. (l995). *Native American Postcolonial Psychology*. Albany, NY: State University of New York Press.

Fleras, A. & Elliott, J.L. (l992). *The Challenge of Diversity: Multiculturalism in Canada*. Scarborough, ON: Nelson Canada.

Helms, J.E. & Cook, D. (1999). *Using Race and Culture in Counseling and Psychotherapy: Theory and Practice*. Boston, MA: Allyn & Bacon.

Samovar, L., Rorter, R. & Jain, N. (l981). *Understanding Intercultural Communication*, Belmont, CA: Wadsworth Publishing Company.

Statistics Canada. (2002). *Population by Visible Minority Population in Canada 2003* [on-line]. Retrieved Jan 10, 2002 from www.statcan.ca/start.html.

Sue, D.W., Arrendondo, P. & McDavis, R.J. (l992). Multicultural competencies and standards: A call to the profession. *Journal of Counselling and Development, 70,* 477-486.

Vinson, T.S. & Neimeyer, G.J. (2000). The relationship between racial identity development and multicultural counselling competency. *Journal of Multicultural Counselling and Development, 28*(3), pp. 177-192.

Walden, S.L., Herlihy, B. & Ashton, L. (2003). The evolution of ethics: Personal perspectives of ACA ethnics committee chairs. *Journal of Counselling & Development, 81*, 106-110.

Part II
Counselling Procedures

The focus of the chapters in Part II of this book is on counselling practices and procedures from a variety of cultural, religious and sexual orientations. We believe that traditional theories of counselling primarily utilized in counsellor training may do more harm than good in working with culturally different clients. We need to be more culturally centered and accept the perspective of the clients we work with by recognizing that in a post colonial world, counselling needs to free itself from its "colonial past." We have included a number of examples of how a culturally sensitive and knowledgeable counsellor can be more effective. In part, we need to recognize that our Eurocentric education has often failed to meet the academic, social and emotional needs of culturally different clients.

Once people understand cultural differences, such as some of the traditional Asian values, we, as a multicultural society can better understand ourselves. Counsellors need to realize the importance of environmental and social influences on behavior and recognize the implications of counselling in terms of attitude, beliefs, knowledge and skills. There are a number of mental health issues that are relevant not only to Asian Canadians, but all the people of Canada. An important part of effective counselling is an awareness of a client's perception of mental health and the therapeutic relationship. Since families often play a large part in influencing the therapeutic process of many minority clients, approaches must be selected that respect this phenomenon. With many people coming from abroad, we need to understand how these unique situations that influence the helping process, such as war, political unrest and human rights violations, affect counselling practice.

An intriguing aspect of a multicultural society is the growth of people of color and of mixed race individuals. Consequently there has been an increased focus on counselling research involving biracial identity development. There are a number of models of identity development for biracial individuals as well as differing cultural groups. Research findings show that growing up in two cultural milieus brings challenges that result in difficulty in trying to integrate two cultures (e.g., inside and outside the home). With more and more immigrants moving to Canada, there is more and more intergenerational conflict between the first and second generations. Consequently, we need to be aware of possible stressors faced by young people as well as their parents with regards to value conflicts. From a multicultural perspective, we need to move beyond the therapeutic role of a counsellor and become advocates of our clients.

Most counsellors from the mainstream have had little experience with what it is like to live as a minority. For example, what are the philosophical foundations of "blackness," identity development and to struggle daily with racism? Theories that describe the relationship between personality and racism, such as Cross's Nigrescence Theory, are just examples of the different frameworks to helping culturally diverse clients. To empower them, we also need to develop counselling strategies that encourage our clients to cope with being different. Anything we as counsellors can do to build a positive and helpful relationship with clients is important if we are to be helpful. One other aspect of diversity is being able to understand differing perspectives in regards to religious beliefs. Counselling has often tried to become value free and dismissive of the spiritual aspects of humanness. Those who have taken the time to become familiar with the part that religion plays in people, particularly with Muslim clients, know that much can be done to empower clients to utilize their religious beliefs for their well being. To include a basic understanding of how religion shapes behavior is increasingly more important as the number of Muslims in Canada increases. This increase has occurred through immigration and through conversion. Multicultural counsellors need to understand the Islamic worldview and the religious teaching of Muslim clients.

We believe that in a truly diverse society, issues associated with sexual orientation become an important aspect of counselling. The traditional support structures that exist within our society often fail visible and invisible minority clients, leaving many of these to face abuse, isolation, rejection and violence. As a starting point, we need to be concerned about the stressors, as well as promote awareness and provide support. In addition, we need to adopt specific counsellor interventions aimed at addressing all of the needs of our clients, regardless of their differences. In a true multicultural society, we must recognize that even within the "white" population there are a variety of people with unique cultural practices, values, languages and religions. Therefore, we need to identify and value what makes people distinct and how these differences impact on our clients. Perhaps we should remember these words from Martin Luther King, Jr: "What we will remember is not the words of our enemies, but the silence of our friends." As such, we believe that counsellors need to be proactive in changing society and advocating for social change in which our children can be free of bigotry and racism.

Chapter 4
Issues in Counselling in the First Nations Community

M. Honoré France, Rod McCormick and María del Carmen Rodríguez

"By keeping the children at school ten months of the year for 12 years, the residential school system succeeded in separating the children from the Nlakapamux adults and the enculturation process which would teach them to be Nlakapamux. This is separation from the cultural self, from parental love and care, from all that is cherished and valued by a hunting and gathering people" Shirley Sterling (1997, p. 11).

The issues that face First Nations people in Canada are quite unique from any other ethnic or racial group, personally, politically and socially. All aspects of well being are fused with these intricate aspects, which makes effective counselling a challenge. Essentially, counselling training as it stands now does not have a solid foundation that would make counsellors effective with the majority of clients that are not only in need of effective counselling, but are demanding culturally competent counsellors both within and outside the First Nations community. All minorities face the prospect of dealing with a Eurocentric counselling paradigm that starts with a worldview and knowledge base that stands as a barrier to effective counselling services. According to Duran and Duran (1995) "a postcolonial paradigm would accept knowledge from differing cosmologies as valid in their own right, without their having to adhere to a separate cultural body for legitimacy" (p. 6).

The population numbers of First Nations people in Canada presently stand between 3-6%, depending on how they self identify: status versus non-status. However, the birth rate for First Nations people is one of the highest in Canada and will continue to grow in the coming years. Dyer (2001) suggests that they will become either the majority or close to it in large areas of Canada (i.e., the north particularly). The study regarding counselling effectiveness with First Nations clients continues to grow. Counselling success has not been present for many minorities, particularly First Nations people, probably because:

...counselors may lack basic knowledge about the client's ethnic and historical backgrounds; the client may be driven away by the professional's counseling style; the client may sense that his or her worldview is not valued; the client may feel uncomfortable talking openly with a stranger; or the ethnic backgrounds of the counselor may create client apprehension (Trimble & Thurman, 2002, p. 61).

While many aspects of the counselling process may be blocked due to differing world-views, there are some approaches and strategies that can enhance trust and promote a healthy relationship between counsellors, regardless of ethnic background, and First Nations clients. There are no definitive strategies, but we believe that counsellors can take proactive steps that will help them be more successful. We agree with what Duran and Duran (1995) stress, that [the difficulty] "...is not so much with traditional practitioners in the Native American community as with the Western practitioners" (p. 9). The lack of understanding of the historical, political and social aspects of oppression and how it disrupts counselling practice has been one reason why counselling has not been as effective as it could be. We hope that with a basic understanding of the Indian Act it will become more evident why First Nations people often feel alienated from Canadian institutions. It is also crucial to acquire some knowledge of the issues, such as the "fall out" from the residential school system that affect First Nations clients. In this chapter, we will describe the diversity of First Nations people and culture as well as common elements that make us unique. We will provide a description and discussion of our counselling approach, including the importance of working with elders, rituals, nature, art and cultural friendly strategies. Finally, we will share some important elements of studies on helping strategies and specific tasks that non-First Nations counsellors can adopt to improve their counselling with First Nations clients.

Who are First Nations people?

Until Europeans came to the Western Hemisphere, the original people who inhabited the lands were a variety of nations with different languages, customs and beliefs. Invariably, like people anywhere else in the world, they were simply the people from this or that place. They were the original people that were mistaken by European explorers as inhabitants of India. The Assembly of First Nations, the major organizational body of native people in Canada, adopted the name First Nations rather than the name Indian. The significance of the name proposes that they came from the earth. Interestingly, this belief is universal in all of the original inhabitants of the Western Hemisphere.

Within Aboriginal groups, there are many nations and many traditions with a variety of languages and customs, yet there are some commonalities such as the relationship between people and the land, wholeness, spirituality and a sense of collectivity or a greater value on the group versus the individual. In Canada, First Nations people have sovereign rights under the constitution, which has allowed them to seek redress from oppressive legislation and practices. Indigenous beliefs emphasize that humankind is interdependent and that there has to be a balance not only in thoughts, feelings and actions, but in the spiritual connection between the self and all creation. Since everything is interrelated, well-being is based on ensuring that one is in harmony with one's surroundings. In counselling, the tribal and the extended family is of utmost importance. Communication is often circular or non-linear, as it is in European traditions. Spiritualism, as a way of knowing the world and as "good medicine," provides guidance and protection through observation, teaching and healing.

Important issues in the First Nations Community

"Teaching First Nations children is really nothing different from good basic teaching with feeling, concern and understanding!" (Council for Yukon Indians, 1993, p. 1). Counselling practice with First Nations clients always starts with competent, effective and sensitive counselling strategies. However, because of the diversity of native people in Canada and their history with non-native people, there are a number of issues that counsellors need to be aware of. That is not to say that these issues will necessarily affect clients, but that the literature reflects these areas of concern.

– Alienation

– Anger towards majority and reservation politics

– Discrimination

– Political & social oppression

– Residential school experience

– Sexual & substance abuse

– Crisis of the spirit

– Loss of culture

The Implications of the Indian Act on the Counselling Relationship

An important implication for counselling First Nations clients can be seen in the historical and political relationship of natives and non-natives as expressed in the Indian Act, which is why we believe that every counsellor should be aware of the major tenets of the law. The legislation was passed in 1876 by Parliament and the aim of the new law as articulated from Canada's first Prime Minister, John A. Macdonald, was "...to wean them [First Nations] by slow degrees, from their nomadic habits, which have become almost an instinct and by slow degrees absorb them on the land" (Beltrame, 2003, p. 37). Not only did this law regulate how the nation of Canada would deal politically with the native inhabitants, but it profoundly affected the social, spiritual and emotional psyche of generations of people to this day. In effect, because of this law and the ensuing relationship that resulted from the law, First Nations clients have by and large developed a sense of mistrust of intentions of major institutions and non-native people in general. Why is it that a law regulating people would have so much impact on people today? The major aspects of the Indian Act:

– Defined who was an Indian: status and non-status Indians. (Status Indians – registered & Non-Status Indians – not registered.);

- Control of the land: forbade the selling or leasing of any reserve land unless it was first surrendered or leased to the Crown;

- Control of government: election of First Nations chiefs. Essentially, these chiefs functioned as agents of the federal government, under federal supervision (Indian Agent);

- Control of the people: An 1880 amendment declared that any First Nations person obtaining a university degree would lose status as a First Nations person and member of their community; In addition people could not leave the reserve without a special pass; Finally, children were taken away to residential schools to be assimilated.

There have been a number of changes over the years, most notably, the loosening of some of the more restrictive aspects, such as the extension of citizenship to everyone, the dismantlement of the residential school system, the freedom to move off the reserves and the extension of educational rights. In addition, Bill C20 changed the definition of who is an aboriginal. Originally, this followed the father's ethnic identity, so if a native woman married a non-native, she lost her rights as a native. Bill C20 changed that by bringing about more gender equality. In terms of day-to-day living, the impact of the laws have had the effect of controlling even small aspects of life. According to WE (2003), "if I want to paint a room in my house on reserve, I have to get permission from the band, who has to get permission from Ottawa! It is so bureaucratic that I just don't want to bother with it!" In the past few years, the government of Canada has introduced the new First Nations governance Act that is presently being considered by Parliament. This act would supersede the original Indian Act by:

- Adopting codes of transparent administration and accountability that would govern elections of chiefs and councils through secret ballot;

- Establishing rules for regulating the making of laws and stipulate requirements for annual, audited budgets;

- Establishing impartial bodies to allow band members to lodge complaints against chiefs and councils;

- Having a companion legislation, which would make it easier for band councils to raise money through borrowing and internal taxation for economic development.

On the surface one could ask why are natives against these changes and the answer is surprising given the recommendations of various Royal Commissions. Essentially, the new governance act (C-7) is a top-down process rather than a cooperative and consultative process. As a result, the government is paying the price because they have left out the very people who might benefit. This Act has implications for counselling, that this process, like many other actions of the government, both privately and publicly, reveals their paternalistic attitude because the values underlying the legislation do not take into account the values of the people. For example, how do these changes work with hereditary chiefs? According to the former Chief of the Assembly of First Nations, Mathew Coon Come, if the government followed what the Royal Commission recommended, that an ombudsperson and auditor general be a part of the new legislation, then there might be some room for accommodations. Chief Coon Come goes further and emphatically states that the new law, just like the old law, goes against the spirit of self-government rights as stated by the Constitution. What upsets the Assembly of First Nations is the assumption behind the act that poverty stems from poor management by the chiefs and councils rather than a lack of resources and an adequate land base (Beltrame, 2003).

The Importance of Building Trust and a Positive Working Relationship

While Canada never had the many Indian wars that characterized the founding of the United States, there has been considerable conflict between First Nations people and Europeans who settled in Canada. Most Canadians, having developed their historical attitudes about the "Indian" from American television, primarily view First Nations people as a "conquered people" (Newman, 1989). As such, many whites expected "Indians" to accept European culture as dominant and therefore, superior. If the "Indians" would only adapt to the white man's way, then everything would be all right. In fact, the "Indians" never fought extensive battles nor were they ever defeated in Canada. They made treaties with the British and French crowns that, at the time, seemed advantageous to all of the parties. Yet the view of a "conquered" people and "conquered" land persists. To First Nations people, humankind has custodianship of the environment. For European settlers in North America, the land was something to conquer and subdue. The land is something that is a part of each person. This idea of the connectedness with the land is eloquently expressed by Carl Jung (Smoley, 1992), who said:

> *"Children born there [a foreign land] would inherit the wrong ancestor – spirits who dwell in the trees, the rocks and the water of that country.... that would mean the spirit of the Indian gets at the [person] from within and without" (p. 85).*

The "road" to technology, strongly associated with European civilization, has led society to pollution and a "scorched Earth policy." While the "road" to spirituality is less scientific, it reflects traditional native people's beliefs; the belief that the environment is reflected in how natives relate to a Higher Being. While there is one Supreme Being, the Great Spirit, there are also spirits of locality, spirits of natural forces and animal spirits. All have distinct powers. For some First Nations people the animal powers are greater than the Great Spirit. In fact, the Great Spirit is rarely invoked, while the spirits under the Great Spirit are routinely involved. Among the Salish people, "almost every action in life is centered around the Spirit Power" (Ashwell, 1989, p. 68). One spirit is not greater than another but they are omnipresent, in Mother Earth, Father Sky and the four directions. Spirits are everywhere. The spirit is in the trees, in the universe, everywhere in life.

One Therapeutic Example: Counselling Residential School Survivors

Residential schools were one of the more odious strategies used by the Canadian Government to assimilate First Nations people. The consequences of this strategy are still haunting the government and aboriginal people today. This failed strategy discontinued only after the Supreme Court stepped in and unanimously condemned residential schools as being disgraceful and even criminal. As a result, the government and the churches, who operated the schools, are paying the price of lawsuits for their despicable behavior. In developing a treatment program for residential school survivors, the authors utilized a therapeutic strategy that was culturally oriented following strict traditional guidelines. When putting together our counselling approach with the various groups we worked with at the healing lodge, we wanted to utilize not only a culturally sensitive approach, but also utilize important elements of the cultures on the West Coast. Our theme, as expressed by Couture (1991), is that:

Being in relationships is the manifest spiritual ground of Native being. In traditional perception, nothing exists in isolation, everything is relative to every other being or thing. As [First Nations people] we are wont to exclaim: And all my relations...(p. 59).

As counsellors we felt it was important to let everyone know in our groups that to make mistakes is a human condition and it is a constant struggle to be on the "Red Road." By this, we meant that as human beings we want to embrace our culture and bring back the true spirit of the "village life," knowing that we live in an industrialized country in a modern world. One of our Elders always reminded us that, "...we do not live in a village anymore, but we can recreate the village in our hearts" (Personal conversation, 2002).

Our approach to healing and helping is holistic, focusing on the:

- Cognitive processes: (e.g., "How are you thinking about yourself vis-à-vis the problem and environment?");
- Affective processes: (e.g., "How do you feel about the problem, people concerned and your relationship to them?");
- Social or action processes: (e.g., "How is your behavior blocking problem resolution in the group?");
- Spiritual processes: (e.g., "How can you fulfill spiritual yearning?).

An important element of counselling and using a cultural approach is to incorporate elders as co-facilitators/counsellors into the therapeutic process. Our experience is that healthy elders provide the traditional well of knowledge and can share their own healing journey. Because they are active in the therapeutic process, they provide valuable support, cultural reinforcement and positive models of behavior. According to Ross (1992), elders can also provide an alternative way of sharing uniquely to them:

Elders favour the use of instructive parables over direct criticism. Criticism focuses almost entirely upon the past and upon failures in the past, while enlightening parables instead serve to coax people forward towards better ways of doing things in the future (p. 173).

We also incorporated a number of rituals that reinforced the cultural-spiritual connections. In each group session we sat in a circle, starting our work with a prayer offered by the elders, which was followed by an invitation for anyone to join us on a pow-wow drum with a traditional song. These songs were given to us to sing and were songs of joy and challenge. The large pow-pow drum was a powerful symbol of the work we hoped to accomplish in our groups. The pow-wow drum can be played by up to ten participants and the drumming creates a focus for energizing the group and reminding everyone that they are united in their healing. There is also an element of the sound, which reminded us of our "heart beat" and how we strive to reunite with the spirit of Mother Earth. We used an eagle feather as a means to allow everyone in the circle to share their thoughts for the day; often times it gave us a clue to the emotional state of a participant thereby knowing if someone was ready to enter the "circle" and work on an issue. We felt that any therapeutic work should be within the circle so that the participants could not only learn from each other's healing while supporting whoever needs it. Sitting in a circle not only reinforced our belief in the power of the circle or the idea, as Black Elk (1961) expressed that all that is holy happens in a circle, but it also corresponded therapeutically with the healing we were trying to accomplish. Our belief is that everyone needs to be heard and they need to say it in their own words. In a sense, the circle was sacred and followed the belief that thoughts and ideas are:

> *…passed from generation to generation through ceremonies, lodges and storytelling. Sacred Circle symbolism is enacted in meetings, sun dances, sweat lodges, sweet grass ceremonies, pipe ceremonies and feasts where participants confer, celebrate and pray. This symbol represents unity, interdependence and harmony among all beings in the universe and time as the continual recurrence of natural patterns (Regnier in Hart, 2002, p. 62).*

Emotional expression or cleansing was an important component of the healing process. Emoting, particularly anger or hurt, was important because these emotions were either suppressed or inappropriately expressed (e.g., towards a loved one rather than towards perpetrators of sexual abuse or racism). Therefore, participants went through the process of learning how to ventilate, express and channel their emotions. The final part of the daily work emphasized resolution and living more constructively. We often "brushed off" a participant with cedar, a sacred plant for people of the Northwest, or with an eagle feather. Sometimes role-playing in which a participant rehearsed a constructive method of dealing with an issue in everyday life was utilized. It was not uncommon for a participant to face their "village elders" or those that they felt they "wronged" in simulation, so that they knew how it felt to tell others of their pain and their sorrow for any mistakes they made in dealing with family or community members. Importantly, we wanted them to understand that absolution goes with atonement. Not surprisingly, at the end of these simulations, there was a great deal of respect shown by the other participants. Finally, we ended our groups with a check out insight and verbal supportive statements from the participants, followed by advice and comments from the elders and a prayer.

Traditionally, First Nations people have practiced informal helping in their community by reaching out to their families, friends and neighbors in times of stress. Accordingly, we try and create a sense of a "family" or "community" within the circle. In the literature, there is even a name for it: "network therapy." This type of therapeutic approach stresses that all of the social forces that affect someone are related to each other. Thus, the family, relatives and friends are included when someone is experiencing emotional distress. Red Horse (1982), a Sioux, developed a "network therapy" program called Wido-Ako-Date-Win, which brought everyone who wanted to be supportive into the helping process. Red Horse stressed that one could not help someone without including those important people in his or her social network. Helping is usually not one-on-one, but the person is helped with significant others available. This idea reflected the notion that the best way to help was to regard everyone in the First Nations community as a family. In fact, many traditional First Nations people stress that mental well-being cannot be separated from the context of the community. In other words, in order to help heal someone's emotional problem, the community has to be involved in the process. To emphasize this further, consider that studies involving help seeking attitudes of First Nations university students, indicated they "would typically seek help from family members before seeking psychological services" (LaFromboise, Trimble & Mohatt, 1990 p. 152). As far as specific counselling strategies, we borrow from Art Therapy, particularly with the carving that is a part of our work. With carving, participants project their ideas and thus have a ready "canvas" of thought and vision that can be utilized for helping. The Nuu-chah-nulth carver and elder, Harold Lucas, said to us, "what is in the heart flows through the hands" (Personal conversation, March, 2002).

We also utilize nature in our therapeutic approach by ensuring that participants experience as a daily ritual the outdoors. In our groups, we take everyone outside for a walk, but we do not just walk and enjoy nature, we show them how nature is a "medicine cabinet" of well-being. There are plants that have traditional qualities, which can be used for different purposes; there are healers who know these qualities and show everyone in the group. We demonstrate how to prepare four-bark medicine and as a group we invite everyone to experience it. The main function of this exercise is to reconnect everyone to the natural world. The implications for counselling is that therapy must go beyond the boundaries of the training and ensure that clients feel a greater connection between themselves and their culture, begin to develop a solid identity, ensure that they can work in a variety of cultural situations and empower them to reclaim themselves as First Nations people. Finally, whenever it was necessary or requested we would "lay hands on" and pray for someone's comfort, thereby reinforcing the power of the spirit in one's well-being.

Facilitation of Healing with First Nations Clients

Research undertaken by McCormick (1995) focused on what traditional First Nations people feel facilitates healing. What is significant about this study is that First Nations people, from traditional healers to clients, shared what worked successfully with their clients and within themselves. The following conditions and actions were the themes identified as facilitators of the healing process:

Anchoring oneself in tradition and participation in ceremonies: This theme consists of being involved and having an active interest in cultural activities such as Pow Wows, ceremonies and gaining traditional knowledge. There is a close relationship between knowing one's culture and being healthy since building a foundation of connectedness, both with those in the community and with the culture, leads to a healthier life style.

Setting goals (medicine wheel) and pursuing challenging activities: Having a clear sense of purpose and balance in all dimensions of life, as exemplified by the medicine wheel, not only brings about a feeling that life is meaningful, but that there is something to work towards for the future. Pursuing activities that relate to completing a difficult project, going back to school or preparing for more a challenging job was found to help people feel better about themselves and their abilities.

Expressing oneself: The ability to express emotions, including anger, love, frustration and other feelings appropriately helps to alleviate stress and express feelings in a healthy manner. The means expressing one's emotions goes from the physical (e.g., screaming in the forest, carving, singing), to the psychological (i.e., reflecting, journal writing, counseling), to the spiritual (i.e., smudging and sweats).

Support from others (collective): Social support is not only feeling connected by blood to others in the community, but it also entails taking more specific actions towards others in the form of acceptance, encouragement, reassurance and validation.

Spiritual connection: Developing a sense of spirituality does not only give one a sense of connectedness, but it also helps develop a sense of morality, constructive living, humility and transcendence. Participating in sacred ceremonies and rituals brings a sense of closeness and interaction, which is different from the relationships one has with other people. Spirituality is represented in different ways in everyday life situations such as brushing oneself with cedar, praying, singing sacred songs and so forth.

Role models: Good role models, such as elders, relatives or successful people in the community, provide inspiration and guidance as to alternative ways for problem solving, decision-making, constructive living or how to conduct oneself in a healthy manner. Among First Nations people stories, myths and legends are elements to teach about morality, good behavior, consequences of one's actions and life in general.

Nature connection: A feeling of being part of the land and therefore, of something greater than oneself provides opportunities for people to reflect on and analyze life situations through metaphoric relationships (e.g., one could use a nature walk to reflect on one's life, obstacles, wisdom along the way and so forth). Nature also offers curative effects such as calming and relaxation. Additionally, roots and plants are often used to make medicine and complement meals.

The implications for practice are that these themes could easily be incorporated into the interventions that counsellors utilize with their clients. "A counsellor with more knowledge might make a more concrete suggestion such as encouraging the client to watch a river flow for a few hours or attend a Pow Wow" (McCormick, 1995, pp. 142-143). Clearly, these themes could easily fit into a variety of intervention modalities and the human resources, such as elders, could be incorporated into the counselling.

Guidelines for Working with First Nations Clients

For a counsellor from the majority community, there are many challenges that confront the counsellor, including his/her own identity development, therapeutic competency, the ability to work within a differing worldview and being culturally sensitive. According to Hart (2002) the relevance of being centered as a counsellor is extremely important for majority counsellors of First Nations people. Essentially, this is focal with any ethnic group, but because of the historical context of First Nations people in dealing with the churches, government and other institutions, genuiness, trust and congruence are important factors for credibility. Establishing a trustful relationship might begin by having an awareness of the different ways of understanding Aboriginal identity. This is exemplified in an anecdote narrated by one of the Elders (Harold Lucas) with whom we worked. He said that a [non-native] counsellor had come to their village once and wanted to get to work with people right away. The Elder asked this young counsellor one question: "Where do you come from?" To which the counsellor replied: "I am from Manitoba." The Elder repeated the question again: "No, where do you come from?" The counsellor's answer was still the same: "I am from Manitoba." The Elder replied: "But who are your people? **Where do you come from?**" (Emphasis given by the authors). The elder then thought to himself: "How can I trust this person if s/he does not know where s/he comes from?"

There is no question that mistrust exists, thus, counsellors need to ensure that they come to the counselling process with a strong sense of self and the ability to project a quality of sincerity. Recently, there is more and more research in the area of what First Nations people want in helpers, whether native or non-native. In a study with Alaskan Inupiat people, Reimer (in Trimble & Thurman, 2002) found that the desirable characteristics in helpers and healers include the following: "(a) virtuous, kind, respectful, trustworthy, friendly, gentle, loving, clean, giving, helpful, not a gossip and not one who wallows in self-pity; (b) strong physically, mentally, spiritually, personally, socially and emotionally; (c) one who works well with others by becoming familiar with people in the community; (d) one who has good communication skills, achieved by taking time to talk, visit and listen; (e) respected because of his or her knowledge, disciplined in thought and action, wise and understanding and willing to share knowledge by teaching and serving as an inspiration; (f) substance-free; (g) one who knows and follows the culture; and (h) one who has faith and a strong relationship with the Creator" (p. 67). Bruce (1999), involving 36 First Nations participants from various Coast Salish communities, explored what counsellors, who are non-native, could do to enhance a positive working relationship. The results of the study provide non-First Nations counsellors with guidelines for building a positive therapeutic bond. The protocol is organized into five themes:

1. Personal counselling skills and personal and therapeutic qualities that enhance counselling;

2. Community relations;

3. Cultural matters;

4. Historical components; and

5. General issues

1. Important counselling skills, personal qualities and therapeutic qualities that enhance counselling include:

Core skills: Genuiness, respect, willingness to listen, effective questioning and positive reinforcement. Although some of these qualities are utilized with both Aboriginal and non-aboriginal people, the counsellor's approach to questioning, for example, might be different as well as the construct of respect, which might entail involving some members of the extended family to demonstrate they are part of the process too.

Personal qualities: Clients always have certain expectation of themselves while in a helping relationship, but they also have expectations of the counsellor as an individual and as a guide. The qualities that clients look for in a counsellor are that she/he is personally healthy, open, patient, non-judgmental, supportive and flexible, compassionate, humble, reliable and one who explains who they are and what they want to do. For some First Nations clients this is vital information as they will establish new relationships of trust and confidence. For those who are dealing with issues of mistrust (e.g., residential schools, being a battered spouse and so forth) and betrayal, self-disclosure from the counsellor could prove to be an additional benefit in the work that is being done.

Therapeutic qualities: Besides the personal qualities that clients need from a counsellor, Bruce's study demonstrates that professionalism, expertise and competency are desired qualities. Additionally, people look for counsellors who use culturally appropriate methods, have a willingness to know and understand the culture and language; have and can set clear boundaries, informalness, confidentiality, rapport, are able to self-disclose and are personable.

2. In regards to what counsellors could do within the First Nations community, Bruce (1999) lists:

Contact the liaison person from the community: Most communities have a designated person who acts as a liaison between their own people and those who do not belong to the community. Establishing such as connection does not only ensure that protocol is followed but also, that people in the community start becoming familiarized with the counsellor(s).

Meet with the Chief and counsellors: In order to follow the appropriate protocol to enter the community, the helper should meet with the Chief and other members to demonstrate respect and follow their suggestions and working approaches.

Be cautious and respectful of protocol: Wait to be invited to work with First Nations people. Some non-First Nations counsellors enter a community with little or no knowledge of how to proceed and interact within the culture. Sometimes, being overly enthusiastic might send an erroneous message. Be visible but cautious and learn how to become part of the community, including attending funerals and other cultural events.

Be open to explaining your role in the community: It is important that the counsellor explains and describes how she/he intends to work with people, what approaches he/she will use and to always let people know their openness and willingness to learn. Self-disclosure is an asset when doing this.

Establish a relationship with other professionals already in the community: Since First Nations people work from a collective perspective where others are involved in different processes and tasks at different times, the counsellor should find ways to establish contact with other professionals already working in the community. This would not only represent willingness to use a team work and collective approach to working but it also denotes professionalism.

3. Culturally, counsellors need to:

Be aware of the culture, including history, beliefs and traditions, stories and legends: It is always important to educate oneself regarding general cultural principles and specific cultural components that belong to the community. The counsellor should know that there are cultural elements that belong to everyone in the community, but there are also elements that belong only to those who have permission to use them (i.e., songs, healing practices, medicine, etc).

Be moderately knowledgeable about cultural and spiritual practices and realize the diversity within a culture: Although many First Nations groups share cultural components and elements (e.g., all of them have their own stories, ceremonies, symbols, rituals and so forth), it is important to know that methods, practices and approaches to teaching, healing and organizing are as varied as are groups.

Know about the extended family you are working with: It is important to remember that extended family members are part of the helping relationship. It is not only polite to invite the family into the helping process, but it is also valuable to ask their input and advice, especially if there are Elders in the family.

Work with healthy elders either as supporters or in conjunction: Elders are respected members in the community as they offer insight, knowledge and advice that is considered part of the cultural transmission necessary to maintain the culture alive. Unfortunately, some elders might not have good health due to issues that might be endemic to the community (i.e., unavailable clinic, substance abuse and so forth).

4. Historical components: Understanding the effect of history on people is vital to learn how to work within a First Nations community. Counsellors would benefit if they understand:

The cultural and political history of the community: Part of the understanding and knowledge that a counsellor must possess before or while getting involved with a community, relates to understanding how socio-political aspects of history influence the way in which people live and relate to others shaping their worldview.

The importance of loss including language, land, land control: After contact with the Europeans, First Nations people lost most of their culture as the result of assimilation, which included sending children to Residential Schools where their language was removed from their daily life; land was seized by the government and laws that damaged their ways of life were created.

Know the impact of the Indian Act and the relationship between the government and the people (e.g., Ministry of Social Service): It is important the helpers have at least basic knowledge of relevant documents such as the Indian Act, in order to have a better and clearer understanding of the laws and actions that affect First Nations communities in several ways (i.e., education, land ownership, health services, housing rights and so forth).

5. General themes: As listed by Bruce (1999), there are some general challenges that face First Nations communities. It is an asset when counsellors are aware of such issues and educate themselves about the causes, alternative ways to reach people and implement preventive actions that are respectful of the individuals and their community.

Residential schools: In the history of First Nations people, Residential Schools and their devastating consequences have brought a plethora of unhealthy issues that have been difficult to overcome as the effect of being physically, emotionally, culturally and spiritually abused have not only affected those who were directly involved but also the subsequent generations. Relationships among family members have been destroyed and changed due to substance misuse, abusive situations where physical force is used (which may result in sexual abuse), impact of acculturation, suicide, racism, and discrimination;

Inconsistency of services: Social services are often inadequate to serve First Nations communities that are isolated and lack the essential health services. While recently children and youth have been the focus of diverse social service agencies, the truth is that, as programs and budgets change, so do the type of available services for First Nations people. Therefore, counsellors must know that people in the communities might be distrustful about the services bring provided by them.

Understand the notion of time: It is vital that helpers working with First Nations individuals value and understand the notion of time in a way, which is different from a non-First Nations' view. People in communities realize that appointments and schedules are related to the moment when people are ready to work. In group work, for example, people can agree on a time to gather for a meeting during the day but it is important to remember that the meeting will begin when everyone gets there and is ready to start. It is respectful on the counsellor's part to wait for everyone to be ready. Furthermore, counsellors would benefit from knowing that family and community affairs are regarded as more important than working with a counsellor.

Conclusion

What we must understand is that this struggle to retrieve and restore the traditional value of respect for all creation is central to the Elders' concerns about the loss of Native culture…. All the outlawed and denigrated facets of traditional culture – the spirit dances, the sweat-lodge and the pipe ceremonies, the regular ritual offering of tobacco as a symbol of gratitude – must be seen for what they really were: tools to maintain and deepen a belief in the inter-connectedness of all things (Ross, l992, p. 183).

As Black Elk stated so long ago, people of all cultures are united "under one tree," working for the good of our children and way of life, but it is vital to continue strengthening our rituals and values. It is fascinating to see all the shared beliefs that we have as First Nations people regardless of our geographic location or our different tribal affiliation. As Ani-yun-wiya, Kikapoo and Mohawk helpers, we have been really fortunate and blessed to have had the opportunity to live and work with different First Nations people in Canada, Mexico and the USA. We know that as we reflect on our experiences and what we have learned from various researchers on First Nations issues and convey our vision for counselling in a "post-colonial" atmosphere, our thoughts are that we need to broaden a sense of community among indigenous people. It means going beyond the roles of what is commonly accepted in counselling, by engaging in a variety of roles from advisors, facilitators and community advocates. We believe that community is more than just a group of people (family, neighbors, colleagues); it is our belief that community has a larger connotation in that communion is necessary to engage with each other. Communion in a spiritual sense where, together, we are able to respond to the guiding principles of the Aboriginal worldview: Respect for all creation, Balance in relationships, Reverence towards the Higher Power and Connection to Nature. These four principles are in themselves a communion and we would like to see them lived and represented in everything we would do together, from culturally appropriate counselling, to supporting community self reliance, ensuring that families have all of the assistance necessary and the ending of institutional actions that limit First Nations development. We believe that acceptance of other worldviews will free counselling from its "colonial past" and ensure that respect is the foundation of counselling practice. Sometimes words, like respect, are overly used and thus, their meaning reduced. Our understanding of respect is related to the many small particles that form it…in the same way in which the sky is made up of millions of stars, planets, asteroids and other life forms we are yet to discover, respect is made of many small elements, some of which we are unable to perceive. Acting with respect towards others is embodied in the way we listen, in how we respond, in how we engage, in how we commit, in how we achieve, in how we love… our elders always reminds us that respect is the simplest form of love….

The literature and our experience tells us that the uniqueness in First Nations people should be respected. That is, family is important and the extended family is usually involved in everyday life. In the first encounter, being respectful, being genuine, fully listening and observing how a person shares his or her experience is vitally important and thus is the foundation of successful counselling. Since trust is a vital key, it has to be built on genuine interest in the culture and life of the clients. While active listening is important, the research also demonstrates that being directive in regards to a recovery plan is equally important. Trimble and Thurman (2002) go on to say that:

> …the directive style seem more effective because many Indian clients, especially more culturally traditional ones, are likely to be reticent and taciturn during the early stages of counseling, if not throughout the entire course of treatment…traditional oriented Indian clients are very reluctant to seek conventional counseling because they perceive the experience as intolerable and inconsistent with their understanding of a helping relationship (p. 75).

All counsellors need to remember that First Nations people are a diverse and unique group of people as any of the nations in the world. They all have differing traditions and practices, but as First Nations people move around the country, we are seeing people from many more different groups. So while we acknowledge that differences exist, we should remember that there are many more similarities, which are much stronger than the many differences we might perceive. If one had to put the idea of similarities in a few words, one might say that what unites First Nations people is the desire to "give voice to our ancestors." What this means is that we have a way of looking at the world in a holistic way, which recognizes and acknowledges all aspects of our existence (mind, body, spirit and feelings). We do not value one part of ourselves over another part since they all are equally valuable and important to make us who we are. In part, one might say that the aim of the helping process is to heal and reconcile these different parts of ourselves to empower and strengthen our identity. From a therapeutic view all counsellors, regardless of background, need to remember that:

> *The idea of self-determination must be allowed to flourish throughout all facets of life including the therapeutic, research and training areas. Self-determination is the sine qua non of having a relevant psychology and is the beginning of the process of absolution for the profession of psychology (Duran & Duran, 1995, p. 198).*

References

Ashwell, R. (1989). Coast Salish: Their art, culture, and legends. Vancouver, BC: Hancock House.

B.T. Personal communication concerning leadership. March 2001.

Beltrame, J. (2003). First Nations: Time of reckoning. *Maclean's,* June 16, pp. 37-38.

Black Elk Speaks (1961). As told to John Neilhardt. Lincoln, NE: University of Nebraska Press.

Bruce, S. (1999). First Nations protocol: Ensuring strong counselling relationships with First Nations clients, unpublished doctoral dissertation, University of Victoria.

Council for Yukon Indians. (1993). *Cross-Cultural Strategies.* Whitehorse, YK: Curriculum Development Program.

Couture, J. (1991). Explorations in Native knowing. In J. Friesen, *The Cultural Maze: Complex Questions on Native Destiny in Western Canada.* Calgary, AB: Detselig Enterprises, Ltd., pp. 53-76.

Duran, E. & Duran, B. (1995). *Native American Postcolonial Psychology.* Albany, NY: State University of New York Press.

Dyer, G. (2001). The visible majority. *Canadian Geographic*, pp. 23-30.

E.W. Personal communication concerning personal issues of living on a Native reserve in BC., March 2001.

Hart, M.A. (2002). *Seeking Mino-Pimatisiwin: An Aboriginal Approach to Helping.* Halifax, NS: Fernwood Press.

La Framboise,T., Trimble, J.E. & Mohatt, G. (1990). Counseling intervention and American Indian tradition: An integrative approach. *Counseling Psychologist, 18,* 628-654.

L.H. Personal communication concerning counselling, February 2002.

McCormick, R. (1995). Facilitation of healing of First Nations people in British Columbia. *Journal of Native Education, 21*(2), 251-322.

Newman, D. (1989). Bold and cautious. *Maclean's,* July 12, pp. 24-25.

Smoley, R. (1992). First Nations spirituality. *Yoga Journal,* January, 84-89, 104-108.

Sterling, S. (1997). Skaloola the Owl: Healing power in Salishan mythology. *Guidance & Counselling, 12,* 2, 9-12.

Red Horse, J.G. (1982). American Indian elders: Unifiers of Indian families. *Social Casework, 61,* p. 80-89.

Ross, R. (1992). *Dancing with a Ghost: Exploring Indian Reality.* Markham, ON: Octupus Publishing Group.

Trimble & Thurman. (2002). Ethnocultural considerations and strategies for providing counseling services to native American Indians (pp. 53-91). In P. Pedersen, J. Draguns, W. Lonner & J. Trimble, *Counseling Across Cultures,* 5th Edition. Thousand Oaks, CA: Sage.

Chapter 5
The Impact of Cultural Misconstruction
on Education

Wendy Edwards

Since the days of initial contact/colonization and enforced Residential Schools, First Nations education has been a contentious issue. Although the era of government paternalism is hopefully being reshaped, we are currently experiencing an age of neocolonialism, which continues in failing to address the needs of First Nations students in the Western public school system. The present-day curriculum still follows the European egocentric blueprint of the past. Our current education system is structured to meet the needs of an individualistic Euro-culture, excluding collectivist cultural values; it is based on curricula developed from a mainstream cultural perspective, degrading to minorities and originally designed to ensure ongoing white (male) privilege. Current government-invoked token strategies of multiculturalism only mask the appearance of racism. The fact remains: First Nations students experience critical displacement and dissension when the culture of their school (education) is different from the culture of their home and community.

Until overt and covert racism in our schools is eliminated, the education system will continue to fail to meet the needs of First Nations students. This chapter proposes the examination of four major issues contributing to this displacement:

– Intercultural communication;

– Institutional racism;

– The influence of culture on learning;

– Why mainstream school's incentives do not work for First Nation students.

Possible strategies for implementing an integrative approach to First Nations teaching/learning are also reviewed.

Having spent many years working with First Nations students at both the elementary and secondary levels and after years of guiding my own children and grandchildren through the education system, I have had extensive opportunities to consider the variety of cross-cultural issues that impact students and families on a daily basis. As an adult woman of considerable years with both Nuu-chah-nulth and Scottish heritage and having experienced a paternal legacy of the Residential School intergenerational impact on the family, it is my intention to use – as a primary source of information - personal observations and experiences of life, including several decades of working with the current public education system. Secondary sources (including both unpublished and professional perspectives) support the proposed issues and suggestions for successful integration without assimilation. Furthermore, I intend to demonstrate in this chapter that responsible educators and counsellors need to understand and address "both the obvious [cultural] differences and the more subtle ones that include different perceptions of time, values, World Views and [epistemologies] ways of expression, learning and aspects of being..." (Cleary & Peacock, 1998; p. 7), in order to provide First Nations students with the opportunity to learn in ways that are consistent with First Nations values, principles and cultures.

Intercultural Communication

The fundamental dimension of individualism versus collectivism constitutes the most basic foundation of cross-cultural communication differences. "This dimension determines how people live together (alone, in families, or tribes;) their values and how they communicate" (Samovar & Porter, 1997; p. 248). An essential difference between individualists and collectivists involves "the amount of psychological distance from, or the importance of emotional closeness with, other people" (Brislin, 1993; p. 49). The words "individual" and "individualized" are constantly used, with people being encouraged to set their own goals, 'stand on their own two feet' and to take the initiative for personal achievement. In collectivist cultures, such as the First Nations culture, people are taught – by the example of generations – to play down individual goals or success in favor of the group's goals or best interests. According to Brislin (1993), "People obtain much of their identity as members of their collective" (p. 48). Whereas Western cultures value personal judgment, initiative and achievement, collectivist cultures such as First Nations emphasize "harmony among people, between people and nature and value collective judgments" (Samovar & Porter, 1997; p. 248). This primary difference between cultures has a profound impact on First Nations students in an individualistic school system and forms the basis for a pyramid of cultural clashes.

"The degree to which a culture is individualistic or collectivist affects the nonverbal behavior of that culture in every way" (Samovar & Porter, 1997; p. 249). Because non-verbal behavior is largely unconscious, non-verbal symbols are used spontaneously without calculation regarding gestures, interpersonal distance, facial expressions or posture. These factors are critically important in intercultural communication, as all aspects of the communication process are subject to cultural interpretation. What might be commonplace in one culture, such as direct eye contact, could be considered a sign of disrespect in another culture. Philips (1993) argues that depending on the ratio of enculturation in mainstream society to enculturation in traditional First Nations cultures, the First Nations students will experience verbal and non-verbal communication difficulties. Proximity or personal space is often misunderstood. Individualistic people are more remote and distant, valuing personal space and not requiring proximity to neighbors, friends or co-workers. Collectivist cultures are interdependent, often living, sleeping, playing and working within close proximity to others in the group (nuclear family and extended family).

Christopher (1992) asserts that individualism is a viewpoint that has shaped modern Westernized lifestyles in diverse ways and that the heart of individualism is a metaphysical position of "the person as a disengaged or abstract self living in a disenchanted world" (p. 105). Intercultural misunderstanding can result in a First Nations student being judged as sad, troubled or antisocial due to a lack of smiling or "happy" facial expression considered necessary for appropriate interpersonal interaction in a individualistic setting. Likewise, avoidance of an issue can be viewed as a negative attribute by individualists, whereas collectivists can perceive avoidance, third-party intermediaries or other face-saving techniques as viable solutions to an otherwise confrontational situation. The First Nations (collective) culture, which is based on relationships, involves high-context (nonverbal cues) communication or implicit messages that do not need to be articulated. "In high context situations or cultures, information is integrated from the environment, the context, the situation and nonverbal cues that give the message meaning unavailable in the explicit verbal utterance" (Samovar & Porter, 1997; p. 253). The low-context cultures include North American as well as Swiss, German and Scandinavian. These cultures regard specific details, literalness and precise time schedules at the expense of context and people from such cultures are often perceived [by collectivists] as excessively talkative, belaboring of the obvious and redundant. On the other hand, people from high context cultures may be perceived [by individualists] as non-disclosive, sneaky and mysterious; they look for, interpret immediately and are affected by the most subtle cues such as facial expression, tensions, movements, speed of delivery and location. They also expect communicants to understand unarticulated emotions and ideas, the slightest gesture and environmental clues unknown to people in low context cultures. "Worse, both cultural extremes fail to recognize these basic differences in behavior, communication and context and are quick to misattribute the causes for their behavior" (Samovar & Porter, 1997, p. 254).

One other source of misunderstanding between First Nations people and mainstream (Western) society is the concept of time. (When discussing traditional ways of time usage, caution against stereotyping should be applied with an understanding that traditional concepts may or may not apply to contemporary First Nations people depending upon where they are on the *continuum of Aboriginality*). First Nations time use is basically polychronic (people or event oriented rather than imposed scheduling). Polychronic people are so deeply immersed in each other's business that they feel a compulsion to keep in touch. Their knowledge of each other is extraordinary and it could be argued that their involvement [relationships] with people are the very core of their existence. However, the polychronic attitude toward appointments, which are "not taken as seriously and, as a consequence, are frequently broken" (Samovar & Porter, 1997; p. 278), is very distressing to the mainstream culture (which tends to be monochronic and follow pre-set schedules). Our schools are run by the clock, literally and there are few, if any, allowances made for circumstances. In a collectivist culture, where people are more important than clocks, a student may arrive at school an hour or more after "bell time" because Grandma needed a ride to town, or the student had to check the family net before attending school. According to family values, both of these events could take precedence over punctuality. Family (cultural) traditions take priority over scheduled lessons and First Nations children are customarily involved in funerals (often for many days), celebrations, Longhouse ceremonies and family visits among many other relationship-based activities.

Being migratory people, it is not uncommon for families to move distances to connect with extended family or community networks. This connection and networking is critical to a culture that has survived attempted genocide and assimilation on the strength of its relationships. In a classroom where teaching and the curriculum are linearly based and where each lesson builds on the one previously taught, educators express frustration at the First Nations student's frequent absences and perceive the absenteeism as a "problem." Without any awareness or understanding of the different perception of time use, teachers take personal affront and alert student support services with a referral for change. Far from being or having a problem, this student is immersed in a people-oriented culture where he or she is being taught the life-skills considered important for childhood.

Institutional Racism

Many First Nations students show little initiative or independence in the classroom. This is primarily based on the teaching they receive from infancy – to watch, listen and practice cooperatively until they have mastered a task before asking for feedback. The individually-based competition for 'excellence' is foreign and distressful to them, often creating feelings of inadequacy and leading to inaccurate assessments by teachers. According to Cleary and Peacock (1998) "… the conscious and unconscious exclusion from the curriculum of [Aboriginal] history, culture, languages, literature and other instruction relevant to these First Nations student's lives" (p. 69) leads to institutional oppression as the result of overt and covert racism and ignorance. The book *The Color of Democracy:Racism in Canadian Society* (1995), by authors Frances, Tator, Mattis & Rees demonstrates yet one more instance where the reality of racism in our schools has yet to be addressed:

> *Perhaps the most serious weakness of multicultural education was its failure to acknowledge that racism was endemic in Canadian society. While schools attempted to "respond to special needs", to affirm ethnic minority children's background and language, to celebrate festivals and to teach "mother" (heritage) languages, multicultural history and non-Western music,*

the real problem of racial inequality was ignored – they maintained that the fundamental issues were not so much cultural as racial; not lifestyles but life chances; not heritage but competence; not diversity but disparity; not prejudice but discrimination. (p. 188)

How often do the books in school libraries depict First Nations people as "past," noble savages, warriors, simple minded children in need of the mainstream culture's care or with names such as Billy Runs-Like-A-Horse and wearing headbands and feathers on a day-to-day basis? Cartoon characters wearing a caricature of First Nations regalia prance across the pages wearing a foolish grin. To be visible only in grade four and grade eleven Social Studies, through pan-Indian curriculum, as a novelty of the 'past', contributes to a First Nations student's sense of invisibility in the school. Institutional racism is also reflected in rules and policies that lack relativity to First Nations communities. The lack of First Nations art in the classrooms and hallways, First Nations teachers and support staff in classrooms and First Nations administrators and board members, all mirror a prevalent Eurocentric attitude that ensures ongoing "white" privilege. Covert racism is expressed by teachers who state, "I don't even notice if my students are from different cultures, I just treat everyone in the class the same." These are assimilation tactics. What those teachers are actually saying is, "I treat all students as if they were of European descent." The need for culturally relevant curriculum is erroneously viewed by some as a "demand for special treatment" rather than required inclusion of First Nations history and contemporary issues. Over the years, many First Nation students have expressed to the writer their sense of invisibility and lack of belonging in an alien system.

The Influence of Culture on Learning

Swisher and Deyhle (1992) recognize the "influence of home and community culture on learning styles – they attribute poor academic performance to the differences between the environment and teaching methods of schools and environment and teaching methods of students' homes and communities" (p. 156). They suggest that education in most First Nations homes is more "casual, informal and unstructured as opposed to the [rigid] formality of most schools" (p. 157). Culturally relevant curriculum can begin to close the gap between home, community and school to develop a truly inclusive education system.

Again avoiding stereotypes, many First Nations students may be visual learners who learn best through the opportunity for initial observation. There are many ways in which the visual learning needs of students can be met within the classroom. Teachers can establish a visual learning environment (Cambell, Cambell & Dickenson, 1996) with a variety of tools (paper, crayons, markers, chalk, videos, etc). Classroom activities can combine the visual arts across the curriculum. Flowcharts, visual outlines, pictures, maps and unit charts should be used to decorate classrooms. The use of learning centres will allow students to change their visual and social perspectives. According to Cleary & Peacock (1998), teachers need to be conscious of the effect of their presence and body language as visual clues to students.

The strong oral traditions of First Nations tribal groups endure and carry solid influence on the way many First Nations students learn, despite the fact that many of these students are first language English speakers or the fact that many have not been directly influenced by traditional storytellers. It has been thought that oral learning was especially significant to First Nations students from a more traditional tribal background, as this was the teaching style they were accustomed to, but research (Cleary & Peacock, 1998) suggests that this learning style may be genetic, "hard-wired" in many First Nations students. The combination of visual and oral learning most aptly describes the traditional way of First Nations cultural teaching and remains an important influence in many First Nations homes today. Acknowledging the diverse learning styles of the students, a teacher could bring to the classrooms traditional storytellers, have students interview Elders or community leaders, teach [and value] listening strategies addressing the students' oral learning needs, read them the newspaper and introduce reader's theatre. Despite the strong influence of oral learning, there is some evidence in existing research that a preference exists for "hands-on" learning among First Nations students. Students need to find personal and practical applications of schoolwork to their daily lives favoring concrete learning; many students cannot "imagine" something unless they can personally relate to it.

A concept of increasing interest in the controversial field of First Nations learning styles is the belief that many First Nations students are holistic learners, coming from the right side of the brain, rather than logical-sequential learners. Ross (1989) expresses the view that our contemporary, North American school system is designed to meet the needs of learners who focus on the left side of the brain, the side that controls "logic, linearity, reading and writing, time orientation and masculine expression" (p. 162). The left side of the brain being dominant in analytical and linear thinking can only see fragmented parts of the whole picture. The right side of the brain begins with the whole picture, being dominant in "instinct, holism, dance, art, spatiality and feminine expression" (Ross, 1989, p. 162). Furthermore, according to Blakeslee (1980) "…a delivery method allowing the right side to function as a doorway to the collective unconscious is that of learning through discovery. By permitting the child to discover his or her own answer, the child's understanding and retention of that experience is much greater" (p. 163).

Why Mainstream School's Incentives Do Not Work For First Nations Students

Some First Nations students get by in mainstream schools; only a few are as successful as their mainstream peers and many more are at the bottom of the continuum waiting to drop out. When examining the possible reasons for First Nations students not being (competitively) successful in the mainstream school system, Cleary and Peacock (1998) suggest the following as relevant cues:

– Lack of parental and extended family support for schooling

– The understandably bitter memories and lack of respect some parents have for education

– Different World Views and priorities in life

– Curriculum that is not relevant to the students' day-to-day life or foreseeable future

– Home and community use of a dialect that causes them difficulty in standard English

– A need not to excel above peers and thus be exposed and ridiculed

– A level of discomfort with analytical writing

– Discomfort with competitive systems

– The need to be comfortable with a concept before performance

According to Good and Brophy (1987):

Student motivation will be affected not only by expectations and attributions concerning level of performance, but also by attributions concerning the reason why they are engaging in tasks in the first place and by expectations concerning goals and objectives. Traditionally, teachers [have offered] incentives for good performance, or by teaching content and designing activities that students find enjoyable – extrinsic strategies do not attempt to increase the value that students place on a task itself, but instead link task performance to delivery of consequences that the students do value. Three common forms of extrinsic motivation are rewards, emphasis on the instrumental value of tasks and competition (pp. 318-319).

The extrinsic incentives that work for many students in mainstream schools (such as a future college career, positive attention for obtaining good grades, enjoyment of competition and potential shame in failing grades) do not work for students "…who have been marginalized by society, who rarely see how academic endeavor has served/rewarded the adults in their community and who do not see real purposes for the knowledge and skills they are supposed to accumulate" (Cleary & Peacock, 1998, p. 203). Rewards, public praise and grades are not effective motivators for many First Nations students; rewards can be viewed as coercion, a strategy used to try to force obedience and conformity under the guise of positive reinforcement. Grades appear to have little relevance or meaning in day-to-day life. The value of homework completed or assignments returned has little to do with the First Nations way of behaving; "…you watch and you observe before you act. You never want to show off because it's not in good taste [respectful] to pound your own drum" (Cleary & Peacock, 1998, p. 204). For the majority of First Nations students, to enjoy praise or appreciation it must be done discreetly so as not to embarrass him or her in front of peers. If one person is singled out as a 'positive example' and receives too much recognition, other students may resent it and that person has then been set up to become an object of scorn. I have observed some students to constantly underachieve in order not to appear more capable or knowledgeable than their peers, specifically to avoid their ridicule.

In turn, criticism must be handled with discretion and sensitivity, always one-on-one and preferably with gentle humor. To verbally criticize a First Nations student out loud in class is personally destructive. First nations students need to feel they have some power in their day-to-day world. Cleary and Peacock (1998) assert that:

> If [First Nations students] don't find meaningfulness and a method of instruction that is responsive to their growing edge, they turn off and tune out and drop out, or get pushed out, or they end up being a 'behavior problem'. Kids don't come that way. We make them that way. I think the system has a responsibility to be more responsive to kids. The curriculum is so linear and structured and you look into our classrooms, even as young as kindergarten and you go in there and the desks are in rows, columns and the kids are doing [identical] sheets and this lock-step curriculum doesn't fit where they are as people. They ultimately get squashed and give up, or they rebel, or they become like little zombies going through the system and that's the worst-case scenario (p. 212).

Similarly, negative reinforcement or punishments commonly used in the Western culture-inspired education system are equally ineffective for Aboriginal students. Using the example of "school suspensions" to illustrate cross-cultural perception, David Rattray (1999) declares that suspensions don't work for First Nations students because they create a separate mind-set in the students which lends to perceive school as a hostile or unbelonging place, resulting in deeper rifts. In addition, he asserts that suspensions create a sense of powerlessness and eradicate a climate of belonging, confidence and self-esteem. Equally unhealthy is the message often received by the parents when their child is suspended. Through generations of negative school experiences, many parents have an unpleasant image of education, the institution and teachers as authority figures. When required to deal with the principal regarding their child's behavior, parents often feel an implied sense of failure, reinforcement of their negative feelings toward school (distrust of power and institutions) and consciousness of cultural isolation. As a result, suspensions only serve to aggravate and accentuate these feelings of being on the outside, looking in.

Multiculturalism (instituted government policy and legislation), as practiced for the past two decades, has failed to meet the needs of First Nations students in the mainstream education system. Taking a "monolithic" or "museum" approach to many living and constantly evolving cultures, "…educators taught students about the material and exotic dimensions of culture, such as food, festivals and folktales rather than the values and belief systems that underlie cultural diversity" (Frances, et al., 1995, p. 187) Important factors shaping cultural identity such as racial, linguistic, religious, regional, socio-economic and gender differences were often ignored. Teachers often had very little knowledge or understanding of other cultures, which led both teachers and students to trivialize and stereotype different ethnic and racial groups. Also not addressed was the critical issue of the sovereign rights of First Nations people versus the immigrant history of others. "Celebrating the differences" did not and does not acknowledge the unique position and needs of First Nations students and provides no relevant motivation for student empowerment and success. Teachers can connect with the intrinsic motivation that stems from a First Nations student's need for feelings of self determination by helping them develop strategies to understand and make sense of the two World Views they live in. The Education Goals and Recommendations in the Royal Commission on Aboriginal Peoples (1997) state that, in the main, Aboriginal people want two things from education:

1. Schools to help children, youth and adults learn the skills they need to participate fully in the economy; and

2. Schools to help children develop as citizens of Aboriginal Nations with the knowledge of their languages and traditions necessary for cultural continuity.

Considering the historical track record of First Nations education in Canada, there is little wonder the current system is not working for First Nations students. During the last quarter of the century, a "band-aid" program approach of 'funded projects' has been considered the solution to Aboriginal education. Funding proposals of vast proportions are submitted regularly for the 'instant solution', the magic pill of the moment to solve all of the problems of First Nations education. Each year, a would-be messiah steps forward with claims of the definitive answer. Monumental amounts of money are spent; meanwhile, the majority of First Nations children are still not finding a sense of belonging in our school system. The majority of these programs have been too late, inadequate or designed to meet a hidden agenda. Racism and cultural ignorance exist in our school system, creating dissension for First Nations students and effectively reducing their opportunities for educational success. According to a report prepared by a First Nations Task Force and presented at a B.C. Teachers' Federation annual meeting for debate:

> As long as the cultural basis of the school and its practices remain unchanged, public schools will have difficulty in serving many students from the indigenous cultures. Public schools primarily teach the culture of European-based peoples... that puts pressure on students to conform by abandoning their culture in order to succeed in school... teachers are asked to bake the notion that forcing Native students to assimilate to majority cultural attitudes and patterns is racist (The Vancouver Sun, p. A8, March 16, 1999).

How Can We Develop Culturally Integrative Education?

There must be a better way to meet the needs of First Nations students and to enable academic achievement without the loss of cultural identity. Making schools inclusive of First Nations students goes beyond the [critical] matters of texts and curriculum. It must be a prerequisite that for true and broad inclusion, the schools – especially their boards and staff – be personally knowledgeable and inclusive of First Nations culture. Before we consider integrating issues and solutions, we need to look at the whole of First Nations education. We cannot prepare students to live in both Worlds (cultural and mainstream) if they are struggling with the characteristics of internalized oppression, anger, hopelessness or passive-aggressive behavior or if schools cannot find the ways to lessen the discontinuity between schools and homes/communities. Making improved changes to curriculum and classroom teaching styles will have little positive effect on self esteem, achievement or graduation rates if the teachers, administration and support staff do not possess the intercultural knowledge and skills necessary to interact with the students. First Nations language programs will have little impact if there are no natural uses of the language in the school and community. First Nations culture and language cannot be integrated effectively into the school curriculum nor can *more First Nations teachers and administrators* be hired if racism in schools is not confronted.

First Nations students experience dissension and displacement when the culture of their school is in conflict with the culture of their home and community. The Eurocentric school system is failing to meet their academic, social and emotional needs and continues to alienate their families and communities. The first impulse is to ask, "Where is it written? Where is the blueprint to create the changes needed in the educational system in order to meet First Nations needs?" It is difficult to capture the essence of an oral culture; its guidelines are not written down, there is no 'pat formula' according to Western culture research styles. The oral culture requires interaction with families and communities to gain an awareness and respect for a World View where all things are connected and based in Nature.

Most important for First Nations students success is the one factor often forgotten: *Involve the family and community in the child's learning experience.* Family support is the deciding factor in student success or failure. By building on existing First Nations curriculum materials, inviting story tellers to the classroom, involving Elders and local First Nations artists in illustrating local stories, the teacher is communicating an attitude of respect and shared teachings. By modeling a circular, holistic belief in all things being related and an abiding respect for balance and harmony, the teacher can establish a student-centered classroom where mutual respect and responsibility for self are the norm. Students must be given every opportunity to feel a sense of belonging and understanding in the two World Views that dominate their lives.

Conclusion

Considering the historical track record of First Nations education in Canada, there is little wonder the current system is not working for First Nations students. Over a relatively short period of time, the colonizing forces eliminated a holistic and natural pre-contact education system based on a meaningful lifestyle, substituting instead the shocking, family-shattering, genocidal Residential School strategy, founded on a premise of cultural destruction and assimilation. Grudging integration of First Nations students into the Eurocentric mainstream school system followed, ignoring the generational ripple effects of the Residential School survivors. Curriculum, developed to meet the needs of an individualistic Euro-based culture and degrading to First Nations peoples, was designed to ensure and perpetuate mainstream privilege, excluding First Nations collective values and worldviews. The Government's educational goals for First Nations students continue to begin with assimilation. Although slightly modified, according to the 'correct' language of the day, curriculum is still Euro-based, leaving First Nations students 'on the outside, looking in'. The Government and its sub-structure continue to substitute money [funded band-aid programs] in place of genuine respect, acknowledgement of sovereign rights and inclusion of First Nations' values and World Views in the education system. In British Columbia there is a 62% drop-out rate of First Nations students. Why? Part of the answer must be that imperialism, racism and cultural ignorance continue to exist in our school system, creating dissension and displacement for First Nations students and effectively reducing their opportunities for educational success and consequently, future economic equality.

Each year that we attempt to seek solutions with the "program approach," is another year of failure for many First Nations students. *The solution lies in people, not programs.* "Schools need to become so integrated a part of the community that there is little discontinuity between them and homes of [First Nations] children. Schools, communities, tribes and individuals need to deal with the remnants of oppression. Schools and communities need to build bridges between the two that go both ways" (Cleary & Peacock, 1998, p. 278). We are not even close to understanding Canadian identity until First Nations history, living culture and values are reflected in educational institutions.

References

Bains, C. (1999). *The Vancouver Sun*, March, p. A8.

Blakeslee, T. (1980). *The Right Brain*. New York: Anchor Press/Doubleday.

Brislin, R. (1993). *Understanding Culture's Influence on Behavior*. Toronto: Harcourt Brace College Publishers.

Cambell, L., Cambell, B. & Dickenson, D. (1996). *Teaching and Learning Through Multiple Intelligences*. Needham Heights, MA: Allyn & Bacon.

Christopher, J.C. (1992). The role of individualism in psychological well being: Exploring the interplay of ideology, culture and social science. In P. Pedersen (Ed.), *A Handbook for Developing Multicultural Awareness*. Alexandria, VA: ACA.

Cleary, L. & Peacock, T.D. (1998). *Collected Wisdom: American Indian Education*. Toronto: Allyn and Bacon.

Frances, H., Tator, C., Mattis, W. & Rees, T. (1995). *The Colour of Democracy: Racism in Canadian Society*. Toronto, ON: Hartcourt Brace and Company.

Good, T. & Brophy, J. (1987). *Looking in Classrooms*. New York: Harper & Row.

Philips, S.U. (1993). *The Invisible Culture*. New York: Longman Publishing.

Rattray, D. (1999). In conversation (Abnet) and with permission. Part I: Why Suspensions Don't Work. October, 1999. On-line abnet-1@etc.bc.ca

Ross, L. (1989). Mitakuye Dyasin (we are all related). Ft. Yates, ND: Bear Publishers.

Royal Commission on Aboriginal People (1997). Nation to Nation. Ottawa, ON: Canadian Commission Group Publishing.

Samovar, L. & Porter, R. (1997). *Intercultural Communication*. Toronto: Wadsworth Publishing Company.

Swisher, K. & Deyhle, D. (1992). Adapting instruction to culture. In J. Reyhner (Ed.), *Teaching American Indian Students* (pp. 81-95). Norman: University of Oklahoma Press.

Chapter 6
Counselling Issues with Asian Youth

David Sue

Mr. S. is a second-generation Canadian whose parents immigrated from India. The Guidance counsellor has requested an appointment with him because his 15-year-old son is being harassed by classmates calling him "Paki," and his grades have suffered. Mr. S is apologetic and extremely embarrassed explaining that "Canada is a good country," and his son has been taught never to cause problems (Christensen, 1989, p. 277).

The opening case illustrates some of the issues that will be addressed in the discussion of problems faced by Asian Canadian youth and their parents. Although Canada has prided itself as a multicultural society, certain groups have had difficulty, not feeling fully accepted. In one study, over one quarter of Southeast Asian refugees living in Canada reported experiencing racial discrimination (Noh et al., 1999). Some of the other problems experienced are more subtle, such as the use of Western standards in evaluating the behavior of various cultural groups.

In this chapter, I will: (1) describe some of the traditional Asian values and contrast them with mainstream Canadian culture; (2) discuss the importance of environmental and social influences on behavior; (3) present the implications of counselling in terms of attitudes/beliefs, knowledge and skills; and (4) offer suggestions for intervention strategies in working with Asian Canadian youth and their families. Before I begin, it must be pointed out that Asian Canadians are a highly heterogeneous group comprised of individuals who immigrated or originated from countries such as China, India, Korea, Pakistan and Vietnam, to name a few. In addition, some are refugees who have faced trauma and a variety of stressors while fleeing their countries. Others may have been living in Canada for generations. Asian individuals can also differ in their degree of acculturation and identification with the host society. Asians are becoming an increasingly visible population as evidenced by the election of Ujjal Dosanjh as premier of British Columbia (Connelly, 2000) and the over 300 000 Chinese Canadians residing in the lower British Columbia mainland (Janigan, 1997). In fact, over half of the children attending Vancouver schools are non-white and most are Asians (Turner, 1997). Clearly, school counsellors are increasingly likely to encounter counselling issues faced by Asian Canadian youth and their families.

Culturally Skilled Counselling

In discussions of appropriate and ethical interventions with Asian populations, minority mental health specialists have identified characteristics of a culturally skilled counsellor within three broad areas: (1) Beliefs/Attitudes – The counsellor is aware of his/her own set of values and assumptions and how these may influence their perceptions of members of other cultural groups. What is considered appropriate or inappropriate is a function of our own set of values and beliefs. The Western perspective is dominant in the Americas. It is associated with individualism, egalitarianism, self-expression and independence. A "good" student is seen as a child who can voice their opinion in the classroom, express differences in views to teachers and who develops self-oriented goals. In contrast, in the Asian community, a "good" student listens to the teacher, carefully writes down the teacher's views and does not challenge ideas presented. In working with Asian children, a counsellor must be careful not to evaluate a culturally accepted form of behavior as "deficient." (2) Knowledge – The counsellor is aware of the sociopolitical history of the cultural group and has information on values and characteristics of the group. It is important to acknowledge, assess and address environmental factors. Both the DSM IV (American Psychiatric Association, 1994) and American Psychological Association (1993) "Guidelines for Providers of Psychological Services to Ethnic, Linguistic and Culturally Diverse Populations" indicate the importance of: (a) determining the impact of social stressors (language problems, discrimination, unfamiliar role expectations and conflicting value systems), (b) assessing the degree of cultural identity of the individual and (c) determining if the problem lies primarily within the individual or the environment.

In the case of the Asian boy who was being racially harassed by his classmates, a counsellor would help the victim develop strategies for dealing with the situation and also evaluate the necessity to change the school environment. If the harassment is not an isolated incident, interventions may include examining the "culture" of the school regarding the ways in which differences are accepted and whether it promotes respect for other cultures. This may need to include an evaluation of staff attitudes and beliefs, teaching styles and strategies, instructional materials and the learning style of the school (Banks & Banks, 1993). In counselling the father about the harassment faced by his son, the counsellor could agree that Canada is a "good" country, but may mention that societal problems still exist and openly discuss issues of racism and discrimination. In this case, it would be pointed out that neither the response of his son or his parenting was responsible for the harassment. Different means of dealing with the problem could be discussed and developed with the aid of the father. (3) Skills – A culturally competent counsellor should have a wide set of intervention strategies and means of communicating effectively with culturally different clients. In the case above, intervention may necessitate a system-wide approach to promote greater acceptance of cultural differences and prosocial attitudes. Counselling strategies and techniques such as empathy need to be changed from a primarily individual focus to one that also includes family and environmental variables.

I will now discuss some of the values and characteristics of Asian populations. Remember that these are generalizations and the counsellor must assess the degree to which a particular child or family adhere to these values. After presenting some of the traditional Asian values, the implications they have for a culturally competent counsellor will be discussed.

Traditional Asian Values and Family Characteristics

As mentioned earlier, there are substantial differences among the different groups subsumed under the heading of Asian Canadians. In addition, there are also within-group differences in terms of generation status, ethnic identity and degree of acculturation. The information to follow involves generalizations. The counsellor is left to assess the characteristics and values and determine how it applies to each particular child and family. Differences between Asian and Mainstream Canadian values and characteristics are noted on Table 1.

Table 1

Values and Characteristics of Asian and Euro-Canadian Groups

Asian	Euro-Canadian
Collectivism – Family and group focus Interdependence. Behavior reflects on the family.	Individualism – Individual or self focus Individual achievement.
Patriarchal Family Relationships Father is not to be questioned. Role of children is to be obedient.	Egalitarian Family Relationships Assent of children is obtained through explanations. Wishes taken into consideration.
Hierarchical Relationships - Respect for authority.	Equality of relationships – Authority can be challenged.
Hierarchical Relationships - Respect for authority.	Equality of relationships – Authority can be challenged.
Restraint of emotions sign of maturity	Expression of emotions is healthy

Collectivism

As opposed to the individualistic orientation of Western cultures, Asian groups tend to be collectivistic – that is, their "self" definition involves relationships with others. The individual is less important than the goals and harmony of the family and group. Because of this,

Asians are more attuned to the social environment and how others are responding to them. They are relatively high self-monitors when compared to North Americans. In a sample of Asian American college students, avoiding shame was a strong motivational factor and 40% conformed to "white society" in order not to be seen as different (Yeh & Hwang, 1996). In countries where aggression is discouraged and qualities such as deference and respect are seen as important to ensure group cohesion, childhood problems tend to be for "overcontrolled" behaviors such as fearfulness and somatization. In Western countries, where independence and competitiveness are emphasized, "undercontrolled behaviors (disobedience, fighting, arguing) are more likely to be reported" (Tharp, 1991).

Characteristics of Asian Families

"When she does something wrong…I will sit down first, think about how to solve this problem. If I have difficulty, I will consult an expert… (Kass, 1998, p. 3).

This statement was made by the father, Hou-Lin Li, after he and his wife were mandated to complete a parent training course after being accused of slapping their daughter for lying and forging their signature on a note to the teacher. The process probably made the parents feel even more inadequate and increased tension with the daughter. If you were the counsellor in this situation, how would you work with the parents?

A strength of Asian families is the interdependency and social ties that can help buffer the youth from environmental stressors. A strong family minimizes the potential destructiveness of minority status. Within this context, the family needs to nurture adaptive life skills among its members (Yee, Huang & Lew, 1998). In Asian families, there is less display of emotion to older children and care is shown by addressing the physical needs of the members. Shame and guilt are used to control the children. In general, Asian parents consider discipline as necessary to prevent delinquency or other behaviors from their children that would bring shame to the family. Overindulging a child is more likely to be considered "child abuse" than disciplining a child (Wu, 1981). As compared to their Euro-Canadian counterparts, Asian male and female undergraduates (85% ethnically Chinese) described their parents' style as more authoritarian and involving both physical and emotional practices (Meston, Heiman, Trapnell & Carlin, 1999). In Asian families, the family structure is hierarchical, with higher status accorded to males and those of the older generation. Sons are responsible to carry on the family name, while daughters are less valued since they will leave the family. Even when married, the males are expected to have their primary allegiance to their family of origin. Children are expected to be obedient and are not allowed to argue with their parents. For example, in one study, Japanese American parents rated "behaves well" as the most important attribute in a child's social competence. In contrast, EuroAmerican parents rated "self directed" as the most important quality (O'Reilly, Tokuno & Ebata, 1986).

Counsellors working with the Hou-Lin Li family might consider their own reactions or attitudes regarding hierarchical family structures where obedience of children is required. Gray and Cosgrove (1985) studied the normative child rearing practices of different ethnic minority groups and concluded that it is likely that some of them would be considered to constitute "abuse" by child protective services. Other cultures may regard Western rearing patterns as leading to selfishness and increased violence. A counsellor might help the family identify different cultural methods of disciplining and explore the possibility that the daughter's misbehaviors stem from conflicting expectations between the family and the school. Acculturation conflicts for both the daughter and the parents could be discussed. In this way, the problem would not be seen as "poor parenting" but as a struggle being experienced by the family in their attempt to maintain traditional cultural values in a society with different expectations.

Acting out problems in school by a teenage Asian student resulted in a recommendation for family counselling. During the family session, the father seemed uncomfortable and non-communicative. The counsellor asked the boy and the mother about their perspectives on the problems. The boy criticized the father, complaining about unfair rules and restrictions. The family did not return for counselling (Sue, 1990).

In the case above, what are possible cultural and value conflicts? According to your own upbringing and values, what constitutes a well functioning family? How might you modify your thinking when working with a traditional Asian family? If you were the counsellor involved, what would be your goals, course of action and rationale for your approach?

In Western societies, parenting is more egalitarian and based on helping children become self-reliant. A child's view is taken into consideration and decisions are either explained to or developed in negotiation with the child. In the family situation above, it is not clear what led to the termination. In counselling the family, it might have been best to work hard to involve the father. Again, reframing the problem as involving difficulties with acculturation conflicts could take the stress of a having a "bad" family. It might also be helpful for the counsellor to modify statements from the son in a way that would show more respect to the mother and father. The counsellor could serve as the mediator and ask for suggestions from the father for ways of resolving the problem.

Ethnic Identity and Acculturation Issues

Asians living in Canada are exposed on a regular basis to mainstream standards and norms. Many begin to adopt Western standards and may denigrate their own background and physical appearance. Among Asian American children and adolescents scores are lower on measures of physical self-esteem compared with their EuroAmerican counterparts (Lee & Eng, 1989; Pang, Mizokawa, Morishima, & Oldstad, 1985). South Asian-Canadian university females scored lower on a measure of body satisfaction than EuroCanadian coeds. They also indicated dissatisfaction with their skin color (Sahey & Piran, 1997). As with many minority children, exposure to the majority culture produces confusion and conflict. They must straddle their own set of cultural values and those of the larger society. Expectations may be different at home and in the larger society. At school, characteristics such as assertiveness and independence are stressed, while at home obedience is expected. On personality measures, Chinese Canadian students scored lower than their EuroCanadian counterparts on assertiveness, need for variety and imaginative fantasy which probably reflects Asian values for practicality and emotional restraint. Attempts to resolve conflicts from competing cultural values may lead to identity issues and questions such as "Who am I?" and "Where do I belong?"

Asian youth may compare their parents' style to those they are exposed to in books and mass media. In Asian families, there are generally less overt displays of affection, especially from the father. A Korean novelist, Chang-Rae Lee, noted the lack of emotional display and writes of his father, "I wasn't sure he had the capacity to love" (1995, p. 58). The evaluation of parents from the majority perspective can result in an estrangement. Lorenzo et al. (1995) found that the majority of EuroAmerican adolescents picked their parents as adult role models. Only 18% of Asian American adolescents made the same choice. It is important for counsellors to remain aware that issues over conflicting cultural values may have a powerful impact of parent-child relationships of ethnic minorities.

Parents are also aware of conflicts between their traditional and mainstream values. They may become worried that they are losing their children. Immigrant parents may have lower English proficiency than their children and require their help in translating during interactions with the larger society. Their dependency on their children can result in a loss of status for the parents. One Asian Indian daughter returned to India with her parents and discovered that their version of "Indian" values and norms was much more restrictive than those currently of India. She described her parent's standards as a "museumization of practices" (Das Gupta, 1997). However, exposure to the dominant culture can also lead to acceptance of mainstream values in raising children (Jain & Belsky, 1997; Lee & Zahn, 1998) and they may begin to feel inadequate as parents. Some parents respond to the situation by becoming more rigid and restrictive.

For Asian youth, culture conflict can result in processes that have been described in different racial and cultural identity development models (Sue & Sue, 1999). These models attempt to indicate the development of racial identity among minority group individuals when exposed to the majority culture. Lee (1994) found four major types of reactions to ethnic identity among Asian American students in high school: (1) "The Korean Students." The Koreans in this group identified themselves solely as Korean and rarely socialized with other Asians. Their parents instructed them to "learn American ways," although they were expected to maintain their Korean identity at home. The youth were encouraged to have a bicultural focus with an accommodation to the larger societal values while maintaining traditional values at home. They were encouraged to succeed academically since it was seen as important for upward mobility. Because of this, the students were expected to work hard in school. (2) "The Asians." Individuals in this group adhered to traditional Asian values and included immigrants, American born Chinese and Southeast Asians; this group most closely resembled the quiet, studious and polite stereotype of the model minority. Students in this group stressed the importance of studying in getting ahead, although they acknowledged that discrimination would limit their opportunities. As with the Korean students, the motivation for study came from the feeling of obligation to the parents because of their sacrifices. Low achievers in this group expressed feelings of shame and the fear that academic failure would cause their family to lose face. (3) "New Wavers." Students in this group identified completely with the majority culture. This group attempted to escape from the stereotypes of Asians by dressing in unorthodox ways and socializing instead of studying. Their primary role was to "party" and get by in their classes with a minimum of effort. They regarded tradition oriented Asians as "nerds." Acceptance by non-Asian students was a primary goal. Teachers viewed members of this group as Asians "gone wrong." (4) "Asian Americans." Individuals in this group had a panethnic identity. They studied and worked hard in school. However, students in this group were outspoken about racism and wanted to use their education to give them tools to fight against racism. Lee's observations of these groups of students indicate some of the different ways Asian students dealt with their minority status. With the exception of the "new wavers," students in the other groups felt pressure to succeed academically. Low achieving Asian students reported feeling ashamed and depressed and unwilling to seek academic help because of the embarrassment such a request would bring to the family.

The observations by Lee indicate that Asian adolescents can respond to their ethnicity, cultural background and the way they interact with the larger society in different ways. The issues found in the different Asian orientations can be quite varied from one another. For example, the "new wavers" would probably not be open to a discussion of acculturation problems. Their attempt to assimilate into the White society may cause them to reject their own ethnicity. The "Asian American" may be suspicious of the counselling staff and consider them to be part of the establishment whose purpose is to make them adjust to a racist society. Those with a traditional Asian orientation may feel intense shame during counselling and present only vocational issues rather than personal ones.

Academic and Vocations Concerns

Among Asian American families there is great emphasis on academic achievement as a means of bringing honor to the family and as a way of ensuring success in society. Japanese, Chinese and Korean parents of 6th and 7th graders had higher educational aspirations for their children than Euro-American parents (Lee, 1987). In the United States, Asian

Americans are underrepresented in special education programs, overrepresented in gifted programs and have the highest rates of college completion of any other ethnic group (Blair & Qian, 1998). The pressure to succeed academically can be extreme and the achievements of Asian American 9th graders appear to be motivated by a fear of academic failure. They report low levels of self-efficacy beliefs even when outperforming their EuroAmerican comparison group (Eaton & Dembo, 1997).

Asian American students have restricted career interests and tend to go primarily into the fields of science, math or other fields that do not require good communication skills. They are underrepresented in the social fields or other occupations requiring forceful self-expression (Park & Harrison, 1995). This may be due to factors such as a lack of facility with the English language, socialization that fosters self-consciousness, or a perceived unreceptivity of society. Asians may need career counselling to help them broaden their search for different educational and employment opportunities. The same is true about academic achievement. Success needs to be redefined more broadly so that low-achieving students and their parents do not feel like failures. Additionally, it may be necessary to reduce the pressure on high achieving students who are experiencing stress and anxiety related to fears of failure.

General Treatment Strategies

In working with Asian students and their families, the following guidelines are suggested for counsellors: (1) Be aware of your own values and how they might affect the way you perceive the problem. (2) Identify strengths and assets rather than only focusing on the problem. (3) Assess the worldview of the individuals involved. (4) Consider the impact of situational, environmental and cultural issues. (5) Consider having culture conflict as the focus of discussions. (6) Determine what are considered to be possible solutions by the student and family. (7) Be ready to act as the mediator family counselling. (8) Help members to broaden their definition of what is acceptable and to consider alternative solutions and ways of dealing with situations. (9) Be willing to offer ideas and suggestions for consideration.

In working with Asians, the overall goal is to help identify and develop a broad range of skills that are acceptable within their cultural orientation. Often there exists a number of useful techniques and philosophies within the Asian tradition. Opening a dialogue to discover and evaluate different cultural strategies can be useful and increase flexibility in dealing with problems. I agree with the view of Ivey, Ivey and Simek-Morgan (1993), who define cultural intentionality as a goal for both the counsellor and client. It is defined as:

"The ability…to generate the thoughts, words and behaviors necessary to communicate with a variety of diverse groups and individuals…to communicate within their own culture and learn the ability to understand other cultures as well…to formulate plans, act on many possibilities existing in a culture and reflect on these actions" (pp. 9-10).

References

American Psychiatric Association. (1994). *Diagnostic and Statistical Manual of Mental Disorders* (4th edition). Washington, D.C.: American Psychiatric Association.

American Psychological Association. (1993). Guidelines for Providers of Psychological Services to Ethnic, Linguistic and Culturally Diverse Populations. *American Psychologist, 48*, 45-48.

Banks, J.A. & Banks, C.A. (1993). *Multicultural Education: Issues and Perspectives* (2d edition). Boston: Allyn & Bacon.

Blair, S.L. & Qian, Z. (1998). Family and Asian students' educational performance. *Journal of Family Issues, 19*, 355-374.

Christensen, C.P. (1989). Cross-cultural awareness development: A conceptual model. *Counsellor Education and Supervision, 28*, 270-286.

Connelly, J. (Feb 21, 2000). B.C. premier breaks racial barrier. Province is first in Canada to elect man of Asian descent to post. *Seattle Post-Intelligencer*, A1.

Das Gupta, S.D. (1998). Gender roles and cultural continuity in the Asian immigrant community in the U. S. *Sex Roles, 38*, 953-974.

Eaton, M.J. & Dembo, M.H. (1997). Differences in motivational beliefs of Asian American and non-Asian students. *Journal of Educational Psychology, 89*, 433-440.

Gray, E. & Cosgrove, J. (1985). Ethnocentric perception of childrearing practices in protective services. *Child Abuse and Neglect, 9*, 389-396.

Ivey, A.E., Ivey, M.B. & Simek-Morgan, L. (1993). *Counselling and Psychotherapy: A Multicultural Perspective* (3d edition). Boston: Allyn & Bacon.

Jain, A. & Belsky, J. (1997). Fathering and acculturation: Immigrant Indian families with young children. *Journal of Marriage and the Family, 59*, 873-883.

Janigan, M. (1997, May 26). That West Coast Difference. *Maclean's*, p. 21.

Kass, J. (1998, May 11). State's attorney needs some sense knocked into him. *Chicago Tribune*, p. 3.

Lee, L.C. & Eng, R. (1989). The world of Chinese immigrant children of New York City. In Proceedings of the International Conference on Chinese Mental Health. Taipei, Taiwan.

Lee, C-R (1995). *Native Speaker*. New York: The Berkeley Publishing Group

Lee, L.C. & Zhan, G. (1998). Psychosocial status of children and youths. In L.C. Lee & N.W. S. Zane (Eds.), *Handbook of Asian American Psychology* (pp. 137- 163). Thousand Oaks, CA.: Sage Publications.

Lee, S.J. (1994). Behind the model-minority stereotype: Voices of high- and low-achieving Asian American students. *Anthropology and Education Quarterly, 25*, 413-429.

Lee, Y. (1987). *Academic Success of East Asian Americans: An Ethnographic Comparative Study of East Asian American and Anglo American Academic Achievement*. Seoul, South Korea: American Studies Institute, National University Press.

Lorenzo, M.K., Pakiz, B., Reinherz, H.Z. & Frost, A. (1995). Emotional and behavioral problems of Asian American adolescents: A comparative study. *Child and Adolescent Social Work Journal, 12*, 197-212.

Meston, C.M., Heiman, J.R., Trapnell, P.D. & Carlin, A.S. (1999). Ethnicity, desirable responding and self-reports of abuse: A comparison of European- and Asian-Ancestry undergraduates. *Journal of Consulting and Clinical Psychology, 67*, 139-144.

Noh, S., Beiser, M., Kaspar, V., Hou, F. & Rummens, J. (1999). Perceived racial discrimination, depression and coping: A study of Southeast Asian refugees in Canada. *Journal of Health and Social Behavior, 40*, 193-207.

O'Reilly, J.P., Tokuno, K.A. & Ebata, A.T. (1986). Cultural differences between Americans of Japanese and European ancestry in parental valuing of social competence. *Journal of Comparative Family Studies, 17*, 87-97.

Pang, V.O., Mizokawa, D., Morishima, J.K. & Oldstad, R.G. (1985). Self-concepts of Japanese-American children. *Journal of Cross-Cultural Psychology, 16*, 99-109.

Park, S.E. & Harrison, A.A. (1995). Career-related interests and values, perceived control and acculturation of Asian-American and Caucasian-American college students. *Journal of Applied Social Psychology, 25*, 1184-1203.

Sahey, S. & Piran, N. (1997). Skin-color preferences and body satisfaction among South Asian-Canadian and European-Canadian female university students. *Journal of Social Psychology, 137*, 161-171.

Sue, D. (1990). Culture in transition: Counselling Asian-American men. In D. Moore and F. Leafgren (Eds.), *Men in Conflict* (pp. 153-165). Alexandria, VA.: American Counselling Association.

Sue, D.W. & Sue, D. (1999). *Counselling the Culturally Different* (3d edition). New York: John Wiley.

Tharp, R.G. (1991). Cultural diversity and treatment of children. *Journal of Consulting and Clinical Psychology, 59*, 799-812.

Turner, C. (1997, November 22). Has Canadian land hit its limit? *The Los Angeles Times*, p. A1.

Wu, D.Y.H. (1981). Child abuse in Taiwan. In J.E. Korbin (Ed.), *Child Abuse and Neglect: Cross-cultural Perspectives* (pp. 139-165). Berkeley: University of California Press.

Yee, B.W.K., Huang, L.N. & Lew, A. (1998). Families: Life-span socialization in a cultural context. In L.C. Lee & N.W.S. Zane (Eds.), *Handbook of Asian American Psychology* (pp. 83-135). Thousand Oaks, CA.: Sage Publications.

Yeh, C.J. & Huang, K. (1996). The collectivistic nature of ethnic identity development among Asian-American college students., *Adolescence, 31*, 645-661.

Chapter 7
Counselling Asian Canadians: Implications for Counsellors and Psychotherapists.

Kelly Sharman

People of Asian descent represent one of the fastest-growing groups in North America (Statistics Canada, 2001; Waxler-Morrison Anderson and Richardson, 1995; Root, 1993). In 1997, over 70 000 people immigrated to Canada from Asian countries; four of the top six countries of origin for immigrants were in Asia (Citizenship and Immigration Canada, 1998). Recent American statistics state that over eight million people are of Asian descent (Kitano & Maki, 1996). Although the terms "Asian Canadian" and "Asian American" suggest a sense of homogeneity, many distinctly different cultures are usually classified under these labels, including people from Japan, China, Southeast Asia, Korea and the Philippines. Considering this wide diversity between and even within cultures, the utility and validity of this classification is questionable. However, as Lin and Cheung (1999) declare, there are enough similarities in religion, cultural norms and social structure to construct some meaningful themes, as religious and cultural influences have disseminated throughout the continent over time. This has resulted in divergent perspectives and schemas between the Western and Asian societies concerning the relationship between body and mind, self and society and self and family. With these differences in mind, this chapter will examine factors influencing mental health services for people of Asian descent. It will focus on resource access, diagnostic and assessment issues, pharmacotherapeutic factors, the role of the family and treatment strategies. Implications for school-based counsellors will be examined as well.

Accessing Mental Health Services

People of Asian descent have demonstrated relatively low utilization rates of mental health services (Paniagua, 1994). This feature occurs with both inpatient and outpatient services, although more research has been conducted on the latter. This may be due to several factors. Root (1993) found that Asians do not come to the attention of the mental health system until invasive treatment is required, so the outpatient and community resources may not be utilized in the early phases of a mental illness. According to Lin and Cheung (1999), Asians often focus on physical symptoms rather than psychological concerns and are more likely to access their primary physician rather than mental health resources. In many Asian cultures, one's capability to control expression of personal problems is a measure of maturity and strength, especially among males (Sue & Sue, 1999). One significant factor in many smaller urban areas may be the paucity of counsellors of Asian descent and a lack of counselling resources within the immediate community. Lin and Cheung (1999) note that there may be a widespread belief that the need and desire for services specific to the Asian population is minimal, but it has been demonstrated that when these services are initiated, they are invariably well utilized. Devore and Schlesinger (1987) noted that generational differences and degree of immersion in the host culture are the primary determinants of receptivity to various types of mental health services. Asians with a low degree of acculturation to the dominant culture and of an earlier generation, are least likely to access services.

Root (1993) offered four suggestions to reduce barriers to Asian clients accessing services: a) provide flexible service hours to minimize conflicts with work schedules, b) offer a range of fees based on income (sliding scale) and provide opportunities for bartering goods for the service, c) use a culturally knowledgeable co-therapist and d) be aware of the need for advocacy and acquisition of tangible needs outside the therapy session. Devore and Schlesinger, (1987) suggest that benevolent societies and churches can play a role in developing culturally congruent and accessible services, as can young Asian students with a renewed sense of ethnic identity. Root (1993) also identifies the common reasons why clients terminate treatment prematurely. They include communication problems, conflict over the direction of psychotherapy, confusion over the workings of psychotherapy and a discrepancy between the client and counsellor perspectives of healthy psychological functioning.

Assessment and Diagnostic Issues

Several related issues affect the assessment and diagnosis of mental health issues with people of Asian descent. Lin and Cheung (1999) state that current psychiatric theories regarding etiology and assessment are primarily based on clinical data gathered from North American and European clients and very little research exists to determine the relevance of these assumptions to other cultures. The application of culturally inappropriate and irrelevant diagnostic tools often results in an inaccurate view of the client's mental health issues. Although the Diagnostic and Statistical Manual of the American Psychiatric Association (1994) recognizes culture-bound syndromes common to Asian populations, there appears to be a lack of correspondence between these indigenous labels and exact diagnostic criteria. This may be due to a radically different view of mental health and dysfunction between East and West.

Somatization of psychological distress in Asians appears to be a salient, yet controversial finding (Sue & Sue, 1999; Lin & Cheung, 1999). One possible explanation is that many

Asian cultures regard body and mind as one entity, as opposed to the Western view that they are separate and require different treatment strategies. Another related factor concerns the reluctance of Asians to speak of private and potentially embarrassing matters of intrapsychic functioning; discussion of corporeal matters may be more culturally acceptable (Lin & Cheung, 1999). Paniagua (1994) has suggested that a focus on somatic symptoms in a mental health assessment may simply be the result of clients selectively presenting symptoms that were congruent with their expectations of a medical setting. Further research is required to determine if this factor is present in non-medical settings such as community counselling agencies. The Korean ailment known as *hwa-byung*, which means both "fire disease" and "anger disease," is one example of a culture bound syndrome originating from psychosocial stressors, but expressed in physical terms (Lin & Cheung, 1999). Essentially, hwa-byung is thought to be caused by chronic unresolved anger that leads to an imbalance of the body systems. It is believed that the fire element becomes dominant, resulting in a variety of symptoms including fatigue, insomnia, dyspepsia and a sensation of a mass in the epigastric area, according to the DSM-IV (1994). Excessive reactivity to the environment, known as shinkeishitsu, is a Japanese syndrome with somatic features. According to Okabe, Takahashi and Richardson (1995), "Individuals suffering from this syndrome tend to be perfectionistic and highly self-conscious; they are also believed to be intelligent and creative. Physical symptoms include fatigue, sleeplessness, stomachaches and headaches" (p. 132).

Contemporary North American culture asserts that many differences exist between beliefs, attitudes and assumptions of Eastern and Western societies. A review of the literature indicates that this contrast also affects beliefs about mental health. Root (1993) identified some common beliefs about mental wellness in Asian Americans. One belief centered on the notion that good mental health can often be achieved through avoidance of morbid thoughts and willpower. There also appears to be a stigma attached to having a mental illness in the family and an attitude of shame and fear dominates. In many South East Asian cultures, common features of mental illness such as delusions and hallucinations, are believed to be caused by evil spirits (Nishio & Bilmes, 1993). Paniagua (1994) states a common belief is that verbal interactions with a clinician are only useful to gather information rather than alleviate distress; only directive behavioral interventions are viewed as helpful. Strong and forceful expressions of emotion outside the family may be viewed as impolite and immodest, especially with non-Asians, in many Asian cultures. Other cultural factors affecting diagnosis and assessment include experiences of prejudice and racism, the subservient roles of children and married women and the expression of respect involving silence, lack of eye contact and humility (Paniagua, 1994).

Pharmacotherapy

Clients of Asian descent may show unique patterns of responses to psychotropic medication, requiring lower doses and closer monitoring of side effects (Lin & Cheung, 1999; Paniagua, 1994). These pharmacokinetic and pharmacodynamic differences appear to be the result of the unique properties of a group of drug-metabolizing enzymes known as cytochrome P-450 isozymes. These enzymes are responsible for the metabolism of many psychotropic medications and appear to operate slower in Asian populations compared to Caucasian groups. Diet is also thought to be a factor in this metabolic process, but research has been unable to establish causal relationships. It is also important to note any herbal preparations that are being used with psychiatric medications (Lin & Cheung, 1999).

The Role of the Family

In contrast with the North American view that mental health interventions are focused on the individual, the family is considered the primary unit of functioning in any supportive intervention (Lin & Cheung 1999; Sue & Sue, 1999). Root (1993) stated that the family will invariably be the identified recipient of service in a mental health setting and two important conditions must be met to satisfy the needs of the family. The therapist must validate the family's feeling and the therapeutic context must make sense in order to ensure positive expectations of therapy. Often, an Asian client's initial contact with the mental health system will have been proceeded by phone calls from one or more family members and family members assume they will take an active role in both the assessment and treatment of the individual (Lin, 1999). Okabe et al. (1995) summarize the superordinate role of the family in mental health interventions:

> *The cultural values of interpersonal harmony and fulfillment of social roles, including service to the family, determine therapeutic goals for mental health problems. In general, the basic objective is to assist the individual to accept and adjust to his social environment rather than to change it (p. 133).*

Treatment Strategies

Asian Canadian clients have unique needs that must be addressed for counselling and psychotherapy to be culturally congruent. Paniagua (1994) underscores the importance of the therapist demonstrating authority and competence overtly by displaying diplomas, demonstrating confidence in a positive outcome and explaining possible causes to the problem. This is consistent with the Asian expectation that health professionals are authority figures, moral exemplars and teachers. Root (1993) also states that a therapist should provide an overview of the therapy plan, explain the types of changes that need to occur and identify tasks for family members to enhance the development of trust.

Sue and Sue (1999) outline seven strategies for counselling Asian immigrants and refugees. Clinicians should use restraint when gathering information, being conscious of the cultural preponderance toward modesty. Some time should be taken to explain the roles inherent in the counselling relationship. Focusing on the specific problem brought to the session and developing goals toward resolution will reduce the likelihood of the therapist's worldview being imposed on the client. The clinician may also need to take a more didactic and active role than usual to provide direction and structure. Financial and social needs may be paramount initially and intergenerational conflicts due to differences in acculturation may be significant as well. Finally, therapy should be as brief as reasonably possible and be focused on the present or the immediate future. Similarly, Paniagua (1994) lists a number of strategies to prevent attrition of Asian clients, including avoiding personalisms (being formal at all times), being aware of the role of shame and humiliation, encouraging dependent relationships between children and parents and avoiding discussions of hospitalizations without first considering less intrusive measures.

According to Lin and Cheung (1999), counselling interventions that emphasize structure and action, such as cognitive and behavioral therapies, appear to be more effective than client-centered or psychodynamic approaches. Simple and easily replicated behavioral techniques such as systematic desensitization and progressive relaxation may be very effective. Progressive relaxation (Cormier & Cormier, 1998) consists of the client tensing and relaxing muscle groups in a sequential manner while focusing on a single soothing thought. It can be done with the aid of a counsellor guiding the process, or clients can be taught to complete the steps by themselves. Systematic desensitization (Kalodner, 1998) pairs a relaxed mind and body with an anxiety provoking thought or image in a hierarchical manner. This has the effect of reducing the degree of disturbance elicited by the thought or image. Progressively stronger stimuli are presented over time to reduce or eliminate anxiety elicited by the thought or image.

Cognitive therapy may be culturally congruent for Asian individuals because of the directive nature of the therapeutic relationship and the emphasis on changing thoughts and behaviors. According to Freeman, Pretzer, Fleming & Simon (1990), the underlying premise of cognitive therapy states that individuals often have immediate interpretations of events known as automatic thoughts. These thoughts may be exaggerated, mistaken or unrealistic, which may lead to larger beliefs and assumptions known as cognitive schemas that shape the perception and interpretation of events. These faulty interpretations, known as cognitive distortions, may lead to feelings and behaviors that are problematic. Cognitive therapy consists of a counsellor labeling and challenging these distortions in cognition and constructing more accurate cognitive schemas, leading to more adaptive emotions and behaviors. This approach is very useful in working with depressed and anxious individuals. Many fundamental concepts in cognitive therapy have their parallel in Asian belief systems and the required didactic features of the therapeutic relationship may be congruent with the expectations of the client.

Asian psychotherapies such as Naikan, Morita and meditation can be adapted to the Western mental health system and provide a respectful and positive experience. Naikan, with its connection to Buddhism, focuses on reflection on past relationships and emphasizes positivity, self-discipline and self-control (France & Allen, 1994). Morita (Walsh, 1995) is a Japanese therapy used in the treatment of anxiety disorders. It is commonly used to assist clients in eliminating social phobia, perfectionism and self-preoccupation through cognitive reframing and interaction with the environment to shift focus away from the self. Meditation is an ancient Asian technique for relaxation, reflection and spiritual enlightenment (Wegela, 1996; Walsh, 1995). It has recently entered mainstream North American culture as a technique to manage stress and enhance wellness.

Certain ethnic groups have specific cultural experiences that warrant consideration from mental health professionals (Waxler-Morrison et al., 1995). Visiting students from Asian countries may feel pressure from parents to succeed academically, resulting in guilt and shame when mental health issues interfere with scholastic pursuits. Older generations of Japanese Canadians, referred to as Issei (Okabe et al., 1995), may have experienced displacement and discrimination because of internment during the Second World War. Political unrest and persecution has been common in many Asian countries in the late twentieth century, resulting in large numbers of refugees coming to Canada from such countries as Vietnam, Laos, Cambodia and China. These refugees often experience depression, anxiety, post-traumatic stress disorder and dissociative disorders because of exposure to trauma and war. They may also have financial, social and legal challenges as they adjust to the receiving culture. The above issues, as well as experiences of racism (in both overt and institutional forms) may exacerbate existing mental health issues for all Asians.

Although the above factors must be kept in mind, the most important tools in any cross-cultural counselling setting may be the beliefs, attitudes and feelings of the counsellor. A related skill is the ability to a view a client as an individual, taking into account uniquely personal characteristics while assessing and acknowledging the impact of both Asian and North American cultures on personal development and mental health issues.

Practical Implications for the School Counsellor

Many of the above factors can impact on the interactions between the school counsellor and the members of an Asian family. As discussed earlier, it is considered impolite and weak to discuss one's personal concerns, so children, youth and families may not engage in the counselling process. As members of many Asian cultures view academic pursuits as paramount, they may view counselling as much less important than scholastic pursuits.

Including extended family in individual or family sessions may be necessary to build relationships. A counsellor may initially be uncomfortable with the family members viewing her as an authority figure and advisor rather than an equal partner in the therapeutic process. Cognitive-behavioral interventions, which require the counsellor to be highly directive, may be more effective with all family members than more egalitarian approaches. Parents may have expectations of children and youths that clash with those of contemporary North American society and local mores. All family members may be experiencing discrimination and racism in both the community and the school environment.

Special consideration must be given to children, youth and parents from war-torn countries that may have experienced harassment, interrogation, family separation and violence. Griggs and Dunn (1996) ventured that many of these youth suffer post-traumatic stress, including nightmares, flashbacks, withdrawal, insomnia and physiological problems. Many of the psychological symptoms of trauma, including problems with concentration, anxiety and depression, interfere with a student's ability to engage in counselling.

Conclusion

The mental health issues relevant to Asian Canadians are complex and varied and may not be served by mental health support systems unless attention is given to the unique requirements of this group. As this demographic group is likely to continue to grow in size, the need for knowledgeable and culturally sensitive counsellors will continue to grow. Factors influencing access to services should be considered when any restructuring of mental health services occurs. The mental health clinician must be aware of the client's perception of mental health and the therapeutic relationship and be aware of the client's expectations of counselling or psychotherapy. Due to physiological differences, psychotropic medications may have a more potent effect and more severe side effects. The important role of the client's family must be respected as well. Many culturally sensitive treatment strategies exist, focusing on clear expectations of both the therapy and the clinician and incorporating dynamics inherent in a collectivist culture to achieve treatment goals. Certain ethnic groups have experienced unique situations that influence the helping process as well. School-based counsellors who interact with children, youth and parents face additional challenges relating to the school environment and cultural factors. Finally, it is crucial that clinicians are aware of their own cultural issues and focus on the individual experience of the client rather than on culture.

References

Citizenship and Immigration Canada. (1998). *Facts and Figures 1997: Immigration Overview.* Available: http://cicnet.ci.gc.ca/english/pub/facts97e/index_e.html.

Cormier, S. & Cormier, B. (1998). *Interviewing Strategies for Helpers*. Pacific Grove, CA: Brooks/Cole.

Devore, W., Schlesinger, E.G., (1987). *Ethnic-sensitive Social Work Practice*. Columbus, OH: Merrill.

Diagnostic and Statistical Manual of Mental Disorders (1994). 4th Ed. Washington, DC: American Psychological Association.

France, M.H. & Allen, E. (1994). Naikan: A western perspective of Asian psychotherapy. *Asian Journal of Counselling, 3* (1&2). 35-42.

Freeman, A., Pretzer, J., Fleming, B. & Simon, K. (1990). *Clinical Applications of Cognitive Therapy*. New York: Plenum.

Griggs, S. & Dunn, R. (1996). Learning styles of Asian-American adolescents. *Emergency Librarian, 4* (1). 8-14.

Kalodner, C.R. (1998). Systematic Desensitization. In S. Cormier & B. Cormier (Eds.) *Interviewing Strategies for Helpers*. Pacific Grove, CA: Brooks/Cole.

Kitano, H.H. & Maki, M.T. (1996). Continuity, change and diversity: Counselling Asian Americans. In P.B. Peterson, J.G. Draguns, W.J. Lonner & J.E. Trimble (Eds.) *Counselling Across Cultures*. Thousand Oaks, CA: Sage.

Lin, K. & Cheung, F. (1999). Mental Health Issues for Asian Americans. *Psychiatric Services, 50* (6), 774-780.

Nishio, K. & Bilmes, M. (1993). Psychotherapy with Southeast Asian American clients. In D.R. Atkinson, G. Morten & D.W. Sue, (Eds.), *Counselling American Minorities: A Cross-cultural Perspective*. Madison, WI: Brown & Benchmark.

Okabe, T., Takahashi, K. & Richardson, E. (1995). The Japanese. In N. Waxler-Morrison, J.M. Anderson & R. Richardson (Eds.). *Cross -cultural Caring: A Handbook for Health Professionals*. Vancouver, B.C.: UBC Press.

Paniagua, F. (1994). *Assessing and Treating Culturally Diverse Clients: A Practical Guide*. Thousand Oaks, CA: Sage.

Root, M.P. (1993). Guidelines for facilitating therapy with Asian American clients. In D.R. Atkinson, G. Morten & D.W. Sue (Eds.), *Counselling American Minorities: A Cross-cultural Perspective* (pp. 211-224). Madison, WI: Brown & Benchmark.

Sue, D.W. & Sue, D. (1999). *Counselling the Culturally Different: Theory and Practice*. New York: Wiley.

Waxler-Morrison, N., Anderson, J.M. & Richardson, R. (1995). *Cross-cultural Caring: A Handbook for Health Professionals*. Vancouver, B.C.: UBC Press.

Walsh, R. (1995). Asian psychotherapies. In R. Corsini & D. Wedding (Eds.), *Current Psychotherapies* (5th ed., pp. 387-398). Itasca, IL: F.E. Peacock.

Wegela, K.K. (1996). *How to be a Help Instead of a Nuisance*. Boston, MA: Shambala.

Chapter 8
The Affects of Biculturalism on Young Indo-Canadian Women

Sukkie Sihota

What does it mean to be Indo-Canadian? I have been challenging and struggling with this question for much of my life. When I occasionally dress up in my *sari* to attend an Indian function, I feel completely Indian. However, more often I dress in my Canadian clothing, not only because it is more comfortable for me, but it is also a part of my identity. While my external appearance may signify an aspect of my identity, how I dress or the color of my skin has not been in the forefront of my struggle. Instead, the conflict lies in my internal sense of self. Are my values and beliefs obtained from my Sikh parents, or do they come from the Canadian culture that I am exposed to and a part of on a daily basis? What are the roles, rules and expectations I am adhering to? These are some of the questions I began exploring in much of my adolescent years and continue to explore as an adult.

Many second generation Indo-Canadian young people are faced with the same struggles and questions about their identity and sense of belonging. Are they Indian, Canadian or Indo-Canadian? They may feel they have two cultures which do not blend together easily. Ghuman (1994) notes that new Indian immigrants to Canada are often firmly rooted in their religion and culture and are sure of their personal identities. Their sense of belonging is not jeopardized because they are certain of their identity as Sikhs. However, the children of these immigrants are less sure of their personal and social identities. The second generation of Indo-Canadians are more likely to question values and beliefs. They more commonly struggle with their sense of self and possibly suffer from culture clash. For many Indo-Canadian students, the values and beliefs at school contradict those of home. Therefore, Ghuman believes the focus should lie on bridging the gap between the culture of the home and the school.

Diversity Among Indo-Canadian Populations

Members of the Indo-Canadian population have also been termed East Indian and/or South Asian. In this chapter I have chosen to label the participants as Indo-Canadians because this term describes the full bicultural experience. To call the participants East Indian or South Asian does not reflect the significance of their Canadian identity. They are products of two cultures, Indian and Canadian and it is important to honor this dualism. The term South Asian is used only to refer to individuals who have spent the majority of their lives in India and are not Canadian citizens.

Also, it is important to note the diversity among the Indo-Canadian population in terms of religion, culture, language and food. In fact, India's constitution recognizes a total of 15 official languages and a recent Indian census tabulated more than 500 mother tongues spoken within the nation's boundaries (Mogelonsky, 1995). So, although the Indo-Canadian population may share the original mother country of India, they do not necessarily share the same cultural backgrounds or personal experiences.

Furthermore, my main focus in this paper is on the Sikh Indo-Canadian population. I have chosen this group for two main reasons. First, Sikhs make up the largest Indo-Canadian group in British Columbia. Second, being from a Sikh Indo-Canadian background myself, my own personal reflections are more accurately expressed from this perspective.

Ethnic Identity

Achieving a sense of identity is an important psychological task for an adolescent. This undertaking includes the ability to know and understand oneself as an individual, as well as recognizing one's particular place in society. The influence of one's ethnic identity is most pertinent in societies that have diverse ethnic backgrounds among the one dominant social group (Rosenthal, 1987). Ethnic identity can be defined as "one's sense of belonging to an ethnic group and the part of one's thinking, perception, feelings and behavior that is due to ethnic group membership" (Rotheram & Phinney, 1987, p. 13). According to Rosenthal (1987), ethnic identity can be conceptualized by two parts: objective and subjective. Objectively, one can relate to their ethnic group in terms of ascribed or external characteristics. These characteristics may include geographical birthplaces, language, religion, race or physical attributes, history and/or customs. These external characteristics may not necessarily meet one's subjective affiliation with the ethnic group. Subjective affiliation is defined as one's sense of identity and feelings of belonging with the ethnic group. The subjective identification with an ethnic group is what leads to the development of a social identity based on ethnic group membership.

So then, what does it mean to have a bicultural identity? Can second generation Indo-Canadian youth be identified as bicultural? and Rotheram and Phinney (1987) state that "bicultural identity refers to an identification of oneself with two ethnic groups" (p. 39). From my personal perspective and experience, it is evident that second generation Indo-Canadian youth indeed have bicultural identities. Given their exposure to both cultures on a daily basis, second generation Indo-Canadian youth tend to relate to and identify with both the Indian culture and the Canadian culture.

Racial/Cultural Identity Development Model

Sue and Sue's (1981) Racial/Cultural Identity Development Model describes the conflicts an individual encounters while trying to find their identity in relation to their own culture, the dominant culture and the oppressive relationship between the two inherently different cultures. In the *Conformity Stage*, "minority persons are distinguished by their unequivocal preference for dominant cultural values over their own" (Sue & Sue, 1981, p. 99). An individual in this stage strives for identification with the dominant culture. Changing appearance, such as dress and hair, in order to be more like the dominant culture is typical in this stage. In the *Dissonance Stage*, the individual is in conflict between appreciating the minority heritage or looking at it as an inhibitor. In the *Resistance and Immersion Stage,* the minority person resists conforming to the dominant culture and instead, strongly values and appreciates the minority ethnic heritage. The individual in this stage may accept the dominant culture as oppressive and consequently, there are strong reactions against it. The *Introspection Stage* involves the individual's deliberation about the cost and benefits of having negative feelings against the dominant culture. At this stage, "the individual begins to discover that this level of intensity of feelings (anger directed toward the White society) is psychologically draining and does not permit one to really devote more crucial energies to understanding themselves or to their own racial-cultural group" (Sue & Sue, 1981, p. 104). Lastly, the *Integrative Stage* involves the individual's acceptance of both his or her own ethnic identity and the culture of the dominant society. At this point, the individual is able to accept and reject the values and beliefs from each culture which he or she does not find advantageous or appealing.

Cultural Conflicts

Sikh people take great pride in their religion and culture. Many of them have overcome great obstacles in order to reside in Canada, a country which is quite different from their homeland. Although the values, beliefs and overall culture in Canada often clashes with the norms that Indian immigrants are accustomed to, they have nevertheless managed to make themselves comfortable and call the Western world their home. So, what does this mean for the immigrants' children who are born and raised in Canada? They seem to be caught in the middle of two distinctly different cultures. As mentioned previously, Indo-Canadian youth may start to question their own identity and wonder what cultural background they actually belong to. Often parents try to preserve their Indian culture by placing traditional values onto their children. At the same time, these youth are challenged on a daily basis to adhere to the norms of Canadian society. Not surprisingly, conflict between parents and children arises because of inherent differences in the Indian culture and Canadian culture. Although there may be many areas of internal self conflicts for Indo-Canadian adolescents as well as many areas of discord between themselves and their first generation parents, the most prevalent themes that have impacted youth in terms of their identity will be discussed below.

Racial Discrimination

Ghuman's (1994) study, which had an Indo-Canadian sample and a British Asian sample, showed a significant difference from the present study in terms of racial comments directed at youth. Although Ghuman noted that the British Asian participants reflected on their personal experience of racism, not one member of his Indo-Canadian sample admitted to having met any overt racial prejudice. This was contradictory to my own study which concluded that the majority of the Indo-Canadian participants had personally experienced racism from white people. Mann-Kahalma's (1997) study reflected the same conclusion as my own. The Indo-Canadian women within her study also spoke of their direct experiences with racism.

In the current study, the racism encountered by participants in their young lives led them to question their ethnic background and their sense of identity. The majority of respondents reported that in childhood and adolescence, they tended to back away from the Indo-Canadian culture and adopt the Western views because of the overt racism. This is congruent with Sue and Sue's (1981) stage of *Conformity* where the individual strives for identification with the dominant culture. The young women showed signs of this stage as they tended not to make friends with Indo-Canadians, refused to speak their native language and spoke of feelings of shame when they were forced to interpret for their parents. Although the women could not change their Indo-Canadian appearance on the outside, they attempted to convince themselves and others they were purely Canadian on the inside. The participants felt there was no easy compromise between the two cultures and therefore, they moved in a direction to fit in with the majority culture.

Dating

All the studies conclusively showed that issues surrounding dating had not changed over the years and they continued to be a source of conflict within the family home. Similarly, Mann-Kahalma's (1997) research found that young women were still expected to adhere to the "good girl" phenomenon, which included being passive, obedient and virginal. The same rules did not apply to their male counterparts because males did not hold the responsibility of the family honor. Often this left females resentful and angry as the same restrictions were not enforced on males.

The issue of dating was something parents were reluctant to change their views on, especially where their daughters were concerned. According to Wakil, Siddique and Wakil (1981), it appeared this was more of a "core belief" rather than a "pragmatic value." The changes in parents tended to be on issues that were more pragmatic in nature rather than the core beliefs of the family. Daughters were considered the repository of the family honour. Consequently, the parents put more restrictions on their daughters in order to prevent the family honor from being tarnished.

Arranged Marriages

On the subject of arranged marriages, the current study was conclusive with the previous research done on this area. It was clear the idea of arranged marriages was evolving to meet the considerations of second generation Indo-Canadians. Parents were lifting their rigid standards around arranged marriages in hopes of finding a common ground that would not eliminate the notion all together. Instead of being the sole determiners of their children's marital future, parents were proceeding only with the approval from their children. Overall, the second generation appeared ambivalent to the idea of an arranged marriage for themselves; although they strongly believed they should be a part of the process. As indicated by this study, the young women still fantasized about finding an ideal match on their own. This idea was conclusive with the study done by Wakil et al. (1981), which found Canadian-born children were generally unwilling to buy the traditional idea that love comes after marriage. Instead, the young women tended to adopt the Canadian culture's emphasis on romantic love.

Although parents modified the arranged marriage to accommodate the wishes of their Canadian born children, they still held the belief that the decision should not be left solely to the children. The change in the traditional marriage is summarized by Vidynathan and Naidoon (1991) as the following: 1) more flexibility in parental authority in the host country as compared to the ancestral country; 2) increase in the independence and decision making powers of the second generation. The studies done on Indo-Canadians clearly showed that they have exhibited adoptive behavior after having discovered that an attitude of compromise and balance is required for optimal functioning with the host country (Vidynathan & Naidoon, 1991).

Gender Differences

Seemingly dating was not the only aspect where males were granted more freedom, rather it was the whole social sphere. As indicated by the present study, although the young women were encouraged to purse their educational and career aspirations, they were restricted in terms of their social freedom. Ghuman's (1994) sample reported a different outcome than what was presented in the current study. Ghuman's Indo-Canadian sample did not find girls and males were treated any differently, although, interestingly, a very high percentage of his British sample agreed with the fact that boys and girls had differential treatment. Ghuman was surprised and skeptical of this finding and attributed the difference to the possibility that the Indo-Canadian sample tended to respond with the "desired" response.

Ghuman's skepticism arose after speaking to teachers and counsellors who indicated these females were resentful of the differential treatment at home.

Drury's (1991) study in Britain was conclusive with the present study in the resentment women felt towards the freedom males were given. However, Drury noted the majority of these women did not rebel from their parents wishes. Only a small percentage noted they secretly rebelled in order to avoid confrontation with their parents. In the present study, the responses were different as the participants noted there was a great deal of secrecy in the lives of young Indo-Canadian women. As one participant reported, "Every one does it, nobody talks about it." Thus, it was possible to conclude from the present study that secret lives were a way for some young Indo-Canadian women to cope with the demands of having two distinct cultures. These women found secrecy as a workable condition which allowed them to maintain the family honor and respectability, as well as fulfill their own needs in the Western world.

Religion

Conclusions from the present study indicated that most participants went to *gurdwaras* (temples) only when there were special religious ceremonies or weddings. The majority of the participants reported that they did not believe in the teachings of Sikhism. Out of the five respondents, only one participant revealed her hope in gaining more knowledge about the Sikh gurus and the history of Sikhism. Wakil et al. (1981) found the same results, as the parents' enthusiasm for their children to learn the religion did not match that of the young people themselves. On the contrary, Ghuman (1994) was left with a different impression in his study with second generation Indo-Canadians. Ghuman felt that although the second generation Indo-Canadians did not know much about their religion, they had a desire to learn more about it.

Evidently the women in the present study did not have positive experiences with the Sikh religion. In fact, some women stated the teaching of Sikhism did not reflect the action of their followers. As a result of this perceived contradiction, the majority of respondents felt Sikhism was not a faith they wanted to follow.

Acceptance of Being Indo-Canadian

As noted earlier, the participants felt they had come to accept their ethnicity as being Indo-Canadian, whereas in the past they attempted to resist the Indian culture by assimilating with the Canadian culture. The comments made by young Indo-Canadians around the issue of their identities were particularly positive in Ghuman's (1994) study as well. Ghuman was encouraged to see the official Canadian policy of multiculturalism as having a positive effect on Indo-Canadian youth. He concluded that the policy helped to foster a sense of pride and security in the youth's bicultural identities.

According to Sue and Sue's (1981) model, these young women are in the *Integrative Stage* of the Racial/Cultural Identity Development Model. Hence, instead of trying to avoid their ethnic heritage, they have learned to accept it and integrate it with the Canadian culture. They have come to embrace both their ethnic identity and the culture of the dominant Canadian society. One participant made an inspiring comment that, "By accepting it [ethnicity], I am accepting myself."

Implications for Counsellors

So, what does this mean for counsellors? In a country where biculturalism in no longer uncommon and an emphasis is being placed on a greater multicultural society, it is essential that counsellors be aware and integrate skills that reflect the changing needs. Counsellors need to be open, sensitive and receptive to new ways of helping which may be different from the conventional methods they are accustomed to. If counsellors choose to remain unaware of Indo-Canadian cultural values and if they feel the Western way of life is superior to the Indian, then it is likely that their attitudes will lead to conflict and alienation for their Indo-Canadian clients. On the other hand, if counsellors are empathic, nonjudgmental and generally cultivate a positive outlook towards their client's ethnic culture, it is more likely the counselling will be a positive experience for the client (Pedersan, Draguns, Lonner & Trimble, 2002).

It may not be often that an Indo-Canadian family comes into counselling for conflicts arising at home or school. Typically, the family relies on relatives or friends to help with conflicts and difficulties they are encountering. Assanand, Dias, Richardson and Waxler-Morrison (1990) state:

> *There is little experience with social service agencies and sometimes distrust of all government servants…South Asian families are likely to use social service agencies only as a last resort, after seeking help from family, friends, the temple, or a physician. (p. 179)*

Likewise, Segal (1991) says, "Even when counselling is sought voluntarily, they often feel they have been reduced to a level beneath their dignity and pride" (p. 239).

Awareness of Values

It may be impossible for counsellors to know all the values and traditions of the Indo-Canadian community and thus, they may need to rely on their ethnic clients to educate them on the issues they bring forth into counselling. Sodowsky, Kwan and Pannu (1995) state some of the inherent values of Asian Americans which seemingly apply to the Indo-Canadian population as well. The values and characteristics that may come forth in counselling sessions are as follows:

- Silence, nonconfrontation, moderation in behavior, self control, patience, humility, modesty and simplicity are seen as virtues.

- Respect for older persons and the elderly.

- Devaluation of individualism: Less value is placed on individualism, higher value is placed on family. The family and society exist to maximize the individual.

- Harmony between hierarchical roles and structured family roles and relationships: Social harmony is achieved through structured family relationships that have clearly defined codes of behavior, including language usage and hierarchical roles.

- Filial piety: There is high respect for parents. Individual family members seek the honor and good name of the family and protect it from shame. Family duties and obligations take precedence over individual desires. Social control is achieved through family demands for obedience and fulfillment of obligations. There is a strong sense of duty towards family.

- High regard for learning.

- Modest about sexuality and not demonstrative with heterosexual affection: Sexuality and sexual relationships are supposed to be treated with modesty and a degree of formality.

- Less need for dating: When an individual is ready for marriage, the family participates in finding a suitable match.

- Marrying within versus outside ethnic group: Importance is attached to preserving the culture and the original religion.

Educational Model

As discussed in this chapter, many Indo-Canadians are faced with the challenges of living in two distinct cultures. Their views and ideas are influenced both by their ethnic culture as well as by the dominant majority culture. Some of the stressors that may come up in counselling include issues around identity, assimilation, intergenerational conflicts, gender role conflicts and concerns about interracial conflicts.

In order to deal with some of these issues, an education model is proposed by Segal (1991). Due to Indo-Canadians' disinclination in coming to counselling, a lecture style which would include group discussions may be an indirect alternative to counselling. First, Segal recommends starting with a clarification of mutual values. Ibrahim, Ohnishi and Sandhu (1997) further explain that this relational style allows the counsellor and the clients to explore both value systems in conjunction. This will increase trust level, as the clients can get to know that the counsellor is objective about his or her assumptions and knows the boundaries of his or her cultural identity. Second, Segal states it is important for clients to understand the myths regarding the Canadian culture and lifestyle. Third, counsellors should review adolescent psychology and peer group pressures within the group setting. Fourth, Maydas and Elliot (as cited in Segal, 1991) state there should be a discussion about cultural conflicts that occur when accommodating, adapting, assimilating and integrating into a new culture. Last, various implications and the inevitable changes of immigration should be addressed.

In dealing with specific bicultural issues, an intervention goal for parents would be to broaden their intellectual understanding of the struggles facing the youth who are evidently torn between two cultures. Also, in relation to first generation Indo-Canadians, this education model is an attempt to help them gain emotional acceptance of the unavoidable changes inherent in their decision to settle in a culture that is often contrary to their own Indian lifestyle (Segal, 1991).

For the second generation adolescents who are struggling with their bicultural identities, one goal would be to bridge the communication gap between themselves and their parents. Often there has been a breakdown in communication due to the turmoil in the home. Hence, a facilitation that opens the gates to communication would be beneficial to both generations. Another goal is to imbue a sense of pride in their bicultural background by exploring the benefits of being bicultural and bilingual (Segal, 1991).

Another option to the conventional counselling style may be group therapy in which adolescents or parents can share their experiences amongst each other and develop support networks (Segal, 1991).

Specific Interventions

Given that the alternative methods proposed by Segal (1991) are not effective, Indo-Canadians may choose to utilize family or individual counselling. Supplementary guidelines are proposed for counsellors by Ibrahim et al. (1997):

1. The client will need the respect of their person, their cultural identity and worldview. Clients will need a mutual respectful relationship and sense of autonomy. They will be less inclined to follow through on interventions that they feel they have not come up with on their own.

2. Understand the client's level of acculturation and identity status before planning a intervention.

3. Clarify the client's spiritual identity before deciding on goals and outcomes. An ideal counselling strategy would incorporate the ideas of both spiritual and identity development because a major source of anxiety involves keeping a balance in both these areas.

4. Multidimensional intervention would be helpful, using cognitive, behavioral, ecological, spiritual and other relevant domains for the client. Use models of counselling that support both individualism and relational aspects.

5. Recognize the importance of the lifestage and age of the client. Within age and lifestage evaluate the impact of gender.

6. Never assume that the client does not or cannot understand your attitudes and nonverbal attitudes. This culture has a high nonverbal content.

7. Recognize the role of humility in the client's cultural identity and do not assume the client has a poor self concept.

8. Respect the integrity and individualism of the clients. Indo-Canadians are individualistic within the familial context.

9. Allow the client to educate the counsellor regarding the client's specific identification level with his or her ethnic subculture, religion, values and worldview and the larger society.

Conclusion

From the studies done, the results were not completely conclusive. In particular the study done by Ghuman (1994) seemed to be contradictory on several issues. Specifically, his study concluded that the Indo-Canadian sample did not encounter any racial discrimination, females were not treated differently than males and that the second generation had a desire to learn about their Sikh religion. The other studies, including the current research, indicated the opposite. However, at the same time, Ghuman did note his skepticism and believed the respondents reported a "desired" response. All studies were conclusive that arranged marriages were evolving to meet the demands of second generation Indo-Canadians and that the parents' stance on dating is something that has not changed in regards to their daughters.

Although Indo-Canadians may not readily seek out counselling, it is important for counsellors to be aware of the group's values and stressors if clients do choose to utilize services. Furthermore, in order to effectively help them through their challenges, it is equally as important for counsellors to know how to help rather than hinder the counselling process.

References

Assanand, S., Dias, M., Richardson, E. & Waxter-Morrison, N. (1990). The South Asians. In N. Waxler-Morrison, J. Anderson & E. Richardson (Eds.), *Cross-cultural Caring: A Handbook for Health Professionals in Western Canada*. Vancouver: University of British Columbia Press.

Drury, B. (1991). Sikh girls and the maintenance of an ethic culture. *New Community, 17*(3), 387-400.

Ghuman, P.A.S. (1994). *Coping with Two Cultures: British Asian and Indo-Canadian Adolescents*. Clevedon: Multilingual Matters Ltd.

Ibrahim, F., Ohnishi, H. & Sandhu, D. (1997). Asian American identity development: A culture specific model for South Asian Americans. *Journal of Multicultural Counseling and Development, 25*, 34-50.

Mann-Kahalma, P. (1995). Intergenerational conflict and strategies of resistance: A study of young

Punjabi Sikh women in the Canadian context. Unpublished master's thesis, University of Victoria, Victoria, British Columbia, Canada.

Mogelonsky, M. (1995). Asian Indians. *American Demographics, 17*, 32-39.

Pedersen, P., Draguns, J., Lonner, W. & Trimble, J. (2002). *Counseling Across Cultures,* 5th edition. Thousand Oaks, CA: Sage Publications.

Rotheram, M. & Phinney, J.S. (1997). Introduction: Definition and perspectives in the study of children's ethnic socialization. In J.S. Phinney and M. Rotheram (Eds.), *Children's Ethnic Socialization: Pluralism and Development.* Newbury Park, CA: Sage Publications.

Rosenthal, D. (1997). Ethnic identity development in adolescents. In J.S. Phinney and M. Rotheram (Eds.), *Children's Ethnic Socialization: Pluralism and Development.* Newbury Park, CA: Sage Publications.

Segal, U.A. (1991). Cultural variable in Asian Indian families. *Families in Society: The Journal of Contemporary Human Services, 72*(4), 233-242.

Sodowsky, G.R., Kwan, K.K. & Pannu, R. (1995). Ethnic identity of Asians in the United States. In J.G. Ponterotto, J.M. Casas, L.A. Suzuki & C.M. Alexander (Eds.), *Handbook of Multicultural Counseling.* Thousand Oaks, CA: Sage.

Statistics Canada (2001). Population by minority population. [on-line] retrieved January 16, 2001 from http://www.statcan.ca.

Sue, W. & Sue, D. (1990). *Counseling the Culturally Different: Theory and Practice.* New York: John Wiley and Sons.

Wakil, R.S., Siddique, C.M. & Wakil, F.A. (1981). Between two cultures: A study in socialization of children immigrants. *Journal of Marriage and the Family, 43*, 929-940.

Vidynathan, P. & Naidoo, J. (1991). Asian Indians in western countries: Cultural identity and the arranged marriage. In N. Bleichrodt and Drenth (Eds.), *Contemporary Issues in Cross Cultural Psychology.* Amsterdam: Swets and Leitlinger.

Chapter 9
Acculturation and Adaptation: Providing Counselling for Immigrants and Refugees

Yali Li, M. Honoré France, María del Carmen Rodríguez
& Elias Cheboud

In the area of immigration, for a nation of its size, 31 million, Canada takes in more different nationalities of migrants than any country in the world. According to Dyer (2001) "Canada takes in about twice as many people, in proportion to its population, as does the United States and four times as many as the United Kingdom" (p. 46). Interestingly, from l995 to 2000, Canada took in 1 246 210 immigrants and refugees. This means that right now more than four percent of Canadians are newcomers and they are from all over the world, starting the complicated process of adapting to the new country. To be effective with these new Canadians, it is important for counsellors to understand the immigrant adaptation process and how it affects adjustment. The trends indicate that the pattern of migration is from developing countries, such as China and India, to developed countries, such as Canada and the United States. The cause of the pattern is complex, which not only emanates from economic and political instability in developing countries, but also from the demand for labor and a declining birth rate in developing countries. The phenomenon is not just an issue in North America, but according to Bemak and Chung (2000), "...the immigrant and refugee populations have been steadily increasing, causing migration to be a global issue" (p. 200).

The experiences of these migrants, whether by choice, such as immigration, or by chance, as in the case of refugees, puts them in a risk category for developing emotional and psychological problems. The government of Canada has encouraged and supported migrants and refugees to come to this country; most recently thousands of Kosovo refugees were airlifted out of the war zone directly into Canadian communities. The process of change for these individuals adds a great deal of individual stress and challenges the social service system to implement culturally sensitive practices. However, in order to help in the resettlement process, multicultural counsellors need to be equipped to deal with a variety of people speaking different languages and valuing different traditions. What part of the world do the migrants come from? According to Dyer (2001), while 62% of all migrants currently living in Canada are of European origin, 74% of migrants who have arrived in Canada within the past 10 years are of non-European origin. The approximate break down from the various continents is as follows:

26% from East Asia	25% from South & South East Asia	10% from the Middle East
14% from Latin America	5% from Africa & Caribbean	20% from Europe & USA

The question of whether adaptation, assimilation or acculturation is the ideal process of adjusting to a new cultural environment is not easy to answer. However, it is one that needs to be addressed by each migrant because this will determine, to some extent, the level of comfort and accomplishment the individual achieves while interacting in a new cultural milieu.

What is Adaptation?

When encountering a new environment and culture, people instinctively respond in various ways. The process of adaptation is conformed by three responses that are generally identified as adjustment, reaction and withdrawal. In the case of adjustment, people make changes in the direction to reduce conflicts and seek for harmony with the environment and a harmony between different cultural groups. Contrary to adjustment, in the case of reaction, migrants try to change the environment and culture according to their needs. Withdrawal occurs when migrants either want to reduce the pressure of environmental factors or are excluded by the host culture.

A further distinction has been drawn between psychological and socio-cultural adaptation. Psychological adaptation refers to a set of internal psychological outcomes including a clear sense of personal and cultural identity, good mental health and the achievement of personal satisfaction in the new cultural context. Social-cultural adaptation is understood as a set of external outcomes that link individuals to their new context, including their ability to deal with daily problems, particularly in the areas of family life, work and school. Psychological adaptation may best be analyzed within the context of the stress and psychopathology approach, while socio-cultural adaptation is more closely linked to the social skills framework (Walton & Kennedy, 1993; Berry & Sam, 1997).

What is Acculturation?

Theoretically, acculturation refers to mutual changes in both migrants and host society as the result of interaction. It can be culture learning or a compromise from one or both groups to find common ground for relating to each other. In practice, most changes occur in the non-dominant group or the group with weak vitality (Berry & Sam, 1997; Bourhis, Moise, Perreault & Senecal, 1997; Kim, 1988). The process of acculturation is characterized by four strategies: Assimilation, separation, marginalization and integration. In the first approach, newcomers voluntarily or involuntarily give up their heritage culture in order to move into the host culture. For the host society, it implies the absorption of the migrant minority into the dominant culture to create a homogeneous society. If the choice is involuntary, it involves a total surrender of their ethnic identity, which imposes a sometimes painful sacrifice on migrants and inevitably brings acculturation stresses (Berry, 1987, 1990; Bourhis, et al., 1997).

In the second strategy, newcomers retain their heritage culture and remain apart from the host culture. When there is separation, newcomers isolate themselves in terms of setting up relationships with other social groups or participating even partially in the host society (Thomas, 1992; ISS, 1993). Separation is indicative of unwillingness to be accepted by the host society and has the nature of reaction.

The third strategy for acculturation is defined as marginalization or anomie, where groups lose or reject both their traditional culture and that of the larger society (Berry & Sam, 1997). This scheme is characterized by little possibility to merge into the dominant culture because of racial discrimination or exclusion. This outcome of acculturation is often accompanied by feelings of alienation, loss of identity and by a good deal of collective and individual confusion and anxiety.

The ideal outcome of cultural acculturation is integration, a strategy most migrants and some countries prefer, such as Canada and Australia. The integration strategy reflects a desire to maintain key features of the immigrant cultural identity while actively adopting the principles and values of the host society and modifying their own (Bourhis et al., 1997; Citizenship and Immigration Canada, 1996).

A good example of acculturation strategies can be found in both American and Canadian history. In North America, European migrants have successfully learned how to function in the new continent although conflict developed with First Nations people over control of the land, resulting in subjection of the original inhabitants. In some cases however, Indigenous people have also modified their structure in order to interact with Europeans.

Both processes, adaptation and acculturation lead migrants and refugees to experience feelings of personal satisfaction once they are able to relate to the host culture or feelings of isolation and anxiety if they are unsuccessful in establishing relationships with the host culture. In essence, the difference between the two processes resides mainly in the way in which individuals view and approach the host culture, the rationale for change and the orientation (outcome) of such change.

Ideologies of Acculturation

From the preceding discussion, two important keywords in acculturation are identified – contact (interaction) and change. Nevertheless, the primary question in acculturation is: Who should change and in what direction? Even though changes inevitably happen in every culture involved as the result of contact, most research discusses the cultural changes of migrants and refugees. This may be simply because the era in which invasion and colonization were a norm is gone and nowadays, in most cases, people migrate for personal safety, peace or pursuing a better life. Migrants and refugees are thought to have an inevitably weak vitality and are supposed to change, no matter how they come to the new land (voluntarily or involuntarily) and no matter which country they migrated to. In contemporary societies, the only realistic alternative is that both refugees and migrants change in order to operate in the host society (Berry, 1990; Berry & Sam, 1997; Furnham & Bochner, 1986; Kim, 1988).

Although these groups are the agents of cultural change, they do not possess complete power to choose the direction of change. There are basically two other main factors influencing the directions or outcomes of acculturation. These two factors are state policies and acculturation orientations of the host society. It is generally agreed that the national immigration and settlement policies can have a decisive impact on the acculturation orientation of migrants and refugees and the members of the host society (Berry & Sam, 1997; Bourhis et al., 1997; Boutang & Papademetriou, 1994).

National immigration and settlement policies are generally shaped within one of four clusters of state ideologies, or philosophies, namely, pluralist, civic, assimilationist and ethnist (Bourhis et al., 1997; Breton, 1988; Helly, 1993). Each of the four ideological clusters is likely to produce specific public policies concerning the acculturation of immigrant and refugee groups. Under the context of state policies, migrants and members of the host community develop their acculturation orientations.

The first cluster is *pluralism ideology*, which expects that migrants adopt the *public values* of the host country. However, this ideology also upholds that the state has no mandate in defining or regulating the *private values* of its citizens, whose individual liberties in personal domains must be respected. One premise of this approach is that it is considered of value to the host community that migrants maintain key features of their cultural and linguistic distinctiveness while adopting the public value of the host majority. Canada is an example of a plural society with multiculturalism as a mechanism for tolerance of minority cultures.

The *civic ideology* shares two important features of pluralism ideology: (1) the expectation that migrants adopt the *public values* of the host country and (2) that the state has no right to interfere with the *private values* of its individual citizens. However, this ideology is characterized by an official state policy of *nonintervention* in the private values of specific groups of individuals including those of immigrant and ethno-cultural minorities. Great Britain is seen as an example of a country espousing a civic ideology.

Similar to the pluralism and civic ideologies, the *assimilation ideology* also includes the expectation that migrants adopt the *public values* of the host country. However, it expects migrants to abandon their own cultural and linguistic distinctiveness for the sake of adopting the culture and values of the dominant group constituting the core of the nation state. The USA, though slowly shifting away from original assimilation policies to a civic position, is still widely viewed as an example of assimilation ideology.

The fourth cluster is *ethnist ideology*. It shares the first two features of the assimilation ideology, namely, (1) migrants must adopt the public values of the host nation and (2) the state has a right to limit the expression of certain aspects of private values, especially those of immigrant minorities. Unlike the other ideologies discussed so far, the ethnist ideology usually defines nation as being composed of a kernel ancestral ethnic group as determined by birth and kinship. Thus migrants who do not share this common kinship may never be accepted as legitimate citizens of the state, legally or socially. Most homogenous countries, such as Germany, Japan and Israel, are seen to belong to this ideology.

Among the ideologies discussed, only plural and civic societies allow people of various cultural backgrounds living together to form a multicultural society. It is undeniable that state policies cannot always represent the choice of every societal member regardless of the setting, whether it is a democratic or an authoritative social setting. Therefore, different attitudes of the host culture will greatly influence the course of immigrant and refugee acculturation. This influence will be further addressed in the discussion of acculturation stress.

In most cases, the culture of the host society is the mainstream culture for groups of migrants and refugees to appreciate, share and live by. It is also known that the acculturation orientations of the members of the mainstream culture will support or constrain such process. One important factor that distinguishes the immigrant's experience from that of refugees is that even though acculturation is very conditional, in pluralistic societies migrants, by and large, enjoy a freedom to decide their acculturation orientations (outcomes) or how to acculturate (strategies). Furthermore, because the reasons for migration are different for migrants and refugees, the acculturation process for the latter group might not reflect a freedom to choose the direction of acculturation. For refugees, for example, assimilation might be the immediate strategy for change since almost inevitably, they will feel an obligation to fit into the culture that has accepted them. However, for both groups, orientations (outcomes) are generally identified within a framework created by researchers.

Relational Acculturation Orientations

Acculturation problems and conflicts emerge when the acculturation orientations of the host community members are different from that of migrants or when both groups experience partial agreement and partial disagreement as a result of their expectations of acculturation orientations. Bourhis et al., (1997) point it out that "exclusionists and segregationists are likely to have very negative stereotypes concerning migrants and to discriminate against them in many domains including employment and housing" (p.384).

In acculturation, Berry (1987) points out that basically both, migrants and the members of host society, have to deal with two issues: 1) culture maintenance and development; and 2) inter-ethnic contact and relationship. Therefore Berry's acculturation framework is built on the belief that the attitudes towards these two issues lead to different outcomes of acculturation. Migrants' acculturation strategies are based on the responses to these questions:

– Is it considered to be of value to maintain cultural identity and characteristics?

– Is it considered to be of value to maintain relationships with dominant society and other groups?

When acculturation is carried out seeking positive outcomes for interaction, harmony appears, social stability is maintained and migrants feel less stressed. If, on the contrary, acculturation is achieved through withdrawal or exclusion, migrants experience high degrees of stress and their mental health is greatly affected. Meanwhile, the host society experiences racial conflicts, problematic migrants and chaotic social order.

For instance, while migrants were working towards an integration policy, a strong desire was found among Canadians, in public consultations conducted by the Department of Citizenship and Immigration in 1994, to see migrants assimilated into Canadian society rather than integrated under the official policy of multiculturalism (Citizenship and Immigration Canada, 1994:41). These differences in the relational outcomes could trigger communication breakdowns between two groups, foster negative inter-group stereotypes, lead to discriminatory behaviors and cause moderate levels of stress among migrants.

Cultural Factors Associated with Migration Stress

According to Furnham and Bochner (1986) there is a connection between geographic movement and a change in psychological "well-being." Even though it has not reached a consensus that there is a positive relationship between long-term migration and psychological disturbance, there is often a particular sense of stress that occurs during acculturation, such as lowered mental health status (especially confusion, anxiety, depression), feelings of marginality and alienation, heightened psychosomatic symptom level and identity confusion (Berry, 1990; Furnham & Bochner, 1986). Acculturation stress is thus a phenomenon that may underlie a reduction in the health status of individuals including physical, psychological and social aspects (Berry, 1990).

Behavior

The individual nature of Canadian society contrasts with the collective nature of many migrants. While individuality and independence are strong values among the majority population, they are often manifested in other areas that reflect culture. Some sports that are team oriented, such as soccer, which is the world's most popular sport, is in marked contrast with sports like hockey, where one player can stand out because of his/her skating abilities. The game now is more oriented towards the strength of the individual and how players can use personal strength to overcome the opponents. It is one of the few sports in which violence is a clear factor, as opposed to cooperative behavior in the way soccer is played. Baseball is another example of the individual, alone, with the bat, capable of turning the game around with a "homerun." The ability of a tall and skillful shooter in basketball changes the whole make-up of the game. To make oneself stand out, whether it be sports or any other area of endeavor, can be contrasted with cultures where this behavior is negatively perceived.

In some countries, affiliation is a behavior that is highly prized, because one may "get ahead" due to various interlocking relationships (e.g., family friends or the "compadre system"). Sharing information or even answers on a test may be seen as acceptable because the society may prize connections. Giving gifts for a favor is not seen as a bribe but another way of showing respect. According to Jay (in Bemak & Chung, 2000) some people live "… in a culture in which they relied heavily on connections, on who could do what for whom" (p. 581). In Canada, using connections has a negative connotation, as does the giving of gifts that might imply someone wants something. Authority is prized in other societies more than it is in countries like Canada where "civil disobedience" is seen as a virtue.

In counselling, collectivist cultures emphasize that decisions which impact the family should be made in consultation or even decided by the group rather than the individual. For example, educational and career decisions that don't reflect an impact on the family are very negatively perceived in many immigrant families from Asia.

Communication

Communication styles are very different from culture to culture. Many cultures see eye-to-eye contact as invasive, while in Canada, it is seen as showing honesty (i.e., "look me in the eye and say that"). Expressing how one feels about something, such as giving an opinion, is not acceptable for people who have come from societies in which it was dangerous to share one's opinion. Framing one's opinion in relationship to the group may seem as overly conforming rather than respective.

Psycho-social and individual factors

Psychological characteristics of acculturation include both pre-contact ones and those that appear during the acculturation process. The former refer to certain experiences that may predispose one to function more effectively under acculturation pressures. The latter are mainly the result of choosing certain acculturation strategies and the lack of a sense of cognitive control over the acculturation process.

Additional to these characteristics, there are other factors affecting migrants' mental health, such as the cultural characteristics of home country, the "departure status," age and gender, adaptation competence, prior expectations and goals. A friendly and supportive political and social environment cannot guarantee a smooth acculturation process because acculturation is, in many ways, a personal journey. For example, those who enjoyed high social status in the home country have to deal with acculturation, making an extra effort because their "entry status" in the host society can never be compared with the economic or social status they enjoyed in the past. When a doctor cannot even get a nurse job or when a professor has to wash dishes in a restaurant, it is hard for them not to have stress and poor mental health, especially those who have very high expectations of the host country. But the problem is as Furnham and Bochner (1986) observe, that high expectations are the very motivation of immigration decision "...apart from refugees, few people would voluntary migrate if their expectations were too low" (p. 175). Therefore, the personal rationale for migrating, personal expectations, choice of strategies and ultimately, outcomes, are key to determine the level of integration into a new society. Consequently, social support is recognized by most researchers as the most important social factor related to increased immigrant psychological well-being and to a lower probability of physical and mental illness. At the initial stage of acculturation, social support is usually perceived to come from the ethnic community and friendship network. Even though social support from the ethnic community is seen to reduce stress (Berry, 1990), the frequent contact with co-nationals might hinder the acculturation progress (Kim, 1988) because newly arrived migrants might not be in the position to offer support and hence get offered very little, which in turn may render them particularly vulnerable to mental breakdown (Furnham & Bochner, 1986).

Impact of Migration on the Family

Migration, like any type of drastic change, can have detrimental effects on the family, particularly if the family came from an agrarian-based society. This is especially true for people with large extended families that are often left behind in the country of origin. Migration not only disrupts the extended family system, but also negates the natural support system that characterizes it. The larger the family, the more likely that some close family members such as older or younger brothers and sisters are left with aunts and uncles and separated from their parents. Because the occupational patterns are different in the new country, the principal "bread winner" and head of the family, the father, has to take a job beneath his educational and occupational training, with the result of loss of self-esteem. In addition, one or more other family members, such as an older child and/or the wife, have to work to provide an adequate income to meet the family's financial needs. Additionally, school aged children might not be able to ask their parents for help since language barriers and different cultural values put the parents in an awkward position of deferring to their children for simple language help. The parents might not feel comfortable in the dominant language and therefore, might not feel comfortable in being involved in their children's education. According to Juntune, Atkinson and Tierney (2002):

> *School districts undergoing rapid increases in diversity often experience a concurrent drop in parental involvement, with school officials blaming cultural values and changing family structures and parents blaming discrimination and insensitivity by school officials (p. 153).*

With cultural differences between the immigrant and host country, issues such as difference in childrearing practices, traditional views on the roles of the mother and father, the perceived hierarchical view of school personnel, differing expectations of gender and the strong emphasis on extracurricular activities in North American schools present migrants with challenges to family structures and values. These issues in child rearing practices can be very challenging for migrants with child abuse laws that prohibit corporal punishment, even though these practices may be traditional and be combined with high levels of empathy, intimacy and support. According to Fontes (2002) "some Latino parents are incorrectly accused of abusing or neglecting their children because non-Latino professionals are puzzled by their unfamiliar yet harmless practices" (p. 31). Interestingly, when different ethnic groups are compared, the following summary of differences in punishment have been noted during the 1980s (Fontes, 2002):

- African-Americans are more likely to use an electric cord, belt or switch applied to the back or bottom;

- Euro-ethnics groups are more likely to use a paddle or open hand to the bottom;

- Asian-ethnic groups may be more likely to slap the face or pull hair.

Over time, migrant children incorporate values much more quickly than their parents, thus creating potential for cultural conflict in the family. Peers start to have much greater influence than family. If the family is racially different, the children may experience overt or covert racial discrimination that impacts the overall family structure. "Whether physical or psychological, racially motivated discrimination can have a devastating effect on student learning" (Juntune, Atkinson & Tierney, 2002, p. 154).

One of the most documented negative effects on migrants is the change of economic expectations. As discussed earlier in this paper, many migrants come to Canada expecting to find better jobs and improved living conditions. The fact that they may have to go into a different occupation or endure many years of "upgrading" of their credentials produces a great deal of stress. Some migrants are helped by extended family members in the "old" country to either send money back to the family or help them immigrate, which is much more difficult if not impossible. With two incomes becoming more and more a necessity, childcare expenses are often an added burden to economically distressed families.

Obviously, stress has a very negative effect on the psychological and physical well-being of all family members. Along with challenges to cultural traditions and values, the family working as a whole to making "ends meet," adds to the overall stress level, therefore contributing to family dysfunction.

The Immigrant Experience: Two Cases

Immigrants who come to Canada come mostly for a better life economically and socially. Many realize their goals, but many face not only challenges of being uprooted from their family and what is familiar, but have to face the prospect of starting over professionally, because their credentials are not acceptable or other factors having to do with the occupational structure of Canada. In 2001, a study conducted by the Conference Board of Canada revealed that, annually, the country loses between $4.1 and $5.9 billion in income due to a lack of recognition of the professional qualifications of 540 000 people, which includes almost 350 000 immigrants. The cases of Antonio and Marianna are typical:

–   Antonio is a 36 year-old physician who has recently migrated to Canada from Mexico looking for a better life for himself and his family. He is fluent in Spanish, English and Japanese and has several years of experience as a medical doctor. However, life in British Columbia has not been easy so far. He aspired to get a job at any of the hospitals in the province but instead has found himself working as a waiter in order to maintain his family.

–   Mariana is a 38 year-old Chilean nurse who came to Canada with her husband several weeks after her third child was born 10 months ago. Mariana did not speak English when she arrived and confesses she went into a depressive episode shortly after moving to Vancouver Island. Although she and her husband had carefully planned their relocation, the difficulties they have faced (i.e., financial constraints, lack of job, weak language skills, etc.), had not been anticipated in the dimension in which they have appeared.

The Refugee Experience

Unlike migrants, refugees arrive at their new country not by choice per se, but by survival. While many factors are similar to the immigrant experience, there are some characteristics that make them a little different. First, refugees come because they feel forced to leave their homeland for any place that would provide them safety. Their leaving is often marked by psychological and physical torture, either by experience or observations. Studies have found that:

> *…many refugees have been subjected to the atrocities of war, such as experiencing and witnessing torture and killing, being forced to commit atrocities, being incarcerated and placed in reeducation camps, starvation, rape and sexual abuse and physical beatings and injury. These events occur during the actual war or conflict, in the subsequent escape, as well as in the refugee camps (Bemak & Chung, 2002, p. 202).*

Experiences that have impacted refugees negatively may not be apparent upon their immediate arrival in the host country due to their survival instinct, but can appear much later, even after the settlement process has been completed. Within the refugee groups, older people are more prone to experience psychological disorder as a result of their experiences. Not only does age and patterns of behavior that are ingrained provide more challenges, but also the language skills are sometimes difficult to acquire. Single men have a difficult time because they arrive at the new country with few family supports and possibly are never able to reconnect with their old families. Bemak and Chung (2002) go on to stress that:

> *…PTSD (post traumatic stress syndrome) among the clinical refugee populations is estimated to be 50% or higher and depressive disorders range from 42% to 89%. Different studies have found depression ranging from 15% to 80% in the refugee community (p. 2002).*

As stated previously, many of the experiences of migrants and refugees are similar with the exception of a few factors. It has been recognized that both suffer from cultural shock and often experience racism.

Helping Immigrants and Refugees Adapt

Additionally, an understanding of the cultural identity of migrants can help in enhancing interpersonal communication and counselling. The basic assumption of the Immigrant Identity Development Model is that counselling can best be achieved by starting at where immigrants are in terms of how they see themselves. Their adaptation to the new culture should not be measured in terms of the number of years abiding in the new society, but how they feel about themselves in relationship to the new society. The higher the levels of adaptation, the greater the possibilities are that cultural approaches reflecting their adaptation will be successful. Consider the following stages of identity:

Stage 1 – Compliance: For migrants and refugees, this stage is characterized by strong desires to adapt and embrace the dominant culture in which the immigrant totally embraces the new country. There is some self-negating about their old beliefs as they try and adapt to the dominant culture that they are in. Adaptation is seen as the only way to survive and they desperately want to fit in and belong.

Stage 2 – Conflict: For migrants and refugees, this stage arises once the reality of minority status and difficulties in blending in economically, psychologically and spiritually are experienced. There is confusion, conflict and changing beliefs and values about the benefits of immigration. They begin to "live" the positive feelings of the old country and see it as superior.

Stage 3 – Defiance: For migrants and refugees this stage is characterized by rejection of the dominant culture, mistrust, anger, endorsement of their life in the "old country." They see the new country as corrupt, dishonest and unaccepting. They either decide to go back to their old lives if they can, create their old lives in the new country or become conservative and traditional in regards to their culture, rejecting accommodation in the new country.

Stage 4 – Introspection and Accommodation: For migrants and refugees this stage is characterized by conflict, but now there is questioning of primary loyalty and responsibility to one's own cultural group. There is the acceptance that they are unique, but now they see that by adapting themselves to the "way of life" is not abandoning their old culture. There is still distrust, but a feeling of accommodation.

Stage 5 – Adaptation and Integration: For migrants and refugees this stage is characterized by awareness of being different, personal identity in their own cultural milieu, a sense of cultural self-fulfillment as an immigrant, greater sense of control and flexibility and an objective outlook on the dominant culture. In essence, they have accepted the multicultural ideal and begin to see themselves as hyphenated Canadians.

People move from stage to stage until they achieve self-acceptance of who they are. Problems occur when they become stuck at stages one to three. In understanding the migrants' cultural background and history, it will also be extremely important to know what their worldview is. In addition, being able to pick up the nuances of their language or ways of describing things will also add to a greater understanding of how they see their problems and issues. Finally, it is important for the counsellor to know if the problem is internal [psychological, cognitive, spiritual or physical] or external [employment, discrimination, financial, etc.].

Implications for Counselling Practice

It is vital that counsellors develop culturally sensitive practices and increase their awareness about the diverse nature of the migrant population. Cultural sensitivity and awareness is not about "isms"; instead, it is about human relationships, interdependency, differences and points of connection. When practice is oriented culturally, the model of practice becomes cross-cultural. The term cross-cultural means a place of cultural intersection where professionals encounter issues of migrants and the approach they use to deal with their clients' problems. A cross-cultural model provides reason for one to understand and examine one's own culture, values, beliefs and most of all identity in order to respect and accept the unique differences they encounter in their professional practice.

Although cultures are maps of meaning through which the world is made intelligible, it is the migrants' experience (their interpretation and the meaning of such experiences) and the understanding of their own culture and its impact on their values, beliefs and choices that should shape counsellors' practice. This is important, as culture is the main source of knowledge that has been passed on from generation to generation and thus, respecting this dynamic enhances professional competency.

In addition, it is important that a cross-cultural approach that encourages counsellors to understand, to be sensitive and to be alert when encountering migrants expands the counsellor's ability to be effective. Hence, the implications as described above provide components to prepare professionals in all human services to be mindful, flexible and open practitioners. This is not implying, however, that professionals are not trained to effectively serve their clients from diverse cultural, ethnic and racial backgrounds. What it suggests is that awareness of the issues associated with diversity and equity, as well as the role of the professional in addressing the migrants' challenges, are necessary ingredients in facilitating opportunities for the individuals' success. According to Das, Kemp, Driedger and Halli (1997) counsellors will have to consider some of the following issues in dealing with migrants:

1. Minority status might predispose people to feelings of social isolation and heightened stress;

2. Young school-age children of immigrants may become the target of negative stereotyping and social rejection;

3. Second generation [immigrants] may experience tension between mainstream American values and their ethnic cultural values;

4. Second generation [immigrants] may find it offensive to be seen as foreigners;

5. In smaller communities, immigrants are likely to feel socially isolated and lonely;

6. A spouse who is staying home and has limited social contact with the outside world is at risk for becoming depressed, or has no avenues for seeking help in the case of abuse;

7. A young, second generation girl who finds her social life unduly restricted by traditional parents may find it irksome and begin to rebel;

8. A successful professional who finds himself in a dead-end job because of racial discrimination and without any remedy may begin to engage in self-destructive behavior like drinking heavily or using drugs;

9. A new immigrant who fails to establish him/herself in the kind of career he/she had in mind (p. 33).

Conclusion

To be effective as a counsellor with migrants it is vital that one understands concepts like adaptation and acculturation, the strategies that guide such processes, as well as the factors that affect them, such as the ideologies of state immigration policies. Furthermore, it is important to identify potential acculturation outcomes, the interactive relations in the acculturation process such as cultural and social components, the impact of migration on the family and how to assist migrants to cope with their shifting status in a multicultural society.

In this sense, Canada is unique, but the challenge will be to help all of the various ethnic and racial groups to reach beyond their own cultural boundaries and enable them to cross cultural borders freely. Under the multicultural policy, people are encouraged to maintain their language and cultural practices. Psychologically, this means that government services will have to help professionals be aware of how cultural identity develops. All people want acceptance, yet their cultural roots bind them and this affects how others perceive them. The multicultural policy reinforces the idea that each ethnic group has a strong cultural identity, which implies that they will have a greater sense of control over their lives. By examining the impact and effect that cultural identity has on people, professionals will be well prepared to assist newcomers in their adaptation process.

The process of acculturation is neither a pleasant experience nor a smooth process. It confronts first of all various state immigration and integration policies, then the different attitudes of host members towards the state policies and towards migrants. These two vital factors will either encourage or constrain acculturation orientations and outcomes.

Although under such (integration) policies migrants are allowed to maintain their own culture in the plural society, their culture is in fact a modified one to be accepted by the host society and to be lived by migrants in the host society. This guest culture is like Chinese food abroad – it is Chinese for local people but not for Chinese people or for people who have been to China. During the cultural modification, migrants keep the parts that are within the tolerance of the host culture, but have to change or give up those that could not be tolerated by others. In order to modify these internalized habits, customs, beliefs and concepts, migrants will inevitably experience inner conflicts and stress.

For those migrants who believe individual efforts can make a difference, stress turned into challenge and acceptance and growth together form the internal dynamics of acculturation. The breaking up of the old internal conditions for these people usually results not in chaos or breakdown, but in the creation of a whole new internal structure that is better fit to the host environment. For some migrants, acculturation can be a painful process but for others, it can represent an opportunity for personal growth and exciting learning. It is important to remember that, in the end, every case is unique and, as a consequence, every migrant experiences a unique acculturation journey.

The different attitudes towards acculturation among migrants and their different coping strategies have important implications for those in helping professions, for they suggest the potential of psychological transformation and the need to learn about philosophies and diverse approaches from other cultures because people have different experiences from culture to culture. With individuals who have come from different stages of acculturation and different cultures, it is necessary to open our mind wider and understand the different ways in which people cope, interact and adjust to a new culture. Additionally, one must be aware of the strategies that are useful in some cases, which ones do not work with certain populations and how personal and societal expectations affect acculturation. A ready example for psychological transformation can be found in an ancient Chinese story of the "Blessing or Bane":

Near China's northern borders lived a man well versed in the practices of Taoism. His horse, for no reason at all, got into the territory of the northern tribes. Everyone commiserated with him.

"Perhaps this will soon turn out to be a blessing," said his father.

After a few months, his animal came back, leading a fine horse from the north. Everyone congratulated him.

"Perhaps this will soon turn out to be a cause of misfortune," said his father.

Since he was well-off and kept good horses, his son became fond of riding and eventually broke his thigh bone falling from a horse. Everyone commiserated with him.

"Perhaps this will soon turn out to be a blessing," said his father.

One year later, the northern tribes started a big invasion of the border regions. All able-bodied young men took up arms and fought against the invaders and as a result, around the border nine out of ten men died. This man's son did not join in the fighting because he was crippled and so both the boy and his father survived.

References

Ananth, J. (1978). Psychopathology in Indian females. *Social Science and Medicine, 12,* 177-8.

Bemak, F. & Chung, R.C. (2002). Counseling and psychotherapy with refugees. In P. Pedersen, J. Draguns, W. Lonner & J. Trimble, *Counseling Across Cultures,* 5th Edition, Thousand Oaks, CA: Sage, pp. 209-232.

Berry, J.W. & Kalin, R. (1995). Multicultural and ethnic attitudes in Canada: An overview of the 1991 National Survey. *Canadian Journal of Behavioral Science, 27,* 301-320.

Berry J.W. & Sam, D.L. (1997). Acculturation and Adaptation. In J.W. Berry & M.H. Segall (Eds.), *Handbook of Cross-cultural Psychology.* Boston: Allyn & Bacon.

Berry, J.W. (1990). Psychology of acculturation: understanding individuals moving between cultures. In R.W. Brislin (Ed.), *Applied Cross-cultural Psychology*. Newbury Park, CA: Sage.

__ (1987). Acculturation and psychological adaptation: a conceptual overview. In J.W. Berry & R.C. Annis (Eds.), *Ethnic Psychology Research & Practice*. Amsterdam: Swets & Zeitlinger.

__ (1974). Psychological aspects of cultural pluralism: unity and identity reconsidered. In R. Brislin (Ed.), *Topics in Culture Learning*. Honolulu, HI: East-West Cultural Learning Institute.

__(1980). Acculturation as varieties of adaptation. In A. Padilla (Ed.), *Acculturation, Theory, Models and Some New Findings*. Colorado, CO: Westview Press.

Bourhis, R.Y., Moise, L.C., Perreault, S. and Senecal, S. (1997). Towards an Interactive Acculturation Model: A Social Psychological Approach. *International Union of Psychological Science, 32*(6), 369-386.

Boutang, Y.M. & Papademetriou, D. (1994). Typology, Evolution and Performance of Main Migration Systems. In the proceding of 1994 OECD Conference: *Migration and Development*. Paris: OECD.

Breton, R. (1988). From ethnic to civic nationalism: English Canada and Quebec. *Ethnic and Racial Studies, 11,* 85-102.

Breton, R., Isajiw, W., Kalbach, W. & Reitz, J. (1990). *Ethnic Identity and Equality*. Toronto: University of Toronto Express.

Citizenship and Immigration Canada (1996). *Finding a New Direction for Newcomer Integration*, [online] Retrieved June 24, 1998 from http://www.cic.gc.ca

__ 1994. *Immigration Consultations Report*. Ottawa: Ministry of Supply and Services Canada.

Das, A., Kemp, S., Driedger, L. & Halli, S. (1997). Between two worlds: Counseling South Asian Americans. *Journal of Multicultural Counseling & Development, 25* (1), pp. 23-34.

Dyer, G. (2001). Canada's visible majority. *Canadian Geographic*, pp. 46-52.

Fleras, A. & Elliott, J.L. (l992). *Multiculturalism in Canada*. Toronto: Nelson Canada.

Fontes, A. (2002). Child discipline in immigrant Latino Families. *Journal of Counseling & Development, 80*(1), pp. 31-40.

Furnham, A. (1986). Economic locus of control. *Human Relations, 39*, 29-43.

Furnham, A. & Bochner, S. (1986). *Culture Shock: Psychological Reactions to Unfamiliar Environment*. New York: Methuen.

Helly, D. (1993). The political regulation of cultural plurality: Foundations and principles. *Canadian Ethnic Studies 25* (2), 15-35.

Hunt, G. (1995). Xenophobia alive and well in New Zealand. *The National Business Review*, Oct. 27-16.

Hunt, G. (1996). Public says no to Asians, Islanders. *The National Business Review,* Sept. 13-16.

Immigrant Services Society of British Columbia, Labor Canada of British Columbia & Ministry of Education and Ministry Responsible for Multiculturalism and Human Rights (1993). *Settlement in the 1990s: An Overview of the Needs of New Migrants in the Lower Mainland and Fraser Valley*. Vancouver: The Society.

Janigan, M. (2003). *Maclean's.* July 2003, p. 41.

Immigrant Canada: Demographic, Economic and Social Challenges. Toronto: University of Toronto Press

Jones, G.W. (1998). "Australia identity," racism and recent responses to Asian immigration to Australia. In E. Laquian, A. Laquian & T. McGee (Eds.), *The Silent Debate.* Vancouver: The University of British Columbia.

Juntune, C., Atkinson, D. and Tierney, G. (2002). School counselors and schoool psychologists as school-home-community liaisons in ethnically diverse schools. In P. Pedersen & J. Carey, *Multicultural Counselling in Schools: A Practical Handbook.* Boston, MA: Pearson Education, Inc.

Kim, Y. (1988). *Communication and Cross-Cultural Adaptation.* Clevedon: Multilingual Matters Ltd.

Moghaddam, F.M. (1987). Individualistic and collective integration strategies among migrants: Toward a mobility model of cultural integration. In J.W. Berry & R.C. Annis (Eds.), *Ethnic Psychology Research & Practice.* Amsterdam: Swets & Zeitlinger.

Neuwirth, G. (1999). Toward a theory of immigrant integration. In L. Driedger & S.S. Halli (Eds.), *Immigrant Canada: Demographic, Economic and Social Challenges.* Toronto: University of Toronto Press.

Thomas, D. (1992). The social integration of migrants in Canada. In S. Globerman (Ed.), *The Immigration Dilemma.* Vancouver: the Fraser Institute.

Walton, B. & Kennedy, A. (1993). Psychological and sociocultural adjustment during cultural transitions: A comparison of secondary students overseas and at home. *International Journal of Psychology, 28,* 129-147.

Chapter 10
Allowing, Adjusting and Achieving: Helping Immigrant Children Deal with Acculturation in the School System

Elias Cheboud

There seems to be an unclear communication between the school system and parents of immigrant children in relation to what best supports their children's learning. While the school might consider that placing immigrant children in a separate classroom (called English as a Second Language-ESL-Resource Room) would be in the students' "best learning interest," parents and students interviewed for this article expressed their anger against what they consider to be a form of exclusion. The conversations with these children and their parents is the basis of this paper where the purpose is to inform counsellors and teachers what immigrant children experience as the result of attending classes in the ESL Resource Room (where most of them are placed regardless of their level of proficiency of the English language). The issue of elementary school children's identity problems – as discussed with these students – is often overlooked by both teachers and counsellors because most of these children are not able to talk about it, either in the school environment or at home. Therefore, there are various questions that arise from this frame of reference. First, do school teachers and counsellors understand the effects of separation from the mainstream classroom on the children's identity development? Second, do they consider the children's culture? Finally, what is the impact on the students' needs when such significant decisions are made?

Advised by the school, the interviewed immigrant children attended two classes: one regular and the other, a special class called an ESL Resource Room, because they were assumed not able to speak English as well as their Canadian White classmates. It was never clear why these students were labelled as different, since most of them were proficient enough in the use of the English language. They believe that they were categorized as ESL students just because they were not White. This leads to one other question that arises from these propositions: How many Canadian children who are White are placed in an ESL Resource Room to improve their grammar, speech, reading or writing? According to the interviewed children who were placed in such ESL rooms, there were none. Furthermore, other immigrant families indicated that they too had to struggle to understand why their children were labelled as different from those children of the mainstream families, given the fact that all these children not only understand but also speak English. Unfortunately, this is the reality for these students. Allingham and Allingham (1988) declare: "The potential of any average immigrant child is equal to that of any average Canadian-born child and to be placed a year or more behind the child's peers, can be degrading" (p. 6).

The Impact of Labelling

ESL classes can debilitate the children's emotional, motivational and psychological well being, setting them up to react against the established norm of the school and their own family rules. If it was all about grammar, vocabulary, writing or reading difficulties, White Canadian students who have difficulty with the language should be taught in the same way as immigrant children; that is, in the ESL Resource Room. Yet, this is not the case when Canadian White children experience difficulty; instead, they get extra help within the main class or they are placed in a resource room not as a language learners, but as needing more concentrated and individual instruction. Immigrant children, on the other hand, are not treated the same and the dissenting experiences expose them to negative self-esteem, damages their cultural pride, forces them to oppose their heritage and ultimately, hate their identity. Consequently, parents and children become overwhelmed and conflicts arise.

Children's schooling experience at times can be painful and as a result, feelings of loneliness, lack of belonging and incompetence are common reactions from these groups of students. In addition, like one of the interviewees suggested: "I feel helpless, because my parents may not share my school experience. In fact, I feel resistant to sharing my experience with my parents too, because they may punish me for not having the interest to learn. They may not understand or even believe how serious and overwhelming my experience is." In this particular case, when assessment, evaluation and placement was implemented, the parents were not aware of it. Perhaps this is because some of the parents do not speak English and therefore the school does not communicate with the family as much as they do with other parents. In other cases, even though the students' parents may speak English very well, the schools often arbitrarily make decisions for the children, and due to cultural constraints, parents do not feel able to question the authority of the professionals within the school system. In this situation, parents merely accept and agree with decisions, which are made for their children and deemed appropriate in terms of the children's educational development.

One factor that the interviewed parents mentioned as particularly important was that they are often unable to interact with teachers and evaluators to discuss in detail the placement of their child, because of language difficulties and due to the feelings of time restrictions placed on them by their employers. Another factor which deters parents from discussing their children's placement with anyone in the school system is their fear of exposing their children to further prejudices regarding their learning abilities. As a result, immigrants are systematically forced to internalize their negative feelings about the decision-making process done by the school personnel. The absence of parents in every aspect of their children's education is disempowering. It is my belief that there are problems in the teachers' (and counsellors') perception of immigrant children and until these misconstrued perceptions are explored thoroughly, the flow of information among parents, students and school personnel will continue to be distorted and these issues will remain a problem. So far, teachers and counsellors have not tried hard enough to acknowledge the children's culture before assigning labels for the sake of 'their best interest'.

The act of sending students to ESL resource rooms without cultural consideration demoralizes, stigmatizes, leads to low self-esteem and makes the children feel punished. More importantly, the experience damages the children's self pride by contradicting the expectations of parents with those of the school and by leading children to react negatively towards their history, heritage and ancestral identity. To some parents, this suggests that when the school separates their children – not based on their need for learning but based on their immigration status and color – the children's culture is either stripped from them or it is used to isolate them, causing the children to react and behave against social norms and/or family rules.

This is All About Perceived Identity

Identity is an important part of school children's development; they learn about self by looking at the way it is experienced. The sense of identity is shaped through the process of knowing and restructuring the relationship between self and others, self and society, self and the country and self and the world. There is, however, a distinction between identity change as a result of growth and identity change as the result of conformity. While the former helps children to know themselves through interplay with others, the latter contributes more to the loss of self. Nonetheless, it is known that children are constantly adjusting and fine-tuning their way of being and becoming in reference to the many influences they are exposed to every single day. One wonders how often school counsellors consult with teachers in regards to students' sense of identity? When there is an appeal for help from children, every teacher and counsellor tries to do their best to help children form relationships with other students and help them become aware of their own identity. However, students who are labelled as failures and unfit by the schools' standards and placed in resource rooms can be discouraged from accepting their cultural/racial identity. When this happens, there is an identity crisis. The image of self becomes unstable and the student's attitudes, opinions and beliefs become negative in nature. Everyone has an inherent desire to be like the group of students in normal classrooms because it is a reference point of acceptance in a society. It is essential for school counsellors to become aware of these identity crises experienced by immigrant children, especially when they perceive themselves negatively after being in the resource rooms.

Because we overlooked the similarities between immigrant and non-immigrant (children) as human beings, we have thought of immigrant education as a very special process, whereas, in fact in its more important aspect notably cultural, social and moral education, "...it should be almost identical for immigrant and non-immigrants alike" (Wolfgang, 1975, p. 16).

In the explored cases, the children were placed in an ESL resource room not because of their linguistic difficulty, lack of language skills or their immigration status, but because of their skin color and ethnic background. This is a historical fact of oppression, which most schools do not recognize. Such actions will always reinforce the belief that immigrant children are less important than the mainstream students. Special education classes impact on children's motivation as well as on their emotional, cognitive and behavioral well-being. The long-term effect of such isolation could be that these children might learn to identify with only a specific group, affecting negatively their relationship with the mainstream.

Counselling Strategies: What to Look For

To better help immigrant children, school teachers and counsellors first need to understand the effects of prejudice, stereotyping and discrimination. Prejudice is an indicator of racism and has four functions. The first is dehumanization to the point where the immigrant students are seen as either a thing or incapable of anything (Klukanov, 1998). Secondly, it is assumed that prejudice may be a way to reduce competition and boost one's standing within one's own school (Hall, 1997). Thirdly, such alienation allows students and teachers to avoid their responsibility to gain some understanding of differences. Fourthly, prejudice functions as a way to celebrate the "good" and show support by opposing the alien (Ho, 1998). While the above indicates the functions of prejudice, there are, according to Hall (1997), five types of prejudice: "blatant, conceit, symbolic, tokenism and arms-length, all of which affect students" (p. 14).

Stereotyping involves categorization of immigrant students based on ethnicity, color, gender and nationality (Graham, 1999). When little is known about a group, there is a tendency to "fill in" the missing information gap, or as Hall (1997) suggests, " there may be too much information and so there is a need to simplify" (p. 1). Mehta and Farina (1994) explain the dimensions of stereotypes. They write of "content, the traits which make up the stereotypes; uniformity, the degree of agreement of these traits; direction, the favourableness or unfavourableness of these traits; and intensity, the degree of favourable or unfavourablness of responses to these traits" (p. 12). The immigrant students' experience seems to be drawn from these characteristics (Abe & Zane, 1990).

Discrimination pushes visible minority students to internalize racism because they cannot escape it or ignore it because it is always there. To be a person of color in the West is to be a problem (Leong, 1984). Immigrant students' cultural attributes, such as formal and informal social behaviors and unique characteristics, not only expose them to stereotyping, prejudice, discrimination and social and institutional racism, but also psychologically handicap them by causing loneliness, helplessness and guilt (Mehta and Farina, 1994).

Allowing, Adjusting, Achieving

There are large bodies of literature about issues associated with adjusting in new social environments. These transitions are often described in the literature as stages, phases or processes to reflect different ways of coping. For example, Furnham and Bochner (1986) discuss immigrant students' experiences in four stages: "honeymoon, crisis, recovery and adjustment" (p. 212). Johnston (1996) highlights the same experiences in five phases: "Honeymoon, culture shock, initial adjustment, mental isolation and acceptance or integration" (p. 13). Furthermore, according to Driedyer (1996), students' transition processes involve six stages, "contact, acculturation, adaptation, accommodation, integration and assimilation" (p. 49). However, no matter how one describes the process, it is obvious that there are phases of difficulties and adjustments. Hanassab's (1991) findings acknowledge that moving from a familiar culture to a foreign culture involves complex and stressful difficulties. The process of learning to understand the competitive, territorial and interactive attitudes of the host society may well be the cause of student's transitional discomfort (Spaulding & Flack, 1976; Pedersen, Druguns, Lonner & Trimble, 2002; Stoynoff, 1997; & Valadez, 1998).

An alternative argument to these processes is that "immigrant students do not need to adjust (e.g., adapt and integrate) to a new culture but instead, need to learn its characteristics (e.g., the social and cultural skills and knowledge) [because] adjusting a person to a new culture is ethnocentric, helping someone to learn a second culture is not" (Pedersen, et al., 2002, p. 213). Klukanov (1998) also questions the interpretation of adaptation and integration because, he writes, "it is not a personal choice; rather it is societal expectation measured by the students' ability to conform to the larger society" (p. 3). Based on these ideas, there are a number of strategies that school counsellors can develop and use to deal more effectively with immigrant children instead of sending them to resource rooms where their self-esteem and self-pride can be seriously damaged. First, the counsellor must acknowledge the different stages that immigrants go through before they are fully integrated. Most immigrants pass through identical stages, but the orders of the stages are not significant as this depends on the families' reasons to immigrate. While the majority of newcomers experience the honeymoon stage first, a few others first experience the culture shock stage. All immigrants go through the adjustment stage, but few immigrants get stuck in the mental isolation stage before accepting the stage of integration. Counsellors must be aware of these processes of adjustment, because it is a starting point to understand in which stage people are when they arrive in a new country and how to elaborate an effective strategy plan for cognitive behavioral restructuring.

Second, counsellors must be sensitive to the impact of these stages on children's and parents' behavior, feelings, thoughts and family dynamics. Additionally, an awareness of the internal and external sources of frustration and satisfaction is important. There are stressors that force immigrant families and their children into one of three negative stages: 1) depression, due to a change in their social and economic status; 2) grief over losses; and 3) social distance due to unfamiliar environmental and living arrangements. Even when they try to connect and create relationship, their language and social skills might make them feel "handicapped." For most immigrant families and their children, disappointment over unfulfilled expectations and homesickness are the cause of behavioral changes inside and outside the family. An understanding of these stages and stressors help teachers and counsellors to adapt appropriate models in the helping process while the lack of this knowledge could make it difficult for students and teachers/counsellors to create a safe environment and establish an enjoyable relationship.

The communication process between students and teachers is subtle, systematic and multidimensional and takes place on two levels: the content (topic) and the relational (feeling and power) (Miles, 1989). Sometimes teachers forget this when they feel trapped in an interracial interaction, when they are being accused of being "culturally insensitive," or when they hear someone say, "This whole school is racist." It is at these moments that teachers and counsellors may feel vulnerable to the interpretations their immigrant students may make. They become conscious of being in an "interracial relationship," of feeling defensive, uncertain, not wanting to offend, wanting to analyze the content and needing to get away from the murky, uncomfortable arena of "race relations." It is no wonder that interracial interactions are described as walking on eggshells or across a minefield (Driedyer, 1996). One of the problems in measuring the extent of difficulties encountered by immigrant students is their reluctance to seek counselling. Thus, it is necessary that teachers and counsellors try to improve their ability, skills and knowledge in order to help immigrant children to identify problems, to construct coping strategies and to show them how to relax and self manage through different counselling approaches within the context of cross-cultural counselling models.

Why a Cross-cultural Approach?

A cross-cultural approach gives students the opportunity to learn by doing, by differentiating and by relating to those differences, thus further connecting their own experiences to what they see as different. In other words, the approach creates and connects learning patterns; relates, unites and differentiates those individuals, the community and the cultural and the spiritual characteristics by enhancing the counselling process and the overall learning environment.

The foundation for cross-cultural views is culture itself, since it has the most profound effect upon human behavior and ways of being. Culture shapes conditions within society and social organization; it governs its member's values, beliefs and choices and it makes for the greatest richness and differences within societies. Within this frame, cross-cultural counselling involves understanding, accepting and respecting complex yet rich cultural differences and modifies models or approaches to meet peoples' needs. It is because of such flexibility that the cross-cultural approach fosters the means to gain the knowledge and the experience necessary for students, teachers and counsellors in the learning environment. In other words, it provides a structure, which allows for the understanding of the numerous cultures, races, belief systems and social organizations that exist in the world. Within such an approach students, teachers and counsellors in the school environment would be open and enriched. Moreover, a cross-cultural approach can connect and transform the different patterns of communication and learning by promoting the common as well as the unique cultural attributes of various areas of knowledge in order to build relationships between students and counsellors from different backgrounds.

In this way, knowing becomes participating, experiencing, imagining and discovering. The cross-cultural approach acknowledges the student's need to share, organize and to be part of the web of learning. The approach involves everyone with no conditions attached and it is open to the creation of patterns of knowledge and experience, which respect all differences and do not involve a hierarchy of knowing.

In a reflective relationship between teacher and student, the teacher does not ask the student to accept the teacher's authority; rather, the teacher asks the student to suspend disbelief in that authority, to join with the teacher in inquiry, into that which the student is experiencing. The teacher agrees to help the student understand the meaning of the advice given, to be readily confrontable by the student and work with the student in reflecting on the tacit understanding each has (Doll, 1993, p. 160).

In the cross-cultural approach, students are given the opportunity to dialogue, to explore and to understand the rationale that makes one different from the other. Cross-cultural counselling focuses on the importance of associating the self with difference, as well as making this experience a different part of the pattern of the learning process. Working within the framework of such an approach, students randomly learn through experience, in preparation for broader future learning. As a result of such experiences, students will most likely understand the nature of their world and the global nature of its political, social, economic and educational structure. Therefore, the cross-cultural approach delivers the knowledge, skills and attitude that are required to participate in learning and actively exchange knowledge.

The cross-cultural nature of human organization is what distinguishes the "otherness" of others, shaping unique and common characteristics, morality, beliefs and perceived worldviews. A cross-cultural approach could transform students' perceptions, values and worldviews about self-in-relation and the unique differences between themselves and others. As a result of using this approach, the counselling, learning and teaching environment could become a place where individual and group stories, sources of ideas and relationships are shared and created.

Students can be encouraged to question and explore beyond class activities. The hierarchy of different ethnicity, gender and cultures can also be deconstructed by means of exploring the cultures of different students as a general foundation. For example, teachers could assign two students a day to interview their parents, asking where their ancestors came from, what is their ethnic mix, what kinds of language people speak in that country and the difference between their father's and mother's cultural background as well as their parents' differences from people of other countries. Such activities create curiosity, the excitement of getting to know their own and their classmates' cultural, linguistic and regional roots. As a result, "the otherness of the other" is not only respected and accepted as part of the pattern of the class and the web of the culture, but it also enhances the individual's self-esteem through strong cultural identification. Recognizing this "otherness" is also an excellent medium for eliminating prejudice and racism and fostering improved intercultural exchanges through increased empathy and understanding.

Conclusion

Teachers, counsellors and decision-making staff should consider the potential negative impact that being separated from the mainstream has on children. Teachers and counsellors play different roles when it comes to helping students. Because they act as advisors, advocates, facilitators, consultants and /or agents of change, it is their responsibility to understand the students' needs to integrate and help them develop a sense of positive identity within the mainstream classroom and not in one outside of it (such as the ESL Resource Room). The cross-cultural approach could help teachers and counsellors retrace the source of problems and difficulties, as well as the cultural, spiritual, family and societal influences. As a result, children's identity crisis could be understood and adequately addressed and restructured. The school's intention to help children should not be undermined. The whole argument here is that immigrant children mistakenly attending the ESL Resource Rooms in schools are being denied the opportunity to grow, learn and experience life in the same way as their White Canadian counterparts.

References

Abe, J.S. & Zane, N.W.S. (1990). Psychological maladjustment among Asian and White-American college students: Controlling for confounds. *Journal of Counselling Psychology, 37*, 437-444.

Allingham, A. & Allingham, P. (1988). *The Education of Immigrant Children in Coastal British*

Columbia: A Case Study (1936-45). Victoria, BC: Eiron Communications.

Doll, E.W. (1993). *A Post-modern Perspective on Curriculum*. New York: Teachers College Press.

Driedyer, L. (1996). *Multi-ethnic Canada: Identity and Inequalities*. Toronto: Oxford University Press.

Furnham, A. & Bochner, S. (1986). *Counselling the Culturally Different*. New York: John Wiley.

Graham, J.M. (1999). The African-centered worldview: Developing a paradigm for social work. *The British Journal of Social Work, 29*:2, 251-268.

Hall, B.J. (1997). Prejudice. *The E-Journal of Intercultural Relations, 1*:1, 1-2.

Hanassab, S. (1991). Acculturation and young Iranian women: Attitudes towards sex role and intimate relationship. *Journal of Multicultural Counselling and Development, 19*:11, 30-49.

Ho, D. (1998). Indigenous psychologies: Asian perspectives. *Journal of Cross-cultural Psychology, 29*:1, 88-103.

Johnston, S.P. (1996) *Culturally Sensitive Mental Health Communities Creating Change: Culture and Health 2000*. Vancouver, B.C.

Klukanov, I.E. (1998). A system approach to multicultural education. *The E-journal of Intercultural Relations, 1*:2, 1-10.

Leong, F.T.L. (1984). Counselling international students (An information analysis paper). ERIC document.

Mehta, S. & Farina, A. (1994). Acculturation and mental health of Asian Indian immigrants. Paper presented at the annual meeting of the American psychological association, Los Angeles, CA, November, 1994.

Miles, R. (1989). *Racism*. New York: Routledge.

Pedersen, P.B., Dragun, J.G., Lonner, W.J. & Trimble, J.E. (2002). *Counselling Across Cultures*. Thousand Oaks, CA: Sage Publications.

Spaulding, S. & Flack, M. (1976). *The World's Students in the United States: A Review and Evaluation of Research on Foreign Students*. New York: Praeger.

Stoynoff, S. (1997). Factors associated with international student's academic achievement. *Journal of Instructional Psychology, 24*:1, 21-53.

Sue, D.W. & Sue, D. (1999). *Counselling the Culturally Different: Theory and Practice*. New York: John Wiley and Sons Publication.

Valadez, J.R. (1998). Applying the college race, class and gender differences. *Journal of Professional School Counselling, 1*:5, 44-71.

Wolfgang, A. (Ed.) (1975). *Education of Immigrant Students: Issues and Answers*. Toronto: The Ontario Institute for Studies in Education.

Chapter 11
Counselling Hispanics: A Multicultural Approach

María del Carmen Rodríguez

It is said that culture is a human necessity and a way of life. It is the core of internal ways in which human beings develop their sense of self, including values, beliefs, thought patterns, perceptions and worldview. All these qualities help determine and shape one's external culture; in other words, the way(s) in which one establishes and maintains a relationship with the environment and others through implicit norms, language, traditions, rituals and loyalties that influence attitudes, behaviors and customs (Gushue, 1993).

In an ever-changing world where cultural roots and heritage represent some of the elements that connect us to our ancestors' past, cultural diversity and the challenges it poses for cross-cultural interaction are vital components of the human experience. Culture has been defined by Falicov (1995) as a set of shared worldviews, meanings and adaptive behaviors derived from simultaneous membership and participation in a variety of contexts including language, age, gender, race, ethnicity, religion, socio-economic status, education and sexual orientation. This definition indicates that cultural values define behaviors and therefore establish norms for attitudes and actions that take place within families and in the larger cultural groups (e.g., religious affiliation, academic community and so forth). As a result, unique individual experiences and commonalties in personality and affiliation across cultures bound the scope of those in helping professions. In the culturally diverse settings of the United States and Canada, as well as those of many other countries, the principles of cross-cultural counselling are applicable to minority groups defined on the basis of visible racial features, historical heritage, language background, history of past discrimination, oppression and exclusion.

Who are Considered Hispanics?

The term Hispanics has been given to the group of people formed by very diverse backgrounds, which are multicultural in their attitudes, beliefs, values and ethnic origins (white, Indigenous & Black, among others). According to Gimenez (1989), the term Hispanic, "does not identify an ethnic group or a minority group, but a heterogeneous population whose characteristics and behavior cannot be understood without necessarily falling into stereotyping" (p .1). Some people identify themselves as Hispanic (see Table 1) based on their heritage and not their country of origin, as they might be third or fourth generation born either in Canada or the United States. Hispanics is perhaps the most common term in the Northwest; it can be used to refer to anyone who is from Mexico, Central America, South America, Puerto Rico or Cuba – or their descendants, even if they were born and raised in the United States. However, some researchers and social activists disagree with the term because of its potential political implications to identify a minority group subject to severe discrimination, so the term Latino or Latin American is sometimes preferred. This paper utilizes the term Hispanics for purposes of discussing the implications of counselling this diverse group of people. The term can be used interchangeably with Latino, but it can have a slightly different connotation.

The Hispanic population has been increasing throughout North America in the last 15 years; initially, people emigrated mostly from Cuba, Puerto Rico, Mexico and Central America. In recent years, people from Chile, Guatemala, Colombia and Ecuador have come to Canada to make it their home (Statistics Canada, 2001). In Canada, the number of Hispanics is 642 548 which corresponds to 11% of the total population of immigrants (5,841,351) and 2% of the total population of Canada. Approximately 50 000 people in Toronto, Canada's largest city, have been identified as having Spanish as their first language (Statistics Canada, 2001).

Even though Hispanics may share similar experiences regarding their work-related and educational opportunities, their history and status, it is important for counsellors to understand that the Hispanic population living in Canada differs, in some ways, from those Hispanics who live in the United States. Among those differences, one can highlight: Rationale for migrating; conditions of migration; and opportunities. Although most of the Hispanic population comes from South America (mainly Chile) and obtain landed immigrant or refugee status, there are many Mexicans who, under the North Atlantic Free Trade Agreement (NAFTA), are granted temporary work permits every year. Lately, Guatemalans, Colombians and Peruvians have also migrated to Canada. Table 1 shows the number of Latin American children and youth living in Canada by ethnic origin and age.

As a result of these changing statistics, it is essential that educators and counsellors become competent and aware of the necessities of this growing minority group and the existing differences among the variety of Hispanics. According to Casas and Vasquez (1989), "race is a very important variable [for Hispanics]...and has a major impact on the life experiences and stressors [or].... the way that they are treated or accepted by non-Hispanic Whites" (p. 150). Recent studies (Damaris, Carrasco & Charbonneau, 1998; Israelite & Herman, 1999; Rockhill & Tomic, 1992; Rublee & Shaw, 1991) conducted in Canada among Latin American populations have demonstrated that the experiences of immigrant and refugee Latin American women are comparable to those of other refugees and immigrants from around the world. Some challenges facing Hispanics in Canada are unemployment, housing and relative poverty (Borjas & Tienda, 1985; Kazemipur & Halli, 1998;

Durst & Lange, 1999). Furthermore, according to Ornstein (1997), in Canada, the children of Latin American migrants often show low academic achievement (only 65% are able to obtain a high school diploma and university graduates account for scarcely 10%).

Table 1: Number of Latin American Children and Adolescents in Canada by Ethnic Origin and Age

Geography Canada	All Ages	Under 5 years old	5-9 years old	10-14 years old
Argentinean	7 115	690	715	795
Central/South American Indian	9 285	965	870	775
Chilean	33 835	3 230	3 210	3 080
Colombian	8 525	1 010	825	725
Costa Rican	1 115	165	120	180
Cuban	4 265	460	445	310
Ecuadoran	6 910	655	615	695
Guatemalan	8 460	1 235	1 090	815
Hispanic	5 275	580	485	485
Honduran	1 820	265	280	170
Latin/Central/South American	30 365	3 320	3 290	3 095
Mexican	23 300	3 110	3 055	2 320
Nicaraguan	4 895	500	555	585
Panamanian	1 690	215	110	155
Paraguayan	705	120	130	80
Peruvian	14 160	1 545	1 650	1 320
Salvadoran	24 125	2 690	3 030	2 570
Spaniard	204 365	18 970	17 875	17 635
Uruguayan	2 940	300	345	235
Venezuelan	4 580	655	495	425
Total (less Spaniard)	397 730	40 680	39 190	36 450

The Three-dimensional Model

Atkinson's, Thompson's and Grant's (1993) multi-modal approach to counselling describes eight alternative roles that involve the counsellor more actively in the client's life experiences than do conventional roles. These roles may be utilized independently or jointly depending on the problems, situation and/or goals of the client. Although they might overlap at some point due to their nature, each of the roles includes some components that make them unique. The model consists of three elements or variables (dimensions) that exist in a continuum and need to be considered when working with minorities: 1) The goal of the counselling situation (preventive/remedial); 2) The etiology of the problem (internal/external); and 3) The client's level of acculturation (low/high).

According to Padilla (1980), acculturation is a central variable in the delivery of counselling services to Hispanics as it encompasses a wide continuum and is affected by a) language proficiency, preference and use; b) socio-economic status; and c) value orientations (Elliot, 2002). Acculturation, however, has the potential to become a risk factor when individuals do not have a support network. As a result of changing life experiences and cultural clash of values, day-to-day situations become unfamiliar, stressful and conflictive. Individuals struggle to maintain a cultural identity while at the same time, try to adapt to their new one. Some factors related to acculturation among Hispanics include:

- Status according to generation (related to family history and educational and occupational opportunities)
- Use of English language (corresponding to needs and preferences [at home and at work] and level of proficiency)
- Frequency of mobility to the original country (maintenance of culture specific attitudes and value orientation).

The Roles of the Counsellor

Atkinson et al,. (1993) identified eight therapist roles to help clients in different ways depending on the interdependent variables and situations: Advocate; Advisor; Facilitator of Indigenous support systems; Facilitator of Indigenous healing systems; Consultant; Change Agent; Counsellor; and/or Psychotherapist. The role(s) assumed by the counsellor will shift based on the three dimensions described above. Figure 1 illustrates how the role(s) would unfold according to the juxtaposition of the dimensions.

Adviser

The counsellor acts as an adviser when the level of acculturation in the client is low, the problem is external and the goal of the treatment is prevention. The counsellor tries to prevent arising difficulties by advising the clients about the problems they or their families might encounter. The counsellor initiates discussion of a potential developing problem and advises the client about some alternatives or options to prevent it from emerging. This approach is utilized mostly with new immigrants who might need some advice concerning the difficulties they might face in the new country. This role of the counsellor serves those clients who want to know what to do to reduce the impact of newly encountered conditions such as culture shock, adjustment, assimilation and adaptation, among others.

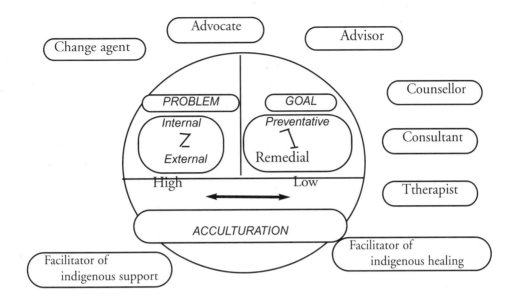

Figure 1: Counsellor's Roles

Advocate

The counsellor serves as an advocate when the level of acculturation in the client is low, the problem is external and the goal of the treatment is remediation. As an advocate, the counsellor speaks on behalf of the client, who could be one individual or a group of people experiencing harsh conditions. In this role, the counsellor represents the individual or the group and must be willing to pursue alternative courses with or for the client. As an advocate, the counsellor has the responsibility to make certain that the person benefits from the diverse resources of the majority culture without losing what is unique and valued in his/her own culture.

In schools, the role of the counsellor as advocate has gained strength among ethnically diverse schools. School counsellors are urged to advocate that their school personnel understand that immigrant children have a legal right to free, appropriate public education and to restructure the policies and practice that sort immigrant students into programs which prepare them for inferior futures. They must also ensure that immigrant students experience a school environment free of victimization, harassment and intergroup conflict and ensure a more equitable allocation of resources to the schools that serve such students.

Facilitator of Indigenous Support System

This role is helpful when the level of acculturation of the client is low, the problem is internal and the goal of the counselling situation is preventive. Counselling can be thought of as a social support system to help prevent and remediate problems; because support systems are more acceptable within many cultures than are professional counselling or therapy, it is likely that clients will trust the counsellor who assumes the role of facilitator of Indigenous support. Some of these support systems are ethnic churches, community centres, family networks and the like. The counsellor is invited to strongly acknowledge the importance of the support systems and encourage the diverse ethnic or governmental organizations to provide the services needed by the individual and/or the community. Additionally, counsellors might facilitate the use of indigenous support systems by referring clients and encouraging them to use the available services.

Facilitator of Indigenous Healing Methods

If the client's level of acculturation is low, the problem is internal and the goal of the therapy is remediation, the counsellor assumes this role. It is the counsellor's duty to honor, acknowledge and respect the client's belief system. Every culture has different effective means to deal with and solve problems once they develop; the effectiveness of such means lies mostly in the members' positive beliefs about the methods. Thus, individuals who believe in certain healing procedures are likely to comply with them. By undertaking this role, the counsellor accepts that healing methods from the client's culture are more likely to be effective than conventional treatments or strategies. When the latter is advised to the client, the result might be a divergence between the need and the help provided, loss of credibility in the counsellor and finally, the client's disengagement from counselling.

Consultant

Hansen, Himes and Meier (1990) have defined consultation as an association that involves a collegial relationship between the consultant and the consultee (client) who work together to affect the behavior of a third party. In this role, the counsellor works in situations trying to prevent problems from developing; counsellors can help minorities to learn skills needed to interact successfully with the dominant society. Because values and the potential to respond in assertive ways differ from one culture to another, minority groups such as Hispanics might struggle with the inability to perform skills valued by the dominant culture which may place them at a disadvantage for coping with the majority culture. Thus, it is advised that the counsellor be able to teach basic coping and social skills to minority group clients. One way for doing this, according to La Framboise and Rowe (1983), is by modelling in small groups since this is a procedure that involves a different way of transmitting knowledge, which – albeit being "indirect" – is effective.

Change Agent

Egan (1985) describes a change agent as "anyone who plays an important part in designing, redesigning, running, renewing, or improving any system, subsystem, or program" (p. 12). In this role, the counsellor attempts to change, modify or adjust the social environment that afflicts racial/ethnic minorities. The counsellor helps the client identify the external resources of his or her own problem as well as methods of resolving the problem. Together, they develop a strategy for eliminating or reducing the effect of affliction on the client's life. Oftentimes, facilitating the formation of racial/ ethnic minority political groups does this. The counsellor serving as a change agent assumes a low-visibility profile, often finding it useful to mobilize other influential persons in the stressful institution so as to bring about change. Lewis and Bradley (2000) identified four ways in which a counsellor can act as a change agent: a) the counsellor can assess community needs; b) coordinate activities and resources; c) provide training in skill-building; and d) advocate change. Ponterotto (1987) described a multi-modal approach for counselling Mexican-Americans and this model includes a change agent component that may be applicable to other ethnic groups. This role as described by Ponterotto (1987), involves identification of the social, environmental and institutional factors that are oppressing the client but that are external to his/her control.

Counsellor

The helper follows the conventional counselling role when the client has a high acculturation level, the problem is internal and the goal is the prevention of problems. The main role of the counsellor is to help the client make decisions considering the client's history, beliefs, attitudes, values and background. Each possible alternative takes into consideration goals and consequences, probability for it to occur, choice and decision-making processes accompanied by decision-making skills. Since the profile of the client concerning acculturation is high, which means that he or she has developed adaptation skills, it is important that the counsellor be aware of his/her own biases that might influence the client's decision for choosing a specific alternative or option.

Psychotherapist

The facilitator serves as a psychotherapist when the level of acculturation of the client is high, the problem is internal and a situation wants to be resolved. Two important elements that the counsellor must consider when taking on this role, is to maintain credibility as a counsellor and to offer clients a benefit from therapy as a soon as possible. Sue and Zane (1987) suggest that three factors are significantly related to maintaining the counsellor's credibility: a) the conceptualization of a client's problem must be congruent with the client's belief system; b) the counsellor's required responses and suggestions from and to the client must be culturally compatible and acceptable; c) the definition of goals must be the same for both the counsellor and the client. By giving, the counsellor reinforces his/her credibility. Giving could be described as a meaningful gain in therapy; it is (giving) reassurance, hope, faith, skills acquisition, a coping perspective and anxiety reduction alternatives among others.

General Considerations When Counselling Hispanics

There are some professional and personal attitudes and beliefs that affect the process of counselling that have negatively impacted minorities. Cultural history and experience of oppression cause changes in behavior, which might have different meanings for counsellor and client. To avoid stereotypes and biases, the counsellor must seek specific information regarding the client such as demographic information (historical and cultural background), professional expertise (what kinds of job experience does the client have) and personal experiences (racism/exclusion/acceptance).

What the counsellor needs to observe

In order to assist Hispanic clients, several factors such as language maintenance, social relationships, family structure and history and religious affiliation should be taken into consideration. Since the vitality of a language indicates how well a group is maintaining itself in society, it should be considered within the broader framework of social, political and ideological factors, as it operates as one of the most important practices within our society wherein cultural production and reproduction take place (Corson, 1998; Darder, 1991).

Despite the many similarities that Hispanics share as a group bound mostly by language, spiritual beliefs and values, it is paramount that counsellors understand that differences in worldview are important to observe in order to best help and deliver their services. In Canada, the reality for Hispanics is different from that of the same population living in the United States, given their history and place of origin. As a result of stereotyping and biases, Hispanics in particular have been diagnosed more often with problems, yet, interestingly, have received less time with helpers than have any other group. The notion of what is considered 'normal' by the various health organizations should be challenged when dealing with non-mainstreams individuals. What is considered to be 'normal' must be evaluated and understood according to the situation, personal history and background, as well as the circumstances under which a particular event occurred. As a result, the counsellor's interpretation or discernment of a situation would benefit from having an awareness of the following:

– Being aware that they might be perceived as authority figures who deserve respect and whose advice is to be followed. In patriarchal societies, people expect to be guided and even told what to do and how to proceed in a variety of situations.

– Knowing that the notion of 'self' as understood in North American [individualistic] societies, operates collectively with Hispanic clients. Understanding the value of connecting, supporting and relying on extended family.

– Be careful not to fall into stereotyping, especially when it comes to anticipating results within the therapy or helping process. Stereotyping uses the racial or ethnic background of an individual as simplistic, straightforward predictors of beliefs or behaviors.

– Finally, it is advised that helpers are knowledgeable of the fact that Hispanic people embrace alternative therapies, such as massage therapists, healers and herbal remedies.

What clients might experience

Among Hispanic clients, history of oppression, personal experiences and specific cultural background cause different reactions and behaviors. What is taken for granted by a counsellor (often times stereotypes) might be a different and unique reality for the client. As a result, clients frequently do not have the opportunity to be understood and treated accordingly to their own experiences. Therefore, it is necessary that counsellors seek more statistical and empirical information that will provide them with more ample opportunities to adequately help Hispanics. From such a foundation, say Casas, Vasquez and Ruiz de Esparza (2002), "…[counsellors] can expand their ability to distinguish between stereotype and truth, bias and health, an effective counselling and cultural oppression" (p. 146). Some general perceptions from the Hispanic client's perspective include:

– Interdependence is viewed as healthy and necessary.

– Family plays an important role in their life in regards to encouragement, educational expectations, critical life events, vicarious learning and work identity (Fisher & Padmawidjaja, 1999).

– Due to the history of poor job opportunities, social relations, oppression, discrimination, access to education and how the Western cultures see or perceive them, some Hispanics might experience low self-esteem that could be reflected in aggressive behavior, isolation and so forth (Mc Neill, Prieto, Pizarro, Vera & Gomez, 2001).

– Some clients may believe that counsellors should go "a step further" helping them to change the environment and not just adjusting or adapting to it.

– Disclosing intimate problems may be difficult since it may impact negatively on the family. Being verbally open and direct is not the norm among Hispanics. This should be understood as a value of the culture and not as a deterring aspect of the counselling process.

– Instant familiarity, especially when meeting a new person (e.g., at the time of the initial office visit), is not advisable. Formality is a sign of respect and deference when you do not know someone well.

– The "history of their past" is important and can effect their immediate feelings and actions.

– Thinking can be linear (cause-effect) or circular (events are viewed as independent of consequent events). It is possible that situations are attributed to God's will or to good luck or to forces beyond their control.

Alternative approaches

According to Casas, Vasquez and Ruiz de Esparza (2002), the counselling process should focus on the client's expectations, preferences, values and attitudes; therefore they suggest taking into consideration the following approaches:

– Use of existential philosophy: This approach enhances and honors, as well as recognizes cultural differences and organizes experiences that reflect universal concerns of humankind.

– Cultural empathy. The counsellor must generate thoughts, words and behavior to communicate effectively with diverse cultural groups..

– Use of a Multi-modal approach: This provides the flexibility to be adaptable to the intra-cultural diversity of Hispanics; it enhances the probability of behavior change and it attends to behavior, images, cognitive processes, sensations and interpersonal relationships.

– Procure a degree of commitment (social responsibility that *should* be embraced). The counsellor could participate actively in some of the activities that the Hispanic community offers and be actively involved.

Conclusion

According to Vanier (1998) "…love and respect, like fear and prejudice, are legacies passed on from one person to another. The movement from seeking approval to taking responsibility, to being open to those who are different, implies a shift of consciousness" (pp. 81-82). The shift for counsellors is viewing cultural identity as a major element of a person's behavior; thus, being sensitive and understanding the cultural background of clients is imperative. As a cultural group that is diverse racially yet shares a common language, Hispanics are in a very unique situation. In fact, Hispanic is one the fastest growing populations in North America, both in the USA and Canada.

The research on cross-cultural counselling is extensive and suggests diverse modes and models for counselling minorities. Atkinson's, Thompson's and Grant's (1993) three-dimensional model for counselling racial/ethnic minorities is one of the most useful paradigms for counsellors working with Hispanic clients. However, it is the helper's judgement and responsibility to choose the procedure(s) that will bring forth the most benefit and positive outcomes for the client. It is in our willingness to be accepting of others that we, as helpers, will begin to understand other people's needs and hopes without forgetting that respect, openness and common sense will always be crucial components of what constitutes a good counselling practice.

Glossary

Hispanic

Probably the most common term used in the Northwest to refer to the people of Mexico, Central America, South America, Puerto Rico or Cuba -or their descendants, even if they were born and raised in the United States. Term created by the U.S. government as a census category.

Latino/Latina

The term Latino can be used to refer to anyone of Latin American descent. It can be used instead of Hispanic.

Chicano/Chicana

This term is often associated with activists and the student movement of the 1960's. Technically, it refers to someone of Mexican descent who was born and raised in the United States. Albeit a politically loaded and sometimes derogatory term, it was created by students who believed neither the terms Mexican nor American, or even Mexican-American, were adequate to describe who they were.

Mexican-American

An American citizen of Mexican heritage.

Mexican

A Mexican citizen (in Mexico or US); some immigrants who are citizens still identify as Mexican culturally. The word is sometimes misused to refer to Mexican-Americans.

Spanish

Either the language spoken in Mexico and throughout South America, or a person from Spain. It is inappropriate to use it to refer to someone from Mexico or South America.

References

Atkinson, D.R., Thompson, C.E. & Grant, S.K. (1993). A three-dimensional model for counselling racial/ethnic minorities. *Counselling Psychologist, 21*, 257-277.

Borjas, G. & Tienda, M. (1985). *Hispanics in the U. S. Economy*. New York: Academic Press.

Casas, J.M. & Vasquez, M.J.T. (1989). Counseling the Hispanic client: A theoretical and applied perspective. In P.B. Pedersen, J.G. Draguns, W.J. Lonner & J.E. Trimble (Eds.), *Counseling Across Cultures* (3rd ed., pp. 153-175). Thousand Oaks, CA: Sage Publications.

Casas, J.M., Vasquez, M.J.T. & Ruiz de Esparza, C.A. (2002). Counseling the Latino: A guiding framework for a diverse population. In P.B. Pedersen, J.G. Draguns, W.J. Lonner & J.E. Trimble (Eds.), *Counseling Across Cultures* (5th ed., pp. 133- 159). Thousand Oaks, CA: Sage Publications.

Corson, D. (1998). *Changing Education for Diversity.* Bristol, PA: Open University Press

Damaris, R., Carrasco, P. & Charbonneau, J. (1998). *The Role of "Weak Ties" in the Settlement Experiences of Immigrant Women with Young Children: The Case of Central Americans Living in Montreal.* Toronto, ON: Centre of Excellence for Research on Immigration and Settlement.

Darder, A. (1991). *Culture and Power in the Classroom: A Critical Foundation for Bicultural Education.* Toronto, ON: OISE Press.

Durst, D. & Lange, A. (1999). *The Social Integration of Salvadoran Refugees in Regina: An Exploratory Study.* Paper presented at the 3rd annual Metropolis Conference, Vancouver, BC.

Elliot, K.A.G. (2002). The Relationship Between Acculturation, Family Functioning, and School Performance of Mexican-American Adolescents. Unpublished doctoral dissertation, University of California, Santa Barbara.

Falicov, C.J. (1995) Training to think culturally: A multidimensional comparative framework. *Family Process, 34*, 373-388.

Fisher, T. & Padmawidjaja, I. (l999). Parental influences on career development perceived by African American and Mexican American college students. *Journal of Multicultural Counselling and Development, 27*, 136-152.

Gimenez, M., (1989). Latino/"hispanic" – Who needs a name? The case against a standardized terminology. *The International Journal of Health Services*, Vol 19, Number 3, 557-571.

Gushue, G.V. (1993). Cultural-identity development and family assessment: An interaction model. *The Counselling Psychologist, 21*, 487-513.

Hansen, J.C., Himes, B.S. & Meier, S. (1990). *Consultation: Concepts and Practice.* Engelwood Cliffs, NJ: Prentice Hall.

Israelite, N.K. & Herman, A. (1999). Settlement Experiences of Recent Latina Immigrants and Refugees: Perspectives on Work. Paper presented at the 16th annual Qualitative Analysis conference, Fredericton, NB.

Kazemipur, A. & Halli, S.S. (1998). Plight of immigrants: The spatial concentration of poverty in Canada. *Canadian Journal of Regional Science, 20* (1-2), 11-28.

La Framboise, T. & Rowe, W. (1983). Skills training for bicultural competence: Rationale and application. *Journal of Counselling Psychology, 30*, 589-595

Lewis, J. & Bradley, L. (Eds.). (2000). *Advocacy in Counselling: Counselors, Clients and Community.* Greensboro, NC: ERIC-CASS.

Mc Neill, B.W., Prieto, L.R., Pizarro, M., Vera, E.M. & Gomez, S.P. (2001). Current directions in Chicano psychology, *Counseling Psychology, 29*, 5-17.

Ornstein, M. (1997). Ethno-racial Inequality in Metropolitan Toronto: Analysis of the 1991 Census. Paper presented at the Urban Forum on Immigration and Refugee Issues, Toronto, ON.

Padilla, A.M. (1980). *Acculturation: Theory, Models and Some New Findings.* Boulder, CO: Westview

Press.

Ponterotto, J.G. (1987). Counselling Mexican-Americans: A multi-modal approach. *Journal of Counselling and Development, 65,* 308-312.

Rockhill, K. & Tomic, P. (1992). *Assessing ESL: An Exploration into the Effects of Institutionalized Racism and Sexism in Shaping the Lives of Latin American Immigrant and Refugee Women in Metropolitan Toronto.* Toronto: Government of Ontario.

Rublee, C.B. & Shaw, S.M. (1991). Constraints on the leisure and community participation of immigrant women: Implications for social integration. *Loisir et Societes/Society and Leisure, 14*(1), 13-150.

Statistics Canada (2001). Immigration by Ethnic Origin [on-line]. Retrieved February 13, 2001 from http://www.statscan.ca

Sue, S. & Zane, N. (1987). The role of culture and cultural techniques in psychotherapy: A critique and reformulation. *American Psychologist, 42,* 37-45

Vanier, J. (1998). *Becoming Human.* Toronto, ON: Anansi

Chapter 12
Counselling African-Canadians

Elias Cheboud and M. Honoré France

My family's history in Canada is one of the many untold stories buried in the margins. My parents migrated to Montreal in the 1940s from areas in Nova Scotia that were economically depressed. They came seeking a better life for themselves and their children but soon discovered that, for Black people, life anywhere in Canada was one of racial discrimination and lack of opportunities (Ruggles, 1996, p. 5,).

The issue of racism described by Ruggles persists at every level of Canadian society from the overt to the covert, yet despite this, African-Canadian people continue to contribute to Canadian society. Most people are familiar with the overt forms of racism embodied by laws that are more reminiscent of Apartheid in South Africa. The more subtle forms are more difficult to recognize. Martin and Warburton (1998) describe one of the more obscure forms of racism in the education curriculum at the University of Victoria in which there is an absence of systematic exposure of students to issues of diversity. What needs to be emphasized in counsellor training is the crucial and complex role that culture plays in becoming competent; that everyone in intercultural training is in process and bound to make mistakes. The call is to be patient and helpful to each other. The idea of a cross-cultural counselling and teaching is to enlighten, inform, sensitize and teach curriculum approaches, theories of helping and strategies that can be used to help others. All people of every culture existing in Canadian society are "brothers and sisters" and so embracing each other and ridding society of racism is the only way of building a "just society." We need to literally teach each other to be more sensitive. The idea of respecting others is a difficult task that is filled with "stumbling" and mistakes. It requires sensitivity to others at a degree that reflects what Ridley and Lingle (1996) identified as cultural empathy. Cultural empathy is a:

...learned ability of counsellors to accurately gain an understanding of the self – experienced of clients from other cultures – an understanding informed by counselors' interpretation of cultural data. Cultural empathy also involves the ability of counsellors to communicate this understanding effectively with an attitude of concern for culturally different clients (p. 32).

The term cultural empathy can also be called multicultural empathy. While helpful, multicultural empathy can supersede factors such as cultural similarity between counsellors and clients. Learning to de-code cultural cues is possible by people of dissimilar cultural backgrounds. This process is not dependent of neutralizing one's cultural values, because not being in touch with one's cultural identity is an insecure personal foundation. And like speaking in a second language, cultural empathy can be learned like any other skill. The process is first learning how to empathize and then decode meaning(s) embedded in culture. This is followed by being able to respond in a culturally appropriate manner that includes the affective, cognitive and spiritual dimensions of human nature. Ridley and Lingle (1993) indicate that in order to be competent in cultural empathy, the counsellor must be able to differentiate between the self and other from a cultural perspective. Cultural sensitivity requires ability to accurately understand cultural information from the client and includes the following processes: perspective taking ("walking in the other's shoes"), experience vicariously (how the client feels things) and be able to respond expressively to client issues.

Who are African-Canadians?

People of African descent have been living in Canada as long as Europeans have, although in comparison to the United States, their numbers are relatively small nationwide. According to Statistics Canada (2001), out of a population of 28 million there were 274 630 who identified themselves as having their origin from the Caribbean or Africa (1% of the Canadian population compared to 12% in the USA). In British Columbia there are approximately 23 275 people who identified themselves as Afrcian-Canadian out of a total population of 3 689 755 (.66% of the population). One has to be careful with these numbers that also do not include people who identified themselves as coming from North Africa or Asia (e.g., Fuji, P.N.G., etc.). However, since African-Canadians are congregated in Nova Scotia and urban areas of Canada, they are more visible in cities such as Toronto (e.g., 25 percent of the total population).

Which is better, calling those Canadians of African ethnic descent Black or African-Canadian? In Nova Scotia, the use of Black to refer to those of African-Canadian decent is more prevalent than the use of African-Canadian. The author of *Black like who?* Rinaldo Walcott (1997), who is of African-Canadian descent, says, "I use the archaic and ancient term black as a way of framing the political discourse that I am structuring..." (p. 2). In that sense, he feels that the use of black becomes more political and thus, goes beyond the narrow sense of identity of someone whose ancestors originally came from Africa. On the other hand, the American political activist, Jessie Jackson, viewed the use of "black" as an outdated term in multicultural America. He often said, when criticized by others, that there was not such place as "black", but there is a place called Africa with a long history and culture. Over a short period, all the critics who at first criticized Jackson began to use the term African-American. We have chosen to use African Canadian and Black in this chapter, because of the use of both terms in the literature; however, we feel that the most useful term is African-Canadian. Not withstanding events in the United States, the term African-Canadian not only includes those "black" loyalists, but more recent immigrants and their children from the Caribbean, Fiji and the many countries of Africa. With few exceptions the term African-Canadian is much more widely cited in the literature than the term "black," although in practicality and usage, it is still widely used and accepted by Canadians of African descent.

Historical Background of African-Canadians

According to Fleras and Elliot (1992), for Canadians to overlook the history of visible minorities is not only to ignore an important cultural heritage; it is to misunderstand the direction of Canadian history in its entirety." Mainstream Canadian history texts have clearly overlooked the place and role of those of African descent. From the very beginning of European immigration to Canada, people of African descent lived and worked in this country. Before slavery was outlawed in the British Empire, in 1834, most were brought to Canada as either slaves or indentured servants. However, there were many exceptions, including over 5000 who came at the end of the American revolution as "loyalists." The history of racism and segregation of African Canadians has been overshadowed by the widely documented experience of African-American struggle against discrimination. The fact is that the government and people of Canada have a long history of discrimination and racism against people because of the color of their skin. While many thousands escaped from slavery in the United States, finding freedom from slavery in Canada, they were still segregated. Even as late as World War I, there were separate battalions for people of color in the Canadian army. Officially, segregation ended in Nova Scotia schools in 1954, but the struggle for equality still persists all over Canada with gradual gains in acceptance and recognition.

More locally, consider that British Columbia's first governor, James Douglass, was a person of mixed British and African blood. His mother, born in the Caribbean, was the daughter of a freeman, who originally was brought from Africa as a slave. Interestingly, Douglas was also instrumental in inviting the first Blacks to the British Colony of Vancouver Island in the spring of 1858. Many settled on Salt Spring Island or in the Central Saanich area. The Colony's first police force was the all-Black African Rifles organized by Douglas, in the summer of 1858. One of the more visible successes in British Columbia was the election in 1972 of Rosemary Brown, the first Black woman elected to a provincial legislature in Canada. While African-Canadians have become an integral part of British Columbia's society, there is a persistence of racism among people in Canada. Moreover, their participation and deeds received little recognition or went unrecorded in the history books. They remained the invisible and yet visible minority. One has to remember that culture is evolutionary and influenced by the historical and social forces around it. Canada's culture, if we can use that expression, is a result of the many varying peoples that have passed through history. However, the influence of the African-Canadian community on that cultural evolution is often omitted or forgotten outright. To fail to acknowledge the contribution is to deny the existence of the contributor. Flerus and Elliot (1992) state that the mass media have portrayed visible minorities "... in unfounded generalizations that bordered on the comical, ... [being] labelled dropouts, pimps, drug dealers ..." (p. 289).

Role of Racism and its Psychological Impact

What the hell do I want to go to a place like Mombasa [Kenya]?...I'm sort of scared about going there...I just see myself in a pot of boiling water with all these natives dancing around me (Times-Colonist, 2001).

The mayor of Toronto Mel Lastman denied being a racist because of what he said during a tour of Africa in support of his city's drive to be awarded the Olympic bid in 2008. However, his statement not only embarrassed the city and Canada, it reinforced many minorities' perceptions that many Canadians just do not understand how racism destabilizes the community and individually humiliates and hurts African-Canadians. Consider the case of Quebec high school teacher William Kafe, who complained to the Human Rights Tribunal in 1993 about his treatment at his school. At the trial:

Kafe testified that over the years students had brought excrement to throw at him; twice the students set fire to his classroom and shouted "we're going to burn down the nigger"; they flooded his classroom and shouted "we're going to draw him and hold him down by his tie, pulling him around like a dog. They told him he was dirty and brought soap and a face cloth to "wash the dirty nigger" (Ruggles &. Rovenescu, 1996, p. 94).

Kafe reported that he was so anxious and depressed with the racial taunts he received from his students, that he was unable to continue teaching. Two days before the judgement was heard, Kafe was arrested for a letter he sent to his local mayor where he complained about racism along with a "shooting rampage" reference. The Tribunal agreed with Kafe that he had been racially harassed and awarded him $10,000. At his trial for writing a threatening letter, he was found guilty, but was released on his own recognizance if he underwent counselling. What the evidence suggests was that the pressure was so intense on Kafe that he suffered from a mental illness, even though his perception about the abuse he was receiving was concrete. The case may be extreme, but again, it may not. What it does illustrate is that racial taunts alienate and make people feel desperate. Ruggles and Rovenescu (1996) describe the following situation to demonstrate how perceived or real incidents of racism affect people on an individual basis by putting them in the position of analyzing situations in regards to racism:

After an exhausting day of sightseeing, I sat down at an outdoor restaurant in a well-to-do [area]. Instead of being approached by an eager waiter anxious to rattle off the specials of the day, I was rudely warned that unless I planned to order something, I was not to sit down. On what basis did he decide that I was not going to eat? As soon as my wife and children appeared from the washroom, his attitude changed dramatically. I wondered, is a black man with a family less suspect? (p. 90).

The internal tension creates anxiety, self-doubt and isolation so deep that many racial minorities desperately look for solace in separation or ways of anaesthetizing themselves. When listening to these types of stories or situations, a counsellor might remember that perception of how it is felt is far more important than wondering if it is imaged or real. The key to being effective is to sensitize oneself to how it feels to be belittled. Racism is often very subtle, but the results are just as damaging as overt racism. Consider the following research results: There are costs of racism that are immense for minorities. In a study of racial awareness preference with whites and African American children in 1947 (cited in Sue & Sue 1999), the researchers found African-American children preferred playing "...with a White doll over a Black one, the Black doll was perceived as being "bad," and approximately one-third, when asked to pick the doll that looked like them, picked the White one" (p. 99). In 1987, a group of researchers reported at the American Psychological Association that their results were similar to the 1947 study.

African Philosophy: The Basis of the African Canadian Worldview

Much has been written about worldviews of different peoples living in North America and how misunderstandings take place when people do not know how other's view the world. Worldview is based on philosophical perspectives and greater understanding can occur with a familiarity of African philosophy. Why would African philosophy be so important many years after the original ancestors of African-Canadians came to North America? According to Nobles (1972):

Its unique status is derived not from the negative aspects of being black in white [North America], but rather from the positive features of basic African philosophy which dictate the values, customs, attitudes and behavior of Africans in Africa and the New World (p. 18).

The following dimensions of African philosophy provide one with a sense of how people act, speak and think in their everyday lives. It is a collective unconsciousness that provides a framework for how people will behave in a systematic and natural manner. Behaviors are derived from all of these aspects of being "black." While there are ethnic and tribal differences among the people of Africa, as anywhere, there is also a communal quality that binds people because of their location (Cheboud, 2001).

Beliefs and Religion: One's humanness is based on being part of the whole, including one's community and the universe. Beliefs and acts are one and the same, thus to live is to be involved in a natural cycle of birth, death and revival (life after death is found in all African societies).

Unity: While god is the center of the universe, every living thing, including animals and humanity, are bound together. Each individual contains the universe within in a kind of collective force.

Time: The present and the past are always bound together, with the direction of the life system from the present to the past. Time always contains these two elements – past and present.

Death and Immortality: Life does not begin with birth, but in naming, puberty, initiation and marriage/ procreation. Immortality is present as long as the person is remembered, thus one lives as long as one is recognized. And procreation ensures one of being remembered.

Relationships: Survival of the family, clan or tribe is basic to all African people, which is dictated by the kinship with others. Kinship is not just vertical (grandparents, parents, child), but horizontal (aunts, uncles, cousins and everyone in the tribe). Finally, the individual is secondary to the family, clan and tribe.

Nigrescence Theory: Identity Development

According to Jenkins (1982) "...blacks reclaimed a proud sense of self as persons or individual self-esteem who are black [or have] pride in group identity" (p. 2) in the political struggles in the 1960s. They essentially moved from "adaptive inferiority," in which they presented a demeanor of humility and emulated whites to "black pride" and "black power." The development of African ethnic identity has its roots in a theory described by William Cross, Jr. in 1971 and revised in 1991 with the publication of his book *Shades of Black: Diversity in African American Identity* called "Nigrescence." Nigrescence is a French word that means the process of becoming Black in a cultural-psychological sense. The theory is designed to reveal the nuances of identity development that are unique to the experiences of people of African descent. The stages of Nigrescence have provided the foundation for thinking about Asian-American identity development, feminist identity development and gay-lesbian identity development. Nigrescence theory has been revised to capture "real-world" identity conflicts and ideological splits found among contemporary Black leaders (Vandiver, 2001). For example, rather than a model that suggests commonalties in the identity dynamics of all persons who reach Internalization, the revised Nigrescence model allows for the existence of ideological "splits"" at that stage or Afro-centric worldview versus a bicultural frame of reference.

One of the most influential theorists on identity development was Erikson (1968) who has influenced generations of psychologists and counsellors. Later, other theorists such as Phinney (1989) modified Erikson's original theory, which is still relevant in terms of understanding identity development of those from European ethnic backgrounds, while Cross' Nigrescence model is considered appropriate for African-Canadians and others. To get an idea of how Erikson's theory compares to Cross' Nigrescence theory see Appendix C (original and revised). The Nigrescence theory, while widely used in counselling, is not the only theory of identity development of those of African ethnic ancestry. Other theories include Baldwin's African self-consciousness, which is sometimes termed a Black Nationalist perspective (Vandiver, Fhagen-Smith, Cokley, Cross & Worrell, 2001).). The model presents four stages of development: pre-encounter, encounter, immersion-emersion and internalization.

Pre-Encounter: Some Black persons at this stage place low salience on Africianness or Blackness. Originally this stage indicated a pro-white and anti-black stance, however, the revised view is that this stage is characterized by assimilation or self-hatred. In assimilation there is "…a low salience for race but a strong reference group orientation centered on being an American" (Vandiver, Fhagen-Smith, Cokley, Cross & Worrell, 2001, p. 176). Self-hatred or possessing a negative self image as an African Canadian was dropped from the definition, although this may be present. Positive psychological functioning or self esteem issues are variables that are not necessarily a part of Nigrescence. Vandiver et al., (2001) go on to describe that those in the pre-encounter stage may have achieved a self image grounded in "mis-education" created by a racist school curriculum. It is possible that some will show signs as a result of "mis-education" of having internalized racist notions about Black people. As a result, they may develop low self-esteem and weak ego development. Both types may undergo Nigrescence once there is an increase of the salience of race in his or her life other than as a corrective to racial self-negativity.

Encounter: The event or events that lead a person to conclude that he or she needs to change in the direction of greater cultural awareness. This is a stage when lack of acceptance, self-examination or experiences of racism leads people to question who they are. It may also occur as one becomes introspective and looks for meaning in life.

Immersion – Emersion: This is the transition stage during which the old and emergent identities struggle for dominance (e.g., pro-black and anti-white). There are two aspects, intense Black involvement characterized by "…the excessive embracing of everything Black…[as]…the first step on the journey toward an internalized Black identity (Vandiver, et al., 2001, p. 177). There is positiveness on African heritage and great enthusiasm on all things African. However, on the other side, Vandiver, et al.,l (2001) stress that there is a price, which is "…rage, anxiety and guilt, emotions that are potentially destructive when uncontrolled…" (p. 177). Sometimes this rage is turned towards others in the pre-encounter stage. Vandiver et al,. go on to say that "anti-white attitudes are an inevitable consequence of immersing oneself in Blackness and becoming fully enamoured with Black people, culture and history" (p. 178).

Internalization: Persons at this stage show high salience for race and culture, however they cluster into divergent ideological camps. Persons in the internalization stage can be expected to have higher self-esteem and healthier ego identity development than persons at Pre-Encounter who show signs of internalized racism. However no differences can be expected with persons at Pre-Encounter who exhibit low race salience but little evidence of internalized racism. The key factors influencing Nigrescence are:

– Individual Differences such as social identity, education level, occupation, sexual orientation and religious affiliation, etc.

– Situational Factors that define a person's context such as family structure, socio-economic status, neighborhood quality and dynamics. In some contexts affiliation with Blackness may be appropriate for optimal psychological functioning. The context in which a person finds him or herself seems to be the explanatory or moderating variable.

The primary shift in this stage is one of identification with reference groups and the development of one of three independent ideological orientations: Black Nationalism (e.g., Black Empowerment, economic independence and heightened awareness of Black history and culture), Biculturalism (identify as being equally both Black and Canadian) and Multiculturalism (acceptance of being Black, but identifying with at least two other characteristics in equal fashion). There is a range of how individuals internalize themselves in relationship with members of other ethnic groups. In addition, there is an uncoupling of self-acceptance and mental health. In other words, healthy psychological function does not hinge on acceptance of "blackness."

Counselling Implications

According to Thomas (1998) for those of African ethnic descent, "the transmission of values occurs through racial socialization within the family" (p. 7). Family not only helps socialize children, but provides them with a strong sense of self in a hostile racial climate. Therefore, the family should be utilized as a resource in counselling. Also, since churches have not only provided a sense of community, but is an institution that has protected and advocated for African Canadians, it too is a valuable resource for the counsellor (Wilmore, 1978). Finally, to be effective and culturally competent, counsellors need to keep the following in mind when counselling African Canadians:

– Avoid presumptions about level of adjustment being tied to one's identity being centered on race;

– Be aware of how context can effect healthy Black adjustment;

– Attempt to understand the client's frames of reference; and

– Base social and other interventions on a multidimensional model of Black psychological functioning

Counselling African-Canadians: Barriers and Challenges

For counsellors to be successful, they need to consider a set of four factors that mediate a presenting problem for African-Canadians. These factors are:

– Reactions to racial oppression;

– Influence of majority culture;

– Influence of Afro-American culture; and

– Personal experiences and endowments.

For a counsellor, particularly those who are not from the African-Canadian community, the acceptance that racism is a part of the client's experience is crucial. While the client may not have experienced racism first hand, he or she needs to be aware of the history of slavery and other violent acts that others experienced. The feeling of oppression manifests itself as a sense of powerlessness, the loss of dignity and the deprivation of human rights. Psychologically, it brings about a sense of helplessness, depression, anxiety and a host of other behaviors that dis-empower a person. Atkinson, Morten and Sue (1993) describe the following examples of types of oppression that many minorities experience: "...include under representation in the 1990 census, sub-minimum wages paid to undocumented workers, the racial/ethnic slurs that permeate written and oral communication and physical attacks upon individuals by racist perpetrators" (p. 12). In addition, the unquestioning acceptance of "black consciousness" reinforces the counsellor's understanding of the struggles that have been made. Recognizing the reality of the situation is important, because pretending to be "color blind" or using a paternal approach in regards to racial background verges on racism. The eloquence of this idea is reinforced with Shanee Livingston's poem:

Stuggle for equality

Racial unrest.

They're trying to kill an idea...

Black consciousness (in Miller, Steinlage & Prinz, 1994, p. 47).

African-Canadians have had to develop a protective mechanism to help them survive in a climate of racial discrimination. These mechanisms are: being guarded, "sizing up" and challenging. These and other mechanisms help keep those who experience racism in a state of defensive balance that maintains sanity. Therefore, not becoming defensive or being put off by these not only helps the counsellor build a "bridge" for communication, but demonstrates that these mechanism are positive qualities. Once the "bridge" is built, the defences are no longer necessary. The qualities that can help counsellors overcome these mechanisms include being patient, natural and straightforward. Obviously, spending time on creating a climate of trust is paramount. Building trust includes not only taking a risk in giving and sharing, but being accepting, cooperative, open, non-judgemental and supportive with others. In essence, being human.

The pressures of racism are enormous and affect psychological levels of functioning, however, African Canadians, just like anyone else in society, face all the human problems that bring about issues in well-being . Racism is a factor of life, but living in society brings about the same problems of relationship, family, self-esteem and so on. According to Wilson and Stith (1993) there are proactive strategies that counsellors, particularly non-African-Canadian counsellors, can utilize to make themselves more sensitive and more effective:

1. Become aware of the historical and current experiences of being Black.

2. Consider value and cultural differences between Blacks and other ethnic groups and how your own personal values influence the way you conduct therapy.

3. Consider the way your personal values influence the way you view both the presenting problem and the goals for therapy.

4. Include the value system of the client in the goal-setting process.

5. Be sensitive to variations in Black family norms due to normal adaptations to stress and be flexible enough to accept these variations.

6. Be aware of how ineffective verbal and nonverbal communication due to cultural variation in communication can lead to premature termination of therapy. Become familiar with non-standard or Black English and accept its use by clients.

7. Consider the client's problem in the large context. Include the extended family, other significant individuals and larger systems in your thinking, if not in the therapy session.

8. Be aware of your client's racial identification and do not feel threatened by your client's cultural identification with his or her own race.

9. Learn to acknowledge and to be comfortable with your client's cultural differences.

10. Consider the appropriateness of specific therapeutic models or interventions to specific Black families. Do not apply interventions without considering unique aspects of each family.

11. Consider each Black family and each Black family member you treat as unique. Do not generaize the finds of any study or group of studies on Black families to all Black clients. Use the studies to help you find your way, not to categorize individuals.

Conclusion

According to Walcott (1997) the African Canadian identity is "…syncretic, always in revision and in a process of becoming [because] it is constituted from multiple histories of uprootedness, migration, exchanges and political acts of defiance and self-(re)definition" (pp. 120-121). In other words, the ending of segregation laws and the implementation of multicultural policies does not necessarily change people's attitudes about race. Much has been made about the changes one sees in the media, with athletes and movies, in very visible places, yet according to Castles (2000):

Racism continues. Distinctions between whites and blacks in income, occupational status, unemployment rates, social conditions and education are still extreme. Racial violence and harassment remain serious problems…the increasing complexity of inter-ethnic relations is leading to new types of conflict and to a politicization of issues of culture and ethnicity. The Los Angeles riots of 1992 were indicative of such trends (pp. 178-179).

Perhaps racism is part of the human condition? However that may be, counsellors will be faced with those traumatized by racism as they try and "bridge" the "color" gap. The research on whether clients are affected by the race or ethnic background of the counsellor are mixed. Many feel that those of European ethnic backgrounds cannot counsel those of African ethnic background. In fact, research indicates that African-Americans prefer some-one who is similar to them (Pederson, Draguns, Lonner & Trimble, 2002). Where one is sit-uated on racial identity stages of development affects one's ability to be sensitive to others. Yet, counsellor competency and style remain important variables in counselling across cul-tures. To match client and counsellor background is a form of stereotyping, with some minority clients resenting it. Even in the best of circumstances those of African descent drop out of counselling more often than those of European heritage (Jenkins, 1982; Pederson, et al., 1996; Aponte & Wohl, 2000).

One of the keys to successfully counselling African Canadians is a thorough understand-ing of identity and how individuals identify themselves. Identity remains a complex and a situational phenomenon that needs more research. The interpretation of '*self*' or one's iden-tity in general seems to be dependent of the degree to which an individual feels connected, the degree he or she relates, feels balanced and is able to transcend racism. These compo-nents help the person to acknowledge the process, where one is involved to design, construct and finally claim a positive sense of identity. Therefore, the development or the transforma-tion of 'self' within the process leads to a broader and specific definition of one's identity. This activity in fact is a process of knowing and restructuring. At the same time, the process helps evaluate the individual's relationship between 'self' and the others, 'self' and society and 'self' and the world. It is important to realize that the notion of identity avoids two extreme theoretical positions: it does not presuppose that one steps into the world a full-blown personal self and only then starts choosing an identity as if from a supermarket shelf. Nor does it presuppose that identity is simply bestowed by fate and that one can merely respond either by being faithful or unfaithful to that destined identity.

According to McRae, Thompson and Cooper (1999), spirituality has been an important element for African-Canadians in that "it is transformative in providing insights and leads to positive behaviors, [but more importantly] it is rejuvenating ... creating hope, faith and love ..." (p. 213). The ability of people to withstand generations of genocidal actions on the North American continent attests to the strength of people of African heritage. The seg-ments of society that have been the most influential and supportive to African Canadians has been the community church. Not only has the church been a place where people could come together as a spiritual community, but a source for political and social action. It was the leaders of the church that lead the civil rights movement in Canada and the United States. People such as Martin Luther King, Jr. (cited in Siccone, 1998) who said:

> *It really boils down to this: that all life is interrelated. We are all caught in an inescapable network of mutuality, tied into a single garment of destiny. Whatever affects one directly, affects all indirectly (p. 91).*

References

Atkinson, D., Morten, G. & Sue, D.W. (1993). *Counseling American Minorities: A Cross-Cultural Perspective*, 4th Edition. Madison, WI: Brown & Benchmark.

Aponte, J. & Wohl, J. (2000). *Psychological Intervention and Cultural Diversity*. Boston, MA: Allyn & Bacon.

Castles, S. (2000). The Racisms of Globalization [on-line]. Retrieved February 2002 from htttp://www.allenandunwin.com/academic/teeth2.polf.

Cheboud, E. (2001). A heuristic study of Ethiopian immigrants in Canada, an unpublished Ph.D. dissertation, Victoria, BC: University of Victoria.

Cross, W. (1991). *Shades of Black: Diversity in African American Identity*. Philadelphis: Temple University Press.

Erikson, E. (1968). *Identity: Youth in Crisis*. New York: Norton.

Jenkins, A. (1982). *The Psychology of the Afro-American: A Humanistic Approach*. New York: Pergamon General.

Martin, Y. & Warburton, R. (1998). Voices for change: Racism, ethnocentrism and cultural insensitivity at the University of Victoria. A report submitted to David Strong, President of the University of Victoria, Victoria, BC.

McRae, M., Thompson, D., & Cooper, S. (1999). Black Churches as Therapeutic Groups, *Journal of Multicultural Counseling, 27(4)*, pp. 207-209.

Miller, L., Steinlage, T. & Prinz, M. (1994). *Cultural Cobblestones: Teaching Cultural Diversity*. London: Scarecrow Press.

Nobles, W. (1972). African philosophy: Foundations for Black psychology, In R. Jones' *Black psychology*, New York: Harper & Row.

Pedersen, P., Draguns, J., Lonner, W., & Trimble, J. (2002). Counseling Across Cultures. Thousand Oaks, CA: Sage Publications.

Phinney, J. (1989). Stages of ethnic identity in minority group adolescents. *Journal of Early Adolescents, 9*, 34-49.

Ridley, C. & Lingle, D. (1993). Cultural empathy in multicultural counselling: A multidimensional process model. In P. Pederson, J. Draguns, W. Lonner & J. Trible (editors), *Counseling Across Cultures*, 4th Edition, Thousand Oaks, CA: Sage.

Ruggles, C. (1996). In the way of introduction. In C. Ruggles & O. Rovenescu, *Outsider Blues: A Voice from the Shadows*. Halifax, NS: Fernwood Publishing.

Ruggles, C. & Roversescu,, O. (1996). *Outsider Blues: A Voice from the Shadows.* Halifax, NS: Fernwood Publishing.

Siccone, F. (1998). *Celebrating Diversity.* Boston, MA: Allyn and Bacon.

Sue, D.W. & Sue, D. (1990). *Counseling the Culturally Different.* New York: John Wiley.

Statistics Canada. (2001). *Population by Visible Minority.* Ottawa, ON: Government of Canada.

Thomas, A.J. (1998). Understanding culture and worldview in family systems: The use of the multicultural genogram. *Family Journal*, Vol. 6(1), 1-19.

Times-Colonist. "Lastman hurts Toronto's Olympic hope," p. A1, Victoria, BC.

Vandiver, B. (2001). Psychological Nigrescence Revisted: Introduction and Overview. *Journal of Multicultural Counseling and Development*, Vol. 29(3), 165-173.

Vandiver, B., Fhagen-Smith, P., Cokley, K., Cross, W. & Worrell, F. (2001). Cross's Nigrescence Model: From theory to scale to theory. *Journal of Multicultural Counseling and Development*, Vol. 29(3), 174-199.

Walcott, R. (1997). *Black Like Who?* Toronto, ON: Insomniac Press.

Wilmore, G. (1978). The gifts and tasks of the black church. In V. D'Oyley, *Black Presence in Multiethnic Canada.* Toronto, ON: UBC & OISE.

Wilson, L.L. & Stith, S.M. (1993). Culturally sensitive therapy with black clients. In D. Atkinson, G. Morten & D. W. Sue, *Counseling American Minorities: A Cross-Cultural Perspective*, 4th Edition, Madison, WI: Brown & Benchmark.

Chapter 13

Counselling the Muslim Client: Identity, Religion and Ethnicity in Canada

Abdullahi Barise and M. Honoré France

The people who call themselves Muslims are not just people originally from Arab countries, but people who represent more than 60 different ethnic groups that include: African-Americans, Europeans, Hispanics, South Asians, African immigrants and even aboriginal people. Muslims of Canada have originally come from a variety of countries including Algeria, Bosnia, China, Egypt, Iran, India, Pakistan, Lebanon, Syria, Somalia and Turkey, but also Muslim peoples from France, Germany and the UK, just to name a few. The list is endless, but it is not just people who have immigrated to Canada who are Muslims, but many native born peoples from a variety of ethnic groups that represent a "rainbow coalition" of peoples. The September 11th terrorist attacks have put renewed light on Muslims in the world and particularly in North America, where some regard them as potential terrorists or people who are so different that there is no possibility that their Islamic faith can be reconciled with the Canadian mosaic. Some publications have suggested that being a Muslim makes one a terrorist suspect (*Time Magazine*, September 30, 2002). But who are Muslims? Who are Muslims and what do they believe and value? Is there a difference across immigrant groups? Despite the recent political events and increased immigration from Muslim countries, Islam is one of the fastest growing religions of native-born peoples of North America. Thus, it is not only the fastest growing religion in the world, but quite profoundly one of the most multicultural religious groups in Canada. What does Islam mean in terms of what a person values? Islam is not just a religious belief or path, but it provides a framework of morality and righteous behavior that is embedded not only in Islamic faith, but is also shared with Judaism and Christianity. According to Sayyid Syeed, the secretary general of the Islamic Society of North America, which is an umbrella organization for Islamic groups throughout the U.S. and Canada, the variety of people of Muslim beliefs face the challenge of the political consequence of governmental policy and their lives as Americans and Canadians. Syeed suggests that:

Islam is Canada's fastest-growing religion and in this year's census, it is expected to surge well past Judaism and be recognized as Canada's second-largest religious group. Even in the 1991

175

census, there were more Muslims than Jews in Alberta and ten of Canada's 25 metropolitan cities (National Post, *September 14, 2002, p. A12*).

Who are the Muslims in Canada and what are their numbers? According to Dawood Hassan Hamdani, an Ottawa economist who has analyzed Muslim immigration and birth rates, the number of Muslims in Canada has more than doubled, from 293 000 in 1991 to 650 000 now. Furthermore, Toronto alone has at least 16 Muslim schools. In short, Muslims are a significant factor in Canadian society.

Islamic Worldview

The word Islam comes from the Arabic salaam that means peace, yet a subtle projection of the word also means submission. When examining Islam as a religion, this second meaning, submission, becomes quite powerful. In other words, to become a good Muslim, one must submit to the will of God; thus religion shapes how one views the world and lives one's life. Farid Esack's book, *On being a Muslim* is very revealing on this point in terms of the role that religion plays in life as a South African Muslim living in Germany. Esack (1999) wrote that:

> …*a number of factors made me carry my 'Islam', my submission to Allah's will in my hand just about every day, factors which regularly threatened to have it fall to the ground, melting into nothingness like snowflakes… we are inexorably tied to each other from the day known as yawmi alast; the day when our souls faced our Lord and we were asked: 'Alastu bi rabbikum (Am I not your Lord?) We said: 'Bala" (Indeed)!…I cannot smother it…I know that my humanness and my Islam depend on how hard I try to discern its message and to live alongside it (p. 59).*

The Muslim consciously submits to the will of God and subsequently gains internal and external harmony, synchronicity and peace. Internal peace refers to one's psychological well-being due to lack of conflict within the self, while external peace stems from the harmonious and loving relationship with God and the environment.

In Islamic cosmology, all creatures exist in compliance with God's will. All creatures, from the tiny atoms to the mighty galaxies, worship God and thus co-exist harmoniously according to God's will. When one accepts Islam, one becomes part of this harmonious co-existence *willingly*. Being a Muslim thus necessitates revolving around God on an assigned course (just like the electrons and celestial bodies do) without transgressing boundaries and infringing on the rights of the self, the environment, and God. Through this pious life the Muslim strives for an all-encompassing peace which is a fundamental concept in Islam. The term *Muslim* means peaceful in Arabic. One of God's names is *Assalaam* which means peace. Both Muslims' greetings and the concluding words of Muslims' daily prayers are *Assalaamu aleikum* which mean 'peace be upon you.' Heaven in Islam is called *Darussalaam* which means the abode of peace (Barise, in Turner, Cheboud, Elvira & Barise, 2002).

There is no separation of religion and politics as is the custom in Canada and the West. It doesn't seem strange that religious leaders, Imams, would be involved in politics or run a government, such as in Iran, or the educational system, as the Wadis do in Saudi Arabia. All schools, following the Islamic tradition, see the study of the Qur'an (Koran) as essential not only to being a good person, but also in being educated. Consider that in Egypt, the largest university, "...Al Azhar, has 350,000 students, 100,000, women and all can recite the Koran [with 114 chapters & 666 verses]" (*National Post*, September 9, 2002, p. A12). Thus the reciting of and reflecting upon the Koran is not only a basis for knowing about God, but of learning good judgment and moral development. In fact, at least one third of the verses of the Qur'an encourage learning or thinking in one way or another (Barise, 1999).

According to Rashid (in Altareb, 1996) there are seven elements that form Islamic worldview. It should be understood that because the roots of Islam are bound up in the Arabic language and the holy places are in Arabic lands, it is difficult to separate Arabic culture from the practice of Islam. In the same way that it would be difficult in Christianity to separate the historical foundations of the Christian faith with the life of Jesus. Understanding the enormous part that Islam plays in the identity of believers goes a long way in working successfully with clients who are shaped by the Islamic worldview. The Islamic worldview consists of the following seven elements:

- Humankind is innately good;
- Morality is absolute;
- The unitary belief in one God (in Arabic Allah);
- One lives in a community of the faithful;
- Women are the source of civilization;
- God (Allah) is the center of the world, thus of human life and thought;
- All wisdom comes from Allah and peace can only be achieved by submission to Allah.

As the central force in life, the spiritual focus of Muslims dominates actions, including what one thinks, feels and how life is conducted. With Islam as the center of life, all actions have the aim of fostering God-consciousness or *taqwa* and becoming closer to Allah. Thus every action, including dress, dietary habits, rearing of children, home life, evolves around the teachings of Islam. There are five pillars that regulate how one lives. These five pillars help the Muslim to become a spiritual whole and develop a good and moral existence.

Declaration of faith (*shahadah*): This is the belief that must be avowed, "that there is no god but Allah and Mohammed is the prophet of Allah";

Prayers (*Salat*): The rituals of prayer is to be performed five times a day facing the Holy Ka-abah in Makkah (Mecca);

Charity (*Zakat*): All Muslims are required to pay a fixed amount of their possessions for the welfare of the whole community and in particular the poor;

Fasting (*Siyam*): During the ninth month of the Islamic calendar, Ramadhan, all Muslims must abstain from all food, drink and sexual activity from dawn to sunset;

Pilgrimage to Mecca (*Hajj*): At least once in life, all Muslims are to make a journey to Makkah (birthplace of the Prophet) during the closing month of the Islamic year, Dhul Hijah.

Islamic Beliefs that Transcend Culture

"Since Sept. 11, Muslims feel that in the minds of the West, devoutness and regular attendance at the mosque implies fundamentalism and a penchant for violence" (*National Post*, September 14, 2002, B6). There is no relationship between being religious and being extremist. A religious person, by obvious intent, is a person of the book, whether it is the Koran, the Bible or the Torah. That is not to say that there are intolerant people in all religions, but because of politics, beliefs about people or attitudes are hard to erase. Because of the nature of what people have experienced in the world, Muslims in Canada, regardless of where they are from, will probably experience some of the following problems (Abudabbeh & Nydell, 1999):

Stress: Either stemming from cultural shock to experiences from the events associated with the Arab-Israeli conflict;

Family: The family is the basic foundation of the individual and thus needs to be "front and center" in counselling;

Dependence: Regardless of the children's age, they are always dependent on the parents and thus counsellors need to adjust their procedures to incorporate this cultural value.

Values: Some values such as roles of women, divulging one's private life and how parents and children are to behave are very different than in mainstream Canadian society (e.g., even those who are born in Canada may adopt the Islamic values);

Islamic ideas of behavior can be incorporated into counselling objectives, thus insuring that clients do not have to reject their cultural ways of thinking and being.

A Muslim is required to believe in and revere all prophets of God from Adam to Mohammed without discrimination. Noah, Abraham, Moses, Jesus and Mohammed are revered by Muslims as the greatest prophets of God. In describing his position in relation to this chain of prophets that God sent at different times in history, Prophet Mohammed says (the *Authentic Book of Bukhari*, Vol. 4, Book 56, no. 735 p. 45, 1999).

My similitude in comparison with the other prophets before me, is that of a man who has built a house nicely and beautifully, except for a place of one brick in a corner. The people go about it and wonder at its beauty, but say: 'Would that brick be put in its place!' So I am that brick and I am the last of the Prophets.

Muslims also believe in all the revealed scriptures. They believe in the original Torah given to Moses to guide the Jews. In addition, Muslims believe in the original New Testament that God revealed to Jesus. Islam is a continuation of the pure teachings of these great prophets. However, it was Mohammed, in the 7th century, that received that last message of God in terms of the Koran that guides all Muslims today. Muslims believe that God revealed the Koran to the prophet, Mohammed, and it is not a work by many different men, which is the case with the present-day Torah and the Bible.

Norms and Values of Muslims

In many ways, the values of Muslims are similar to others in Canada yet, some values predominate. Consider this quote from a recent *Time* magazine (September 9, 2002): "I watched Oprah the other day. She was talking to pregnant 13-year old girls who were unmarried. I am glad I don't have those complications in my life" (p. 53). With strict views about chastity and remaining pure, Islamic views can come into conflict with Western ways of life. Alcohol and all other intoxicants are strictly forbidden in the Koran. In many traditional Islamic societies, as they exist in Kuwait or Saudi Arabia, the sale of alcohol is strictly forbidden, while in other Muslim countries only foreigners and non-Muslims can buy it with a special permit. The following are some Islamic values that exist in many Muslim traditions around the world:

1. Children and marriage are essential for happiness;

2. The man is considered head of the family, with the authority to direct and protect the family[1];

3. Mothers are three times more deserving of their children's good treatment as compared to fathers;

4. Respect is given to older generations and siblings, thus everyone in the extended family is valued;

5. Children should not only take care of older members of the family, but also show respect to everyone in the extended family (widowhood is especially important);

6. Women have a greater responsibility to the family and their behavior can easily damage the family, thus their honorable behavior is important;

7. The family has more importance than the individual, including the career aspirations of individual members;

8.   The belief in Islam is particularly valued above all other ideas.

The Family, Gender and Marriage

Americans talk about protecting women's rights. But have you seen that George Michael video where he has these woman with leashes, likes dogs? Give me the burqa any day (Time Magazine, *September 9, 2002, p. 93*).

There is much debate in the West about how women are regarded in Islam and Muslim countries. Sometimes the reality gets lost in the cultural maze of traditions and values. It is clear that for many Muslims, the West is morally corrupt, where drugs, teenage pregnancy, incest, alcoholism and the family breakup are rampant. For many in Islamic countries, the relationship between the genders in the West seems to have not only undermined the family, but also has contributed to the decline of social moral values. No doubt the debate cannot be resolved as to whether separating God from the schools or the state leads to moral corruption. Muslim societies are presently in a state of transition, where the modern influences, traditional values and Islamic values are competing for supremacy. Islamic teachings encourage dynamic interactions and mutual learning between nations. According to many historians of science and philosophy, when correctly interpreted and implemented, Islam has an in-built great power in not only absorbing every form of human progress but spearheading it (see Hitti, 1970). The Western Renaissance was greatly influenced by Islamic scholars who not only assimilated the positive aspects of Greek and Persian civilizations, but also formed their own distinctive thinking in science and philosophy. Many talk about the Judeo-Christian-Islamic heritage of the West. However, Menocal (1987) argues "Westerners – Europeans – have great difficulty in considering the possibility that they are in some way seriously indebted to the Arab [Islamic] world, or that the Arabs [Muslims] were central to the making of medieval Europe" (p. xiii). Presently, most Islamic societies are in the developing world where high illiteracy still persists. There are secular Muslim states such as Turkey that claim to have created an egalitarian gender society. However, many believe that Turkey falls short of both Islamic principles and Western democratic principles when it comes to respecting women's basic human rights. For example, a Turkish woman wearing a headscarf is not allowed to attend a university or hold a government office.[2] There are Muslim countries that have separate, but equal schools for men and women; yet, just as in the West, gender inequity is an issue. What is clear for counsellors is that for many with an Islamic identity, the teachings of the Koran, as they see them, affect their belief about the primacy of the family and how gender relations in and outside of marriage are practiced. In the Koran, it is very clear, women have all the rights that men do "And women shall have rights similar to the rights against them, according to what is equitable" (Koran, 1989, Chapter 2, Verse 228). However, just as it was historically in the West, women were treated differently. In law, in most Muslim countries, women have the same rights that men do, but here is where the controversy lies. The idea is not that men and women are the same, but that they are different because of their sex, thus treated differently. Yet, they are still equal in the sight of God. According to Safaa El Meneza, professor of pediatrics at Al Azhar, Islam does not make women suffer "…it's true that in some Muslim countries the cultural tradition is for a man to try to control and dominate their wives, but that has nothing to do with Islam. Islam actually preserves women's rights" (*National Post*, 2002, p. 12).

Not all women in Islamic societies agree that they are equal to men. Javed (1994) suggests that in some Islamic societies "…the concept of hijab (a dress that is from head to toe covering) is used as one of the strategies for coercing women to live an imposed identity rooted in misogynistic assumptions" (p. 58). However, the use of the hijab or even the burqa (completely covering including the face and hands) is seen by many Muslim women as a garment that made them feel more free. These women believe that the hijab makes the people they are interacting with focus on their intelligence rather than on their body. Here is another explanation of why a woman has chosen to wear the hijab:

> …*because that was how the West had made me feel. I was put on the defensive by the assumptions of the Western media that we were the guilty parties and I wanted to show that I was proud of Islam"* (Time Magazine, September 9, 2002, p. 36).

Clearly, Islam teaches that men and especially women, should dress and act in a modest manner. It is evident in the Koran that Islam has freed women from the former practice of female infanticide, given inheritance rights long before Christian women had them and brought about financial and social supports. On the other hand, growing extremism at times reinforces cultural mandates in regards to gender (e.g., the Taliban in Afghanistan). Interestingly, Javed (1994) emphasizes that women's roles have always been subservient in the past or the present. For example, Muslim women need to remember that there have been three (female?) heads of state in Muslim countries in recent years (e.g., Bangladesh, Pakistan and Turkey). She advocates that the women's movement, to retrieve gender egalitarianism, can come from increasing levels of literacy in which women become aware of narratives that "…celebrate women's power and accomplishments in the public domain [in Muslim countries]" (p. 67).

Counselling Muslims

Only recently have people with Islamic backgrounds been given consideration as being distinct and different. In part, it is because of recent political events such as the Gulf War, the terrorist attack in New York City, the Israeli and Palestinian conflict and the American-Iraqi war. People with an Islamic background have either been grouped according to culture, country of origin or as international students. The fact is that, as the fastest growing religion in Canada, counsellors need to have a greater awareness of how Islamic identity influences individuals living in Canada.

Mental Health Issues

According to Abudabbeh and Nydel (1999) and our own investigation, the most frequent issues concerning Muslims are:

1. Blaming all Muslims for the events of "9-11" or the breakdown in the Israeli and Palestinian dispute;

2. Discrimination and racism for being Muslim;

3. Differences between generational values (first and second generations);

4. Differing parenting styles of strict religious and secular values;

5. Physical abuse;

6. Gender cultural differences such as assertiveness or agoraphobia (especially among women unaccustomed to going out alone);

7. Identity confusion;

8. Differing social and economic status among immigrants;

9. Loss of extended network of family support.

Communication Style

A counsellor who has competent multicultural therapy skills needs to be sensitive to cultural differences and have a strong personal identity. The work of Abudabbeh and Nydell (1999) focused on questions that counsellors need to address in counselling Arab-Americans, but it also has relevancy to all those of Islamic background. Consider the following issues:

Recognizing the difference between direct and indirect communication: A counsellor needs to know that sharing of feelings on certain issues relating to the family are not given directly, but with subtle clues in an indirect fashion;

Becoming sensitive to non-verbal cues: Various gestures, such as eye contact, may suggest that what is being said in the session is difficult, thus the eyes may be diverted;

Awareness of differing Islamic cultural and linguistic groups: Generally people of Arab extraction speak directly or even aggressively on an issue, while Bangladeshis speak more softly and indirectly about a concern;

Understanding basic Islamic values and how they impact counselling: The family is of central importance and elders are held in high esteem not only for their age and experience, but also because they are thought of as sources of wisdom and Islam is seen not just as a religion, but also as a way of life;

Knowing how social and political events affect and perpetuate stereotypes that Canadians hold about Muslims and conversely, identify the common stereotypes of majority Canadians by Muslims: The events, particularly around the "9-11" attacks, make Muslim people vulnerable to racism and discrimination, thus creating a sense of personal mistrust and self doubt;

Recognizing personal biases about Islam and Muslims: Differing ways of thinking and believing evoke misunderstanding, thus, issues like a strong belief in Islam doesn't equate with anti-western feelings.

Interacting with various people of Islamic backgrounds can be perceived by some as challenging, yet people of Arab or Somali ethnic groups, just to name two ethnic groups in Canada, are very open and welcoming to all people regardless of ethnic or religious backgrounds. The demonstration of friendliness is inherent in the culture and religion. For example, a frenzied handshake becomes very important, for it is not only a greeting, but also a way of allowing, "…guilt to slip away through the hands, for any hostile or revengeful feelings evaporates when you greet people in that way" (National Post, 2002, p. 23). Consider that many people with Islamic backgrounds, such as Arabs, tend to use euphemisms when sharing feelings or even facts about their family in regards to illness, death or any bad event. For example, Abudabbeh and Nydell (1999), provide the following example:

They often say that someone is tired when the person is sick ("He's in the hospital because he's a little tired), hesitate to state that someone is growing worse or dying and hesitate to predict or even discuss bad events. Such events can be discussed more comfortably, however with appropriate benedictions such as "May he/she soon be better or "God willing, may this never happen" (pp. 274-275).

Implications for Counselling

Counsellors need to know that, although mutual helping is a central value in Islam, many Muslims might be unfamiliar with professional counselling as practiced in Canada. From the Islamic point of view, God is the ultimate source of help, although this help comes through the environment, including humans. Reliance on God and on oneself is expected in Islam. However, if there is a need, seeking help from others is encouraged to the extent that the help seeker would see helpers as means only and God as the ultimate help-provider. Practicing Muslims pray to God "we worship You and we seek help from You" at least 17 times every day.

The challenges for counsellors working with clients who are Muslims are very complex because the diversity within the Islamic society is so great. In addition, there are many factors within these differences that can shape intervention. However, for counsellors to be successful with the Muslim client, they first need to be aware of their own personal stereotypes about Islam. With all of the turmoil in the Middle East, the growth of worldwide terrorism not only from the Arab-Israeli conflict, but its impact on the West, particularly after the attacks in New York City on September 11th, 2001, openness to diversity is of primary importance. Interestingly in recent years the issues around working with Islamic identity, even in the multicultural counselling literature, there is little information despite the Islamic presence in North America going back to the growth of Islam among African-Americans and the rise of immigration to Canada from the Islamic world. It is not surprising that not only is the average Canadian unfamiliar with Islam, but also that they may have a negative view of the Muslim world. Research on prejudicial relations found that values:

> *...especially those favoring both openness to change and self-transcendence – improve the willingness of persons who hold these values to be open to inter-group contacts of the sort that might reduce prejudicial relations. In contrast, those who favor values of conservation are less interested in having these contacts with differences (Sampson, 1998, pp. 102-103).*

Along with the diversity that exists within Muslim clients, counsellors need to address different circumstances of those who immigrated versus those Muslims born in Canada. For immigrants, levels of acculturation need to be ascertained along with levels of religiousness, including the particular sect that clients belong to. The process of acculturation brings clients more in-line with values that are consistent with values of the Canadian majority. The lesser the acculturation, the greater the differences; thus, clients who recently immigrated reflect traditions and values of their 'home countries." Because of the central place that religion has for Muslim clients, the degree of religiosity will affect not only what clients want to focus on, but also how counsellors can prescribe treatment. Obviously, the acceptance and working within Islamic religious values will help counsellors' work more effectively with their clients. For the multicultural counsellor, this cannot be over emphasized. More importantly, using religious values to solve problems will greatly enhance the ability of counsellors to work for solutions. That means becoming acquainted with the Islamic viewpoint on issues of importance. Many in the Canadian Islamic community are in a double bind; while they support Arab and other Islamic causes, which may not be popular in the larger society, they also feel love for the Canadian state. In a world in which people are often forced to take sides, being a devout Muslim is very difficult.

As a result, three of the most important issues facing Muslims are discrimination, racism and lack of acceptance of Islamic ideas and views. Along with these is the perennial problem of color against visible minorities. The turmoil in the Middle East exacerbates these problems. In addition, clients may be under stress because of what is happening to their families in their country of origin. Traumatic events, particularly for refugees, such as those from Kosovo, contribute to a sense of alienation and isolation. Therefore, it may be helpful to incorporate or consult with Imams (religious leaders), Muslim organizations and/or individuals during the counselling process. Religious and community leaders are greatly respected in the Islamic community and their help and support can go along way not only in helping clients solve their problems, but can help bring extended support after clients leave counselling. In addition, Imams can enlighten counsellors on basic Islamic worldviews and values. Traditionally, the Mosque has always been open to outsiders, regardless of religious background, as has the adaptability over the years of Islam.

Finally, it is vital that counsellors be able to separate cultural issues from spiritual or Islamic issues. Sometimes these seem so intertwined that it is a challenge to separate one from the other. For example, Altareb (1996) provides the example of a Muslim woman client who is "...struggling with the desire to work outside the home...because such a practice was not supported within their native culture" (p. 36). The Koran never prohibited such a practice, but yet religious reasons are sometimes more cultural in origin. The challenge is to help reconcile the reality of Canadian society, with cultural norms of the previous way of life. In addition, issues of gender equality are often misunderstood as being religious in nature, rather than culturally derived. One way of reconciling this issue can be addressed through the stories of early historical Muslim women. Altareb (1996) goes on to suggest to counsellors working with Muslim women raising their children alone "...that what they do for their children or families can be considered acts of worship" (p. 36). Counsellors should also broaden their perspectives in regards to counselling practices that are only Euro-centric. For example, there are a number of Sufi meditation strategies derived from Islamic traditions such as:

1. *zekr*, a contemplation on the 99 names or attributes of God;

2. *takhliya*, a meditation aimed at obviating one's moral weaknesses;

3. *tahliya*, a meditation designed to strengthen one's virtues so that vices become weak and ultimately die (Sheikh, Kunzendorf & Sheikh, 1989, p. 477).

Conclusion

The collapse of the Soviet Union and the demise of the cold war have led some analysts to debate whether the next arena of global confrontation would be between the Islam and West. This argument, however, is profoundly flawed as Islam is deeply divided...(Samad, 1996, p. 90).

All of the literature in regards to working with Muslims shares some general themes. First, a distinction needs to be made between religious Muslims and non-religious Muslims, between the various foreign countries that people immigrated from or whether individuals are native born and the level of acculturation in Canada. Cultural differences vary widely (e.g., Saudi Arabia vs. Bosnia) as does religious affiliation (e.g., Sunni vs. Shi'a). However, the Islamic faith has general principles and customs that transcend cultures and religious affiliations. According to Abed al Jabri (1994):

...No matter what framework is being considered, be it religious, nationalistic, liberal or left-

*ist, each one possesses a "known" (*shahid*) over which it will trace an "unknown" (*gha'ib*). The unknown is the case of the future as it is conceived or dreamed of by the adherents to these schools. The known is the first part to the double question that they all ask (e.g., for the fundamentalist movement)... (p. 17).*

Working within the Islamic identity does not mean that counselling methods that are used with other multicultural groups will not work. Clearly, any counselling strategy that brings about a solution and reinforces clients' Islamic values will be helpful in solving personal issues that affect clients. The strength of the Islamic identity lies in how the values that are inherent in the Koran guide everyday interaction, but that does not imply that there will be no problem. Problems coming from within, such as depression or low self-esteem, or external problems such as marital discord, discrimination and unemployment need to be addressed with solutions and strategies that will help bring resolution. Counsellors who work with a multicultural flavor are much more likely to succeed within the Islamic framework, than outside it. Javed (1994) emphasizes that women's empowerment lies in:

Literacy modes that facilitate a desire for rearming [and] must include storytelling as a major technique. Storytelling can be done in several ways including popular theatre. The content of the stories, however, must be drawn from Islam and the past and contemporary role models and women's lived experiences (p. 68).

Canada's Muslims, whatever their ethnic backgrounds, need to be understood first in terms of Islamic identity rather than cultural aspects. That is, counsellors need to understand Islam as a way of life, not just as a religion. It is a set of values that guide Muslim people; thus, to adequately counsel Muslims, one must understand their values. Finally, regardless of ethnic backgrounds, Canadians need to realize that Islam is growing, not only among those from Muslim countries, but also among the general population. In fact, they are doing "...well in adapting and involving themselves in practically all spheres of the country's economic, educational and cultural activities (*National Post*, 2002, p. 13). Islam has been able to adapt to a variety of cultural settings over the years and there is no reason that it cannot be at home in Canada, Europe and other countries of the world. After all, ...

Reason is a beacon that we must not only light in the middle of darkness but also learn to carry around well into broad daylight. Mohammed Abed al-Jabri (1999, p. 6).

References

Abed al Jabri, M. (1994). *Arab Islamic Philosophy: A Contemporary Critique*. Austin, TX: Center for Islamic Studies.

Abudabbeh, N. & Nydell, M. (1997). Transcultural counselling and Arab Americans. In J. McFadden (editor) *Transcultural Counselling*, pp. 261-284. Alexandrea, VZ: American Counseling Association..

Altareb, B.Y. (l996). Islamic spirituality in America: A middle path to unity. *Counselling and Values, 41*, p. 29-36.

Authentic Book of Bukhari (1999), Vol. 4, Book 56, No. 735. Dubzi, UAE: Religious Press.

Barise, A. (1999). *Thinking and Learning in the Qur'an.* Unpublished manuscript.

Esack, F. (l999). *On Being a Muslim: Finding a Religious Path in the World Today.* Oxford, UK: One World Publications.

Hitti, K.P. (1970). *History of the Arabs.* New York: St. Martins Press.

Javed, N. (l994). Gender identity and Muslim women: Tool of oppression turned into empowerment. *Convergence, 27*(2/3), pp. 58-68.

The Koran (1989) (English Translation), Al-Munawarah, Saudi Arabia: King Fahd Holy Qur'an Printing.

Menocal, M.R. (1987). *The Arabic Role in Medieval Literary History: A Forgotten Heritage.* Philadelphia, PA: University of Pennsylvania Press.

National Post. (2002). September 14, p. A12-13.

Sampson, E. (1998). *Dealing with Differences: An Introduction to the Social Psychology of Prejudice.* Orlando, FL: Hartcourt College Publishers.

Samad, Y. (1996). The politics of Islamic identity among Bangladeshis and Pakistanis in Britain. In Ranger, Samad & Stuart, *Culture, Identity and Politics.* Aldershot, UK: Avebury.

Sheikh, A., Kunzendorf, R. & Sheikh, K. (1989). Healing images: From ancient wisdom to modern science (pp. 470-515). In A. Sheikh & K. Sheikh, *Eastern & Western Approaches to Healing.* New York: Wiley-Interscience.

Time Magazine. (2002). September 9.

Time Magazine. (2002). September 30.

Turner, D., Cheboud, E., Elvira, R. & Barise, A. (2002). Challenges for Human Rights Advocacy and Conflict Resolution: The Case of Racism and Racial Conflict. Paper presented at the Conference of International Schools of Social Work, Montpellier France, July 15-18.

Endnotes

[1] Man's authority is conditional on following Islamic principles such as *Adl* or fairness and *Shura* or mutual consultation.

[2] Surprisingly, there is a debate going on in France about whether to ban women with headscarf from French schools!

Chapter 14

Biracial Identity Development: A Reflection on Current Models

Robert Awai

As the product of a racially "mixed" marriage myself, I have always been extremely focused on my own identity in relation to other biracial individuals. I have often wondered where the "sameness" of our experience lies in relation to those of others. This has led to a review of the literature pertaining to models of identity development for biracial individuals. Of these, I have chosen three which best represent the range of opinions (Stonequist, 1937; Poston, 1990; Kerwin & Ponterotto, 1995); further reflection on the validity of these models from my personal perspective follows. I also present some of the implications these models may hold for cross-cultural counselling and I have put forward some areas for future research.

The Need for a Biracial Identity Development Model

Identity development is crucial for those of minority backgrounds and can be seen as even more complex for those of more than one racial heritage (Gibbs, 1987). Although it has been pointed out that all ethnic/racial minority groups "must negotiate some degree of biculturality" (Ponterotto, 1989, in Kerwin & Ponterotto, 1995), biracial individuals have the added challenge of reconciling identification with two opposing groups while belonging fully to neither. Adding to this challenge is living with society's desire to classify biracial individuals into one or the other of their differing backgrounds. This dilemma of choice is reflected in the words of Carmen Braun Williams (199), who said in regards to her own biraciality:

I have been queried about my racial identity (erroneously, my 'nationality'). People, mostly White, have wondered why, I do not choose to pass as white. Other people, mostly Black have demanded to know why I say I am biracial instead of 'just admitting' I am black....People have given me advice on how I should talk, think, act and feel about myself racially. Repeatedly, people have tried to define my existence for me. (Braun Williams, 1999, p. 33)

Current/Historical Models of Biracial Identity Development

The earliest model of biracial identity development is Stonequist's (1937) concept of the "marginal personality," and there are few others. Poston's (1990) proposition for an "updated" model of biracial identity development is the first in a small series of such theories put forward in the more recent past. Kerwin and Ponterotto's (1995) contribution attempts to address some of the problems created in adapting the other models to every situation. One important thing to note around all of these models is that they attempt to deal with the issue from the American perspective and that most of the research is drawn from studies involving those of African-American/Dominant White descent. This is markedly different from the Canadian context because of the differing national policies regarding multicultural issues and holds implications for future research.

The "Marginal Person" Model

Stonequist's (1937) model of the 'marginal person' is what can be termed a 'deficit model' (Poston 1990; Kerwin & Ponterotto, 1995). Drawing mainly from research which focused on the pathology of black families in the U.S., this model assumes that people who are of "mixed race" have problems with identity development because they are associated with two worlds, but belong fully to neither and they are "deficient" of the ability to do so. Normal processes of identity development are exacerbated within this model (Gibbs, 1987). The individual is thrust into a state of internal conflict through the desire to hold both identities simultaneously, while at the same time being unable to commit to either.

Poston (1990) notes that being marginal as an individual "does not necessarily lead to a marginal personality" (p. 153) and that such conflict may be more a factor of social structural prejudice rather than internal conflict. It has also been shown to be possible for a person to have a healthy integration of both their parent cultures without such conflict (Gibbs, 1987). One large factor influencing the sense of marginality within the individual is the level of support given to each aspect of racial heritage by the individuals' parents; another is the level of acceptance and exposure for either parental race/culture within the individuals' immediate community (Brown, 1990). These problems aside, the concept of marginality has had a large hold over the literature involving biracial individuals and continues to do so (Kerwin & Ponterotto, 1995).

Poston's Five Stage Model

Up until Poston's (1990) call for an update, the best modern model available had been adaptations of Cross's (1987) model of Afro-American self-actualization model of Minority Identity Development (MID). Although this model has been updated (Cross & Fhagen-Smith, 1996), it doesn't address the issues faced by biracial individuals specifically. This model is somewhat general in approach. This leads to a lack of application to individual minority groups.

In particular, Poston (1990) felt that development would be different in biracial individuals for several reasons. First, models based on homogeneous minority development do not acknowledge that the individual might choose one set of cultural values over another at a given stage. Second, the individual may come from both minority and dominant culture groups. Third, the integration of several identities is not recognized. Finally, these models assume "some acceptance into the minority culture of origin" (Poston, 1990, p. 153). Biracial individuals may feel that they are "rejected by both the majority and minority groups because they fit neither in terms of physical appearance, family background and loyalty" to specific groups (Gibbs, 1987, p. 269).

What is proposed in Poston's (1990) model is a five-stage process during which attitudes towards the varying 'reference groups' within the individual's background are developed. These 'Reference Group Orientations' (RGO's) are based around Cross' (1987) five stage model, more recently elaborated in the work of Cross and Fhagen-Smith (1996). Poston's (1990) five stage model involves group identification, racial preference and attitudes, while personality traits examining self efficacy are excluded. The five stages of Poston's theory are:

1. **Personal Identity:** The individual has developed independent of RGO attitudes which have not been integrated. Identity is based largely on self-constructs originating within the family. Poston noted that parental attitudes towards race or racialization would have greatest effect at this stage.

2. **Choice of Group Categorization:** The individual is 'pushed' to choose an identity through society's need for definition. This can cause "crisis and alienation for the individual" (Poston, 1990, p. 153). The choice is primarily limited to the minority or the dominant culture group. Poston characterized this stage as taking place before individuals have a level of cognitive development allowing them to hold multiple cultures concurrently within their identity.

3. **Emeshment/Denial:** The individual becomes confused through guilt at having to choose/deny one identity. A large portion of this stage is seen as the result of feelings of 'disloyalty' to the parent whose heritage is secondary for the individual. Gibbs (1987) outlined this as a cause of various pathologies in biracial adolescents within the social service system and Poston adapted these findings in his development of this stage (Kerwin & Ponterotto, 1995).

4. **Appreciation**: The biracial individual in this stage begins to broaden the RGO's to include both groups. Identification is still with one main culture/group, yet there is significant effort invested in the exploration and involvement with the secondary heritage.

5. **Integration:** Individuals at this stage "tend to recognise and value all of their ethnic identities" (Poston, 1990, p. 154). The individual continues to acquire knowledge of both backgrounds and develops from the secure space of the 'integrated' individual.

Poston's model is important in that it recognizes the role that the internalization of outside prejudice and values has on the individual's self-conception. It also examines the way in which family and peer influences affect identity choice. Kerwin and Ponterotto (1995) note that this limits the biracial individual in that it suggests that periods of confusion and resultant maladjustment are mandatory. The model also outlines the need for strong family and community support as essential in resolution of conflicts. Poston sees this aspect of the model as a particular benefit in the development of preventative programs building support through parent and counsellor training and awareness building.

The Kerwin-Ponterotto Model

The model proposed by Kerwin and Ponterotto (1995) draws upon those previously discussed, as well as attempting to integrate further research which shows that personal, societal and environmental factors are further enmeshed in the process than originally accounted for (Kerwin, 1991). It attempts to recognize the individuality of both situation and resolution of self-concept for the biracial person. This outlook contains six stages based around the developmental milestones of Pre-school, Entry to School, Pre-adolescence, Adolescence, College/Young Adulthood and Adulthood. The specifics for each stage are:

1. Preschool: Racial awareness emerges earlier than is generally found in the individual population (Kerwin 1991). The authors theorized this as the result of higher levels of difference within the child's immediate social groupings (i.e., the family). There is also the supposition that parental anxiety of the biracial status of the child may play a role in awareness and there is some indication that a lack of such anxiety may have differential effects on the development of racial awareness.

2. Early School: The sense of self developed by the child through the limited social communities of family and friends is challenged upon entry to school. The authors note that questions such as "What are you?" (Kerwin & Ponterotto, 1995, p. 211) may be asked more frequently to multiracial children. Self-identification with a given group or social category begins to become a factor in the biracial child's development. The way in which children speak of their biraciality is largely dependant on parental input. If the parents provide good self-concept, or at least a unified self-concept for the child, Kerwin and Ponterotto (1995) state that this is the label which children will "typically use to describe themselves" (p. 212). The attitudes of the school community in terms of role modelling and prejudices begin to play a larger role as well.

3. Pre-adolescence: An increased identification of group membership as being factored upon skin color, appearance, language and culture is apparent; however, the tendency is to use

societal labels as descriptive terms. Awareness of difference between the parents typically occurs at this stage (Kerwin, 1991).

4. Adolescence: This stage is characterized as the "most challenging for biracial youngsters due to both developmental factors characteristic of this age group and societal pressures" (Kerwin & Ponterotto, 1995, p. 212). The pressure to chose one strain of the individual's background over another is related to Erikson's (1968) conception of "ingroups" and "outgroups." The pressures of dating add to this mix. Brown (1990) and Gibbs (1987) note that this last factor is especially important to biracial adolescents. Issues of interracial dating may bring out race in a way the individual has never before conceived.

5. College/Young Adulthood: Continued immersion or rejection in one or the other of the individuals may continue, although rejection of societal limits and an acceptance of the dual nature of biraciality is more likely. This is due to increased self-efficacy accompanying this stage of life generally. The advantages of a biracial heritage become clearer at this stage, as do the disadvantages (Kerwin & Ponterotto, 1995).

6. Adulthood: Development of a biracial identity is conceived as a lifelong process. Continuing integration is necessary throughout the individual's life span. Kerwin and Ponterotto (1995) state that "...with the successful resolution of earlier stages there will be a continuing exploration and interest in different cultures, including one's own" (p. 213). The individuals may be much more flexible in terms of their individual identity as a result of their experience and be able to accept a wider range of interpersonal relations.

This latest model of biracial identity development has been "presented as an integrated framework" of development (Kerwin & Ponterotto, 1995, p. 215) and attempts to specifically outline racial awareness and biracial acceptance as a factor of social expectations and individual processes. It attempts to move away from the 'labelling' associated with the marginal person model and the idea of "necessary conflict" in "choosing" one parental heritage over the other as in Poston's (1990) model. There is also an attempt within this model to publicize the fact that biracial individuals are willing and able to discuss their experiences in holding a dual identity (Kerwin & Ponterotto, 1995).

A Personal Reflection on the Models

The concept of claiming race and heritage is not easy for the biracial individual, according to what has been presented. This has certainly been my own experience. I am the first-born child of a Chinese man, whose nationality is Trinidadian and a white Anglo/Scottish Canadian woman. I grew up in a small town in British Columbia where the majority were of white European descent. At the same time, many of the interactions within my extended "family" involved interracial couples and their offspring (cousins and family friends).

As a biracial individual, I have felt conflicting emotions, varying levels of discrimination and have been faced with choices regarding how I identify myself and my heritage. As I have read and re-read the models presented, my own struggle for self-definition is highlighted in varying and – sometimes – conflicting ways. Each of these models has a certain "ring of truth" yet none encompasses fully my own experience in developing a solid and definable identity; nor does any model reflect the reality that I am and have always been, biracial and have never been able to separate this into "parts." Although I have certainly felt the strain, in social situations, of "not belonging," this has not been (for me) a matter of my being the "tragic" figure from Stonequist's (1939) model of the "marginal person." Like Poston (1990), I see this as having to do with the systems and structures that surrounded and supported me in my development. Little mention was made of race or socialization issues – either within my immediate or extended family. Instead, the focus of difference was on my father's cultural heritage as a person from Trinidad. Trinidadian culture is an amalgam of many different heritages, influenced greatly by the European colonialist structures which shaped and formed its social systems. Although not a racially harmonious society by any stretch of the imagination, each root culture has grown and adapted a distinct personality within the whole. For one take on the hybrid nature of this culture, an interested reader may wish to view Amitava Kumar's film *Pure Chutney*, which focuses on the post-colonial experiences of ethnic Indians in Trinidad. I personally find myself identifying with this variegated aspect of my dual nature in a positive way and actively dislike the idea of being called "marginal."

The individuality within the biracial experience is mentioned (i.e., Gibbs, 1987) as being a large limiting factor in the model. The fact that my father presented as bicultural and came from a society which has developed a multi-ethnic heritage, has allowed me to escape the labelling necessary for Stonequist's ideas to be fully applicable. "Marginality" in my experience had to do with not being completely within the "white" community in which I grew up, although this had more to do with my darker skin-tone. It is my personal proposal that the social structures of Trinidadian society and the legacy of British colonialism, fit well with the Canadian experience in which I grew up and keep the differences in my cultural heritage largely limited to culinary or musical exposure.

The concept from these models which resonates most in my own life is that of feeling "pressure to choose" (Poston, 1990, p. 153) between one heritage and the other in my own identification. Certainly, the largest struggle I have felt within my life has involved commitment to definition, both in myself and in my attitudes. Far from having the negative influences possible, this has instead led to an appreciation of my double heritage and a flexibility in my personal outlook, which I feel goes beyond that of many of my mono-racial peers. The difficulty lies in what Poston (1990) aptly describes as *integration*. The ability to claim an integrated identity – what Braun Williams (1999) aptly describes as the "I" – is individual and is an inherent part of being biracial from birth. Claiming this identity is what is important in being able to develop a sense of self and in being able to present oneself as a whole, authentic person. What is needed is the social and structural support within the family and within the individual's community environment, to allow an exploration of the various aspects of the self which make up the reality of a biracial individual.

The Reference Group Orientation that is most important can only be discovered and defined by the individual. This is consistent with the need for "community education" and support throughout the developmental span, as advocated through the Kerwin-Ponterotto (1995) model. The biracial individual is then free to discover and become energized about the uniqueness of his or her reality. One of my former co-workers reported to me that her eight year-old son thought of his biracial status as "way cool," and I have had numerous conversations with other biracial individuals highlighting both the similarities and the differences within that experience. There is a definite need for the models of biracial identity development to further include this range of difference and to further integrate the interplay between cultures and race instead of being focused largely on race alone.

Implications for Counselling and Research

One of the most important aspects of cross-cultural counselling is the ability to hold an awareness of client worldview and experiences (Arredondo, 1999). This includes not only being aware of the client's own processes with Rogers' (1961) concept of "unconditional positive regard"; instead, as counsellors, this involves actively exploring with the client the effects that cultural/racial difference has had on their lives and becoming aware of one's own position as cultural/racial beings. Although the conflicts experienced by biracial individuals are to some degree universal and to another the product of their minority status, there are definite similarities which allow the process to be seen as discrete. In particular, the "dual" nature of the biracial individual disallows simply following a homogeneous model. Braun Williams (1999) notes that "it is our preconceived notions and unresolved feelings about race and culture that present some of the most formidable barriers to expressions of empathy in therapy" (p. 75). Truly effective cross-cultural communication allows for the unique position held by biracial individuals in holding more than one identity simultaneously.

Recently, there has been a focus on highlighting the implications of cultural diversity on counselling practice. Witness the recent issue of *The Journal of Counselling and Development* (vol. 77, 99, special issue) along with the ACA's recently developed guidelines for multicultural competency (Arredondo, 1999). As discussed, very little of this literature focuses on the biracial population. Given the ever-increasing percentage of the population which is able to claim biracial status (Poston, 1990), along with the need to include biracial status as a context for counselling, this is an unrealistic state of affairs.

Several possibilities for research exist in this area. The social factors which affect biracial individuals and the degree to which these variances influence experience should be examined. Poston (1990) calls this examining the "salience" of the social factors involved within the choice process. This would include a more comprehensive examination of the interaction between cultural and racial factors. It would also be useful to investigate the degree to which biracial individuals identify with the above models through an exploration of their present identity. Similarities and differences in the formation process could be drawn from their individual experiences to form a more cohesive model of biracial identity development. In much the same way, the communication processes and styles of interactions within interracial families could be examined to gain a better understanding of the structures and support needed to develop a more integrated biracial identity. A stronger effort should also be made to investigate the topic within the Canadian context, given that the governmental policy of "multiculturalism" is somewhat different from the "melting pot" ideology existing within the United States.

Conclusion

Although few models of identity development specific to biracial individuals do exist, these lack a comprehensive integration into the "dual" heritage that biraciality imparts. In my personal experiences, it is true that the dichotomy of my parentage has led to a questioning search for identity; it is, however, equally true that my dual nature has always been simply a "fact of life." This integration can be reached only after certain developmental processes within the existing models occur and this is not consistent with the reality of existence. New ways of thinking about identity development in the biracial individual must be explored. This has many implications for counselling. Without an awareness and the understanding of the context of the biracial individual we – as counsellors – are limiting our ability to work in empathic and understanding ways.

References

Arredondo, P. (1999). Multicultural counselling competencies as tools to address oppression and racism. *Journal of Counseling and Development.* Vol. 77, 102-109.

Braun Williams, C. (1999). Claiming a biracial identity: Resisting social constructions of race and culture. *Journal of Counselling and Development,* Vol. 77, (32-35).

Brown, P.M. (1990). Biracial identity and social marginality. *Child and Adolescent Social Work,* Vol 7(4), 319-337.

Cross, W.E. Jr., (1987). A two-factor theory of black identity: Implications for the study of identity development in minority children. In J.S.Phinney, and M.J. Rotheram (Eds.), *Children's Ethnic Socialisation: Pluralism and Development* (pp 117-133). Newbury Park, CA: Sage Publications.

Cross, W.E. Jr. & Fhagen-Smith, P. (1996). Nigrescence and ego identity development. In Pedersen, P.B, Draguns, J.G., Lonner, W.J. and Trimble, J.E. (Eds.), *Counselling Across Cultures* (4th ed.), (pp. 108-123). Thousand Oaks, CA: Sage Publications.

Gibbs, J.T. (1987). Identity and marginality: Issues in the treatment of biracial adolescents. *American*

Journal of Orthopsychiatry, Vol. 52(2), pp 265-278.

Kerwin, C. (1991). Racial identity development in childeren of black/white racial heritage (Doctoral dissertation, Fordham University, 1991). *Dissertation Abstracts International*, Vol. 52, 269-A.

Kerwin, C. & Ponterotto, J. (1995). Biracial Identity Development. In Ponterro, J., Cascas, J.M., Suzuki, L.A. & Alexander, C.M. (Eds.), *Handbook of Multicultural Counselling* (pp. 199-217). Thousand Oaks, CA: Sage Publishers.

Poston, W.S.C. (1990). The biracial identity development model: A needed addition. *Journal of Counseling and Development,* Vol. 69 (pp. 152-155).

Rogers, C. (1961). *On Becoming a Person: A Therapist's View of Psychotherapy.* Boston, MA: Houghton Mifflin Co.

Stonequist, E.V. (1937). *The Marginal Man: A Study in Personality and Culture Conflict.* New York: Russell and Russell.

Chapter 15

My Multiracial Identity: Examining the Biracial/Multiracial Dynamic

Natasha Caverley

Identity is a simple word yet it raises many complex issues and causes introspection. We grapple not only with ourselves, men and other women, but also with broader influences of history, society, cultural heritage and traditional structures. (from Making Waves, *cited in Featherston, 1994, p. 7)*

As children develop an appreciation of their inner mental world, they begin to think more intently about themselves. During early childhood, they start to construct a self-concept, "the sum total of attributes, abilities, attitudes and values that individuals believe define who they are" (Berk, 1997, p. 428). Over time, children organize these internal states and behaviors into dispositions that they are aware of and can verbalize to others. The knowledge that we exist as individuals, separate from everyone else, emerges by the age of 18 months (Stipek, Gralinski & Kopp, 1990). As children get older, they soon develop a sense of themselves as separate individuals, ultimately forming a self-concept. For some multiracial individuals, development of their ethnic identity between two or more racial backgrounds can cause cultural conflicts and struggle in defining who they are. Some multiracial individuals may feel lost between two or more worlds. The purpose of this article is to explore and gain insight into the family life and social development of multiracial individuals as it relates to their self-concept and racial identity. Also, it is important to examine the implications of these aspects in the area of cross-cultural counselling and teaching.

Personal Perspective

In this chapter, I have chosen to focus on multiracial individuals where one parent is Caucasian and the other parent is a member of a visible minority group. The reasons for this specific focus are to examine the dynamics that occur when an individual is both a member of the dominant culture and a marginalized group. Secondly, as a person from a multiracial background (Caucasian, West Indian and Aboriginal), my own personal reflections and experiences will be more accurately expressed from this perspective.

Forming One's Racial Identity

Self-concept is the set of beliefs about one's own characteristics. One's self-concept comprises one's sense of identity, the set of beliefs we hold about what we are like as individuals (Breakwell, Hattie and Stevens, 1992). The development of one's self-concept leads to the formation of self-esteem, or the judgments that one makes about one's own worth (Baumeister, 1993). An individual's self-concept affects identity formation; thus, reflecting a combination of one's social identity, the roles or group membership categories to which a person belongs and one's personal identity, the traits and behaviors that people find descriptive of themselves (Tajfel & Turner, 1986).

According to Erik Erickson (1956), personality develops through a series of eight stages. He examined the integration of the biological, psychological and social aspects of development and his theory of development holds that at each stage of life, we face the task of establishing an equilibrium between ourselves and our social world (Erickson, 1956). For some multiracial individuals, an implication of this theory would be the fifth stage which revolves around identity versus role confusion.

The fifth stage of development occurs from ages 13 through 19. At this stage, the adolescent experiments with different roles, while trying to integrate identities from previous stages. Self-examination occurs as many adolescents examine their roles in their family, school and peer groups. At the same time, adolescents are trying to figure out who they are and who they want to become within their larger society (Erickson, 1956). It is during this time when some multiracial adolescents may struggle with the uncertainty of their racial and ethnic identity. This conflict and confusion that some multiracial adolescents may be going through could be an example of Erickson's identity crisis. This refers to individuals who are struggling to find out who they are (Erickson, 1956). Youths who have not adequately resolved their conflicts may develop a negative identity in which they act in scornful and hostile ways toward roles considered as proper and desirable by the community. Lacking a clear sense of identity, some multiracial individuals may exhibit a range of negative emotional states, including shame, anger, personal confusion and feelings of helplessness (Fukuyama, 1999). Key parts of multiracial individuals' identities rests on the support they receive from their society, their family and on their internalization of the ideals of their race and their culture. Braun Williams (1999) believes that racial identity for multiracial individuals is fluid, seamless parts of who they are. Racial identity, especially for multiracial people, tends to be centered in the person, not in societal constructions. There is no one correct identification for multiracial people, it is the person who gets to name his/her experience. Therefore, some multiracial individuals may choose to align themselves with one or more ethnic groups which complement them in personal characteristics such as birthplace, language, race/physical attributes or customs. I realize that race is not concrete, it is only a label, a term that individuals create to describe how they see themselves in relation to others. The various cultures and racial backgrounds are only elements of who I am as a multiracial individual. I am free to define myself as I see fit. As stated earlier, it is important to realize and encourage multiracial individuals to value freedom to choose what aspects of their cultural and racial backgrounds they wish to embrace.

During my teen years, I was approached by various individuals who said, "So, where are you from?" "I live here in Victoria" I said, but I realized that was not what some of them wanted to hear. "No, what nationality are you?" They would clarify and say, "What is your ethnicity?" "What color are you?" or "What is your race?" I was never bothered by these questions as I felt I could do one of two things: feel victimized/threatened by the questions or choose to educate these individuals about what it is like being multiracial. I chose the latter. By briefly describing my ethnic background to these individuals, I felt I was doing my part in enlightening others about multiculturalism and diversity; thus, making them more aware of the unique population which I am part of. I realized that no one meant badly by asking me to define myself, they were merely curious because I did not look like anyone they had ever seen and perhaps my parents were not like any other couple they knew.

One of the frustrating things that I had to go through during my adolescence was being excluded on certain questionnaires when applying to various universities and for scholarships. The statement concerning race usually stated, "Please fill in one of the following boxes" but my race was never there. As a multiracial individual, I do not easily fit into any racial group. I am not ONLY Black, not ONLY Aboriginal and not ONLY White, I am all three races simultaneously! I was bothered by this question on scholarship and university application forms because these organizations or educational institutes appear to be saying, listen, you have to pick out a portion of your identity and deny the other. Are you Black, Aboriginal or White? You cannot be all three. There appeared to be no consideration or understanding on the part of these organizations that some of the population did not view these existing racial categories as valid in terms of their identity or affiliation.

In order to gain a clear sense of identity, an individual needs a sense of continuity of their self over time. According to Erickson, a sense of identity requires a consistency between that which individuals conceive themselves to be and that which they perceive others to see in them and expect of them (Erickson, 1956). For multiracial individuals, "simultaneity" should be stressed and acknowledged as a means of empowerment and pride of their multiple racial backgrounds (Braun Williams, 1999). For multiracial individuals, one environment where "simultaneity" should be encouraged is in the home.

Family Life

The family performs important functions for their children. Parents should ensure that they provide their children with an adequate foundation for socialization and emotional support. A key element to the family is the promotion of positive family interactions, which in turn will aid in enhancing a child's development (Berk, 1997). During adolescence, young people know that they are an integral part of the family and yet they also have a budding sense of independence and personal efficacy. They are realizing and recognizing their own competence, can take initiative and are able to see a variety of tasks through to completion. Thus, they enter adolescence with a variety of loosely related segments of identity based on experiences in the earlier stages (Conger & Galambos, 1997).

Growing up as a multiracial individual, I was raised embracing all aspects of my cultures equally. I was exposed to my Canadian and Jamaican roots, fascinated by the differences and similarities between these two Commonwealth nations. My parents instilled in me at an early age never to judge people based on their racial/ethnic/cultural backgrounds. Through the years I have lived with them, they have taught me that there is more to learn from other nations than to fear. It is through my parents' actions letting me value all aspects of my racial and cultural backgrounds that really made me feel like I was somebody. Another component to my upbringing was the fact that my parents provided emotional support and freedom to explore within my multicultural heritage from letting me play with my black Barbie dolls, visiting my relatives in Ontario who shared with me their stories of their early years in Canada to reading the *Daily Gleaner* (the national Jamaican newspaper). As I am recently finding out more about my aboriginal ancestry, my father and I are exploring our Algonquin cultural heritage and history, especially through the process of genealogical mapping and connecting with distant relatives in the Greater Golden Lake region of Canada. I am appreciative that my family served as a secure base from which I could confidently develop my racial identity which was enhanced by my many positive life experiences.

Social Development

Identity development also depends on schools and communities that provide young people with rich and varied opportunities for exploration (Tajfel et al., cited in Feldman, 1998). Within society, multiracial individuals transgress the racial boundaries and put into question the entire basis of social order, the racial hierarchy entrenched in history. Multiracial individuals have the opportunity to reveal how artificial the color/racial line is within society (Kawash, 1997).

Society differentiates and discriminates on the basis of color; one's ascribed color may denote acceptance or nonacceptance in various social circles. Braun Williams (1999) stated that, "...in a world where socially constructed categories of race are misconstrued as biological, little encouragement is offered to multiracial people like me to claim an identity that falls outside prescribed frameworks" (p. 33). As a result, groupings in society tend to be based on physical characteristics tied to skin color/race. In Western influenced culture, skin is the greatest signifier. It is the first thing people see and is used to define who one is

(Kawash, 1997). The privileges, or their lack, attached to different shades of skin color, texture of hair, shape of one's eyes are encoded into the social fabric. For some multiracial individuals, this social pressure can force them to identify themselves with the racial group of one parent as opposed to the other which may lead to confusion, guilt and resentment.

The dynamics which surround white privilege and power express the realities of cultural/ethnic group status and categorization within society. The term privilege "confers dominance, gives permission to control, because of one's race or sex" (McIntosh, 1992, p.77). In addition, power represents an ability to control and shape the behavior of others. Through historical relationships and perceptions between various cultures, what tends to result is some type of separation of "us" versus "them" – resulting in the classification of "other." Groups such as multiracial individuals have been classified as "other" and are believed to be different from the dominant groups in society. The categorization of "other" can become an expectation, based on stereotypes which may have arisen from personal experiences, media and/or social messages that are used to classify groups within society. It appears that being "other" can stem from any trait that contributes to a groups' social identity or emphasizes privilege differences from the dominant group – such as class, sex, color, ethnicity, nationality, socio-economic and political status (LeBaron, 2003).

There may be tendencies for some biracial individuals to experience something called biracial guilt. This occurs when the biracial individual feels terrible guilt, wondering if he/she has the right to call themselves, for example, "African-Canadian," even though they were not raised within an African-cultural environment. Other questions stemming from biracial guilt are: "Can I really say I am Black even though my skin color is white?" "By saying I am White based on the color of my skin, am I therefore, rejecting the Black parent that I have come to love?" For those biracial individuals who have a Caucasian parent, there may be feelings of guilt as they associate themselves with the oppressive majority who have caused much pain for those individuals of color.

Fukuyama (1999) described how as a young adult, she felt a need to fit into the dominant White culture. At one point in her life, she changed her name to the Anglo-American name of her husband so as to assimilate into the dominant culture as much as possible. Some multiracial individuals may feel the pressure from society to fit in with the dominant culture and conform in what is called "passing/crossing over". Passing/crossing over means that an individual internalizes the values and beliefs of the dominant culture and rejects the other aspects of their ethnic and racial heritage (Parrilla de Kokal, 1997). Socially, an individual would laugh, ignore or join in the disparaging remarks made about their ethnic group. Some of the reasons why one may deny part of their racial identity may be because of such things as racial stereotypes, racial epithets and discrimination faced by them personally or to family and friends. When some individuals pass/cross over, they truly believe that they are making themselves more desirable with the dominant group to obtain the privileges afforded to them at the expense of recognizing and embracing all aspects of their racial identity (Kawash, 1997).

An interesting twist to passing/crossing over was a time when I went to meet with a human resources advisor for a potential job interview. The session was going well and then I asked what kind of support networks were offered at this organization for a visible minority like myself. The human resources advisor stated, "You are a visible minority!" I replied "Yes I am!" She proceeded to tell me that it would be in my best interest not to mention that I was multiracial as "You have a good thing going with your scholastic achievements and work experience, you do not want to jeopardize your chances by bringing something up like that!" That was my definite cue to remove myself from that interview session and look for work else where. Though I have fair skin, I am very much a Caucasian, West Indian and Aboriginal woman who has and will not let someone else tell me to deny my racial and cultural heritage!

Peer relations play an important role in adolescent development. Peers serve as socialization agents through the use of modelling, reinforcement and direct pressures to conform to social behaviors, whether they are positive or negative (Conger & Galambos, 1997). I think another reason for feeling comfortable living among three races was my parents' decision that I attend an international school for girls. By attending an international school (from Kindergarten to Grade 12), I happily embraced all aspects of my racial heritage on an equal level. At this school, Caucasian, Asian, Hispanic and Multiracial women were treated as equals who came from diverse backgrounds. It was through my years at this school that I came to solidify my racial identity, realizing that I did not have to choose between being Black, Aboriginal or White, I could happily be all three. As a result of these experiences and fostering of multiculturalism, I have found that I have developed quite a comfort zone in the community and at the university with individuals who come from different cultural/ethnic backgrounds. I have been told by these acquaintances that my warm, non-judgmental manner has made them feel very much at ease with me and easy for them to approach me. Again, I contribute these abilities to the fact that by being multiracial, I too can identify with various needs and concerns of other visible minority groups in the community.

Benefits of Being Multiracial

From a psychological perspective, some multiracial individuals feel empowered to incorporate and accept all aspects of their racial and cultural backgrounds. This may result from interactions with friends and/or family members who provide the richness of diverse cultural knowledge and experiences regarding the many facets of the multiracial individual's racial/cultural heritage. In *The Identity Development of Multiracial Youth*, Schwartz (1998) brings forth other positive aspects of being multiracial, such as having greater intergroup tolerance, language facility, appreciation of minority group cultures and ties to single-heritage groups than do monoracial people (Thornton, 1996, cited in Schwartz, 1998). In addition, some multiracial individuals are able to identify diverse aspects of a situation; thus, recognizing and seeing all sides of a conflict (Kerwin, Ponterotto, Jackson & Harris, 1993, cited in Schwartz, 1998).

Implications for Cross-cultural Counselling & Teaching: Strategies and Interventions

The role of culture is becoming more recognized in the area of counselling. The growing multicultural factor continues to be ever present in our lives. In a world where communities have expanded to include individuals who are from different nationalities and racial backgrounds, the natural byproduct of this interaction are multiracial children. According to the 2001 Census data, 11 331 490 of the total Canadian population self-identified that they were of multiple ethnic origin (Statistics Canada, 2001). Therefore, cross-cultural counselling and teaching becomes a fundamental helping tool. The following considerations should be observed when working with multicultural individuals:

Teachers

Use stories, role playing, films, photos and picture books, show students how people have effectively mixed religions, national heritages, ethnic, racial, political and linguistic differences through marriage. For example, accessing multiracial children's books at www.comeunity.com/adoption/books/0multiracial.html.

Lead a family tree project in your classroom, allowing the students to research as far back as they can with each side of their family. Note the differences and origins of each child – nation, language, culture and so forth. Use photos and artifacts and encourage parents, grandparents and other relatives to come to the classroom and talk with the children.

Encourage and support discussions about individual differences (Wardle, 1992). Children are very curious, they are also uncertain and sometimes afraid of the unknown. "Why do you look different from your mommy?" "Why is your daddy white and you're not?" "Can I touch your hair?" "Are you adopted?" Respond to these questions and use the interest to talk about children getting their physical characteristics from their parents. Use both biracial and non-biracial children to make this point. This activity will naturally lead to a project on different families. Develop a bulletin board or collage showing every variety of family – foster, adoptive, two-parent, single families, interracial, extended and minority. Invite as many of these families as possible to visit your classroom.

Counsellors

It is important to realize that multiracial individuals have the same amount of concerns and questions about their ethnic and racial origins as any other visible minority group.

When working with multiracial clients, remember to reinforce the counselling philosophy of having a non-judgmental way of thinking in therapy sessions. Do not assume that because a client has a certain skin tone, he/she would identify more with respect to ideals, values and morals of the racial group that reflects their skin color.

Validate the experiences and identity of multiracial individuals such as the client's feelings (i.e., anger) about racism (Fukuyama, 1999).

Familiarize yourself with the client's multiple racial and ethnic background to determine values and characteristics that may be rooted in the person's cultural background as opposed to a general personality trait.

When appropriate, look for multiracial role models for clients as a means of finding someone in the community (e.g., family members or friends) or in society at large (e.g., celebrities) who acknowledge and embrace their multicultural heritage (i.e., singers Mariah Carey and Amanda Marshall; Academy Award winner Halle Berry and New York Yankees baseball player Derek Jeter). Often multiracial individuals may feel the pressure from society to choose role models who are from one specific ethnic group or another (Braun Williams, 1999). Opportunities of this nature to discuss and share experiences would allow for those who are uncertain of their self-concept to identify with other members of the multiracial community; thus, feeling more at ease with their racial heritage. Some key multiracial websites that can be used in the multicultural counselling experience include:

Biracial Portraits (www.pbs.org/wgbh/pages/frontline/shows/secret/portraits)

Interracial Voice (www.webcom.com/intvoice/)

MixedFolks.com (www.mixedfolks.com)

Multiracial Activist (www.multiracial.com)

"Demonstrate ability to interpret assessment results including implications of dominant cultural values affecting assessment/interpretation, interaction of cultures for those who are biracial and the impact of historical institutional oppression" (Arredondo, 1999, p.108).

Be aware of the use of language in the sessions. The power of language and terminology in describing multiracial individuals is another important aspect to note. Some terms like "hybrid," "mixed," "half-breed" or "mulatto" have been used to describe some members of the multiracial community. These terms are derogatory in nature and can lead to one having a negative self-image/self-concept. With respect to the term "mulatto," it is used to refer to individuals who are both Caucasian and Black. This term has the same negative/politically incorrect connotation as calling a Black person a "Negro." The word "mulatto" was initially coined to refer to the sterile mule, the progeny of a mating between two diverse species. Thus, this term was used as a means of evidence that members of the black community and members of the white community were indeed separate and distinct species (Kawash, 1997). The terms "bicultural/biracial" and "multiracial/multicultural" are now being used in reference to people who are of multiple racial and ethnic heritage. Word choice/terminology in identifying others is crucial and necessary to ensuring a positive image of oneself.

In general, as a counsellor working with members of various ethnic groups you may wish to consider the following:

Empathy should be a foundation to all counselling. Clients want to be understood and validated by the therapist (Braun Williams, 1999).

Recognize and realize that counsellors are powerful agents of change in affirming ethnic and racial identity (Fukuyama, 1999).

Commit to being a lifetime learner of cross-cultural issues (whether it is informal or formal training) such as multicultural competency training. Cross-cultural training will allow counsellors to recognize their own feelings of defensiveness, resistance, mistrust and vulnerability regarding the subject of race (Robinson, 1999).

Self-awareness. An emphasis should be placed on examining one's own cultural heritage as it relates to comfort and positive orientation to cultural differences (Braun Williams, 1999).

Leading from behind by feeling comfortable as a counsellor in exploring racial issues with the client (Braun Williams, 1999).

As counsellors and teachers, we should continue to reflect interventions that acknowledge the diverse community in which we live. One must view these cross-cultural issues not as barriers for the clients but as challenges brought before us; challenges for which we are ready.

Conclusion

The development of a multiracial individual reflects many needs that are necessary for all people. Hopefully, the integration of my first hand experiences and analysis of current literature will allow some insight into the struggles and concerns which face those who are multiracial. It should be noted that my personal experiences are in no way reflective of the family life and societal development of all multiracial individuals. By gaining first hand knowledge of the developmental aspects of multiracial individuals, we hope to move away from social labels and stereotypes associated with individuals who are multiracial. The thoughts expressed in this paper wish to serve as means of shedding some light on how multiracial individuals are influenced by their family and society in the development of their self-concept and racial identity.

References

Arredondo, P. (1999). Multicultural Counselling Competencies as Tools to Address Oppression and Racism. *Journal of Counselling & Development, 77*(1), 102-108.

Baumeister, R. (1993). Self-esteem: The puzzle of low self-regard. In R.S. Feldman (1998), *Social Psychology* (2nd ed.). Upper Saddle River, NJ: Prentice-Hall.

Berk, L.E. (1997). *Child Development* (4th ed.). Needham Height, MA: Allyn and Bacon.

Braun Williams, C. (1999). Claiming a Biracial Identity: Resisting Social Constructions of Race and Culture. *Journal of Counselling & Development, 77*(1), 32-35.

Breakwell, G.M., Hattie, J. & Stevens, R. (1992). Social psychology of identity and the self concept. In R.S. Feldman (1998), *Social Psychology* (2nd ed.). Upper Saddle River, NJ: Prentice-Hall.

Conger, J.J. & Galambos, N.L. (1997). *Adolescence and Youth: Psychological Development in a Changing World* (5th ed.). New York: Addison Wesley Longman.

Erickson, E. (1956). The problem of ego identity. In J.J. Conger & N.L. Galambos (1997). *Adolescence and Youth: Psychological Development in a Changing World* (5th ed.). New York: Addison Wesley Longman.

Featherston, E. (1994). *Skin Deep: Women Writing on Color, Culture and Identity.* Freedom, CA: Crossing Press.

Feldman, R.S. (1998). *Social Psychology* (2nd ed.). Upper Saddle River, NJ: Prentice Hall.

Fukuyama, M.A. (1999). Personal Narrative: Growing Up Biracial. *Journal of Counselling & Development, 77*(1), 12-14.

Kawash, S. (1997). *Dislocating the Color Line: Identity, Hybridity and Singularity in African-American Literature.* Stanford, CA: Stanford University Press.

Kerwin, C., Ponterotto, J.G., Jackson, B.L. & Harris, A. (1993, April). Racial identity in biracial children: A qualitative investigation. In Schwartz, W. (1998). *The Identity Development of Multiracial Youth.* New York: ERIC Clearinghouse on Urban Education. Retrieved on May 28, 2003 from http://ericcass.uncg.edu/virtuallib/diversity/1015.html

LeBaron, M. (2003). *Bridging Cultural Conflicts: A New Approach for a Changing World.* San Francisco, CA: Jossey-Bass.

McIntosh, P. (1992). White Privilege and Male Privilege: A Personal Account of Coming to See Correspondence Through Work in Women's Studies. In Margaret L. Andersen and Patricia Hill Collins (Eds.), *Race, Class and Gender: An Anthology* (pp. 70-81).

Parrilla de Kokal, M.D. (1999). "White Chocolate": An Inquiry Into Physical and Psychological Identity. *Journal of Counselling & Development, 77*(1), 27-30.

Robinson, T.L. (1999). The Intersections of Dominant Discourses Across Race, Gender and Other Identities. *Journal of Counselling & Development, 77*(1), 73-80.

Schwartz, W. (1998). *The Identity Development of Multiracial Youth.* New York: ERIC Clearinghouse on Urban Education. Retrieved on May 28, 2003 from http://ericcass. uncg.edu/virtuallib/diversity/1015.html

Statistics Canada. (2001). *Ethno-cultural Portrait of Canada (2001 Census).* Ottawa. ON: Government of Canada. [on-line] Retrieved May 28, 2003 from http://www12.statcan.ca/english/census01/products/highlight/ETO/Table1.cfm?Lang=E&T=501&GV=1&GID=0

Stipek, D., Gralinski, J.H. & Kopp, C.B. (1990). Self-concept development in the toddler years. In L.E. Berk (1997), *Child Development* (4th ed.). Needham Height, MA: Allyn and Bacon.

Tajfel, H. & Turner, J. (1986). The social identity and intergroup relations. In R.S. Feldman (1998), *Social Psychology* (2nd ed.). Upper Saddle River, NJ: Prentice-Hall.

Thornton, M.C. (1996). Hidden agendas, identity theories and multiracial people. In Schwartz, W. (1998), The Identity Development of Multiracial Youth. New York: ERIC Clearinghouse on Urban Education.

on-line] Retrieved on May 28, 2003from: http://ericcass.uncg.edu /virtuallib /diversity/1015.html

Wardle, F. (1992). Supporting Biracial Children in the School Setting. *Education and Treatment of Children, 15*(2). 163-172.

Chapter 16

Upon Arrival: Ordeals and Challenges in Working with International Students

María del Carmen Rodríguez

Being a foreigner does not only mean to find one self in a different geographical place but it could also mean to find one self without the familiar cues that tie people to their most cherished belongings: a sense of trust, intimacy, self-confidence, self-worth and empowerment. Foreign student is a term that must go beyond the simple description of someone who studies overseas, since it conveys much more than just living and studying abroad. According to the New World Dictionary (1999), foreign means: "...situated outside one's land; relating to or dealing with other countries; strange" (p. 763). However, this definition does not embrace all the processes an individual must undergo to adequately function in an environment that is dissimilar to his or her own. Loneliness, depression, homesickness, academic concerns, language proficiency, discrimination, cultural differences, personal characteristics and financial concerns are just a few of the difficulties experienced by many international students (Surdham & Collins, 1984; Heikinheimo & Shute, 1986). On the other hand, willingness to learn about another culture, establishing relationships, opportunities to learn English and sharing common interests are viewed as stimulators (Heikinheimo & Shute, 1986).

Representing over 180 countries and many more cultural groups, foreign – or international – students compose a heterogeneous group of individuals with diverse needs and concerns that face relatively common issues and challenges related to the acculturative experience. Although the extensive growth in the international student population has been positive for colleges and universities in North America, it has exceeded the ability of those in helping professions to assess, comprehend and address their needs (Pedersen, 1991). Even when the United States continues to be the preferred destination for foreign students (National Association for American Foreign Students Affairs, 2001), the increasing number of student mobility programs has opened possibilities and opportunities to people for studying abroad. Within the frame of reference that outlines who international students are, it is important to notice that there are no subgroups or categories that take care of their specific characteristics. For example, one may find single or married students (with or without a family); those who form part of a Co-op program and those who have no job; students who were sent from their country of origin or those who chose to study abroad; students who will return home or those who are planning to make North America their home. Notwithstanding the individual struggles for acculturation, the ordeals and adversities that international students face are similar. It is due to these characteristics, needs and challenges that academic advisers and counsellors should be prepared to guide and assist international students in this cultural transition.

Contrast and Variance: Premises

The most severe culture shock does not result from dealing with external matters... but rather from status change and status loss in responding to the new situations (Alexander, Klein, Workneh & Miller, 1981). Dealing and coping with loss and newfound independence when first arriving into a new culture could be interpreted as a first sign of culture shock. The concept implies that the experience of visiting or living in a new culture is an unpleasant surprise or shock, partly because it is unexpected and partly because it may lead to a negative evaluation's of one's own and/or the other culture (Furnham, 1989). Students are on their own and they must ponder, choose and decide over an extensive range of possibilities that go from finding a place to live, to deciding what they are to do with all the options that lie ahead. However, it might not be soon when they understand that culture shock goes beyond dealing with bus routes, money matters or finding buildings at the university. The anthropologist Oberg (1957) was the first to have used the term culture sock. He identified four stages and six aspects to this reaction, which has been seen as a normal part of a routine process of adaptation to cultural differences and the manifestation of a longing for a more predictable and understandable environment. The stages, according to Oberg (1957), are:

1. **Initial euphoria:** Most people begin their new responsibility with great expectations about themselves and a positive frame of mind towards the host country. Anything new is intriguing and exciting but soon, disappointment is inevitable.

2. **Irritability and Hostility:** Gradually, the focus shifts from the excitement of being in interesting places with fascinating people to the difficulty of living amongst them. People seem to focus on the differences (which suddenly seem to be everywhere) and begin to emphasize them.

3. **Gradual Adjustment:** The crisis is over and people seem to be more open to others and willing to share. Once students are able to interpret some of the subtle cultural clues, which were overlooked earlier, the culture seems more familiar. One becomes more comfortable in it and feels less isolated. Interestingly, a person's sense of humor returns and there is a realization that the situation is not a hopeless one after all.

4. **Adaptation or Biculturalism**: Full recovery will result in an ability to function in two cultures with confidence. Students might even enjoy a great many customs, ways of doing and saying things and personal attitudes to which they have acculturated (to some extent) and which they might even miss when the time comes to pack up and return home.

Oberg (1957) also described six aspects that accompany and affect culture shock: 1) Sense of loss and feelings of deprivation (in regards to friends, status, profession and possessions; decrease of social interaction); 2) Strain (anxiety as a result of the efforts to make the necessary adaptations); 3) Ejection (being rejected by and/or rejecting members of a new culture due to stereotyping); 4) Confusion (mixed feelings in role, values, feelings and self-identity); 5) Surprise and distress after becoming aware of cultural differences; and 6) Feelings of being less important or capable (low self-esteem; perceived inability for not being able to cope with the new environment due to language limitations). The levels of anxiety, stress and rejection vary from one individual to another and from culture to culture. However, there is not enough research yet to explain for whom the shock will be more or less intense (e.g., older people, young men/women, less educated individuals, university or college students, etc.); what determines which reaction a person is likely to experience; how long will they remain in a period of shock; and so forth. Nevertheless, culture shock is not always an unpleasant experience. Paradoxically, according to Adler (1975) "…the more one is capable of experiencing new and different dimensions of human diversity, the more one learns of oneself" (p. 22).

Students' ordeals

Oberg's (1957) description of the six aspects that accompany culture shock serve as a starting point in describing the ordeals that international students face when living and interacting within a new culture.

Loss

In moving to another country for the first time, international students experience a profound sense of loss that is unique in its nature. There is loss of social support and status, loss of familiar cues, loss of certainty and self-worth. As a consequence, they often feel less confident and more tense, tend to take less time off, become preoccupied with academic demands and may even become confused over how to live day to day. Financial restrictions are also part of this sense of loss; this might create tension while the person learns the best ways in which to utilize the money (e.g., grocery shopping, transportation options, movies and so forth). Such responses can give rise to behavioral dysfunction in new cultural contexts (Heikkinen, 1981). In the increasing number of cross-cultural counselling studies, self-esteem, self-efficacy and social concern have been identified as some of the biggest problems that face international students (Day & Hajj, 1986; Heikinheimo & Shute, 1986; Meloni, 1986; Pedersen, 1991). As an initial reaction, international students lose the shared identity that comes from being with family and peers (Pedersen, 1991; Romero, 1981). Having to identify and develop functions necessary to their future well being as participants in the host culture as well as the need to develop new roles and rebuild a support system intensifies the students' levels of anxiety (Putney, 1981). "To be alone amongst strangers, with whom there is no historical association, can be an alienating and negative experience which threatens identity and self-esteem" (Wheeler & Birtle, 1993, p. 110).

Detriment of Social interaction

Since individuals vary widely in their ability to achieve success in various relationships (such as family, romantic and friendship), individual differences must be considered when attempting to understand why some students are more likely than others to encounter barriers to potential support. Understanding how these factors interact with one another to create barriers that hinder the successful adjustment of individual students can help counsellors to intervene more effectively. Similarly, appropriate social behavior is associated with self-esteem and interpersonal control. Students who are confident in their capabilities in dominant, ambitious and extraverted domains do not experience much general anxiety (Paulhus & Martin, 1987). International students experience more anxiety in the new and unfamiliar cultural environment, thus their abilities to succeed socially are limited. Making friends is one important factor in successful adaptation. Unfortunately, host students neither make themselves available nor make an effort great enough to create a bridge for international friendship (Bochner, Hutnik & Furnham, 1985; Furnham & Alibhai, 1985). In addition, host nationals generally recognize that international students have language difficulties, but hosts are often insensitive to the need of the international student for conversation. Recognizing that the contribution of the partner in conversation plays an important part in adapting, host nationals can be seen as sharing equal responsibility with international students for building cross-cultural friendships. Therefore, counsellors are exhorted to look at personal social networks as attributes of individuals rather than simply as environmental characteristics.

Stress

International students will relate to others in order to develop active strategies such as "learning new skills" and "talking with others to learn the language" and might even choose direct counselling over indirect methods as a means for socializing (Exum & Lau, 1988; Leong & Sedlacek, 1986). Yet, most international students deal with stress in isolation. This is a difficult endeavor since it is an unconscious affair where one might not be able to identify the symptoms or the origins of distress and restlessness, which in turns makes emergence more difficult. As a result, students may estrange themselves from potential sources of social support such as cultural and sports groups. They isolate from others who can help them learn about the new environment and from co-nationals with whom they can discuss similar problems. Consequently, peer counselling becomes an important helping strategy for counsellors and academic advisers.

Stereotypes

The particular prejudices that members of the host culture may hold for the various international students they encounter can serve as powerful obstacles to establishing social networks. International students are often well aware of the meanings of non-verbal or verbal cues that convey intolerance and discomfort. In addition, different students will encounter different prejudices in the form of stereotypes, depending on their own specific stigmatized characteristics. This tendency to think of members of other cultures in terms of stereotypes (i.e., the excitable Arabs; the amorous French; the touchy Italians; the lazy Latinos; the volatile Hungarians; the materialistic Americans; and so forth) might be considered as another stumbling block that compounds the problems of culture shock. Some psychologists think that anxiety-prone people cling to stereotypes, because it lessens the threat of the unknown by making the world predictable (which is exactly what the foreigner needs). The only difficulty is that such apparent or created predictability might block any realistic assessment of the person's environment, thus delaying the emergence from the state of culture shock.

Self-esteem

Pedersen (1991) mentions that a person's self-esteem and self-image are validated by significant others who provide emotional and social support in culturally patterned ways and that moving to a different culture deprives a person of these support systems. "A normal response to the withdrawing of support is anxiety, ranging from irritation and mild annoyance to the panic of extreme pain and the feelings of disorientation which accompany being lost" (p. 12). Furthermore, Belenky, McVicker, Rule and Mattuck (1986) say that: "If one can see the self only as mirrored in the eyes of others, the urgency is great to live up to other's expectations, in the hope of preventing others from forming a dim view" (p. 48). Affective factors encompassing the students' personal realm (e.g., family-related worries, illnesses, economic constraints and so forth) are likely to impact on their studies, especially where there is an ambience with little or no understanding and support for these concerns. Literature on self-esteem suggests that an established identity will remain as such until a threat to the established internal order interferes, or a crisis comes along to upset the preconceptions and self-perceptions that an individual has built up so far. Being an international student may be perceived by some as a "crisis."

Self-identity issues

Among the difficulties that might delay their growth and adaptation, international students are mostly afraid to disclose their concerns and anxieties before strangers and consequently, affect their adjustment to a foreign country. As described by Pedersen, Draguns,

Lonner and Trimble (2003), "Relationships with co-nationals become an extremely important resource for success, with international students far more willing to disclose a 'personal problem' to a co-national than to any other counselling resource on campus" (p .21). Therefore, counsellors and advisors are challenged to help students work through their modified self-image, their diminished self-esteem, loss of social support experienced as the result of studying abroad and the academic requirements in order to succeed. They need to help students develop the necessary social networks to support them both personally and academically. Steinglass, DeNour and Shye (1985) suggested that the size of the social network is the best predictor of social adjustment. The positive functions of a cultural subgroup provide a place where international students can establish new primary relations, thereby developing a sense of belonging and a place to share familiar traditional values and belief systems.

Language limitations

Additional to the loss of social support is the student's ability to communicate in the host culture. Not surprisingly, English proficiency has also been found to be an important factor in social interaction and adjustment (Meloni, 1986; Pedersen, 1991; Schram & Lauver, 1988; Surdham & Collins, 1984). Language restrictions and other affective and situational factors are detrimental to academic performance and to the overall educational experience. Although studies suggest the need for social contact with host nationals, such contact among international students seems limited by their language proficiency level which, in turn deters communication with peers, teachers and counsellors (Bochner, Hutnik & Furnham, 1985; Furnham & Alibhai, 1985). Many studies support the finding that the inability to speak the host language fluently is a primary inhibitor to becoming socially involved in the host society (Furnham & Alibhai, 1985; Heikinheimo & Shute, 1986; Meloni, 1986; Ray & Lee, 1988). Dryden and Ellis (1987) declare that language is a fundamental characteristic due to "... the powerful effect that language has on thought and the fact that our emotional processes are heavily dependent on the way we, as humans, structure our thought by the language we employ" (pp. 130-131). Moreover, Albert and Triandis (1991) maintain that language is "...intimately connected with the way in which experience is interpreted and with the cognitive and affective categories which are used to conceptualize the world" (p. 412). Counsellors working with international students should be reminded that it is their own desire to work with the students and the quality of their contribution to the conversation and exchange of trust and empathy that are most significant to the developing relationship.

Gender Differences

Manese, Sedlacek and Leong (1988) conducted a study to examine differences in the needs and perceptions of male and female undergraduate international students from a variety of countries. The results of this study reported sex differences, with women expecting to have a harder time, being more easily discouraged and questioning their self-efficacy more than men. Furthermore, Mallinckrodt and Leong (1992) conducted research to examine level of stress symptoms and sources of social support in male and female international graduate students. They found that female students exhibited more stress symptoms, experienced increased stress and were less satisfied with social support received from family and academic departments. Since women are generally encouraged more than men to develop greater sensitivity to the needs of others (Gilligan, 1982), women are expected to have superior support resources. Even though research results demonstrated a reality different to the expectations, it is generally those individuals with an expressive orientation (i.e., warm, compassionate and nurturing), who seem to have more social support and are more likely to use these resources in times of need (Burda, Vaux & Schill, 1984). These notions have provided some insight for counsellors and academic advisers, alerting them about the impact of stress and stress-related issues faced by international students. One additional implication is that men, who are less likely to be seen by others or themselves as needing support, are most likely to need it and least likely to know how to get help or be willing to take the steps necessary to get it.

Despite gender differences, literature demonstrates that the more different the student's cultural background is from that of the host culture, the more likely it is for them to develop emotional problems of adjustment (Domingues, 1970). Alexander, Klein, Workneh and Miller (1981) researched the adaptation of international students from Third World countries to life on a U.S. campus. Their findings demonstrated that the students experienced stress and feelings of vulnerability throughout their time of study in the United States. An important variable in this group of students was the lack of a familial support system, which is frequently found in people from Third World countries (Arredondo-Dowd, 1981). For these students, initial expressions of happiness about studying abroad can soon turn to feelings of sadness and even disappointment (Arredondo-Dowd, 1981). In a different study, Ying and Liese (1990) used a longitudinal perspective to examine the process of adaptation in a group of Taiwanese international students where adaptation was conceptualized as a subjective sense of adjustment (result oriented, cognitive appraisal of one's life) as well as emotional well-being (process oriented, level of distress experienced while engaged in the process of making the adjustment). The researchers wanted to know what differentiated international students who benefited and grew from the experience of studying abroad from those who were overburdened and unable to cope with the experience. Their findings showed that superior adjustment after arrival was significantly correlated with post-arrival emotional well being. Hence, they suggest that it may be possible to predict adaptation to a new culture because it is largely a self-fulfilling prophecy.

The Challenges

Klineberg and Hull (1979) studied strategies related to dealing with culture shock with 2536 international students from 139 nations; they found that the two most important factors in the coping process were social contact with local people and prior foreign experience. Klein (cited in Pedersen, 1991) identified four coping strategies in international students: Instrumental adaptation, Identification adaptation, Withdrawal adaptation and Resistance adaptation. The findings of his research suggested that: a) culture is important in defining role conflict and identifying elements of stress, but adaptive coping responses are similar across cultures; b) environmental factors are more powerful than personality in determining adaptation; and c) self-esteem and self-confidence with positive reinforcement of social skills and the learning of new skills, can facilitate a successful adaptation. Taft (1977) also listed four predictors of successful adaptation: 1) Size of gap between familiar and unfamiliar culture (inversely proportional); 2) abruptness of discontinuity; 3) salience of changing to functioning; and 4) encompassing degree of new culture.

The academic adviser

As a person who will be in charge of guiding the student throughout his/her program, the academic adviser should be committed to possess a certain amount of information (i.e., on/off campus resources) that will assist the student. The adviser also has the responsibility to develop skills and competencies to help the student during this transition. Differences in how advisers are perceived by international students may be a source of tension in the relationship. These perceptual differences may arise from the ways in which various cultures view men and women in their gender roles. Depending on the country of origin, for example, male students may feel insulted or find it humiliating to have a woman as an adviser. In other cases, some female international students may find it difficult to look male advisers in the eye (Idowu, 1985), a practice that is quite normal and even expected in North America. Because of the differences among cultures in the perception of authority figures, some international students may expect a more formal relationship with their academic advisers or instructors than do most American students. They may be more dependent, demanding or both, believing that advisers or professors should show, tell or even do for them that for which they would be expected to assume individual responsibility in a North American culture. The adviser, in some cases, takes in a mentor role instead. An empathic understanding towards the transitional experience, which involves a sudden self re-evaluation (on both the student and the adviser) is required.

Probably two of the most fundamental objectives in advising international students are to help them adjust to the demands of their respective academic programs and help them achieve academic success. The academic adviser serves as a link between the institution and international students to realize these important goals. Given the seriousness with which the students typically view academic achievement (Heikinheimo & Shute, 1986), the academic adviser may be the central figure in their life. Whether or not this is an accurate description of the adviser's role, advisers must be cognizant of certain issues (e.g., administrative procedures, resource availability and so forth) if they hope to be successful in dealing with this special group. However, the role that an adviser must fulfill goes beyond assisting students with their academic programs. It is the cultural diversity among international students that may prove to be the greatest challenge for academic advisers and counsellors. The challenge comes from the knowledge that whereas diversity must be understood and addressed, "advising must be highly individualized" (Weill, 1982). Common cultural threads may run among students sharing a similar cultural background, but ultimately, each student is an individual with different motivations, needs and disposition. It is in this context that international students must be accepted, helped and advised. By considering the students' cultural background and unique needs, the advising process becomes meaningful and effective for international students. Academic advisers should be prepared to provide ready access to services, help students cope with and balance their emotions and help them anticipate possible challenges and difficulties (being careful not to predispose students), which form part of the adaptation process.

The counsellor

Unfortunately, North American institutions still have a long way to go in order to accommodate to the needs of this special and diverse student group. According to Sue (1981), the cultural adjustment of international students follows a developmental course similar to that of members of minority groups. Early experience with the host culture is likely to result in efforts at conformity, in which the international student follows the lead of the dominant culture. As cultural conflicts arise, values are disturbed and conformity gives way to disharmony. Resistance follows as the student withdraws from the dominant culture. Struggle for a personal locus of control leads to increased introspection, which is followed, for those who will be successful, by a mutual awareness that leads to successful bi-culturalism. Understanding the course of this journey and identifying the student's progress along the way helps the adviser to select appropriate intervention strategies for the student's developing needs. In addition, advisers must transcend their own personal background if they are to be effective in a multicultural society (Heikkinen, 1981; Pedersen, 1991).

International students do have concerns and problems that are different from those of North American students. As a consequence, North American colleges and universities have a special responsibility to international students to provide special services or the customary services in special ways (Locke & Velasco, 1987). After all, counsellors accept a legitimate role in helping international students in the period of cultural transition. However, helping skills must be developed and worked at in order to be effective. Thus, professional counsellors ought to make conscious efforts to increase their cultural awareness and learn the skills and knowledge appropriate to helping students in an international context. Recognizing someone as an international student calls attention to the need to take care differently (Locke & Velasco, 1987). Being an international student, however, does not make these needs different from those of other host students on campus. Counsellors who accept the challenge to work directly with international students are not only likely to help make coming to North America a fulfilling experience for these students, but are also likely to rediscover themselves in the process.

Essential Attributes

Establishing rapport

Being empathic with international students is much easier when the counsellor has the experience of having lived abroad. In some ways it is easier for him/her to understand the students and be patient with them. Counsellors could initiate a conversation by asking students to express how they feel and what they fear. It would be less convenient for counsellors to lecture about their personal experiences since personal accounts are never similar (although pointing them out might help). Counsellors know that acculturation requires time and interaction with the host culture; therefore, it is fundamental that they promote activities where the students feel comfortable and safe to explore their fears, doubts, changes and improvements.

Cultural sensitivity

Cultural sensitivity is a fundamental element, helping international students. It requires that counsellors ignore ethnocentric ways of perceiving differences in behaviors and opinions. International students may demonstrate cultural differences in terms of their concept of time, their use of space, their understanding of self (Hall, 1981) or their value orientations (Sue & Sue, 1999). Regardless of the differences manifested by international students, counsellors must have an attitude of genuine caring (Bargar & Mayo-Chamberlain, 1983) and interest about these students as individuals. Cultural sensitivity is a quality that takes time and effort to develop since it involves an opening of the mind (and the heart) to different worldviews, as well as seeking a deeper understanding of one's own worldview as a helper. Cultural sensitivity is a commitment. It must be remembered that the presence of international students on university campuses represents a commitment on the students' part to achieve academic success. Therefore, counsellors must be similarly committed to helping the students adjust to life in the new culture and its academic demands. Multicultural feasts could be an inviting way to encourage international students to gather and share aspects of their culture by utilizing different forms of displays (i.e., family photographs, recipes of typical foods, traditional/modern kinds of music, stories and/or stereotypical myths followed by historical and accurate facts, etc.). Potlucks can be part of the feasts; after all, food is a key component that brings people together regardless of their cultural background.

Trust

Counsellors should understand that homesickness, academic goals, obtaining housing, the level of the host language and finances are only some of the problems generally faced by international students (Stafford, Marion & Salter, 1980); thus, referring them to the different services on campus might be an appropriate response in helping them resolve some of these problems. However, prudence is advised since, although making referrals is standard practice in American culture, simply referring international students to a particular department for specialized services may not be enough to meet their needs. Developing a sense of trust and credibility might prove to be more helpful since many of them, for cultural reasons, may not be assertive enough to search for help on their own, so making a phone call on their behalf or taking them to the department as a way of introduction may be very useful. Some international students may wait longer than the average North American student before seeking professional assistance because of a strong conviction to obtaining help through the traditional family system (Dillard & Chisolm, 1983). There is reluctance on their part to discuss their problems with individuals who, although professionals, are perceived to be strangers (NAFSA, 2001). Therefore, counsellors should maintain close contact with international students in order to follow their progress. Counsellors who do this are more likely to gain confidence and respect as well as being more effective in helping students to find future help if needed.

Accepting Ambiguity

The cultural dimension of working with international students may create ambiguity that may not exist in counselling relationships with North American students. The codes of communication that counsellors may be familiar with and might even expect in an interaction, may differ from those of their international students for cultural reasons. In instances where these differences create misunderstandings, counsellors must be willing to be patient and do everything possible to encourage clarity. Probably the first step in avoiding such dilemmas is to realize that limited proficiency of the English language or poor social skills in American culture is no reflection of the intelligence of international students. Speaking slowly, carefully articulating words and being willing to repeat oneself when necessary could go a long way in helping to promote understanding and avoid conflict. The same effort put forth by counsellors in an attempt to be understood better should be no different when attempting to understand better. Displays of restlessness or disappointment when students are not sufficiently articulate simply build barriers in the communication process and may even damage the relationship. However, despite the efforts to maximize mutual understanding, there may still be aspects of a particular relationship that may be ambiguous. Counsellors must be prepared to accept this, hoping that as the newly established relationship improves, the level of ambiguity will decrease. It is fundamental that they promote activities where the students feel comfortable and safe to explore their fears, doubts, changes and improvements.

Communication

Students from non-English-speaking countries usually have problems with English speech and comprehension. Although they are required to earn scores on the Test of English as a Foreign Language (TOEFL) at or above a level believed to be adequate for them to understand lectures and do their assignments, many still report English to be a problem (Heikinheimo & Shute, 1986). Counsellors could advise students to take an English support course that would help them improve their proficiency level. Moreover, counsellors could examine and help students with their articulation and comprehension skills during encounters. A cross-cultural group work could evolve from the counsellor's meetings with other international students. This group could be a safe place to explore feelings and emotions that might otherwise not emerge and it could provide opportunities for international students to talk amongst themselves about related adaptation issues. The purpose of the conversation group could aim towards supporting personal growth and self-exploration, encouraging the expression of students' sense of identity, enhancing self-esteem and confidence while concurrently tending to their learning needs by creating effective conditions. The group would also provide support to other members by establishing new connections based on common needs, creating a learning community where individuals can benefit from the group as an environment conducive to personal and professional development. The group would not only be a resource for international students to raise cross-cultural awareness but it would also aid host nationals to become more sensitive to the multicultural context of their relationship with international students. Additional activities (for the more advanced) might include providing the students with opportunities to act as guest speakers for other classes or groups of people (community organizations such as retirement homes, schools, tourist agencies and so forth). Even though some of these activities might require a certain level of language proficiency, they represent opportunities for international students not only to promote their culture and their country, but also to practice English and appear as "visible" components of the university student body.

Implications for Counselling

International students enrich the educational and cultural environments of universities and colleges; they help North American students to gain an appreciation of the vast array of human traditions throughout the world and they help foster a sophistication and cosmopolitan identity in the student body (Weill, 1982). The field of cross-cultural counselling has already built up a considerable frame of research, yielding insights for those concerned with international student support (d'Ardenne & Mahtani, 1989; Eleftheriadou, 1994; Lago, 1996; Pedersen, 1991; Sue & Sue, 1999). However, in many universities, there may be no relationship occurring for students with those who have been designated their academic advisers. This suggests a need for developing more natural channels to be opened up and incorporated within the context of cross-cultural counselling through more open communication and exchange. The experience in which international students are involved cannot be reduced to a purely cognitive journey, but should also allow opportunities for the expression and integration of the personal, emotional and "redefined" self. A support group lead by the academic adviser or the counsellor could be an effective venue for addressing the students' needs for integration, a context in which to establish their sense of belonging and to find a facilitating climate of trust and understanding, that will in turn promote personal and professional growth.

Research on groups (Aveline & Dryden, 1988; Henderson & Forster, 1991; Whitaker, 1987) has shown that the commonality of being with people who share an experience is vital in helping them feel less isolated and provides a strong incentive to group members to seek alternative resolutions to common concerns. If we consider the learning experience in its academic domain as fostering self-actualization and growth, then the process of growth cannot be achieved solely through the academic milieu, but has to be accompanied at the same time by the self-perception that an individual achieves as a fulfilled self. The process of growth involves communication, interaction, sharing experiences and being able to display the affective side of a cognitive being. Unfortunately, when it comes to counselling or guiding international students, it appears that attention is directed almost entirely towards their academic experience (i.e., complying with academic requirements and being successful) leaving little or no room for exploring personal growth and the changes that accompany it as a result.

Conclusion

During the past decades Canadian universities have become a preferred location for foreign students, including American and European students. Nearly 70% of the international students enrolled in Canadian universities are from Third World countries (Statistics Canada, 2000) and research has demonstrated they have had to make more substantial adjustments to North American academic and cultural life than their American, European or Caribbean counterparts. Mickle (1984) mentions in his research that foreign students are more likely to have positive academic and nonacademic experiences if they enjoy a satisfying contact with the host community and that such an achievement is more likely if the emotional and social atmosphere is pleasant and the environment congenial. Domingues (1970) described in her research the need for full-time foreign student advisors in the universities and colleges; she stated that the more different the student's cultural background was from that of North America, the more likely it was for them to develop emotional problems of adjustment. Working with international students in small numbers and groups could mitigate the feelings of isolation and despair that arise as the result of leaving behind what is familiar and known. Pedersen (1991) warns that by making a 'special case' of international students, counsellors and educators run the danger of isolating and stereotyping them by not recognizing the unique problems international students present.

Although universities often provide counselling services for their international (and local) population, these might not be enough nor completely adequate to assist students from up to 200 nationalities. It is understandable that cross-cultural counsellors are not entirely prepared to handle international students under an individual and exclusive approach regarding their country of origin. Hence, international students should be strongly encouraged to adopt a receptive, intuitive and open view concerning their life-style in the host country. As one international student points out: "As a result of having lived in a foreign country, I changed and grew. Facing culture shock, language misunderstandings, monetary constrains (which derived in dietary restrictions, limited resources for academic purposes and inside traveling) and academic disadvantage (because of the difference in programs and requirements), originated in me the need to express everything I was feeling and what was happening around me, to me and inside me. I found that writing about these events and sharing them with other international students alleviated these happenings. I utilized my writing to talk to my adviser about my feelings and emotions. It was not an easy process but I thought that if I was to make out of this experience one of the best of my life, I had to be authentic and true to myself. Being aware of what this meant was not simple nor was it enjoyable at times. Describing to myself and sharing with others what I was feeling and unveiling my limitations were not easy endeavors. There were many feelings attached to every day events and talking about them sometimes meant jeopardizing my own values, beliefs and convictions. However, being specific and authentic about my feelings and emotions thoroughly aided in my adaptation to a new culture. I had to learn how to live in a society that, by being multicultural, shares different worldviews, ideologies, religions and customs. But this was not all; I also had to be aware of the academic requirements of the university and I firmly desired to succeed. Being an international student was not easy at all; however, this experience allowed my self-awareness to emerge and my self-reflection to develop. I was rendered with the opportunity to concurrently review, analyze, challenge and develop my skills, my knowledge, my abilities, my maturity and my common sense...although, according to my mother, it's the least common of all senses."

References

Adler, P.S. (1975). The transitional experience: An alternative view of culture shock. *Journal of Humanistic Psychology, 15*(4), 13-23.

Albert, R.D. & Triandis, H.C. (1991). Intercultural education for multicultural societies: Critical issues. In L.A. Samovar and R.E. Porter (Eds.), *Intercultural Communication: A Reader* (6th

Edition). Belmont, CA: Wadsworth.

Alexander, A., Klein, M., Workneh, F. & Miller, M. (1981). Psychotherapy and the foreign student. In P. Pedersen, J. Draguns & J. Trimble (Eds.), *Counseling Across Cultures* (2nd ed., pp. 227-243). Honolulu, HI: University of Hawaii Press.

Arredondo-Dowd, P. (1981). Personal loss and grief as a result of immigration. *The Personnel and Guidance Journal, 2*, 376-378.

Aveline, M. & Dryden, W. (Eds.) (1988). *Group Therapy in Britain*. Milton Keynes: Open University Press.

Bargar, R. & Mayo-Chamberlain, J. (1983). Advisor and advisee issues in doctoral education. *Journal of Higher Education, 54*(4), 407-432.

Belenky, M., Mc Vicker, B., Goldberger, N. & Mattuck, J. (1986). *Women's Ways of Knowing*. USA: Basic Books.

Bochner, S., Hutnik, N. & Furnham, A. (1985). The friendship patterns of overseas and host students in an Oxford student residence. *Journal of Social Psychology, 125*, 689-694.

Burda. P., Vaux, A. & Schill, T. (1984). Social support resources: Variation across sex and sex role. *Personality and Social Psychology Bulletin, 10*, 119-126.

D'Ardenne, P. & Mahtani, A. (1989). *Transcultural Counselling in Action*. London: Sage.

Day, R. & Hajj, F. (1986). Delivering counseling service to international students: The experience of the American University of Beirut. *Journal of College Student Personnel, 7*, 353-357.

Dillard, J. & Chisolm, G. (1983). Counseling the international student in a multicultural context. *Journal of College Student Personnel, 3*, 101-105.

Domingues, P.M. (1970). Student personnel services for international students. In Wehrly, B. (1986), *Counseling International Students: Issues, Concerns and Programs. International Journal for the Advancement of Counseling, 9*, 11-22.

Dryden, W. & Ellis, A. (1987). Rational-emotive therapy. In W. Dryden & W.L. Golden (Eds.), *Cognitive Behavioral Approaches to Psychotherapy*. New York: Hemisphere Publishing.

Eleftheriadou, Z. (1994). *Transcultural Counselling*. London: Central.

Exum, H. & Lau, E. (1988). Counseling style preference of Chinese college students. *Journal of Multicultural Counseling and Development, 16*, 84-92.

Furnham, A. (1989). Communicating across cultures: A social skills perspective. *Counseling Psychology Quarterly*, No. 2, 205-222.

Furnham, A. & Alibhai. N. (1985). The friendship networks of foreign students: A replication and extension of the functional model. *International Journal of Psychology, 20*, 709-722.

Gilligan, C. (1982). *In a Different Voice*. Cambridge, MA: Harvard University Press.

Hall, E. (1981). *Beyond Culture*. New York: Anchor Press, Doubleday.

Heikinheimo, P. & Shute, J. (1986). The adaptation of foreign students: Student views and institutional implications. *Journal of College Student Personnel, 27*(5), 399-406.

Heikkinen, C. (1981). Loss resolution for growth. *The Personnel and Guidance Journal, 59*, 327-331.

Henderson, P. & Forster, G. (1991). *Groupwork*. Cambridge: National Extension College.

Idowu, A. (1985). Counseling Nigerian students in United States colleges and universities. *Journal of Counseling and Development, 63*(8), 506-509.

Klein, M. (1977). Preliminary overview: Adaptation to new cultural environments. In P. Pedersen, *Counseling International Students. The Counseling Psychologist*. No. 1, January, 1991, 10-58.

Klineberg, D. & Hull, W.F. (1979). *At a Foreign University: An International Study of Adaptation and Coping*. New York: Praeger.

Lago, C. (1996). *Race, Culture and Counselling*. Buckingham: Open University Press.

Leong, F. & Sedlacek. W. (1986). A comparison of international and U.S. students' preferences for help sources. *Journal of College Student Personnel, 27*, 426-430.

Locke, D.C. & Velasco, J. (1987). Hospitality begins with the invitation: Counseling foreign students. *Journal of Multicultural Counseling and Development, 7*, 115-119.

Mallinckrodt, B. & Leong, F.T.L. (1992). International graduate students, stress and social support. *Journal of College Student Development, 33*: 71-78.

Manese, J.E., Sedlacek, W.E. and Leong, F.T.L. (1988). Needs and perceptions of female and male international undergraduate students. *Journal of Multicultural Counseling and Development*, 24-29.

Meloni, C. (1986). Adjustment problems of foreign students in U.S. colleges and universities. Washington, DC: ERIC Clearinghouse on Language and Linguistics.

Mickle, M. (1984). The cross-cultural adaptation of Hong Kong students at two Ontario universities. In Heikinheimo, P.S. & Shute, J.C.M. (1986), *The Adaptation of Foreign Students: Student Views and Institutional Implications. Journal of College Student Personnel, 27*, 399-406.

National Association for Foreign Student Affairs. (2001). *Guidelines: Academic and Personal Advising*. Washington, DC: Author.

Oberg, K. (1957). Culture shock and the problem of adjustment to new cultural environments. In Pedersen, P., Draguns, J., Lonner, W. & Trimble, J. (Eds.), *Counseling Across Cultures*. Thousand Oaks, CA: Sage Publications.

Paulhus, D. & Martin, C. (1987). The structure of personality capabilities. *Journal of Personality and Social Psychology, 52*, 354-365.

Pedersen, P. (1991). Counseling international students. *The Counseling Psychologist, 19*, 10-58.

Pedersen, P., Draguns, J., Lonner, W. & Trimble, J. (2003). *Counseling Across Cultures*. Thousand Oaks, CA: Sage Publications.

Putney, R. (1981). Impact of marital loss on support systems. *The Personnel and Guidance Journal, 59*, 351-354.

Ray, M. & Lee, M. (1988). Effects of stigmas on intergroup relationships. *Journal of Social Psychology, 129*, 855-857.

Romero, M. (1981). Multicultural reality: The pain of growth. *The Personnel and Guidance Journal, 59*, 384-386.

Schram, J. & Lauver, P. (1988). Alienation in international students. *Journal of College Student Development, 29*, 146-150.

Stafford. T. Jr., Marion, P. & Salter, M. (1980). Adjustment of international students. *NASPA Journal, 18*(1), 40-45.

Statistics Canada. (2000). Available at http://www.statcan.ca

Steinglass, P., DeNour, A. & Shye, S. (1985). Factors influencing psychosocial adjustment to forces in geographical relocation: The Israeli withdrawal from the Sinai. *American Journal of Orthopsychiatry, 55*, 513-529.

Sue, D.W. (1981). *Counseling the Culturally Different.* New York: Wiley.

Sue, D.W. & Sue, D. (1999). *Counseling the Culturally Different – Theory and Practice.* New York: Wiley.

Surdam, J.C. & Collins, J.R. (1984). Adaptation of international students: A cause for concern. *Journal of College Student Personnel, 25*, 240-244.

Taft, R. (1977). Coping with unfamiliar cultures. In N. Warren (Ed.), *Studies in Cross-Cultural Psychology* (pp. 120-135). London: Academic Press.

Vaux, A., Burda, P. and Stewart, D. (1986). Orientation towards utilization of support resources. *Journal of Community Psychology, 14*: 159-170.

Webster's New World Dictionary of the English Language. (1999). New York: Collins/World.

Weill, L. (1982). Advising international students at small colleges. *NACADA Journal, 2*(1), 52-56.

Wheeler, S. & Birtle, J. (1993). *A Handbook for Personal Tutors.* Buckingham: Society for Research into Higher Education. Buckingham: Open University Press.

Whitaker, D. (1987). *Using Groups to Help People.* London: Tavistock/Routledge.

Ying, Y.W. & Liese, L.H. (1990). Initial adaptation of Chinese sojourners in Canada. In P. Pedersen, J. Draguns, W. Lonner & J. Trimble (Eds.), *Counseling Across Cultures.* Thousand Oaks, CA: Sage Publications.

Chapter 17

The Invisible Minority: The Role of the School Counsellor in Serving the Needs of Gay and Lesbian Students

Heather Roberts

Everyday We wake up and get ready for work.
We drive our cars on the same roads, the same highways.
We park right next to your cars. We use the same bathrooms.
We listen to the same music.
We breathe the same air.
We live in the same society.
So, why do you abhor us when we share so many of the same things?
Okay, so we love differently!
Why does that matter?
There is really nothing to fear from us except the pain that comes from your ignorance!
Brett, a high school student (Sears, 1992, p. 31).

Gay and Lesbian youth are a forgotten minority in our society. To many, these teens do not exist (Savin-Williams, 1990). The traditional support structures that serve other adolescents fail lesbian and gay youth; leaving many of them to face an inordinately high risk of suicide, parental rejection, violence, sexual abuse, school drop-out, drug abuse and prostitution.

Adolescence is a time of tremendous physical, emotional, social and intellectual change. Regardless of sexual identity, this is often a period of turmoil as teens cope with physical and sexual maturation, while at the same time striving for independence as they separate emotionally from their parents. This process is further complicated for the gay or lesbian youth whose primary developmental task becomes adjustment to a socially stigmatized role (Hetrick & Martin, 1987). Usually this adjustment occurs in isolation; without adequate information. While other adolescents are becoming aware of their interest in the opposite sex, gay and lesbian youth are often frightened, confused and ashamed by their emerging sexual feelings.

The invisible nature of lesbian and gay adolescents is also evident in the lack of empirical studies of this group. For the most part, research either ignores sexual minority youth entirely, or relies on retrospective data, substituting recall for teen's experiences (Anderson, 1995; Herdt, 1989).

This chapter examines many of the unique stressors and challenges facing gay and lesbian adolescents and offers some interventions that school counselors can use to meet the special needs of this invisible minority.

Issues Gay and Lesbian Students Face

Isolation

Isolation is frequently cited as the most prevalent and, potentially, the most serious problem gay and lesbian adolescents face (Besner & Spungin, 1995; Hetrick & Martin, 1987; Martin & Hetrick, 1988; Murphy, 1992; Uribe & Harbeck, 1992). Much of this isolation stems from the stigma and confusion associated with society's negative attitudes towards gay and lesbians. In adopting a sexual identity that is often considered abnormal, immoral or pathological, many teens internalize the negative stereotypes, thereby believing they are psychological and/or social deviants. Many gay and lesbian youth react by hiding their homosexuality, which contributes to an even greater sense of loneliness, as fear of discovery becomes an integral part of life. The options available are less than optimal. To hide means living a double life based on a lie and never feeling truly accepted, while to disclose means risking disapproval and discrimination (Murphy, 1992). The gay adolescent feels completely alone, with no one to talk to; no source of emotional support. The critical nature of this emotional isolation is evident in the high incidence of suicide among gay and lesbian teenagers.

In 1989, gay and lesbian adolescents accounted for an estimated 30% of all completed suicides among youth (Besner & Spungin, 1995). Equally alarming, Uribe and Harbeck (1992) found that half of the participants in their study of 50 self-identified gay and lesbian teens acknowledged that they had attempted suicide. Hetrick and Martin (1987) report that 20% of their clients at the Institute for the Protection of Lesbian and Gay Youth had either attempted suicide or had strong suicide ideation, with the incidence even higher for those teens who had only telephone contact with the Institute.

Not only has isolation been identified as a primary factor in predicting suicide, but it frequently leads to other high-risk behaviors, including running away, substance abuse, dropping out of school, unhealthy sexual behaviors and others (Besner & Spungin, 1995).

Family Difficulties

Family difficulties can lead to increased isolation and alienation and range from feelings of rejection and denial to actual violence and expulsion from the home. Problems within the family appear to be linked to stigmatization and misinformation (Hetrick & Martin, 1987). Adolescents depend on their parents for emotional and financial support. Family acceptance is important to both heterosexuals and homosexuals, however, many gay and lesbians fail to disclose a significant part of themselves to those they love. Fears of coming out to family indicate internal fears of emotional rejection and guilt, along with cognitive dissonance, as they fear disappointing their family by failing to live up to parental expectations (Gerstel, Feraios & Herdt, 1989). Coming out also elicits fear of external threats of being expelled from the home, being physically abused or being forced into psychotherapy (Gerstel, Feraios & Herdt, 1989). These fears are realistic. Half of all gay and lesbian youths interviewed in a 1987 study reported that their parents rejected them for being homosexual (Besner & Spungin, 1995). It is also startling to note that one in four gay and lesbian teens are forced to leave home because of conflicts with their families about their sexual orientation (Besner & Spungin, 1995).

Unlike adolescents of other minority groups who can find support and acceptance within their families, gay and lesbian teens almost never have the same sexual orientation as their parents (Gerstel, Feraios & Herdt, 1989). Therefore, even those parents who are aware and supportive of their child's emerging homosexuality, lack personal experience dealing with the related problems and issues and thus fail to serve as their child's advocate. Despite evidence that indicates familial background appears to have nothing to do with development of sexuality, when disclosure occurs, parents often blame themselves for their child's emerging gay or lesbian identity (Martin & Hetrick, 1988; Carl, 1990). Many parents dismiss their child's feelings as a "passing phase" on the way to a heterosexual destination; communicating a negative message to the gay or lesbian teen (Uribe & Harbeck, 1992).

Violence

Violence is another issue that gay and lesbian youth are confronted with daily. Martin and Hetrick (1989) report that over 40% of their clients have experienced violence because of their sexual orientation. 49% of the violence occurred at the hands of the family; most often from parents, but occasionally from siblings. Running away or expulsion from the home often result when violence occurs within the family, with prostitution a secondary consequence.

The perpetrators of violence against gay and lesbians are most often young men, making high schools a frequent site for homophobic violence (Lipkin, 1995). When violence occurs within the school environment, many gay and lesbian teenagers view dropping out as the only solution. Each of the respondents in Uribe and Harbeck's (1992) sample knew at least one or more gay or lesbian student who had dropped out of school because of the physical and verbal abuse he or she had suffered. A recent article in the *Vancouver Sun* (Bolan, 1997) reports of a 16-year-old gay youth who was driven out of his school by both taunting and threats. "I was afraid to go. I was petrified. I even had a knife pulled on me"

(p. A6) stated the teen. In the same article, a 17-year-old gay male described the harassment he faces daily, "People call me names. Everyday I've been followed from my school by guys in a car who came to beat me up" (Bolan, 1997, p.A6)

Sexual Abuse

Sexual abuse of gay and lesbian youth is widespread. 22% of the adolescents that Martin and Hetrick (1988) work with eventually report sexual abuse. The abuse is often not mentioned initially out of shame, self-blame and a failure to recognize that what happened to them was abuse.

Sexual abuse of adolescent gay and lesbians living at home is likely to be by a family member, while teens who run away or are expelled from the home face a high risk of rape and prostitution (Martin & Hetrick, 1988). When it occurs at home, teens often blame themselves. In particular, the young gay male tends to feel he has brought it on himself because of his sexual desires for men. Many gay males become involved with older men because they feel that there is no one else they can relate to. Often the relationship continues even when the young male is forced to perform acts he does not want to perform or to perform them with people he does not desire (Martin & Hetrick, 1988). The early sexual experiences of gay males are often recalled as violent, guilt ridden encounters, rather than happy events (Uribe & Harbeck, 1992). The phenomenon of self-blame and lack of recognition of abuse for gay and lesbian adolescents is often exploited by adults who prey on these isolated teens.

HIV Infection

Adolescent gay males face a higher risk of HIV infection than any other group (Cranston, 1992). The rates of infection in young gay and bisexual males range from 4%-47%, with a median rate of 25% (Cranston, 1992). Unprotected sexual activity, along with sharing drug needles, account for the increased risk. When alcohol and other drug use are combined with sexual activity, unsafe sexual behaviors are even more likely to occur. None of the gay males in Uribe and Harbeck's (1992) study had practiced "safe" sex during his first sexual experience. A factor that is often overlooked when accounting for increased risks of infection among lesbian and gay youth is their lower self-esteem. Individuals with a poor sense of personal worth lack personal empowerment and support and therefore, have less ability to pursue healthy behavior options (Cranston, 1992).

Despite being at risk, the special needs of these youth have received little attention; few resources are available. In recent years, the majority of HIV prevention has been directed towards heterosexual adolescents, excluding the concerns of gay and lesbian youth. The absence of information informs learners that sexual minority youth either do not exist or are not important.

Counselor Interventions

Addressing The Needs of Gay and Lesbian Students

If we accept the widely quoted estimate that 10% of the population is homosexual, it is easy to recognize that the number of gay and lesbian teens in the school counsellor's caseload is significant. While gay and lesbian students do not differ from heterosexual youth in their need to make use of the basic counseling and guidance services available, in order to effectively meet the needs of lesbian and gay teens who may be feeling alone and isolated, the counselor may need to adapt his or her role (Reynolds & Koski, 1995). Counsellors attempting to satisfy the needs of gay and lesbian students require certain competencies beyond the everyday core skills of listening, empathy, facilitation, consultation and individual and group counseling. To work effectively with gay and lesbian teens, counselors need to be able to tolerate ambiguity and conflict, be able to confront homophobia and heterosexism and deal openly with issues of sexuality (Reynolds & Koski, 1995). The school counsellor is in a position to understand the stressors gay and lesbians face, to promote awareness and to provide appropriate support. The remainder of this article offers specific interventions the school counsellor can implement to work towards addressing the needs of this under-serviced population.

Practice of Self-Awareness

Sears (1991) conducted a two-year study of the perceptions and attitudes of school personnel toward homosexuality. According to this study, nearly two-thirds of school counselors expressed negative attitudes and feelings about homosexuality and gay and lesbian individuals. It is important for counsellors to examine their own feelings and attitudes regarding homosexuality (Krajeski, 1984). Any biases need to be explored honestly, in order to remain a neutral source of information and support. Students and counsellors alike are both affected by homophobia and heterosexual bias, therefore counsellors must become conscious of their own homophobia and overcome their negative attitudes and stereotypes towards gay and lesbians. In addition, counsellors are encouraged to explore their comfort level with their own sexual orientation to ensure they are able to provide an appropriate environment for the adolescent to explore his or her feelings about sexuality.

Provide Accurate Information and Referrals

It is important that school counselors familiarize themselves with issues that surround gay and lesbian youth and be able to provide accurate information on vital topics, such as the coming out process, debunking myths and safe sex. Misinformation must be replaced with accurate knowledge. We have all been exposed to myths and stereotypes, therefore, the students' understanding of homosexuality should be assessed and any necessary clarification made. Counsellors can develop a list of relevant books, videos and articles for teens and parents in need of further information and support.

Practical knowledge of community resources is essential. The counselor should be aware of local organizations, youth support groups, help lines and gay and lesbian publications. Part of the counsellor's role is to serve as a liaison between the school and outside agencies. Counsellors require a strong referral network when additional services for their gay and lesbian students are necessary. A list of physicians, therapists and other health care professionals who are sensitive and supportive of the needs of gay and lesbian teens is essential.

Create a Supportive Environment

Establishing an office environment that is sensitive and open will help develop trust, increasing the likelihood that students may eventually confide in the counsellor. Gay and lesbian students require role models who can help foster a more positive, accepting climate. School counsellors can take on this role by actively combating homophobia and heterosexism within the school.

The counsellor can begin to create a supportive environment by using non-judgmental language when speaking with teens about dating, relationships and sexuality. Gay and lesbian teens will feel more comfortable discussing their feelings if they hear the counsellor refer to their "partner" rather than using either "girlfriend" or "boyfriend" to refer to a member of the opposite sex. This indicates an awareness of sexual diversity and lets others know that they do not assume that all teenagers are heterosexual (Besner & Spungin, 1995).

The counsellor should be accepting of the student as a whole person. It should not be assumed that all gay and lesbian students' problems stem from issues of sexuality (Dulaney & Kelly, 1982; Krajeski, 1984). Sexual orientation does not define whether an individual is psychologically healthy, nor does it define any particular background, beliefs, abilities, values or lack thereof (Krajeski, 1986). All teenagers are faced with complex developmental tasks, therefore, integration of sexual orientation should be viewed as only one aspect of an individual's identity.

In addition, by displaying posters and books on the subject of homosexuality, counsellors will identify to students that they are open to discussing the topic. This small gesture goes far in conveying a message of acceptance and affirmation. Referral information displayed on a bulletin board also provides a non-threatening means of reaching students who do not feel comfortable asking for information.

Provide In-Service Training to Staff

A necessary step in helping lesbian and gay students is to establish an awareness of sexual diversity and homophobia among school personnel. School staff are in a position to create a positive learning environment of support, acceptance and understanding, or a negative atmosphere of rejection and discrimination that may lead to further isolation (Kaplan &

Geoffroy, 1990). Demonstrating an open and accepting attitude and responding positively to the diversities among students will promote the trust and communication which are critical to the emotional growth of all (Besner & Spungin, 1995).

When developing workshops for staff, it is important that experienced and knowledgeable trainers be used, because the level of knowledge and individual biases will likely be varied. When possible, gay and lesbian individuals of differing ages and backgrounds can be invited to share their experiences. This will expose school staff to first-hand information and help dispel many of the myths and stereotypes. Facilitators must create a safe climate for discussion and an acceptance of diverse opinions. The issue of sexual orientation should be presented as another part of normal development, rather than as a "problem" (Reynolds & Koski, 1995).

Data from a workshop on gay and adolescent youth suggest that education can improve awareness and result in more accurate and positive attitudes (Newman, 1989).

Start a Support Group for Teens

Support groups provide a safe, comfortable place where students can deal with the emergence of their sexual orientation, family problems, peer relationships and other issues. They offer a non critical atmosphere in which participants can be themselves and explore their feelings. Sharing experiences with peers can enhance self-esteem and facilitate emotional growth (Gerstel, Feraios & Herdt 1989). This is especially important for gay and lesbian youth who often believe that no one else is experiencing the same feelings. A supportive peer group validates sameness and celebrates differences of gay adolescents. The groups offer a healthy environment where teens can develop necessary social skills, learn about others and obtain unbiased information (Robinson, 1991). The effects of both internal and external homophobia are lessened as teens become confident in discovering who they are and what being gay means to them (Robinson, 1991).

In Vancouver, which has one of the highest concentrations of gay and lesbians, has 10 drop-in groups a week operating throughout the lower-mainland area. The Vancouver Gay and Lesbian Centre recommends that counsellors who are interested in starting a youth group begin by promoting gay/straight alliances. The general goals of gay/straight alliance groups are to encourage acceptance, support and collaboration of all sexual orientations and to provide a safe place for teenagers to be themselves. Such alliances promote recognition that homophobia is something that affects all students. "…alliance groups are steadily becoming an important piece of an over all strategy to ensure that schools fulfil their mandate of providing the best education possible in a safe and welcoming environment for students of all sexual identities" (Blumenfeld, 1995, p. 212).

Educate All Students

While it is important to provide support groups to those students who want to attend, it is also necessary to educate the entire student population about gay and lesbian issues. Schools can have a positive impact on how students construe differences among themselves. Not only does broad education of the entire student population help make schools safer for minority students, but the general student body appreciates the additional information, they become proud of the friendships they have with gay and lesbian peers and are better prepared for life in our diverse society (Harbeck, 1995). Everyone benefits and grows if given the guidance and opportunity. Presenting homosexuality without embarrassment signals an acceptance of sexuality in general, an attitude that may facilitate important communication with gay and lesbian and heterosexual students alike.

While the Vancouver Gay and Lesbian Centre (VGLC) will deliver workshops to interested classes throughout the province, this may not be true in other areas of Canada. However, it does provide some idea of what can be done. The workshops are facilitated by both teens and adults and focus primarily on issues of homophobia, labeling and the role all students can play in dealing with these issues. Sex is not discussed. The VGLC has found that their education programs can improve awareness and attitudes towards gay and lesbian teens in schools, as well as adults within the community. In their study, Uribe and Harbeck (1992) found that the majority of the general student population felt homosexuality was an appropriate topic for discussion.

Consult and Share Experience with Colleagues

No discussion of counselling interventions would be complete without the inclusion of collegial consultation. The process of sharing information and ideas, comparing, observing and providing a sounding board can assist counsellors in strategically planning for effective intervention with gay and lesbian students. Through collaboration and joint planning, counsellors can benefit from the knowledge and first hand experiences of colleagues, share resources, distribute work equitably, develop competencies and provide support for one another. Harbeck (1995) advocates a multi-layer approach in dealing with these educational and social concerns, whereby teachers from elementary, middle schools, high schools and post-secondary institutions form alliances and work together to share information and develop programs for gay and lesbian students.

Conclusion

This chapter serves merely as a starting point for the concerned counsellor. While the lack of research on gay and lesbian youth is problematic, counsellors are in a unique position within the school to ask questions and gather and assess information, thus determining the needs directly from the students themselves (Kaplan & Geoffroy, 1990). While confronting gay and lesbian issues within the school may be controversial, the alarming risks sexual minority youth face daily demonstrate that the issue needs to be dealt with directly. Breaking the silence concerning homosexuality is essential in preventing suicide, substance abuse, violence and school drop-outs. "The pain and hardship suffered by adolescent gay, lesbian and bisexual youth is no longer invisible and our lack of action is no longer professionally or ethically acceptable" (Uribe & Harbeck, 1992, p.27)

References

Anderson, D.A. (1995). Lesbian and gay adolescents: Social and developmental considerations. In G. Unks (Ed.), *The Gay Teen: Educatinal Practice and Theory for Lesbian, Gay and Bisexual Adolescents* (pp. 17-28). New York, NY: Routledge.

Besner, H.G. & Spungin, C.J. (1995). *Gay and Lesbian Students: Understanding their Needs.* Washington, DC: Taylor & Francis.

Blumenfeld, W.J. (1995). "Gay/straight" alliances. In G. Unks (Ed.), *The Gay Teen: Educational Practice and Theory for Lesbian, Gay and Bisexual Adolescents* (pp. 211-224). New York, NY: Routledge.

Bolan, K. (1997, March 17). Demonstrators face off over homosexuality issue. *The Vancouver Sun*, pp. A1, A6.

Carl, D. (1990). *Counseling Same-sex Couples.* New York, NY: W.W. Norton & Company.

Cranston, K. (1992). HIV education for gay, lesbian and bisexual youth: Personal risk, personal power and the community of conscience. *Journal of Homosexuality, 22*(3/4), 247-259.

Dulaney, D.D. & Kelly, J. (1982). Improving services to gay and lesbian clients, *Social Work, 27*(2), 178-183.

Gerstel, C.J., Feraios, A.J. & Heerdt, G. (1989). Widening circles: An ethnographic profile of a youth group. *Journal of Homosexuality, 17*, 75-92.

Harbeck, K.M. (1995). Invisible no more: Addressing the needs of lesbian, gay and bisexual youth and their advocates. In G. Unks (Ed.), *The Gay Teen: Educational Practice and Theory for Lesbian, Gay and Bisexual Adolescents* (pp. 125-133). New York, NY:Routledge.

Herdt, G. (1989). Introduction: Gay and lesbian youth, emergent identities and cultural scenes at home and abroad. *Journal of Homosexuality, 17*, 1-41.

Hetrick, E. & Martin, D. (1987). Developmental issues and the irresolution for gay and lesbian adolescents. *Journal of Homosexuality, 14*, 13-24.

Kaplan, L.S. & Geoffroy, K.E. (1990). Enhancing the school climate: New opportunities for the counsellor. *The School Counsellor, 38*, 7-12.

Krajeski, J.P. (1984). Psychotherapy with gay and lesbian patients. In E.S. Hetrick & T.S. Stein (Eds.), *Psychotherapy with Homosexuals* (pp. 76-88). Washington, D.C.: American Psychiatric Press.

Krajeski, J.P. (1986). Psychotherapy with gay men and lesbians. In T.S. Stein & C.J. Cohen (Eds.), *Contemporary Perspectives on Psychotherapy with Lesbians and Gay Men* (pp. 9-25). New York, NY: Plenum Medical Book Company.

Lipkin, A. (1995). The case for gay and lesbian curriculum. In G. Unks (Ed.), *The Gay Teen: Educational Practice and Theory for Lesbian, Gay and Bisexual Adolescents* (pp. 31-52). New York, NY: Routledge.

Martin, A.D. & Hetrick, E.S. (1988). The stigmatization of the gay and lesbian adolescent. *Journal of Homosexuality, 15,* 163-183.

Murphy, B.C. (1992). Educating mental health professionals about gay and lesbian issues. *Journal of Homosexuality, 22*(3/4), 229-246.

Newman, B. (1989). Including curriculum content on lesbian and gay issues. *Journal of Social Work Education, 3,* 202-211.

Reynolds, A.L. & Koski, M.J. (1995). Lesbian, gay and bisexual teens and the school counselor. In G. Unks (Ed.), *The Gay Teen: Educational Practice and Theory for Lesbian, Gay and Bisexual Adolescents* (pp. 85-93). New York, NY: Routledge.

Robinson, K.E. (1991). Gay youth support groups: An opportunity for mental health intervention. *Social Work, 36*(5), 458-459.

Savin-Williams, R.C. (1990). *Gay and Lesbian Youth: Expressions of Identity.* New York, NY: Hemisphere Publishing Corporation.

Sears, J.T. (1992). Educators, homosexuality and homosexual students. Are personal feelings related to professional beliefs? *Journal of Homosexuality, 22* (3/4), 29-79.

Uribe, V. & Harbeck, K. (1992). Addressing the needs of lesbian, gay and bisexual youth. The origins of Project 10 and school-based intervention. Journal of Homosexuality, 22)3/4), 9-28.

Chapter 18

Ethnic Canadians: A Multicultural Perspective

M. Honoré France and Steve Bentheim

In a pluralistic and multicultural society it is vital to help make people aware that there is not just a large majority on one side and visible minorities on the other side. In fact the "white" population, which has been referred to in the research literature as the "majority," is made up of a variety of different peoples with differing cultural practices, values, languages and religions. When many of them came to North America they were escaping persecution for being different, either because of their language, beliefs, religion or ethnic identity. They came to Canada in the last 150 years, as many people who immigrate today, to find justice and a safe place to rear a family. The first wave of European immigration was primarily composed of English and French peoples. Later, Irish, Southern and Eastern Europeans came to the shores of Canada. Today, the primary groups of immigrants come from China, with other large segments coming from such diverse places as Trinidad, Ethiopia and El Salvador. In Canada, many of these people have been labeled allophone, to show the distinction from being neither Francophone nor Anglophone. We need to get it into our consciousness and into our counselling and teaching practices that in a true multicultural society, every group of people is different. So what does it mean to be pluralistic or multicultural? It means to become aware and knowledgeable about everyone, regardless of their color, ethnic background, language or religion. This chapter will cover the European immigrants to Canada including Anglophones, Francophones and white ethnic that includes people who originated from other parts of Europe, such as Eastern and Southern Europe. To highlight some of the differences between peoples, we have chosen to provide some specific aspects of those from the Italian and Jewish communities.

Acculturation and Assimilation

According to Dyer (1994), the concept of national identity is not only recent, but fluid in nature. That is because the nation state is historically a recent phenomenon that goes back to a time when people started to live in large groups. Before that, people identified with their families or clans. Nation-states are not permanent, but rise and fall according to historical events. Canada is not unique in that regard, having not only a very recent history, but also having a dramatically diverse population that has changed since Confederation. The various people who immigrated to Canada have adapted themselves to the new land and created over time a national identity that is changing as the diversity of its people change. The forces that forged Canadian society can be better understood by examining the concepts of acculturation and assimilation. Acculturation is an internal process of accepting the values of the majority society at the expense of one's traditional culture. It often occurs slowly over time. According to Berry and Sam (1997), there are four strategies of acculturation: assimilation; traditionality; integration; and marginality. These dynamic forces that have shaped people to become who they are today should not been seen as negative or positive, but rather as processes that were either chosen (e.g., Irish), forced (e.g., First Nations) or circumstantial (e.g., refugees from a variety of countries).

Assimilation

Generally, most peoples, particularly those of European origin, have assimilated into the mainstream of Canadian life with little difficulty. Assimilation is a process where people are absorbed, either passively, deliberately or by government policy, losing their cultural differences and blending into society. For example, people of German ancestry give up the language and custom of their ancestors either by choice or over time and become Anglo in language and culture. In the United States, this process is sometimes positively viewed as a "melting pot" in which everyone blends together to make something new or different. The Canadian government, on the other hand, has stressed that it is committed to encouraging groups to maintain their identity, so there can be a pattern of distinct differences among peoples. In actuality, this has sometimes been an idealized view that is not shared by the general population nor by various societal institutions that would still prefer people to behave in a way similar to their own. Despite whether the "mosaic" or "melting pot" is better, the fact is that many people, when they go to work, must give up what makes them distinct.

Traditionality

Traditionality, unlike assimilation, occurs when people choose to hold on to their language and culture, often rejecting or avoiding interaction with the majority culture. Traditionalists, while maintaining their own culture and traditions, have little knowledge or appreciation of the majority culture. Groups like the Doukhobors, who have kept the Russian language and customs, or the Mennonites, who kept the German language and customs, have maintained them by keeping themselves apart from mainstream Canadian culture. Interestingly, traditionality is much more difficult to maintain when there is frequent contact, even in Doukhobor society, which by the late 20th century was assimilated, unlike the Mennonites. When the same action is forced upon people, it is called segregation. Segregation occurs when those in power force separation on the powerless (i.e., Apartheid).

Integration

Integration, on the other hand, is a process of maintaining one's language and culture, while gaining knowledge and an appreciation about the majority culture. Thus, having this bi-cultural stance makes it is possible to have knowledge about or even an appreciation of the majority culture while maintaining one's own culture and traditions. This ideal of integration is more demonstrative of the mosaic philosophy. Berry and Kim (1988) go on to stress that those who have a strong sense of their cultural identity, while being able to function successfully in majority society, are the least likely to suffer from mental health problems.

Marginality

Marginality is the process in which the original or traditional culture is not maintained and there is a rejection of majority culture. It has to be understood that sometimes the process of acceptance or rejection may be determined or affected by the historical experience of discrimination. Marginalized people have lost their language and traditions and have not replaced them by accepting the dominant culture's values. People who are marginalized, by rejecting themselves and others, are not surprisingly led to acculturation stress, sometimes accompanied by alcohol and substance abuse. According to Robinson and Howard-Hamilton (1999), this relationship between marginalization and substance abuse can be seen in some Hispanic and Aboriginal groups, which have been culturally devastated. The case of the Inuit of Davis Inlet is a good example of the effects of people who have been marginalized by majority society.

What needs to be remembered is that dealing with different ethnic groups successfully is being able to adopt helping strategies that can exist with acculturalization differences. Culture plays a fundamental role in people's lives that take in beliefs, behaviors and traditions. Effective counselling can only occur when one becomes aware, accepts and values the differences in others. This is what accepting the "diversity" in society is all about. It is important to remember that while diversity encompasses the traits that distinguish one group from another group, ethnicity "is the consciousness of a cultural heritage shared with other people" (Bucher, p. 13, 1999).

Anglo-Canadians

Anglo-Canadians include not only those people whose parents originated from English-speaking peoples, but also Germanic and other northern Europeans. In addition, it also includes those who acculturated into English speakers. After the defeat of French forces on the Plains of Abraham in Quebec, Canada was an integral part of the British Empire, with every "white" person born during this period considered English or a citizen of the British Empire and thus identifying themselves as British. The concept of Canadian started only after Confederation and even then, Canadian identity was firmly rooted in Anglo-Saxon tradition. Other early groups, such as Scandinavians and Germanic peoples, quickly adapted and became English in national consciousness. Before the turn of the century more than 80% of the peoples who immigrated to Canada from Europe came from the British Isles or Germanic countries. Later generations of immigrants from other European ethnic groups, regardless of origin, have assimilated to the point that their ethnic identity can be consider Anglo-Canadian.

Immigration and Racial Identity

Other than Francophones, the English-speaking peoples, who were primarily Protestant, saw themselves as the founding people of Canada. In fact, up until the Pearson years, most elements of Canadian government and cultural practices were primarily English in origin. Peoples from other parts of Europe, particularly Southern Europe, were considered as "not measuring up" to English standards. Interestingly, people of British ancestry are multicultural in ethnic origin. Anglo-Saxon, often used to describe people of "English" origin, are actually Germanic and Scandinavian. When Canadian immigration laws were changed in 1947, with the passing of the Canadian Citizenship law, all citizens of Canada were considered British subjects. In other words, new immigrants were supposed to assimilate, which Fleras and Elliott (1992) called "Anglo conformity." In fact, the political nature of the Canadian government, laws, social traditions and other aspects of culture were primarily British. Even the Canadian national flag had the British Union Jack as its most distinguished feature. Immigration up until this point favored those from Western Europe and discriminated against those from other parts of Europe and the world. Early immigration laws were not only racist in nature, but assimilationist in content and segregationist in intent (Walker, 1985). The government of the time realized that this "white only" policy was morally and politically indefensible. While those from Eastern Europe were considered acceptable, Mediterranean and Jewish immigrants needed a special permit and those of color, Chinese, Japanese and Indian had exclusionary laws designed to keep them out. Economic demand for labor often allowed these groups into Canada to work, but then shut off when the labor demands lessened. Immigrants were expected to comply with Canadian (British) culture and values. After World War II, this began to change and for the first time, the Canadian government:

> ...*eliminated the preference for suitable minorities from the selection process and introduced a set of universal criteria for entry. Applicants were admitted on the strength of their capacity for self-reliance (Fleras & Elliott, 1992, pp. 42-43).*

In 1967, the immigration laws changed with the criteria for entrance and replacing ethnic and racial background with a point system. Four classes of immigrants were defined: family, independent, entrepreneur and refugee. These classes of immigrants could apply under three categories: sponsored, independent or nominated. Under this system, "discretionary powers" were given to the immigration officers who implemented the plan. Skills, language ability, age and education determined the suitability of the immigrants. Under all categories the primary core of the immigration policy was family reunification, with the independent category being fairly low (i.e., only 4% until 1988 when it increased to 28%). The laws are continually being changed to suit the times, but the result is the changing face of the people of Canada. At the time of Confederation in 1867, only 8% of the population was neither British nor French (Fleras & Elliott, 1992). By the year 2001 less than half of the population of Canada was neither British nor French. However, despite the change, British traditions predominate. Consider the fact demonstrated by the important symbol – Canada's head of state is the British monarch. In comparison with the United States, Canada is very "British." For instance, Benedict Arnold is a "hero" in Canada, while in the U.S. the name Benedict Arnold is synonymous with a traitor. In the city of St. John's, New Brunswick, there is a statue to commemorate his heroic deeds. With just a few exceptions, all of the Canadian Prime Ministers have been of British heritage and Protestant. Interestingly, Canadians, unlike Americans, with some exceptions (i.e., Hutterites) define themselves in relationship to language, in that descendants of Europeans who have been in North America for two or more generations see themselves as Anglo or Franco rather than ethnic.

Historical Phases in Group Relations

In order to put in perspective the multicultural nature of counselling, the relationship of minorities and new Canadians needs to be understood. Historically, there appears to be three aspects of relationships: Conquest (differing national groups competing); Anglicizing and the two solitudes (assimilation); and finally, the Cultural Mosaic (diversity). According to Axelson (1993) "conflict is especially likely when the dominant group exerts its influence on minority groups for conformity or when misconceptions are perpetuated by both groups" (p. 76). Consider the following historical phases and how they may affect issues of trust and cooperation between majority and minority groups:

1. Initial Meeting: This type of situation occurred when people met as equals and engaged in some mutual exchange or interdependence (e.g., during the fur trade).

2. Subjugation: One group exerted dominance over the other through theft of their land, controlling their culture and restricting cultural norms by outlawing or marginalizing their language (reservations, English only or covenants against certain religious groups);

3. "Melting Pot": this idea was based on the notion that Anglo-Saxons would be the dominant cultural group with all groups conforming to it as the "master" culture (this notion excluded visible minorities);

4. Canadian Identity: this was based on the idea that a new identity would emerge based on the "melting pot" theory, accepting all cultural groups, including the so called "founding races" (French & English), still excluding visible minorities;

5. Multiculturalism: based on the idea that all peoples, regardless of color, creed or national identity, are equal partners. This not only included the stressing of bilingualism, but inclusions of "heritage languages" (aboriginal languages, Chinese, Ukrainian, Japanese, Punjabi, etc.) in the curriculum and national policies. To redress earlier discriminatory practices, equal employment opportunities and other educational opportunities are made available to accelerate advancement.

Cultural Pluralism and the Process of Inclusion

While the idea of a pluralistic or multicultural society occurred officially in 1972 with a bill introduced in the House of Commons by Prime Minister Pierre Trudeau, people of different cultures have been living side by side maintaining cultural diversity (e.g., French, English, those of African and Asian origin and aboriginal peoples). However, there were problems and outright hostilities. Today, laws bring greater protection and have gone a long ways to alleviate past injustices. One way of viewing how cultural diversity and ethnicity is explained by Gordon's theory (McLemore, 1980). There are four components to the theory:

1. Secondary structural assimilation: consists of sharing by the majority with minority in education, business and other areas of living that are often imposed or developed because of the circumstances. The atmosphere is characterized as cold and impersonal (e.g., desegregated facilities or equal employment opportunities).

2. Primary structural assimilation: the mixing of different cultural and racial groups, majority and minority, in social and living situations in which relationships are close, personal and warm.

3. Cultural assimilation: this occurs when minority groups lose their cultural identity by adopting the majority cultural norms (e.g., value preferences, language, religion, family practices and interest in heritage.) Interestingly, McLemore (1980) found that among immigrant groups, there is less hostility to the majority and shorter periods of time of assimilation. However, there is also some cultural resurgence by the 3rd generation. Among "conquered peoples" there is more hostility and longer periods of time of assimilation. In addition, there is a strong tendency towards separation or secessionist activities.

4. Marital assimilation: this occurs as the final step in the process of assimilation when members of either the majority or minority marry. One aspect of this phenomena not discussed in Gordon's theory involves those who choose between one culture over another and those who choose to be bicultural. Research suggests that it takes 3 generations to assimilate into the majority population.

The Protestant Tradition

According to the literature (Fleras & Elliot, 1992; Axelson, 1993; Alladin, 1996), one's views on life stem in part from one's religious beliefs, which in turn influence one's social reality. Protestantism in Canada was largely Anglican, when churches were available, but there were also Methodist and other Calvinistic churches that had a strong influence. When churches were not available, people conducted their own services by reading the bible or having prayer meetings. In the early days, before the middle of the 18th century, 98% of people outside of Quebec were Protestant. Their belief system and customs were interwoven into the fabric of society and culture. There was a "deep mistrust" of Catholics. The influence of culture and religion is evident in the "Protestant work ethic." What is it and how is it expressed in everyday life? "According to the ethic, work and productive activity in the society are an expression of one's spiritual being and one's eventual self worth" (Axelson, 1993, p. 79). If one's life was predetermined, then one had a "calling" or a sacred duty to accomplish certain things. If one was successful, then it was because of God's will, if not, then some "sin" one might have committed caused one's failure. Working hard and being productive became important aspects of the work ethic that determined whether one was good or bad. In fact, the notion of being good or bad was an important value preference among Anglo-Saxon peoples. This sometimes translated into seeing situations in terms of "black or white."

In examining the majority worldview, which by and large refers to those with a European ethnic heritage, the world is seen as a place where one has to work hard to survive. Even in times of plenty, work is seen as one's obligation to family, society and God. Since the early exploration of the Americas, in order to survive, immigrants had to sacrifice and labor long hours. Thus, being productive and advancing personally and economically (doing) was a duty. An interesting question is, how do these values of productivity and control impact counselling? Obviously a great deal of pressure is put on the individual to succeed. Consider the following influential quotes from a variety of European and North American literary, social and political leaders:

"It is work which gives flavour to life." Amiel

"To youth I have but three words of counsel – work, work, work." Bismarck

"There is no substitute for hard work." Edison

"I look on that man as happy, who, when there is question of success, looks into his work for a reply." Emerson

"Every child should be taught that useful work is worship and that intelligent

labour is the highest form of prayer." Ingersoll

Canadiens and Franco-Canadians

At one time the largest European ethnic group were the French who first settled in the "New World" in 1604 along the territory of what became known as St. Croix Island. The harsh conditions motivated the colonists to move to the Port-Royal area of Nova Scotia, which eventually lead to the move to Quebec City, which is the oldest continuous European settlement in Canada. The settlers of New France grew and prospered until the Seven Year War, in which the British Army defeated the French Army, ending French rule in North America. The 1763 Treaty of Paris was typical of the harshness toward defeated peoples, but an unusual event occurred in the British colonies south of Canada. A revolt by American colonists forced the British government to make accommodations to the French-speaking people. In exchange for their support against the Americans, the victorious British passed the Québec Act guaranteeing *Canadiens* freedom of religion and maintenance of the French civil code. In effect, it granted them the same territories that they had enjoyed under the French Régime and control over their daily lives. The people of Quebec more or less lived their lives in a French world, developing separately from English Canada with a separate and distinct identity. Their culture and traditions have become very unique, with their linguistic survival being paramount. As the balance of power shifted with the growing population of English Canada, there was greater desire for protection. The distinctness grew into dissatisfaction with their English neighbors over the years, with numerous cultural and political movements to ensure of their survival as a people. It wasn't until the election of the Parti Québecois in 1975 that the dream of a separate nation became a possibility. Consider the words of René Lévesque, the founder of the Parti Québecois who said:

> Being ourselves is essentially a matter of keeping and developing a personality that has survived for three and a half centuries. At the core of this personality is the fact that we speak French. Everything else depends on this one essential element.... We are...heirs to the group obstinacy which has kept alive that portion of French America we call Québec. More is involved here than simple intellectual certainty. This is a physical fact. To be unable to live as ourselves, as we should live, in our own language and according to our own ways, would be like living without an arm or a leg – or perhaps a heart (Handler, 1984, p. 60).

The ensuing political debate in Canada about language and separatism has brought to the surface deep feelings of anger and distrust. From the English perspective, there is a sense that the government has given too much to the province of Quebec, while in Quebec there is a perceived sense that French-speaking people are not accepted. The traditional view from English Canada of French-Canadians is that they are "obedient Catholics who have large families and never divorce" (Donnelly, 1996, p. 1). However, like most people who live in Canada, this imaged has evolved over the years with very different characteristics. There has been large scale immigration to Quebec, just as in other parts of Canada, except those who settled in Quebec became Francophones and thus adopted the culture of the people living there. Donnelly goes on to describe some unique aspects of the French Québécois perspective by saying that like all immigrants to North American, their perspective is Eurocentric, however, because of their survival in what has become a mass of English-speaking peoples in North America, they have a natural tendency to want to protect their culture and language. There is an historical sense of distrust of Anglophone society, which in the past tried to diminish their cultural and linguistic choices, hence a very strong separatist movement that still desires a nation separate from Canada. From a cultural perspective, counsellors need to recognize the historical differences that have produced a view of the world from another perspective. Unless the counsellor is bilingual and or the client is bilingual, the degree of proficiency of languages will color the degree of understanding. In addition, the catholic tradition, while weaker these days than in the past, is still a dominant force in French-Canadian culture. Accepting the distinctness of French Canadians and ensuring that one proceeds from the perspective of the client's perspective, there will be little difference in counselling French-Canadians from counselling other white ethnic clients.

White Ethnic Canadians

Up until the twentieth century, Canada was predominately populated by First Nations and the first European settlers – British and French. The nature of the Canadian federation created geographic pockets of cultural acculturation that confronted later European immigrants (Upper and Lower Canada). As the new immigrants from Eastern and Southern Europe settled in the various areas dominated by the traditional "founding nations," they often assimilated into either the English or French society. However, many kept their cultural traditions that make them distinctive from either of the two earlier groups. The following are some examples of some of these distinctive or white ethnic groups.

The Catholic Experience

The worldview of Catholics is different from those of Protestants. According to Axelson (1993), "Catholicism functions as influence in the adaptive process for many of the new White Ethnic groups and perpetuation of spiritual and ideological ties with Catholicism in one form or another is an important characteristic of many of the southern and eastern European peoples who migrated in masses to [North America]" (p. 85). Is Catholicism a religion of the heart and mainstream Protestantism a religion of the rational mind? If so, this may mean that some preferences or ways of acting are different because of the differing religious "upbringing." For new immigrants and those living in French Canada, the Catholic Church plays a big part in their lives. Politics and where the Church stood on a particular issue often determined how people would vote. There was a pervasive influence in the lives of new immigrants in the following ways: conscientious fulfillment of duty; awe of higher powers; deep reflection; inner sacred preoccupation; a close and lasting relationship with the supernatural (that is, the ultimate structure of the universe, its center of power and human destiny). As a result of 19th- and 20th-century immigration, the Roman Catholic church in Canada grew rapidly and was removed from mission status in 1908. The newcomers, however, changed its character. Irish immigration in the early 1800s reduced the French-Canadians to a minority among Catholics outside Quebec and led to conflict over language and Episcopal appointments. Such tension continued in the 20th century with the arrival of southern and eastern Europeans. In the early 1990s the Roman Catholic Church was the largest religious group in the country, with about 45% of all Canadians. It still had some government recognition, especially in Quebec and in provinces where Catholic schools received tax aid. Its clergy included 3 cardinals and 118 other prelates (Encarta, 2001).

Persistence of White Ethnic Cultures

The literature presents a number of examples of white ethnic groups that continue to identify with their culture through language, religion or other cultural practices. In Canada, these can be diverse ethnic groups such as Greek, Russian, Ukrainian and Polish, to name a few. A summary of two distinct examples follows:

Italian-Canadians

Many of the Italians who came to North America were from southern Italy, where they were poor and often experienced repression. As a result, these Italian immigrants identified more with the family and villages rather than the Italian nation. Because they were different and uneducated, they were exploited and thus most of these immigrant sought refuge in the family or "village atmosphere" of their communities in the large cities where they settled ("little Italy"). Their neighborhoods were close knit, with strong family ties and deep allegiance to the Catholic Church. This probably helped them maintain their separateness and uniqueness and lessened the tendency to be assimilated by the larger culture. The family structure often was extended to the community structure, that was hierarchal in nature. At the top was the "padrone" or Godfather. This is not the same as the various depictions of organized crime, but a social system brought over from southern Italy in which those on top helped others in time of need. "Making it" in Canadian society often meant a clash of culture in which the individual had to put his or her welfare ahead of the group. According to Axelson (1993) "the mainstream culture emphasizes individuality and material achievement, often at the cost of breaking away from the family, old friends and the culture of parents and grandparents." (p. 89).

Jewish-Canadians

One of the distinguishing characteristics of Jewish immigration to North America is that they came highly educated, literate with experience in living as a minority society. In Europe they had been forced into ghettos and restricted from the larger society except in certain occupations that serviced the larger society (e.g., merchants, bankers, artisans) and in less restrictive countries they served as doctors, teachers and other professionals. As a people experienced in being persecuted, they developed coping mechanisms that assisted in their survival, particularly reliance on their faith and their communities.

"Jewish devotion to family life was and is, highly valued and loyalty to kin, along with a strong spirit of ethnocentrism, offered strength in confronting many environmental obstacles" (Axelson, 1993, p. 91). Historically, this begins 2000 years ago, with the destruction of Israel's Second Temple in 70 **i.e.**, and the dispersal of the Hebrew people from the Holy Land. Many of the rituals that had been performed in the Holy Temple were then performed in the family home. The dining table replaced the holy altar for the eating of ritually blessed foods. The synagogue, as a community prayer center, was not meant to fully replace the ancient Temple and the holiest of the rituals, particularly surrounding the Sabbath day, always took place in the home.

Immediately after the destruction of the Temple, the great Rabbi Akiva began to offer the written and oral traditions of ancient Judaism in the first academy-in-exile. Rabbi Akiva maintained that one could fulfill the ancient obligations of the Temple through prayer and studying the Torah (scriptures). Interestingly, he argued against his critics that the "Song of songs" not be expunged from the canon of Holy Scripture and maintained that the "Song of songs" was akin to entering the "Holy of Holies." By this, he was referring to the conjoining of the religious couple and marital couples become "doubly blessed" when consummating their love during the evening of the Sabbath. (Jung, L. in Litvin, 1987).

This is a central illustration of how Jewish ritual is devoted to maintaining the sanctity of couple relations, believing that it fulfills the Creator's very first commandment to man and woman; "Be fruitful and multiply and replenish the earth" (Genesis 1:28). It is taken even further to mean that the sexual urge, as part the sexual act, was placed in humankind for a blessing, not a sin. Mystical Jewish teaching then elevates the sexual act, when properly consecrated, into the spiritual dimensions, as a joining of the sacred male and female principles.

Jewish people are expected to be married, in order to fulfill their generative, social and spiritual life. However, contemporary Jewish feminists, such as Rosa Kaplan, has examined the position of women who are single, divorced or widowed and who then have difficulty integrating into the family-oriented religious community. She warns the traditional religious community to be accepting of those who are not within a mainstream family life-style, saying: "Unless individuals learn to relate to each other inside and outside the family as human beings rather than as role-occupant, the family that stays together may well decay together." (Kaplan in Heschel, S., 1983).

In the year 2000, Canada has 362 000 self-described Jewish people, living primarily in the major urban centres. Forty percent are religiously Orthodox, 40% are Conservative and 20% consider themselves Reform, the most liberal of the three (American Jewish Yearbook, 2000). Jewish people were not permitted in Canada at all under the French Catholic rule, but entered Montreal with the British soldiers in 1768. A few merchants settled in British Columbia during the Gold Rush, while some Jewish farmers from Eastern Europe settled in the Prairies during the late 19th century. In 1832, full civil rights were granted, but many institutions, including universities, had quota systems to bar most minority peoples. It is now acknowledged that Canada acted shamefully in denying Jews into Canada during the holocaust, but Canada now has the largest population of holocaust survivors in the diaspora (Abella, 1990).

Today, Jewish people in Canada are a combination of assimilated, traditional and integrated into the Canadian mosaic. While the strong sense of ethnocentricity has given them certain advantages, it has also made them a target for "hate" by "skinhead and neo-nazi" groups, despite the gains over the years. With the current unrest in the Middle East, many Jewish people are concerned that their relatives abroad will be targeted by terrorists, or that religious and political hatreds may flare up here in Canada.

Implications for Counselling

Multicultural counselling is not just about counselling minorities, although counselling initially did not embrace cultural differences in theory and practice. This acceptance of the new reality of diversity in society has changed the nature of counselling. The traditional theories have had to be revamped to reflect the multicultural nature of society, including those theories that deal with Anglo and white ethnic groups. Axelson (1993) defines multicultural as the interface between counsellor and client that takes the personal dynamics of the counsellor and client into consideration alongside the emerging, changing and/or static configurations that might be identified in the cultures of counsellor and client (p. 13). In working with clients who are different, it is important to consider the following rules, identified by Pedersen (1994):

1. Consider that conflicting cultural views are equally right;

2. Consider that one can have multiple views or even conflicting views, depending on the situation;

3. Try "seeing" what the situation is like from another cultural perspective;

4. Listen for the cultural perspective in dealing with another ethnic group;

5. Develop the ability to shift to another cultural perspective by learning behavioral expectations and values;

6. Learn to accurately identify culturally appropriate feelings in specific rather than general terms (i.e., cues, signals and patterns of emotional expression);

7. Explore multiple levels of support that are possible within a given cultural group;

8. Develop the ability to identify culturally learned criteria being used to evaluate alternative solutions;

9. Develop the ability to generate insights for the culturally different client from his/her culturally learned perspective.

Conclusion

According to Alladin (1996) Canadians have to realize that "a serious study of racism in schools and society will inevitably create controversy (since) racist practices have been so integral in our history that they have gained acceptance" (p. 160). However, in a multicultural society, such as Canada, all cultural groups add to the "cultural mosaic" and work as partners in the development and growth of the nation. Increasingly, other cultural groups are replacing the original groups who immigrated to Canada, the French and English. In the major Canadian cities, Chinese and Indo-Canadian groups are becoming the dominant ethnic groups, while in the north and in places across the Prairies, First Nations groups are becoming the dominate ethnic groups. Immigration to Canada is coming more and more from Asia rather than Europe. However, to understand the important contributions that the English and other white ethnic groups have made, I have summarized material from the literature on these groups. While it is easy to generalize and see the majority population as one monolithic group, there is a great deal of difference that I hope this paper summarizes. I also feel that revisiting the "majority cultural identity model" is a good place to start in order to understand cultural norms and how the dominant culture has shaped many of the political and social institutions. What I have here summarized by describing the Anglo-Saxon and white ethnic groups is simply scratching the surface. The struggle for national identity is part of being Canadian and it is constantly being redefined. However, in light of all this, it might be wise to keep one's sense of humor. Consider this statement by Canadian novelist, poet and critic, Margaret Atwood (1990): "The beginning of Canadian cultural nationalism was not 'Am I really that oppressed?' but 'Am I really that boring?'"

References

Abella, I. (1990). *A Coat of Many Colors: Two Centuries of Jewish Life in Canada*. Toronto, ON: Lester and Orpen Dennys.

Alladin, M.I. (l996). *Racism in Canadian Schools*. Toronto, ON: Harcourt Brace & Company, Canada.

American Jewish Yearbook. (2000). Vol 100. New York: The American Jewish Committee.

Atwood, M. (1990). "Dancing On the Edge Of the Precipice," interview with Joyce Carol Oates published in *Ontario Review* (fall-winter 1978; reprinted in *Conversations*, ed. by Earl G. Ingersoll, 1990).

Axelson, J. (l993). *Counseling and Development in a Multicultural Society*, 2nd Edition. Thousand Oaks, CA: Brooks/Cole.

Bucher, R.D. (l999). *Diversity Consciousness: Opening Our Minds to People, Cultures and Opportunities*. Upper Saddle River, NJ: Prentice-Hall.

Berry, J.W. & Kim, U. (1988). Acculturation and mental health. In P.R. Dasen, J.W. Berry & N. Sartorius (Eds.), *Health and Cross-Cultural Psychology: Toward Applications* (pp. 207-236). Newbury Park, CA: Sage.

Berry, J.W. & Sam, D.L. (1997). Acculturation and adaptation. In J. Berry, M. Segall & C. Kagitcibasi (Eds.), *Cross-Cultural Psychology* (Vol. 3, pp. 291-326). Boston: Allyn & Bacon.

Dyer, G. (l994). *The Human Race: Tribal Identity*, Ottawa, ON: National Film Board.

Donnelly, G. (1996). Counselling French-Canadians, an unpublished M.A. thesis, University of Victoria.

Encarta. (2001). Roman Catholic Church, Microsoft.

Fleras, A. & Elliot, J.L. (l992). *Multiculturalism in Canada: The Challenge of Diversity*, Scarborough, ON: Nelson.

Handler, R. (February, 1984). On sociocultural discontinuity: Nationalism and cultural objection in Quebec. *Current Anthropology, 25*(1), 55-71.

Heschel, S. ed. and intro. (1983). *On Being a Jewish Feminist: A Reader*. New York: Schocken Books.

Jung, L. (1987). Married Love in Jewish Law. In Litvin, B., *The Sanctity of the Synagogue: The Case for Mechitzah – Separation Between Men and Women in the Synagogue*. New York. Ktav Publishing House.

McLemore, S.D. (1980). *Racial and Ethnic Relations in America*. Boston, MA: Allyn & Bacon.

Pedersen, P. (l994). *A Handbook for Developing Multicultural Awareness*, 2nd Edition. Alexandria, VA: ACA.

Robinson, T.L. & Howard-Hamilton, M. (2000). *The Convergence of Race, Ethnicity, and Gender*. Upper Saddle River, NJ: Prentice-Hall.

Walker, J. (l985). *Racial Discrimination in Canada: The Black Experience*, Booklet #4. Ottawa: The Canadian Historical Association.

Part III

Applications and Practical Approaches

The focus of the chapters in Part III of this book is the practical application of multi-cultural counselling approaches. We believe that cultural friendly theories and approaches have not been given adequate attention in most counselling theory courses and we hope that the selective inclusion of these approaches will highlight the fact that differing cultural approaches have a lot to offer the counsellor practitioner. The theory of Multicultural Counselling and Therapy (MCT) is a Meta theory that offers a unique way of working with diverse people. We believe that the integration of MCT principles into counsellor training and research can effectively increase counsellor awareness of personal values and biases and the "person-in-relation," frame of reference. This awareness can also help validate a myriad of multicultural worldviews, leading to more varied and effective strategies, assessment, treatment and research. Another element often overlooked as counsellor educators, in our drive to be "scientific," is the lack of attention to the spiritual dimension. We believe that when these approaches that emphasize spirituality are examined, there is much that could be gained from including this important dimension of being human. Counselling in relationship to spirituality and healing methods that are culturally appropriate are significant for many people who are thirsting for this type of counselling practice. Two spiritual approaches to multicultural counselling are discussed in this section and they offer ideas that can be adapted into other types of counselling. For example, Sufism assumes that as people experience the full range of the spirit of God, they acquire insight into their "greater selves." Included in this therapeutic process, which is highly individualized, is meditation, dance, dreams and parables. Naikan is a Japanese psychotherapy with philosophical roots in Buddhist spiritual practices. Another important strategy is the inclusion of nature and how it can be used to improve personal and inter-personal well-being. Our view is that separation from nature in our modern world increases stress and leaves people with a sense of psycho-social, emotional and spiritual isolation.

While we have been critical of traditional counselling approaches, our feeling is that with diverse populations these are the least helpful, although some theoretical approaches offer a great deal to diverse clients. Among the traditional approaches that have been shown to be highly adaptable to diverse groups is the Cognitive-Behavioral approach to counselling. The cognitive behavioral counselling approach is the least value laden and one of the more cultural friendly counselling models. Another important theory, often overlooked, is the Transpersonal theory. This approach includes awareness, compassion, emotional transformation, ethical training, motivation, meditation and wisdom as fundamental components of the helping relationship. Finally, as an extension of our belief in compassion, tolerance and acceptance as ingredients of sensitive counseling, we have included ideas on Restorative Justice as an alternative approach within the context of cross-cultural counselling. Our view is that exploring alternative ways of healing brings another element into differing counselling roles. We believe that the inclusion of the approaches in this section is only the "tip of the iceberg," so we urge counsellors to be more open to approaches from different cultures and approaches that are inclusive of differing worldviews.

Chapter 19

The Positive Effects of Integration of MCT Theory into Counselling Practice

June Saracuse

Changes to the immigration act 30 years ago opened Canada's doors to people of every color, faith and language. Without much fuss, we've become the most spectacularly diverse country in the world (Dyer, 2001).

Canada's population demographics continue to change, reflecting a trend from homogeneity to heterogeneity and according to Dyer (2001), we are doing it well. We all have a responsibility to ensure continued good relations with each other. Counsellors, in their capacity as helpers, must learn to accept and understand differences and learn to provide varied support and treatment to a multitude of people with diverse needs. One way to do this is to ensure that those in the helping field are receiving thorough, competent and on-going multicultural education. The Theory of Multicultural Counselling and Therapy, otherwise known as MCT, would be an asset to the curriculum in counselling programs. Its basic principles could easily be integrated into all subject matter. In addition, it encourages a new and promising perspective on researching multicultural populations.

This chapter will briefly introduce the Theory of MCT and its basic tenets. The major counsellor-training model of the MCT theory and the benefits of learning this theory to counselling students and their potential clientele will be discussed. Finally, the need for more research in the area of multiculturalism and how the MCT theory can support this will be addressed.

Basic Tenets of MCT

MCT asserts itself as a metatheory; a theory of theories. It comes from a particular worldview, just as all theories do. It posits that the appropriate frame of reference for seeing a client is as "person-in-relation" and that counselling strategies should be directed toward what is meaningful for the client. In opposition to the Eurocentric importance of individualism, MCT asserts that a client should not or cannot be viewed as a single entity. "A person's identity is formed and continually influenced by his or her context. Working effectively with clients requires an understanding of how the individual is embedded in the family, which in turn requires an understanding of how the family is affected by its place in a pluralistic culture" (Sue, Ivey & Pedersen, 1996, p. 15). The dominant culture makes the assumption that all people strive to be independent and individual. It does not recognize that many people from other cultures strive for connection with family, group and even the universe.

Speaking to counselling strategies, MCT sees the ultimate goal of a therapist as expanding his/her repertoire of helping responses, in order to address what is meaningful for the client, regardless of the counsellor's theoretical orientation. An effective multicultural counsellor may utilize traditional methods of healing from a particular culture, should that be appropriate and meaningful to the client and involve significant others. Inclusion of a shaman, for example, as well as extended family, to help counsel a Native Indian youth, may be more personally relevant and meaningful for the youth, than one-on-one cognitive-behavioral therapy. A First Nations youth may see him/herself as part of a family and a group, as well as the universe, not as a separate entity. To make decisions based solely on what he/she wants may not be an option to consider. His/her learned experience and consequent worldview may be one of person-in-relation. MCT counsellors would draw on both Western and non-European strategies of assisting.

There are many cultures that have magical explanations for psychological problems. In Vietnam they use a method of healing called "Thuoc Nam." The person's body is covered with camphor and they are struck all over with spoons or perhaps a bag of coins. Many Vietnamese believe that this method helps "the poison" rise out of the body. A magical solution for a problem that is perceived to have a magical explanation may be more fitting with the client's beliefs and worldviews and perhaps be more meaningful and helpful in solving the problem. MCT theory recognizes that using traditional Western methods of helping with populations that do not understand or believe in them is not effective.

An introduction to the basic tenets, at least, is necessary to understand the possible benefits of MCT theory to counselling students. MCT bases its theory on six propositions. The propositions are as follows:

1. MCT is a metatheory of counselling and psychotherapy.

2. Both counsellor and client identities are formed and embedded in multiple levels of experiences (individual, group and universal) and contexts (individual, family and cultural milieu). The totality and interrelationships of experiences and contexts must be the focus of treatment.

3. Development of cultural identity is a major determinant of counsellor and client attitudes toward the self, others of the same group, others of a different group and the dominant

group. These attitudes are strongly influenced not only by cultural variables, but also by the dynamics of a dominant-subordinate relationship among culturally different groups.

4. The effectiveness of MCT theory is most likely enhanced when the counsellor uses modalities and defines goals consistent with the life experiences/cultural values of the client.

5. MCT theory stresses the importance of multiple helping roles developed by many culturally different groups and societies. Besides the one-on-one encounter aimed at remediation in the individual, these roles often involve larger social units, systems intervention and prevention.

6. The liberation of consciousness is a basic goal of MCT theory. MCT theory emphasizes the importance of expanding personal, family, group and organizational consciousness of the place of self-in-relation, family-in-relation and organization-in-relation. This results in therapy that is not only ultimately contextual in orientation, but also draws on traditional methods of healing from many cultures (Sue et al., 1996, pp. 23-29).

Major Training Model

Also of importance is the major training model for MCT theory (Sue et al., 1996, pp. 46-49). It focuses on three areas of counsellor expertise:

Being aware of one's own assumptions, values and biases.

Developing understanding of the worldviews of culturally different clients.

Developing varied and appropriate helping interventions and strategies.

Benefits of Cultural Awareness – Assumptions, Values and Biases

"We can state that cultural therapy is a process of bringing one's own culture, in its manifold forms – assumptions, goals, values, beliefs and communicative modes – to a level of awareness that permits one to perceive it as a potential bias in social interaction and in the acquisition or transmission of skills and knowledge….At the same time, one's own culture, brought to this level of awareness, is perceived in relation to the "other" culture, so that potential conflicts, misunderstandings and "blind spots" in the perception and interpretation of behavior may be anticipated. One's own culture as well as the other's culture become a "third presence," removed somewhat from the person, so that one's actions can be taken as "caused" by one's culture and the interactions with "other" and not just by one's personality" (Spindler & Spindler, in Sue et al., 1996, p. 52).

Being aware of one's own assumptions, values and biases is imperative to being an effective counsellor. Perhaps the biggest lesson to learn as a student of counselling is the danger of not examining one's values and biases. According to the Canadian Code of Ethics for Psychologists, (1997) Principle 1: Respect for the Dignity of Persons, section 1.9, states that psychologists will "not practice, condone, facilitate, or collaborate with any form of unjust discrimination (p. 41)." Although it might be assumed that counsellors would not intentionally be discriminatory, unintentional racism can do as much harm as intentional racism. Martin Luther King Jr. upholds that "Shallow understanding from people of good will is more frustrating than absolute misunderstanding from people of ill will" (cited in France, 2002).

Counselling courses must reiterate the importance of ongoing examination of one's beliefs and values, especially in relation to multicultural issues. The fundamentals of MCT theory encourage students to pursue lifelong learning and critical thinking in relation to their cultural beliefs and values. It encourages development of cultural identity, recognition of dominant-subordinate relationships, recognition of what is culturally meaningful to the client, exploration of alternative methods/strategies of helping, expansion of consciousness, and this list is not exhaustive. The students' whole world opens up when they examine the above issues and realize that there are many other worldviews besides their own and each and every one is valid. Through examination of one's worldview and the impact it has on the treatment of clients from diverse groups and backgrounds, "we are better positioned to work ethically, effectively and respectfully" (Ivey, D'Andrea, Ivey & Simek-Morgan, 2002; p. 5) as counsellors. Our perspectives greatly influence how a client's problems are understood and the strategies that are used to help.

Benefits of Understanding Others' Worldviews

Counselling students who learn to question and critically analyze their own and other cultural worldviews are less likely to perpetuate the status quo. If counsellors believe that their learned assumptions and values are universally shared, they can unwittingly or purposely impose them on their ethnic minority clients (Sue et al., 1996). For example, incorrectly and negatively assessing a client from a collectivist culture as being too attached to his/her family, would be confusing and damaging to the client's own worldview. Asian clients, who according to Dyer (2001) make up about 50% of Canada's immigrants, are from a collectivist culture. If an Asian-Canadian student went to her university counsellor to discuss her unhappiness with pursuing being a lawyer, a counsellor who is not culturally sensitive and/or educated may make the mistake of trivializing the situation and advising the student to simply change her path. The counsellor may not realize that the student does not think only of herself and her own future in deciding a career path. Most children from collectivist cultures learn that they must respect their parent's decisions for them and bring honor to the family. To disobey one's parents is to shame the family. Advising this student to change career paths based on her own needs and desires may go against what she has learned and subsequently used to form her worldview. In other words, based on a Eurocentric perspective, the counsellor may judge the client as having a personal failing, not recognize the collectivist perspective and advise incorrectly.

Another example of the importance of recognizing others' worldviews and the impact on client's healing is in relation to contrasting cultural definitions of health and well-being. For example, Western beliefs of well-being may differ from Native-American beliefs about well-being. Most Native-American concepts of healing incorporate the concept "that wellness is harmony and unwellness is disharmony in spirit, mind and body" (Sue et al., 1996 p. 195). Whereas Western medicine tends to treat the body and mind separately and does not treat the spirit at all, Native-American treatment includes healing of the body, mind and spirit. Therefore, a Native-American with a broken leg may not only seek help from a doctor for the physical injury, but may also see a medicine man or woman to help care for his/her spirit.

> *Treating the spirit is the process of finding out why the broken leg occurred, understanding the events in a spiritual rather than a physical sense and then beginning the process of changing whatever it was in the body, mind or spirit that was out of harmony enough to warrant a broken leg (Locust in Sue et al., 1996, p. 195).*

Counselling students must understand the implications of culture in relation to assessment, diagnosis and treatment, or risk making grave errors in judgement (Porter, cited in Sue et al., 1996). According to Williams (as cited in Caverley, 2000), counsellors who work with members of a variety of ethnic groups should "lead from behind." Leading from behind means that the counsellor is able to feel comfortable asking about and learning about possible racial/ethnic issues for the client. Only then, can the counsellor start to grasp the perspective of the client's worldview.

Looking at each existing theory from a cultural point of view, as MCT suggests, highlights the Eurocentric, individualistic, scientific arena that students of the Western world learn from. Counselling students may be able to curtail perpetuating these learned culture-bound values, through thorough examination of the values, biases and assumptions about human behavior that underlie each theory. It is important to note that MCT theory stresses recognition of how different theories describe different aspects of the human condition. They maintain the importance of preserving the integrity of each theory. What is fundamental to MCT theory is learning to examine each theory from a cultural perspective, in order to recognize and respect that there are many ways to frame a problem other than one's own. It is important to be aware that the questions asked about the human condition, when developing theories about human nature, cannot help but be influenced by our specific culture and of course, our worldviews.

Benefits of Learning Varied Helping Interventions

It makes sense that if recognized or unrecognized biases' continue, the techniques and strategies that counsellors employ will be static. If counsellors are not open to other worldviews, they are certainly not open to alternative or non-Western methods of helping. Being restricted in perspective and helping strategies severely limits the variety of culturally different clients that counsellors are able to help effectively, especially in any way that is meaningful to the client. Arthur and Stewart (2001) explicate: "For different cultural groups, counsellors need to…expand the boundaries of helping. They need to learn from models of helping that are holistic in perspective, accent the spiritual dimension and use diverse ways to view reality" (p. 9). It is interesting to note that in Sue et al. (1996), "Cultural Group Comparative Worldview Profiles" (pp. 144-45), Anglo-Americans are described as being more concerned with "doing," whereas African-Americans, Latino/a, Chicano/a, Native Americans and Asian Americans are more concerned with "being" or "becoming." This fundamental difference in conceptualization of what is important to accomplish as a human being has enormous implications for counselling interventions. A therapist who does not understand what it means to "become" cannot effectively help a client striving for this harmony. More education is needed to help expand perspectives and in turn, helping interventions.

In order to develop varied and appropriate helping strategies, as MCT theory suggests, there must be more than one multicultural course offered in a counselling program. According to McGuire (1999), educators need to offer more multicultural training to assure that graduates are able to be effective and culturally competent with minority clients. He asks: "But how are you going to go out and work with folk of color when you've had just one course?" (McGuire in APA Monitor, 1999).

Students cannot possibly deal with the multi-leveled, multifaceted issues of multiculturalism in one course. As learned in cognitive-behavioral theory, a person must process on thinking, feeling and behavioral levels in order to learn thoroughly and this does not speak to the additional cultural, spiritual or political aspects, that Western theories so often ignore. Sue et al., (1996) maintain that cultural issues are currently little more than add-ons to existing counsellor training in many programs and that this must change. "…all the actions, research and practice of counsellors must be reexamined and reinterpreted through the lens of culture" (p. 45). By re-examining and re-interpreting educational learning from a cultural perspective, our worldviews, our methods of helping and the applicability of counselling to a wider variety of populations, cannot help but expand. Research too can benefit from new perspectives and alternate assumptions of the study of human behavior.

How MCT Theory Can Support More Multicultural Research

In relation to research, there are those in the counselling/psychology field who argue that biases in psychological research discourage research on ethnic-minority populations as well as allotment of available funding. Stanley Sue, (1991) asserts that the research community is more interested in internal validity than external validity. They prefer a lab setting for research to ensure that effects of one variable on another are indeed causal. This necessarily omits the kind of research required for studying ethnic-minority groups, which requires study in the field, in order to generalize the results to wider populations. Much research of culture and related beliefs, values and traditions can be done by observing populations in their natural families, communities and environments. This kind of research is by necessity more flexible, subjective and holistic.

MCT theory encourages the questioning of whether trying to isolate each confound is the most effective way to study human behavior.

The psychological research community traditionally prefers methods of investigation to be objective, quantitative, linear, reductionistic (Sue et al., 1996). The study of the elaborate intricacies of human nature combined with the complexity of culture lends itself to what Ponterotto and Casas (1991) refer to as "qualitative methodology." This methodology is more inductive, holistic, humanistic and more concerned with the person-in-relation and the given situation. MCT theory encourages consideration of alternative research methods such as field observation, in-depth interviewing, case studies and narratives in order to support culture-centered research. MCT theory points out that traditional research theories depend on assumptions that may not be shared by non-Western cultures. For example, research in Western cultures aims at an objective, scientific model, limiting subjective elements as much as possible, whereas the Japanese perspective emphasizes the subjective elements of person-in-relation to family, group, etc. as being indispensable when studying human behavior.

Interestingly, Sue (1991) points out that: "In America, the overwhelming subject of research is white Americans. The U.S. constitutes less than five per cent of the world's population, yet from that population we develop theories and principles assumed to be universal" (p .89). Sue points out that if treatments have not been tested with other populations, we cannot say that the method is empirically validated, yet we do. This example demands our attention. MCT theory is nicely trying to point out that we have gone by the Eurocentric, scientific model for a long time and perhaps not played by our own rules. We need research with ethnic minority groups worldwide if we truly want to understand people from cultures other than our own. We cannot become effective helpers to people whose worldviews we do not know nor understand.

Conclusion

In an ideal world, this knowledge and understanding would be incorporated into our life learning. Being the complicated human beings that we are, there are many reasons why negative learning about other cultures or no learning at all takes place. It is imperative then, for those in the helping field, to address these issues in their education. It could be considered unethical for counselling training programs not to address multicultural issues in detail and at length. Educational institutions have a responsibility to ensure that their trainees are culturally knowledgeable and competent and that they do not inflict psychological harm on their clients, intentionally or otherwise.

MCT theory advocates awareness of the multiple levels and interconnection of experiences, relationships and their contexts. Culture is an integral part of this web. Counsellors need to be able to consider the appropriate factors when assessing, diagnosing and treating ethnic-minority clients. Improperly referring could be a by-product of lack of knowledge about other cultures, but awareness of different worldviews may lead to appropriate questions being asked by the counsellor and the client being pointed in the right direction.

MCT theory raises many new questions. There is much that counsellors, psychologists and other helping professionals need to learn about ethnic-minority people in order to service them effectively. There is also much learning and debate to take place concerning qualitative versus quantitative research and multicultural study.

Most importantly, MCT theory promotes examination of one's values and biases, recognition and respect for alternate worldviews and openness to varied and appropriate interventions, generating a new kind of vision. Counsellors will be less likely to categorize clients, to simplify their situations and to judge and be more likely to listen patiently and to ask appropriate questions, so that the bigger picture might be seen. Counsellors are more likely to accept that how and what the client's experience is, is very real and very valid and connected to the development of their worldviews. Counsellors will learn to listen in a whole new way.

References

Arthur, N. & Stewart, J. (2001). Multicultural counselling in the new millenium: Introduction to the special theme issue. *Canadian Journal of Counselling, 35,* pp. 3-13.

Caverley, N. (2000). What color are you? Reflections on My Multiracial Identity. *B.C. Counsellor,* vol. 22, # 2, 73-82.

Canadian Code of Ethics for Psychologists (1997). Ottawa, ON: Canadian Psychological Association.

Dyer, G. (2001). The New Canada: Visible Majorities. *Canadian Geographic,* Jan/Feb. pp. 45-51.

France, M.H. (2001). *Nexus: Transpersonal approach to groups,* Calgary, AB: Detselig Enterprises Ltd.

Ivey, A., D'Andrea, M., Bradford Ivey, M. & Simek-Morgan, L. (2002). *Theories of Counseling and Psychotherapy: A Multicultural Perspective* (5th ed.). U.S.A.: Allyn & Bacon.

McGuire, P.A. (1999). Multicultural summit cheers packed house. *APA Monitor Online,* 30, Retrieved May 12, 2000 from http://www.apa.org/monitor/mar99/foster.html.

Ponterotto, J.G. & Casas, J.M. (1991). Handbook of racial/ethnic minority counseling: A systematic five-year content analysis. *Journal of Multicultural Counseling and Development, 17,* 23-37.

Sue, D.W., Ivey, A.E. & Pedersen, P.B. (1996). *A Theory of Multicultural Counseling & Therapy*. U.S.A.: Brooks/Cole.

Sue, S. (1991). Ethnicity and culture in psychological research and practice. In J.D. Goodchilds (Ed.), *Psychological Perspectives on Human Diversity in America*. Washington, DC: American Psychological Association.

Chapter 20

The "Red Road": Culture, Spirituality and the Sacred Hoop

Honoré France, Rod McCormick & María del Carmen Rodríguez

When I was standing on the highest mountain of them all, around about beneath me was the whole hoop of the world. And while I stood there I saw more than I can tell and I understood more than I saw; for I was seeing in a sacred manner the shapes of all the things in the spirit and the shape of all shapes as they must live together like one being. And I saw that the sacred hoop of my people was one of many hoops that made one circle, wide as daylight and as starlight and in the center grew one mighty flowering tree to shelter all the children of one mother and one father. And I saw that it was holy. Black Elk speaks (1961)

When Black Elk spoke these words almost a century ago, he was expressing the most fundamental belief of all First Nations people of North America. The idea that all living things are related – brothers and sisters. The philosophical essence of this idea can be expressed in one word: respect. Respect for the land, respect for the animals, respect for the plants, respect for other people and finally, respect for the self. This is the essential ingredient for living life. According to Russell Means (Smoley, 1992) the development of respect among First Nations people can be compared to the idea of love for Christians and enlightenment for Buddhists. The notion of respect is that humankind is not separate from any other thing in the world, but just another living, breathing creature among many. Thus, the environment, as a brother or sister, is not something to be exploited or harmed, but is to be considered an integral part of everyone. When this does not exist, then nature is separate. As a separate entity, nature becomes like a machine – something to be mastered – something to be exploited.

Disease is caused when people are out of harmony with the land. This idea of harmony can be seen in the hot-cold belief in curing illness. In the human body, sickness will ensue if an excess of hot or cold foods are ingested. The hot-cold scheme is applied to foods, diseases and remedies. The terms hot and cold do not necessarily refer to the temperature of such foods or remedies. Qualities are assigned on the basis or origin, color, nutritional value, physiological effects of the food or remedy, as well as therapeutic action (i.e., bananas and sugar cane are considered cold, whereas garlic and corn meal are hot). Cold-classified illnesses such as arthritis, colds and gastric complaints must be treated with hot foods and remedies. Their hot counterparts are constipation, diarrhea and intestinal cramps, which require treatment with cold substances. First Nations people believe that humankind has a choice of two roads: the "road" to technology [blue] or the "road" to spirituality [red]. In this chapter we will explore counselling in relationship to spirituality and culturally appropriate helping and healing methods that can be utilized with First Nations people. However, it is important to remember that Indigenous people, like European ethnic groups, are just as diverse in their customs and language. Yet, there exist among First Nations people elements of beliefs and actions that are universal. To be successful with First Nations people, counsellors must take the time to find out about their culture and to be open to adapting or replacing the models they presently relate to with those that are more appropriate for the First Nations person. It is our belief that counsellors, regardless of their ethnic background, can work with appropriate elders and traditional healers in situations in which some of the following strategies can be utilized.

Basic Values Underlying Actions

Among First Nations people are beliefs about the world that shape how they view themselves and how they interact with majority culture. Hart (2002) lists the following values that are common among First Nations people: "vision/wholeness, spirit-centered, respect/harmony, kindness, honesty/integrity, sharing, strength, bravery/courage, wisdom and respect/humility" (p. 45). Values not only drive people, but also contain important information on how we experience the world. Among the most important elements in understanding values is the exploration of worldview, interconnectedness, balance and spirituality. An understanding of these beliefs can help counsellors work more effectively with Aboriginal people.

Worldview

To be effective with First Nations people, it is important to understand differing worldviews and be able to incorporate such understandings into a helping and learning framework. Despite the naive wish to be seen as 'value free', the Western educational system makes inherent assumptions, which are rooted in philosophical views of human nature and people's place in the world (Wachtel, 1977).

Worldview deals with a culture's orientation and ways to see and understand the world in relationship to humankind, nature, the universe and other philosophical issues that are concerned with the concept of being (Rodríguez, 2001). Our worldview helps us locate our place and rank in the universe; it influences the sense and understanding of culture at a very deep and profound level since it affects the beliefs, values, attitudes, interpretation of time and other aspects of culture. Our worldview affects our belief systems, value orientation, decision-making processes, assumptions and modes of problem solving. Lafromboise, Trimble and Mohatt (1990) state:

> *Knowledge of and respect for an Indian worldview and value system, which varies according to the client's tribe, level of acculturation and other personal characteristics is fundamental not only for creating the trusting counselor-client relationship vital to the helping process but also for defining the counseling style or approach most appropriate for each client (p. 629).*

An important point that was made in this statement concerns the need to recognize the diversity among First Nations people. Thus, worldview and personal value systems will vary according to a person's tribe, level of acculturation and other personal characteristics. But how, then, can counsellors assess worldview? Ibrahim (1984) has developed a scale for assessing worldview across cultures based on a value orientation scheme developed by Kluckhohn and Strodtbeck (1961). The Kluckhon framework considers both philosophical and psychological dimensions, including beliefs, values, assumptions, attitudes and behavior of individuals and groups. These conceptions influence human behavior, motivations, decisions and life-styles. Kluckhon proposed five universal or existential categories that pertain to a general, organized conception and understanding of:

Human nature: good or bad, or a combination of both;

Social relationships: lineal-hierarchical, collateral-mutual and/or individualistic;

Nature: subjugate and control nature, live in harmony with nature, accept the power and control of nature over people.

Time orientation: past-present-future

Activity orientation: being, being-in-becoming and/or doing.

An examination of these schemes would further our understanding of any culture or an individual's worldview. An example of how First Nations people relate to these categories would be the scheme of people-nature orientation. Traditionally, aboriginal people attempt to live in harmony with nature, whereas non-aboriginal people attempt to control nature to meet the needs of the people. Time orientation also differs among cultural groups. According to Sue and Sue (1999), time orientation in traditional native culture has always been towards the present incorporating the past, in contrast with the western tendency to focus on the future. This is often confusing to those who have not shared this perspective.

Balance

The Native Medicine Wheel is a ready-made model of the First Nations Worldview. The medicine wheel shows the different entities of the emotional, mental, spiritual and physical elements of people as being equal and part of a larger whole. This reinforces the concept of interconnectedness and the lesson that one part cannot be the center of existence but must instead learn to work in harmony with all of the other parts. The medicine wheel represents the balance that exists among all things. The First Nations worldview as represented by the medicine wheel has balance as one of the basic tenets of healthy living, as this is a paramount value. The medicine wheel represents the all-encompassing cycle of creation, from birth to death, in which balance between animals, nature, humanity and spirits co-exist.

Traditional medicine incorporates the physical, emotional, psychological and spiritual being. As a result, it is difficult to isolate any one aspect, because these parts exist in a harmonious balance. Aboriginal people become ill when they live life in an unbalanced way. Balance is essential for the First Nations person because the world itself is seen as a balance among transcendental forces, human beings and the natural environment (Hammerschlag, 1988).

Interconnectedness

The collective orientation of First Nations people is something that has been stressed continuously by leading Native mental health researchers (Trimble & Hayes, 1984; Lafromboise et al., 1990). It is unfortunate that Western counsellors still stress the role of individual responsibility when helping First Nations clients. The role of healing in traditional Aboriginal society has been not only to reaffirm cultural values, but also to consider the individual in the context of the community (Trimble & Hayes, 1984; Lafromboise et al., 1990). Katz and Rolde (1981) found that the goal of traditional healing was not to strengthen a person's ego, as in non-First Nations situations, but to encourage people to transcend the ego by considering themselves as imbedded in and expressive of community. Traditional ceremonies such as the Vision Quest and Sweat Lodge reinforce Aboriginal people's adherence to cultural values and helps to remind them of the importance of keeping family and community networks strong (Lafromboise et al., 1990).

Traditional helping approaches, unlike Western approaches, usually involve more than just the counsellor and the client. Relatives and community members are often asked to be part of the healing process. Trimble and Hayes (1984) found that First Nations people would usually turn to their relatives and community members when they were experiencing personal problems. This raises serious doubts as to the usefulness of using Western approaches such as Client-centered counselling with Aboriginal clients. The one on one interaction characteristic of many Western helping approaches is isolated outside of the context of the community and family and must therefore be questioned as a valid means of dealing with First Nations clients.

Spirituality

Traditional American Indians believe that mental health is much more spiritual and holistic than western psychology would suggest (Locust, 1988). Many traditional aboriginal healing ceremonies emphasize the spiritual aspect of healing. It is to the Great Spirit, perceived everywhere, that the Indian turns to in times of need (Dugan, 1985). Different ceremonies stress the need for reconnection with one's spirituality. In the Vision Quest ceremony the First Nations people make contact with their spiritual identity. The Medicine Wheel symbolized by the circle represents spiritual ties that bind human beings to each other and to the natural world. This spirituality or holiness is seen as the essence of healing for Native people. This represents the manifestation of wholeness in spirit, bringing it into our bodies, our families, our communities and our world.

There is a oneness in the First Nations life philosophy, that is reflected in the Salish belief of the creation of the world. Ashwell (1989) emphasizes that the Salish believe that the human soul is characterized by that: " ....indestructible spark, which once departed went to the sunset, where it remained forever, that which was left behind was the earthly body and its shadows – these shadows held a three-part existence and remained on the earthly scene with either good or evil intent, depending on the characteristic of the person in life" (p. 60). This continuity of life is often represented by the circle, which appears in many of the symbols used in First Nations ceremonies (e.g., the drum, the Ghost Dance, etc.). According to Smoley (1992), this idea of spiritual power is conceptualized in "....si si wiss, which means sacred breath or sacred life (p. 85)." When people respect everything, there is love of all things because in the trees, animals and all living things, we see and perceive more than our own humanity. Everything has experienced the same sacred breath. When there is respect, which is the essence of the healing spirit, then we appreciate the "...love of God we feel in our hearts" (Smoley, 1992, p. 85). First Nations spirituality demonstrates how humanity can harmoniously coexist with the environment.

Various Methods of Helping and Healing

Working With Dreams

According to Duran and Duran (l995) "as early as 1668 there was documentation as to the importance of dreams in Native American culture" (p. 46). People around the world have long used dream exploration, because it is a straightforward method of looking at the unconscious. Consider one of the dreams of Black Elk (1961), one of the principal philosophers of the First Nations tradition. He was a Lakota [Sioux] born in the 19th century, but lived a long life, enabling John Neilhardt to record his thoughts on his life, the struggles to revitalize Native American culture and his belief in the continual survival of his people after decades of fighting the US army. One of Black Elk's early dreams or visions provides an excellent example of the transcendent experiences. Before one of the battles of the Little Big Horn (1867), the young Black Elk had a vision of two men descending with flaming spears. They kidnapped Black Elk and brought him to a great plain on a cloud, where horses of different colors greeted him: **black** [West: releases water from the clouds], **white** [North: cleaning, endurance and courage], **red** [East: power of the sacred pipe and the power of peace, to awaken others, through knowledge and wisdom] and **yellow** [South: growth and healing]. These colors represent, in First Nations spirituality, the four directions of north, south, east and west. From there, Black Elk went into a rainbow-covered lodge of the Six grandfathers. These are the powers of the four directions, father sky and mother earth. The first grandfather, of the West, gave Black Elk water to sustain life and then handed him a bow and said he could use it to destroy. The second grandfather of the north gave sage, cleaning power and a white wing, cleaning power of the northern snow. The third grandfather gave the power to awaken others by bringing wisdom, peace and knowledge. The fourth grandfather of the south gave him the power to heal others. The fifth grandfather, the spirit of the sky, became an eagle and told him that all living things were his relatives. The sixth grandfather, who was really mother earth spirit, told him that salvation was within the earth (nature). Later Black Elk was shown the hoop of the world that was made of many hoops, representing all people, but that they were one and the same. When Black Elk actualized his dream upon awakening, he spent his life using his powers to help his people. In the end, as an old man, well into the 20th century, he thought that the dream had failed. He was wrong, because much of what was predicted came true, perhaps through his efforts, but the real gift was what he said and did to revitalize the spiritual revival not only of the Lakota, but of all First Nations people. It was just a dream that Ed McGaa, Eagle Man (1990), stresses has become a blooming tree with the:

> ...*bright rainbow, symbolic of the flowering tree...now blooming among the environmental and spiritual gatherings of enlightened peoples that have begun to flourish throughout the land. The rainbow-covered lodge of the six Grandfathers is a strong symbol of the old holy man's prediction [dream] that, someday, the flowing tree would bloom. The blooming has begun and will continue – if only some blue man (creed, corruption and user of the land] doesn't push the wrong button"* (p. 17).

Among the Ani-yun-wiya First Nation people, dream sharing is a vital part of their lives, because it links them to the real world they experience to the world beyond themselves. It is where the conscious self meets the unconscious self. Thus to talk about dreams after they occur is important, since it is easy for dreams to be gone by the time one awakes. Dreams "talk" about strange actual events that have impacted them and events past. And some dreams are not just for one's self, but might even foretell the future. These dreams are about unusual happenings and they transcend life as it really is and can provide a sense of awareness about things that might otherwise be unknown. The history of the Ani-yun-wiya people, whose language was one of the first indigenous languages to be written, shows that dreams were a pathway to other spiritual dimensions. However, not many of the ancient Ani-yun-wiya signs, presages and dreams have pleasant associations; in fact, it seems as if they are fixated in death, illness and misfortune. In the study of such portents and dreams, there are four important characteristics to consider:

Some dreams are about things that seldom happen, they caused little concern among the observers;

Through dreams and signs, people found ways in which to deal and come to terms with unexpected deaths without accusing the Above Beings for being unfair to them;

Signs and dreams prepared people to accept death as a natural consequence of living. It was better to be ready than to be suddenly seized;

People were kept from attempting to solve their problems on their own by seeking the help of a priest for cleansing and restoration and they believed that this action pleased the Above Beings [the Creator].

For the Ani-yun-wiya, dreams and signs were thought to be among the causes of things happening. To see in a dream the sign of death was to cause the death, the illness or any other matter; and even when most dreams defy recall, the Ani-yun-wiya utilize seven ritual stones to help in this important act, since this is a vital practice in their lives. These are some examples that foretold sickness or death among the Ani-yun-wiya:

Seeing anyone with an eagle feather in his hand or to dream of possessing such feathers was a sign of death;

Seeing a person with very clean clothes meant that the person would not live long;

Dreaming of a living person or an animal that was dead in the dream was a certain sign of sickness to come and those who dreamed of seeing a woman would have fever.

Other dreams had to do with good fortune, good luck and greatness. If hunters dreamed of having bread, peaches, or any kind of fruit, they were told they would kill a deer, and if someone dreamed of flying, it was implied that a person would live a long life. In addition, there were dreams and signs that had to do with strangers and visitors. For example, if a little bird called Tsi ki lili flew over in the direction of someone who was traveling, that person would soon meet a stranger; if a bird flew into the house, it announced that a visitor was coming. There were also signs that had to do with enemies and warfare. If a Tsa wi sku bird was heard singing very loud and fast, it meant that enemies were in town and if an owl rested on a peach or any other tree in town and sang, enemies would approach shortly after. And yet, not every aspect of the Ani-yun-wiya dreams has a negative connotation; there is a lingering belief that dreams do indeed speak of positive human attributes and of how people must be centered in their spirituality and the Great Spirit. The dream work process works towards understanding the meaning in the dream and we recommend the following sequence (France, 2002):

Hearing the dream with the idea of exploring feelings, thoughts, actions and experiences that can clarify meaning;

Exploring the dream structure, elements, symbols, issues and qualities of the dream characters;

Dialoging about the symbols, by examining one's outer life and if possible, by expressing the dream in an art form;

Amplifying the symbols by analyzing their cultural and personal meaning in one's external life;

Bringing resolution and actualizing the message of the dream in everyday life.

In the transpersonal sense, the traditional way that Ani-yun-wiya people embraced dreaming and then incorporated the messages and signs into their everyday life illustrates how the unconscious world can be a part of everyday existence. Essentially, one looks for the message or meaning in the dream by exploring the symbols, story and other aspects of the emotions in the dream. However, Duran and Duran (1995) advise caution, because:

> *The notion of living out dreams is a cross-tribal phenomenon. There are rules and taboos about reporting dreams, which makes the discussion of dreams a concern for the Western therapist who is naïve to this practice. The therapist must become informed as to the different rules of reporting and discussing dreams within the tribal context in which s/he is working (p. 50)*

Working with stories

Stories have the power to transform and heal by creating images that are as vivid as life itself. These images faithfully mirror one's journeys through the ordinary and the unexpected experiences of daily life, for it is in stories that one discovers eternal truths, clarification, rectification, meaning and ultimately, purpose. In telling stories, traditional folktales, myths and legends rich in archetypal imagery, we unveil profound spiritual truths to the listener reflecting the journey of the soul. As a result, the story becomes part of our own personal spirituality. In listening to stories, one discovers eternal truths that seem to escape amidst a rushed life. Stories carry life, history, traditions and culture. It is not surprising then, that 15 minutes of storytelling or listening can reveal and clarify 15 years of living.

Since stories carry universality, peoples' shared experiences can be found in their qualities, which serve diverse purposes:

Sharing and creating a common experience in storytelling aids in the development of people's ability to interpret events beyond their immediate experience. Stories can be used as ways to understand one's life through looking at symbols, creating analogies and bringing closure to diverse issues.

Stories contribute to one's social, emotional and cognitive development through shared experiences (i.e., to feel joy for another's happiness or sadness at their misfortunes).

Stories contribute to the client's mental health and help people cope with their own conscious and unconscious self by giving them the structure for their own daydreams and fantasies.

Stories aid in the development of an ethical value system, helping people appreciate and reinforce their own cultural heritage.

Helping Strategies: Skaloola (an example)

Among First Nations people, legends, myths and stories are more than just stories or fairy tales. The story of Skaloola, as shared by Shirley Sterling (1997), demonstrates how stories were used in a traditional context by Elders or parents to teach their children. Stories maintain a continuity from one generation to the next, ensuring that the values and standards are not only shared and transmitted vertically but also horizontally. In other words, while Elders and parents might tell the story with a certain purpose (i.e., to teach about personal safety), children share stories with others to strengthen relations among themselves and to share information and life experiences. In this way, the story reinforces values that are relevant to the storyteller and to the listener, thus creating a sense of understanding, caring and acceptance.

> *Skaloola was an owl who stole children. He hid watching boys and girls to see if they wandered far from camp or stayed out too late after dark. If they did, Skaloola would grab them, put them into a big basket on his back and run away to the mountains. Although hunters chased after him, for some reason at some point the tracks always disappeared and there was no sign of Skaloola or the children. They were never seen again.*

According to Sterling (1997), this story was used by parents as a device for social control and personal safety. It taught children about some social dangers such as abduction, sexual abuse, or encountering enemies. Additionally, the story taught moral values and reminded children about the consequences of lying and not obeying their elders. It also provided explanations for existence and respect for all creation based on kinship ties as it allowed to engage in conversations about taboos, harm and life in general. From the child's perspective, the myth of Skaloola the Owl provided children with opportunities to engage in conversations about safety and danger issues, ways to respond and be careful, help and teach the helpless, as well as to comfort and protect each other. Since respect for self and others is the basis for living a healthy life, fearful reaction of loved ones for breaking such balance served as a warning to transgressions of the moral code. In this sense the myths become a preventative means to help keep the family in spiritual, mental, physical and emotional balance.

The myth about Skaloola also provides a powerful analogy with regards to how the government "stole" First Nations children to take them to residential schools, made them adopt different beliefs, values and language, live within a different culture and be the victims of physical, spiritual and emotional abuse. This parallel offers clarity in understanding the seriousness of the crimes committed against First Nations people. Additional to orally presenting a story, journal writing, visual artwork and dramatization can form part of the process of analyzing and responding to stories. Writing and/or drawing evoke one's own images, emotions and interpretations, helping create a tangible image of what was verbalized. Drawing exploration becomes a powerful tool to reveal concerns, difficulties, joy and delight. The counsellor can assist the individual in the search for symbols and signs that might be absent in other forms of exploration and interaction. Journal writing offers similar possibilities; by "anchoring" the images in words that have been transferred on to paper, the individual is able to explore feelings and emotions in a different way, find symbols and make meaning of the experiences.

The Sweat Lodge

According to Duran and Duran (1995), counselling programs that have mixed traditional methods, such as the sweat lodge, with therapy have been very successful in the therapeutic process. The authors go on to say that counsellors should work in collaboration with traditional colleagues. The sweat lodge ceremony is a basic method of purification, in which a temporary structure is used to enact the ceremony. The sweat lodge is built out of willows around a hole dug in the center. The willows are covered with canvas or plastic and a fire is built to heat the rocks, which are put in the center of the pit. Essential to partaking in the Sweat Lodge ceremony is to be respectful to the "spirits." Before beginning one prays to the guardian spirit. In fact all aspects of nature are respected and symbolically represented in the ceremony (i.e., such as the rocks, which are called the bones of Mother Earth). In a sense, the sweat lodge is a symbol of the womb of Mother Earth, while the fire represents the Father Sun. The rocks represent the act of conception. As the participants enter the sweat lodge they have the opportunity to experience their own birth or to feel reborn. Thus it is a chance for a new beginning in life. Every action is performed with deference, because the ceremony is sacred. Essentially, it is the demonstration of respect to "Mother Earth" and all creation. Before the ceremony begins, the leader instructs everyone what is to happen. Upon entering the sweat lodge, all movement is clockwise and circular. Participants turn to the left and either walk or crawl to where they will be seated. Once a spot is chosen, then on succeeding rounds, this will be where they will sit. There are four complete rounds in the ceremony. Upon entering, participants are given a prescribed prayer, which is a method of demonstrating respect and putting participants in the proper state of mind. As participants become closer to the elements, they enter a spiritual space, in which insights or messages can be received. The duration of the round depends on the leader of the ceremony, who enters with the participants. The fire person brings the stones, as required by the leader, while the door person brings in the water. Once the door is closed, the leader burns dried sage, sweet grass, or pieces of cedar. These herbs clean the lodge, symbolic of the world. It is felt that sage smoke affects all the colors of light spectrum, thus touching everything in the universe. Physically, the sweating cleanses the body of toxic elements and is symbolic of cleansing the mind (e.g., when the body is clean, then the mind is clear). At various times during the round, the leader sprinkles water over the stones while everyone meditates and stays in a respectful frame of mind. The leader explains what the round is for (e.g., thanksgiving for the earth, universe, etc.) The leader starts by praying for whatever has been chosen. Each person has the opportunity to follow suit. When finished he will say "all my relations" to acknowledge all creation and the connectedness. Between each prayer, more water is sprinkled. Once the round ends, participants leave in a clockwise fashion in the same order that they entered, thus completing the circle. As the participants leave the womb, they are symbolically reborn. The new beginning creates a new state of mind and a change in attitudes. Those who have cleared their minds during the ceremony can now see the power of the animal spirits and all of the hurt, anger and negative feelings are released. After they have departed from the sweat lodge, participants can enhance the experience by taking a dip in a cold stream or pond. It takes strength to move from heat to cold and back, yet it is thought that the contrast is curative. The complete process is repeated four times. Once again, the symbolic recognition of the four directions, elements and races is enacted as a means of reinforcing the natural cycles in the natural world. "Steam comes up; that's the breath of life. It cleanses out our negative thoughts and fears. Our whole body is crying; it's a very powerful experience. The sweat lodge (Initi), is said to 'strengthen the ghost' of a human being and drives away all evil things" (Smoley, 1992, p. 87).

In the Lakota culture, a sweat lodge ceremony is undertaken before any major endeavor. The ceremony takes place in a dome-like structure, which may look like a teepee. Large poles are bent and put into the group to match the sacred directions of N.S.E.W. northwest, etc. Since the sun rises in the east, the opening of the door is always east. The frame can be covered by blankets or mats or even plastic, as long as the sun is blocked out. Inside the structure, a three-foot hole is dug to hold the stones. Outside the sweat lodge, a fire is built to heat the rocks (lava rocks are the best). At one side of the fire is a mound of fir boughs for participants to place personal items to be cleansed and blessed. Inside the sweat lodge, cedar or fir branches are placed around the hole for people to sit on. Also there are four pieces of cloth to show the four directions, their four races (red, white, black and yellow) and the four elements (air, fire, earth and water). The cloths are usually the colors red, white, blue or yellow. Most often, the sweat lodge is built near a lake, pond or creek to allow the participants to immerse themselves in water between each round. Participants prepare themselves by giving thanks to the boughs, rocks, twigs, water and sage, because these elements are giving themselves up in the ceremony. The ceremony can be for women only, men only, family members only, or in mixed company. If the ceremony is for women only it is led by a woman, or if for men only, it is led by a man. The clothing that participants wear depends on the occasion or the wishes of the participants. If they choose not to wear clothes, it is fine. The only instruction given to participants is that they remove negative thoughts and open their hearts and minds to any messages they receive during the ceremony. Besides the one leading the ceremony, one person is chosen to be the fire keeper and one to be the door keeper. The door keeper must make sure that no outside light comes inside and to listen to the participants. It is important for the symmetry of the ceremony, that when someone wants to leave he or she chants: "all my relations." Once the participants have cleansed their minds, bodies and spirits, they are led in a prayer of appreciation and thanks to the Creator, the great grandfathers, mothers and ancestors. It is believed by First Nations people that those who have gone on before are watching over all from the spirit world.

The Vision Quest

The vision quest is a method of opening oneself up to the spirit world by a process of isolating oneself in the wilderness. Among the Coast Salish people it is called a spirit quest (Jilek, 1982). A person might go off into the forest alone and stay there without speaking to anyone or even eating or drinking. The seeker is to open the self to a vision. Vision quest embodies much of what is most characteristic in First Nations spirituality: exposing the individual to the forces of nature and the supernatural; most crucial perhaps, is the search for one's inner truth (Smoley, 1992). The vision quest resembles an inner journey, where the spirits are confronted.

In all of the dancing, healing or shamanistic ceremonies the theme of rebirth and restoration is always constant, for it is believed that in order to attain personal change, there must be a "kind of death." "Death," as a metaphor, is always followed by rebirth. Whether the method is the sweat lodge or the vision quest, the process is always unfluctuating. When a client approaches the healer, the healer always attempts to look inside and decipher the client's state of "existence." The goal is to destroy the patient's faulty and diseased "old self"; in a sense, a reawakening of what is called "baby" and the "helpless" part of the self. The initial ceremonies produce a kind of infantile dependence, which help in rebirth, reorganization and the beginning of a "new self." In effect, according to Jilek (1982) there is a revival of a "...new human being, that's why when they club you, just go and pass out, but you come back....there is not be evil thinking after they're through with you, all you think is I'm starting life all over again" (p. 66). What happens is a personality rebuilding that facilitates self-exploration in a totally different light.

In the new birth, people have a different, more powerful sense of self. The old self, which might have been addicted, diseased, or confused, now with the help of the guardian spirit or animal spirit, becomes "stronger." The past falls away and only what is "new" is important. The effect is to teach rules of personal and social behavior, indirect reinforcement of coercive group suggestion, the reinforcement of cultural pride (ancestral authority) and the reinforcement of cultural supernatural sanctions. However, despite this, there is a sense of equality as a factor in helping First Nations people to be "new people."

The Traditional Healer

Those who lead ceremonies are often medicine men or women. A medicine man or woman can be of three types: priests, who perform ceremonies; storytellers, who pass on the legends and wisdom from the past; and healers, who use herbs or psychic medicine. However, only a healer would be a shaman, who is someone who can enter into another sate of consciousness to heal or to divine some type of answer. Medicine men or women, as the name denotes, are powerful, but they are still different from a shaman. All shamans are medicine men or women, but not all medicine men or women are shamans. Interestingly, the word shaman comes from Tungus language of Siberia and so is a word that is new to First Nations people of North America (Smoley, 1992). In Coast Salish society, there are two different classes of shaman. The greater shamans are those who have powers of clairvoyance, can cure the sick and control the ghosts and shadows of people. The lesser shamans are those who have the power to heal minor illnesses and deflecting negative influences (Ashwell, 1989). Often, the lesser shaman is a woman who also practices midwifery.

Paramount to a shaman's training is an intimate knowledge of First Nations culture, values, traditional modes of conduct and how people cope with illness. The practices are most often used to alleviate the distress of disease and restore harmony in people who are emotionally or physically ill, or both. However, a shaman does not just rely on the past, but will introduce new ideas about sickness and healing practices that are borrowed from traditional or modern medicine. Shamans have an intimate knowledge of roots and herbs and their medicinal properties; knowledge that is gained through a teacher or known from birth (Harner, 1989). Among some Salish peoples there is the belief that shamanistic skills are not developed, but are present at birth. For others, long years of apprenticeship with a shaman is required to develop such skills. Shamans employ a variety of ceremonies and methods in their repertoire of skills. They are expected to lead an exemplary life and are frequently required to provide demonstrations of their powers. According to Ashwell (1989), a shaman "has an animal helper who had been revealed to him [or her] in a dream during his [her] days as a novice and this animal becomes his [her] relative and could be invoked by him [or her] at any time when assistance was needed" (p. 70). Illness, physical and mental, is thought to be caused by an interference of harmony caused either by external forces, such as the winds, animals and ghosts, or by internal forces, such as the breaching of taboos. Shamans can heal using herbs, through divining, or through specific healing ceremonies, such as ritual sweat baths, drinking of herbs and so forth. Ashwell's (1989) description of a shaman working with a patient is quite revealing of how the Shaman enters the patient's world:

The patient lay in a coma on rush mats inside the long house. The Shaman had first to make a diagnosis. He went into a spirit dance calling on his spirit helper to help him see what was afflicting the sick man. Everyone in the village had gathered to beat on the roof with poles to help him achieve his power. The [Shaman] masked and wearing a headdress of cedar bark and shaking his rattle, bounded in and danced around the patient. His helpers followed him repeating a song, until finally the Shaman went into a trance, showing that his spirit was with him. When he came out of it, weary and exhausted, he had full knowledge of what was causing the patient's ailment (p. 71).

A Caution: Outside Interest in First Nations Helping

Smoley (1992) suggests that it is "natural that whites should look to Indians to revitalize their spirituality. Mainstream Judaism and Christianity have failed to kindle a spark in many earnest seekers raised in those traditions and Eastern traditions, with roots in foreign lands, are sometimes difficult for Westerners to assimilate" (p. 84). Yet because of the past history of exploitation, First Nations people are suspicious of white peoples' interest.

Particularly, Natives have had potent negative experiences with anthropologists and others from the majority culture who claim knowledge about them. Even some Native spiritual leaders, who teach native spiritual ways, have been criticized by many of their own people for selling out to whites (Smoley, 1992). The rationale is that as outsiders, they can never learn the teaching since the teachings are rooted in culture. To remove the teaching from its point of origin is to bring damage to it. Yet others native spiritual teachers believe that those who have come close to the Earth can follow some of the teachings (e.g., vision quest and sweat lodge). However, some ceremonies and practices, such as the Ghost or Sun Dance, should not be open to outsiders. This does not preclude that these approaches not be included in therapeutic intervention with First Nations clients, only that it been done with those qualified to do it and that it be done in a way that is respectful.

Conclusion

Many Native American clients have been so acculturated that many times the focus of the therapy is merely to reconnect them to a traditional system of belief and make sense of their life world from a traditional perspective (Duran & Duran, 1995, p. 89).

While reconnecting with culture is vital, Duran and Duran (1995) go on to say that: "…for the most part the client must be able to adjust and work in a white environment as well as still maintain a sense of identity" (p. 89). Thus, a sensitivity to the historical and political struggle of First Nations people is a must for those who are working with aboriginal people or who wish to work cooperatively with elders or traditional helpers. However, at the same time, the counsellor needs to empower clients to cope with the reality of the world. There are a number of healing practices that can be incorporated in counselling, but in doing so it is vital that it be done in a respectful and sensitive manner. Consider that when one becomes respectful and sensitive to the land, then one can communicate with the spirits that inhabit the land and everything in it. What distinguishes First Nations helping approaches are the rituals that are full of cultural symbols that in themselves have a healing affect. Symbols provide not only important meaning in ceremonies, but have a curative effect. Each act in a ritual is a reminder of humanity's relationship with the spirit world. For example, when Black Elk (1961) spoke, he described the four ribbons on his sacred pipe as representing: " ....the four directions of the four spirits (e.g., the black one is for the west whence the thunder beings live to send us rain; the white one is for the north, whence comes the great white cleansing wind; the red one is from the east, whence springs the light and where the morning star lives to give men wisdom; the yellow for the south, whence come the summer and the power to grow. But these four spirits are only one spirit after all" (p. 39). Thus, when the pipe is smoked, the tobacco is smoked not as it is in white civilization, as an amusement or an addiction, but as an offering to the Great Spirit in the four directions.

Chief Dan George said: "there is a longing among all people and creatures to have a sense of purpose and worth...to satisfy that common longing in all of us we must respect each other" (George, 1982, p. 11). Among many First Nations people there is the sense of a loss of control over their everyday lives. Many social initiatives that have been taken to help them by the majority society have sometimes reinforced the feelings of powerlessness. Even many of the counselling methods that are standard in the helping profession are viewed as inappropriate for First Nations clientele (LaFromboise, et al., 1990). That is why using appropriate methods is important for counselling to be effective. According to Jilek (1982), what characterizes First Nations helping and learning, such as in the Salish spirit dance, is that it provides participants "…with meaningful collective activity, ego-strengthening group support and an opportunity for socially sanctioned emotional reaction" (p. 159). Yet the power of these ceremonies is that it brings about a sense of renewal or rebirth in its participants. It is not just the healing of a particular problem, but the beginning of a "new person." Thus, culture is an important ingredient in successful psychotherapy, particularly with those from indigenous cultures. Interestingly, the vision of Black Elk (1961) is a wonderful symbol of the re-emergence of traditional culture in the life of First Nations people in North America. The sacred hoop that he spoke of is the restoration of the "hoop" of the nation after seven generations, which is the time that we are living in. Finally, the words of Chief Seattle, a Squamish First Nations leader, epitomizes the essence of what is basic in First Nations helping:

> *Every part of this country is sacred to my people. Every hillside, every valley, every plain and grove, has been hallowed by some fond memory or some sad experience of my tribe. Even the rocks, which seem to lie dumb as they swelter in the sun along the silent sea shore in solemn grandeur, thrill with memories of past events connected with the lives of my people. The noble braves, found mothers, glad, happy-hearted maidens and even the little children, who lived and rejoiced here for a brief season and whose very names are now forgotten, still love these*

somber solitudes and their deep vastness which, at even-tide, grow shadowy with the presence of dusky spirits. Our dead never forget this beautiful world that gave them being. (Ashwell, 1989, p. 6)

References

Ashwell, (1989). *Coast Salish: Their Art, Culture and Legends.* Surrey, BC: Hancock House.

Black Elk Speaks (1961). As told through John Neilhardt , Lincoln, NE: University of Nebraska Press.

Campbell, M. (l979). *Half-breed.* Toronto, ON: Seal Books.

Dugan, K.M. (1985). *The Vision Quest of the Plains Indians: Its Spiritual Significance.* Lewiston, NY: Edwin Mellin Press.

Duran, E. & Duran, B. (l995). *Native American Post-colonial Psychology.* Albany, NY: SUNY Press.

France, M.H. (2002). *Nexus: Transpersonal Approach to Groups.* Calgary, AB: Detselig Enterprises Ltd.

George, D. (l982). *My Spirit Soars.* Surrey, BC: Hancock House.

Hammerschlag, J. (1988). The Dancing Healers: A Doctor's Journey of Healing with Native Americans. San Francisco, CA: Harper & Row.

Hart, M.A. (2002). *Seeking Mino-Pimatisiwin: An Aboriginal Approach to Helping.* Halifax, NS: Ferwood Publishing.

Harner, M. (1989). *The Way of the Shaman.* New York: Harper and Row.

Ibrahim, F.A. (1984). Cross cultural counseling and psychotherapy: Existential psychological perspective. *International Journal for the Advancement of Counseling, 7,* 59-169.

Jilek, W. (1982). *Indian Healing: Shamanic Ceremonialism in the Pacific Northwest.* Surrey, BC: Hancock House.

Katz, R. & Rolde, E. (1981). Community alternatives to psychotherapy. *Psychotherapy, Theory, Research and Practice, 18,* 365-374.

Kluckhohn, F.R. & Stodtbeck, F.L. (1961). *Variations in Value Orientation.* Evanston, IL: Row Peterson.

Lafromboise, T., Trimble, J. & Mohatt, G. (1990). Counseling intervention and American Indian tradition: An integrative approach. *The Counseling Psychologist, 18,* 628-654.

Locust, C. (1988). Wounding the spirit: Discrimination and traditional American Indian belief systems. *Harvard Educational Review, 58,* 315-330.

Medicine Eagle, B. (1989). The circle of healing. In R. Carlson & J. Brugh (Eds.), *Healers on Healing* (58-62) [City?: Publisher?].

Newman, P. (l989). Bold and cautious. *Maclean's,* July, 24-25.

Rodríguez, C. (2001). Worldview and developing multicultural skills. *Connections,* University of Victoria, 52-58.

Smoley, R. (1992). First Nations spirituality. *Yoga Journal,* January, 84-89, 104-108.

Sterling, S. (1997). Skaloola the Owl: Healing power in Salishan mythology. *Guidance & Counselling, 12,* 2, 9-12.

Sue, D.W. & Sue, D. (1999). *Counselling the Culturally Different: Theory and Practice* (2nd ed.). New York, NY: John Wiley & Sons.

Trimble, J.E. & Hayes, S. (1984). Mental health intervention in the psychosocial contexts of American Indian communities. In W. O'Conner & B. Lubin (Eds.), *Ecological Approaches to Clinical and Community Psychology*, 293-321.

Wachtel, P.L. (1977). *Psychoanalysis and Behavior Therapy: Toward an Integration*. New York, NY: Basic Books.

Weenie, A. (1998). Aboriginal Pedagogy: The Sacred Circle Concept. In L. Stiffarm (Ed.). *As We See ... Aboriginal Pedagogy*. Saskatoon, SK: University Extension Press.

Chapter 21

Pre-contact education and the role of storytelling

Wendy Edwards

First Nations people unanimously emphasized a logical and realistic teaching and learning style that relied on looking, listening, and learning (Miller, 1997). Despite their differences, the educational system of the First Nations reflected a common philosophical or spiritual grounding, as well as a similar approach. Because all First Nations based their educational instruction within the deeply ingrained spirituality of their Worldview, it is not uncommon to find striking commonalties, including the total absence of anything resembling the Europeanss punitive, competitive, institutional approach to schooling. The traditional methods of First Nations education involved family *and* community as teachers and caregivers.

The common elements in Aboriginal education were the shaping of behavior by positive example in the home, the provisions of subtle guidance towards desired forms of behavior through the use of games, a heavy reliance on the use of stories for didactic purposes and, as the child neared early adulthood, the utilization of more formal and ritualized ceremonies to impart rite-of-passage lessons with due solemnity....All of these approaches shared enough assumptions, methods and objectives to be described collectively without doing violence to the individualism of the groups as an Aboriginal system of education. All of them relied on looking and listening to learn (Miller, 1997, p. 89).

In childhood, appropriate or desired behavior was encouraged by indirect and non-coercive means, in direct contrast to European child-rearing methods. Discipline more often consisted of embarrassment or warnings rather than hurtful blows or penalizing deprivation. In similar spirit was the use of storytelling to teach an indirect lesson to a contrary child (Miller, 1997).

An illustration

In an oral society, it is an unforgettable lesson to be the subject of an embarrassing story that may be retold for years to come. Such a story might sound like the following:

Big Brother and Little Brother are Coast Salish boys who live in the village of Snaw Naw As on the East coast of Vancouver Island. One fine, sunny day Big Brother asked Grandpa if he would take them fishing at the Bear Pool. This pool was the site of a fine fish camp and there were always big, fat salmon hiding in the dark water. "Yes," Grandpa replied, "it is time we caught some fish for Grandma and your aunties to prepare for winter eating. And we will catchour supper," he said "and have a tasty feast at the camp."

The boys were very happy and quickly got ready to go. "Grandpa," said Little Brother, "Can our cousin Max come too? He knows how to fish and he can help us catch salmon for Grandma and the aunties." "Yes," said Grandpa, "Max can come too. The more hands we have, the faster the work goes." Little Brother ran to get Max and Big Brother went out in the yard. Looking skyward he called, "We're going to the Bear Pool, Eagle will you fly with us?" Then, looking in the direction of the Bear Pool, he called, "We're going to the Bear Pool, Salmon will you wait for us?"

Little Brother returned with Max, who was carrying a good fishing rod and a big net. They all set out for the Bear Pool. It was going to be a fine day. Grandpa and Big Brother and Little Brother fished that pool all day. They walked further down the river, meeting other relatives who were also inviting the fat salmon to come and keep their winter stomachs full. Max left his rod and net on the bank and went off to play amongst the trees. Several times during the day, Big Brother called to him, "Max, there is work to be done. Your rod and net sit there alone. Come and help us." Max would reply, "Not right now. There is plenty of time. I want to play for awhile." Big Brother was getting tired and he grumbled to Grandpa, "This is not right, he knows he is supposed to help. If everybody helps, there will be enough fish for everyone to eat during the winter." "Never mind," said Grandpa, "just do what you know is right." As supper time approached, Grandpa built a good fire on the river bank. He had saved a particularly fat salmon for their feast. The boys were all hungry. With growling bellies they watched Grandpa prepare their meal. Soon the wonderful smell of roasting salmon was in the air. Yum! Now Grandpa said "Big Brother and Little Brother, you have done a fine day's work. There are many fish to take home to your Grandmother. Come and share in this feast." "Max," said Grandpa, "you can go and play amongst the trees. I know that is where you would rather be. Don't worry about us." And Grandpa turned his back to Max. Max was horrified! He was hungry! He could not argue with Grandpa. Slowly, he walked back to his playing ground and sat down. His belly was growling hard and he could smell the roasted salmon. Max was very sad. Grandpa and Big Brother and Little Brother had a wonderful feast. They felt full and very satisfied. It had been a good day's work. When they were finished eating, they began to pack up the fishing gear and the salmon harvest. Still, Max sat by himself amongst the trees. Grandpa called to him, "Max, come and eat. We saved some of our feast for you. We will not let you go hungry." Although Max was very hungry, he walked slowly back to the fire. Quietly, he ate his delicious meal.

Advantages of Storytelling

Children hearing this story would recognize the lesson of cooperation immediately. To ensure that knowledge did not get separated from experience, or wisdom from divinity, Elders stressed listening, watching and waiting, not asking why. According to Beck and Walters (1997), training began with children who were taught to sit still and enjoy it; they were taught to use their sense of smell, to look when there was seemingly nothing to see and to listen when, presumably, all was quiet. A child who had to ask 'why' was not paying attention in the approved manner. Storytelling was also an effective means of preserving the origin histories. In these stories, individuals are told where the people came from, how the stars were created, where fired was discovered, how light became divided from darkness and how death originated. Curled up with Grandmother, under a blanket, children learned lessons about life through the experiences of the animal characters in the teaching stories. Gently, they acquired the tools and ways of knowledge with which to survive the world. Since there were no books, movies, radios or television, these stories were the libraries of the people and included the human voice, hand movements and facial expressions. The human memory is a great repository which we ordinarily fill with only a fraction of its capacity; the Elders knew this and tested and trained the memory along with the other senses, so that the history and traditions of The People could be preserved and passed on. Oral tradition was one of the principal means The People had to maintain stability over the years in the tribal community. In each story, there was recorded some event of interest or importance, some happening that affected the lives of the people. There were calamities, discoveries, achievements and victories to be kept. But not all our stories were historical; some taught the virtues of kindness, obedience, thrift and the rewards of right living.

Characteristics of a Storyteller

A good storyteller is able to communicate the universality and the timelessness of certain themes we know will never change. Sometimes the story is like a code, the more often it is told over the years, the more a person listens and the more it reveals. According to Beck and Walters (1997), the 'coding' of knowledge in stories is like listening more closely to the narration of events that happened, creatures and characters that are encountered that may be symbolic of something besides what they appear to be or do. Storytelling is a very flexible method of education in the ways of generational knowledge since the traditional forms – style, delivery, tone and words – can be employed not only with traditional content and traditional symbols but with modern themes and content, as well as gradual dimensions of meaning. Knowing when the child is ready, at certain points in his/her life, to be exposed to certain knowledge is the responsibility of the storyteller. It is important to avoid knowing too much too soon, before the child's maturity to handle the information is in place.

Teachers could use storytelling time to achieve their curricular goals and objectives, to teach students about geography, world literature, vocabulary and so forth. However, a good storyteller must also emphasize the inherent values that lie in each story that is being told. If teachers take advantage of their students' "thirst" to learn and if teachers know how to instill a desire for transmitting oral stories, much could be gained in terms of raising students' awareness about the importance of maintaining, valuing and honoring traditions; after all, oral traditions are part of every cultural group. A tradition is something that is lived out and is communicated in its being – lived out to those who come within its circle of influence (Phenix, 1964). Moreover, what is traditional should not be viewed as old-fashioned or unenlightened old ways but as a means to find reassurance that somehow, those who come after us will find common ground in sharing the tradition. It is also indispensable to mention that storytellers would be at an advantage if they use their whole body to express the feelings and ideas behind a story (i.e., hand movements, voice pitch, facial gestures and posture). Finally, it must be said that not only teachers can have the abilities to be storytellers; opportunities and acknowledgement must be given to those children who have a family story or an event to share because, at any rate, we all have stories to tell.

Conclusion

The ways people relate to one another and behave toward one another are as important today as they have always been. Consequently, the teaching stories remain viable in today's world of fast-paced technology. Though some stories might be seen as cautionary tales, the outcome of right or wrong behavior is not always what might be expected even when the attitude towards good and bad adds a wonderful complexity to the stories. The characters must undertake some form of the classic journey, beset with dangers, challenges and the sacrifices that heroes are often called upon to make for personal or communal benefit. In the real world, we too make our journeys for personal or common gains. Some journeys gain knowledge for society and some others yield self-knowledge. Like the Haida youths (in traditional stories) who prepare themselves for any feat of will or body, we too test ourselves in the search for perpetually elusive truths.

Transcending time and culture, the metaphors of journeys, challenges, quest and triumphs in stories envision man's constant struggle to understand and experience the mysteries of the universe. Storytelling, the ability to tell a story, is a universal practice, a means of passing on a wide variety of skills and ways of knowledge from one generation to the next.

References

Beck, P.V. & Walters, A.L. (1997). The Sacred: Ways of Knowledge, Sources of Life. Arizona: Navajo Community College.

Miller, J.R. (1997). *Shingwauk's Vision: A History of Native Residential Schools*. Toronto, ON: University of Toronto Press, p. 16

Phenix, P. (1964). *Realms of Meaning*. New York: McGraw Hill.

Chapter 22

Sufism and healing: An Islamic Multicultural Approach

M. Honoré France

...the cry of animals, or the quivering of trees, or the murmur of water, or the song of birds, or the rustling wind, or the crashing thunder, without feeling them to be an evidence of Thy unity and a proof that there is nothing like unto Thee (Nicholson, 1922, p. 12).

There is considerable debate as to what the word *Sufism* means. The most widely accepted meaning is probably derived from the Arabic suf or "wool," thus sufi is "a person wearing an ascetic's woolen garment." It is thought that Sufism first appeared in the late 7th and 8th century Persia as a movement against the worldliness and loose morals of the ruling Umayyad family. The Sufis "...denounced the luxury of caliphs, viziers and merchants and proposed to return to the simplicity of Abu Bekr and Omar I" (Durant, 1950, p. 258). They not only denounced the government, but the rigid rituals of the mosque. Sufis saw these rituals as an impediment to the "mystic state in which the soul, purified of all earthly concerns, rose not only to the Beatific Vision but to the unity of God" (Durant, 1950, p. 258). One of Sufism's early thinkers was Hasan of Basra (d. 728), who exhorted the Islamic world to return to the strict tenets of prophet Mohammad. Hasan taught that people should prepare for judgment day, heed to the original teachings of the Koran and remember the transitory nature of life. This emphasis on the love of God brought the transition from asceticism to mysticism. Another early teacher of Sufism was the woman who is considered a saint by Sufis, Rabia of Basra (d. 801), who emphasized the love of God neither out of the hope for heaven nor the fear of hell, but "for its own sake."

One of the most prominent exponents of Sufism was Al-Hallaj, a Persian Islamic mystic, who was born about 858 and died in 922. Al-Hallaj broke early with Sufism, when he began to preach publicly, revealing the secret experiences after a pilgrimage to Mecca. When he uttered the phrase *ana l'haqq* ("I Am the Truth") in Baghdad, charges of blasphemy were brought against him. He was accused of heterodoxy and charlatanism and was burned to death. Interestingly, the manner of his execution gave rise to legends of a resurrection that are remarkably similar to that of Jesus.

It is not surprising that Sufism was criticized by traditionalists who feared that the Sufis' focus on personal experiential knowledge of God might cause people to neglect established religious observances. What bothered these critics most was Sufism's ideal of unity with God as a denial of the principle of the separateness of God. As a result, believers in Sufism who claimed mystical communion with God were persecuted. Later followers, such as Ibn Arabi (d. 1240) and Jili (d. 1428), did teach a kind of theosophist monism. They combined the traditional Islamic theological position with a moderate form of Sufism. This led to the wide acceptance of mysticism in the Muslim world. Sufism became more widely spread through the mystical poetry of Jalal al-Din al-Rumi and through the formation of religious brother-hoods. These brotherhoods grew out of an intensive study, by the participants, of the Koran under a mystical guide or "saint," who helped them achieve direct communion with God. In addition, many of the brotherhoods had a significant impact on the spread of Islam.

Another early teacher of Sufism was Farid al-Din Abu Hamid Attar, a Persian poet. Attar was born around 1119 and died around 1230. His works on Sufism are considered definitive. His Biographies, composed of delicately balanced rhymed prose are considered some of the most beautiful in the Arab world. His most famous is the mystical epic, *Conference of the Birds*, in which he created many metaphorical stories used by many later poets. According to Attar, the seeker does not submit to God, but becomes one with God:

> *And if they looked at both together, both were the Smurgh (a name for the seeker and sought), neither more nor less. This one was that and that one this; the like of this hath no one heard in the world (Arasteh 1980, p. 92).*

One of the most interesting practices of Sufism is the whirling dervish. Those who practice this differed in their living style from Christian counterparts, in that they did not live in monasteries but wandered as mendicant teachers. They advocated mystical practices, which included ecstatic and hypnotic rituals of singing and dancing (dervish). The most extreme forms were the howling and the whirling dervishes. These dervishes were generally led by a sheikh who possessed esoteric knowledge. The followers of these sheiks thought they possessed a *silsila* or "chain" which linked novices to their immediate teacher through a series of saints all the way to Mohammad himself.

Stages of Self Realization

Stories are often used in Sufism to explain important beliefs and concepts. Consider one of the following stories by Rumi about a group of Chinese and Greek artists, although their nationalities are unimportant to the story. Both groups claimed that they were the best painters, so the King gave both groups a room to paint. The Chinese painters requested hundreds of paint pigments to paint their room in elaborate colors and intricate designs. However, the Greek painters said they needed nothing and they spent all of their time pol-

Figure 1 - Stages Leading Towards Self-Realization

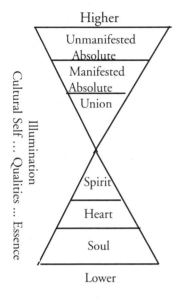

-- Akhfa (innermost consciousness of Divine essence of the unmanifested absolute)

-- Khafi (attributes of the Divine emanating grace to the spirit)

-- Sirr (union with the Higher Spiritual self)

-- Ruh (plateau of concensus and creative nature)

-- Qalb (beatific vision / divine love and rational native)

-- Nafs (egotistical passionate / animal nature)

ishing the walls. Finally, their walls shone like a mirror, while the Chinese painters had their walls beautifully painted with elaborate pictures. Both were beautiful, but when the King saw the room that was like a mirror, he determined that it was the most beautiful. This polished room reflected the Sufi idea that one's hearts and minds should be clear and reflect openness and purity of numerous realities. In the same way, each person must discover the drive or passion for power and wealth and then trancend those drives by refocussing on a path of self realization. According to Harvat (2003) the process follows a path of seven stages that are psycho-spiritual "organs," facilities of suprasensory perception that could also be described as a means of contemplative experiences. Figure 1 describes the stages of self realization. There is considerable debate on these stages but Figure 1 combines what the majority of Sufis believe.

The Sufi Therapeutic Experience

Sufi is at heart a helping process that emphasizes the experiential over the didactic. Wholeness is found by developing a spiritual attitude and seeking fulfillment by becoming more aware. Sufism assumes that as people experience the full range of the spirit of God, they can have insight into their "greater selves." That is, people must strive for greater spiritual perfection by developing what Kahlil Gibran (1933) calls the larger self. According to Gibran:

You are not enclosed within your bodies, nor confined to houses or fields...that which is in you dwells above the mountain and roves with the wind...it is a thing free, a spirit that envelops the earth and moves in the other (p. 91-92).

As an experiential process, Sufism values experiencing as the only means for achieving sensitivity to self, others and the world. Learning and gaining knowledge does not occur through conditioning, but through exposure and experiencing something or someone in its totality as a vital living force. To learn about nature, people cannot simply observe it, but experience it by becoming a part of nature. According to Arasteh and Sheikh (1989), "...those who (are) prepared to take the path of Sufism must first uncondition themselves" (p. 150).

The inner experience is not only mystical, but a means that leads to the reclamation of naturalness or a rebirth. The "inner journey" is a process of transcending the "sinful" self that is caused by living in a materialistic world. Carnal desires, substance addictions, greed, covetousness, selfishness and other worldly desires can be let go if people will it. The process is the identification with the all-knowing power of God as manifested in the "creative self conscious." Arasteh and Sheikh (1989) have described it as being similar to the Gestalt "I-Thou" concept:

Thou can be any object of desire and "I" can be any person at any stage who is incited by the proper object of desire. In the process of union of I and thou, the essential point is the inner motivation of the seeker. The heart must be motivated from within. The thou, the object of desire, must be worthy enough (p. 151).

It is the purity of the heart, with the corresponding innocence of intention, which is the most important aspect of the seeker. Essentially, the heart should become like a mirror, which reflects the attitude of the creator or what is essentially "truth." If this does not happen, then the mind becomes cloudy with negative qualities, such as anger, rigidness, selfishness, greed, envy, etc. (Arberry, 1961). The "truth" is always highly personal, so is never explained to another person. Each person must seek their own "truth" by total concentration in which the object or state becomes you. The duality results in "An" or a new state. This is a "...situation in which one becomes aware of one's previous states and can communicate symbolically, holistically and through experiential media" (Arasteh & Sheikh, 1989, p. 153).

The Sufi Therapeutic Process

The "seeker" following the Sufi therapeutic process must approach the process in a completely open and sincere manner. The reason is that the Sufi way is a highly individual process. To transcend one's individual nature, the seeker must be purified (e.g., to become innocent). There are three stages of the process: the illumination of the cultural self, qualities of self and self essence. The process follow two interlocking steps. First, there must be a disintegration (Fana) of social-self, self-intellect and partial soul. Secondly, there must be a reintegration (Baqa) of the cosmic or universal self. Everyone possesses the power to be a positive or negative force for personal development. The struggle for everyone is to get beyond either emotion or reason and harmonize these discordant elements of being. According to Arasteh and Sheikh (1989):

> *Disharmony appears most often between (1) nafs e amareh (the force with us that commands regressive and evil acts) and reason; (2) reason and nafs e mutma'ana (which confirms certainty); and (3) intuition and reason in the final state of personality growth. (p. 153)*

The result of disharmony causes people to act in self serving ways (e.g., lust robs people of intelligence and reverence and materialism robs people of growth). The purpose of life is union with all and comes only after the abandonment of the "social self" and the embracing of the "universal self." In a sense, each person has the potential to become "god like." That is, everyone possesses the power for bringing about good if they so choose. Yet it is not so easy for some to understand what is beyond themselves. It may require a great deal of effort or it may appear suddenly. The answers are always elusive, but it is clear that awareness can only be found within and not through someone else. It is important, therefore, to be introspective and remove the mental barriers that have been interjected through socialization. With awareness of the universal self comes a realization of what one is.

The Helper as a Guide

While the answers lie within, Sufis' feel that since the journey is difficult, seekers should have a guide (or Pir). The guide shares his or her experience and acts as a touchstone to measure feelings, thoughts and actions. The guide, as helper or therapist, assists with the traps that befall the seeker (e.g., self delusions). While the guide has experience of the journey, the guide is not a teacher. Arasteh and Sheikh (1989) stress that the guide:

> *…cannot teach through instruction but only can set up a situation in which the inspired novice experiences what he or she should. Of course, he or she can experience only those situations that come close to his or her mental state (p. 156).*

The guide should be able to communicate through "tele" or reciprocal empathy ("heart to heart"). The guide gives and the seeker receives and conversely the seeker gives and the guide receives. The process of change is evolutionary and as the seeker transcends the social self, there is less need of guidance from the guide. "This guidance promotes rebirth; the guide serves only as a transfer in this path" (Arasteh & Sheikh, 1989, p. 156). As the seeker becomes more aware or stronger, one's vision (mirror) becomes less cloudy. The stages of rebirth start with the:

1. awareness of the blocks;

2. repentance (*tubeh*);

3. avoiding behaviors that block (*vara*);

4. achievement of piety (*zohd*);

5. becoming patient (*sabr*);

6. trust (*tavakul*);

7. and finally satisfaction (*reza*).

During this therapeutic process, seekers learn to become observers of their psyche or develop the ability to measure self with the object of their search. As they move towards enlightenment, they experience rapturous states of consciousness. The goal of their search intensifies and they develop a divine state of unconditional love for all. What they feel is an intense state of intimacy with the "larger selves." They will spend a great deal of time in contemplation as they become more secure and comfortable with the "self." Finally, they achieve a state of unification with the cosmic. In this state, they will desire to live more genuinely, without need for things materialistic.

Therapeutic Methods of Sufism: Meditation, Dance and Dreams

"Lamps are many, but light is one," wrote the Sufi poet, Rumi. There are a number of methods that Sufis' utilize to bring about the realization of one light. With acceptance of that one light, one can gain enlightenment, redemption, unification and rebirth. These methods may range from hypno-therapeutic experiences to mediation. Hallaji (1979) describes one method used by Sufi healers in Afghanistan, for inducing hypnotic trances, in which the healers started by leading the clients in chanting and then rhythmically blowing on them. This was followed by more meditative and relaxation training. Not only mental disorders are treated, but also physical disorders. In effect, it is the spirit within that is believed to have curative powers. The practitioner speeds the process and focuses the energy.

Sufi Meditation

One representative method for achieving self-realization is through meditation. While meditation practices may differ from practitioner to practitioner, meditation techniques start with learning to concentrate. According to Shafii (1985), there are three types of Sufi meditation: silent meditation (*zikr*), mindful meditation and outward meditation (*zikr-i-jali*).

Silent meditation is basically a passive kind where one focuses on breathing or something else, such as the names of God (e.g., repeating all the names that could be used to call God in Arabic). Mindful meditation is the sense of being free from thoughts, sensations and feelings. Outward meditation uses a poem or music, name of God, or a *pir*, where the goal is to work towards a sense of "emptiness" (*Zen*) or Kundalini arousal (Yoga), which the Sufis call *fana*.

Consider the Ceremony of Rememberance, which utilizes these three meditative processes. The Koran emphasizes that by practicing *Zikr*, individuals can expand their aliveness, increase spiritual attunement and a peaceful soul. Essential to Sufism is meeting on a regualr basis with a *pir* and other seekers. Sometimes, two seekers are matched and asked to meet on a regular basis to study a common theme. The idea is to help everyone to become attuned to others or their partner. In the next phase, seekers learn to direct their energy at will with the guide, followed by regular practice with different seekers. Thus, "...it is believed by the mystics of the Chishti, Qadiri and other schools, the human capacity for connection with superior cognition is practiced and brought to fruition" (Khan, 1979, p. 262). Essentially, meditation moves the seeker beyond the self, transcending what is material and on to the union of all truth. In meditation, the mind becomes empty and allows the seeker to observe mental states, experiences and imperfections. What occurs is an explosion of energy that culminates in a state of rapture and finally, the state of emptiness where one becomes "nothing" or above all things, including "god." The seeker might suddenly engage in whirling dances (*sama*). The Arabic meaning of *sama* is listening to and hearing. It happens when one reaches ecstasy from singing and hearing music while in a whirling dance.

Sufi Dance

"Sama were adopted to actualize these peak experiences" (Arasteh & Sheikh, 1989, p. 158). In fact, movement, particularly circular motion, leads to a deeper awareness. Positive energy is "stoked as a fire" and the seeker moves to a different state. Once again it is the experience or passion that remains dominant as seekers move toward rebirth. As emotions peak in the dance, the seeker is filled with love towards all things. This occurs because seekers realize that they have become "whole." The separation of mind, body and spirit that society reinforces falls away and a new sense of power emerges. When seekers realize the wholeness of all things, then conflict is past. Arasteh and Sheikh (1989) describe the insight as the realization that "...the basis of evolution is not conflict (or competition), but rather the positive force of love (and) they discover that the lover and beloved come from love" (p. 190).

According to Ghazzali (in Shafii, 1985) Sufis have used used *sama* throughout their history. Their is a mystery within everyone, which the seeker must uncover:

Almighty God has placed a secret in the heart of human beings. This secret is hidden like fire in iron. When a stone hits the iron the hidden fire will become evident...Sama and listening to beautiful and pleasant music moves the hidden jewel within. It creates a spontaneous situation which connects the heart of human beings with the Universal and spiritual world. The Universal world is the world of beauty and harmony. Any rhythm, beauty and harmony is the manifestation of that world...a beautiful voice and a delightful song are reflections of the wonder of that world. Sama creates awareness in the heart and brings total joy (shauq). In a person's heart is filled with the intense love and total joy of the Beloved, sama will fan the fire within (l985, pp. 155).

Sufi Dream Work

Dreaming is another popular method for achieving understanding. Sufis have always honored dreams and view them as a means in which the unconscious mind leaves the conscious world (social self) and enters a more pure world of the self (true self). Since the true self is uncluttered with the logic and culturalization of society, wisdom can be revealed through intuition and messages. As insights increase and knowledge unfolds, seekers experience a renewed sense of consciousness in which:

> *…their minds are illuminated and vision increases…now universal trust appears; imagination, perplexity, fantasy and suspicion disappear entirely;…they become the mirror of all. All that remains is to become all truth;…they grasp truth intuitively…thus they have a direct relationship with evolutionary events…they seem unconscious, although they experience a dream like awareness (Arasteh & Sheikh, 1989, p. 159).*

Conclusion

The traditions of Sufism go back to the very beginnings of Islam, however, Sufism is still evolving as a spiritual force for healing the mind. Sufis exist everywhere in the world that values the spiritual aspect of humanity. While it is important to traditional Muslims who practice Sufism to accept the "one true God," Islam, as a religion, is also tolerant of other religious beliefs. Judaism and Christianity have been traditionally recognized by Islam as important contributors to their beliefs. The traditionalist may say that you must accept Allah (God), while more liberal believers say that you must accept God and whatever you call God is immaterial. It is more important to seek the truth. Yet Sufism does not have the nontheistic form of mysticism as does Buddhism. The focus of Sufis is always towards the union with the "creator" (God). Thus Sufism, as a mystical experience, is directly related to the immediate experience of what knowledge is derived from such an experience. Sufism, as a mystical form of healing, is not only highly emotional, it is also highly philosophical. Poetic language, which is a common expressive approach in the Middle East, is frequently the vehicle of expression in all the great writings describing Sufism. Not surprisingly, images like a fire, the dark, an inner journey, twilight of the soul, knowing the unknown are common descriptions of the mystical experience.

Humans becomes alienated by separating themselves from nature, dualistic thinking and fragmentation. The methodology is mystical, yet uses practices that are common to being human (e.g., dance, meditation, music and poetry, just to name a few.) However, it is meditation that is the primary technique of the *pir* or Sufi guide. Humans have become misguided, thus by refocussing their energy, they can become more in harmony with themselves, the world and God. In fact, joining with the purity exemplefied by God is a primary goal of Sufism. What attracts many healers in the West to Sufism, is that Sufism values more than just the emotional and the intellectual. Sufism values the spirit, which Deikman (1979) likens to a house that has been taken over by the servants. In Deikman's view, the servants are the intellect and emotion, while the Master/Mistress is the spirit. Without the spirit, people are incomplete. In that sense, helping or healing cannot be accomplished without the spirit. The method, whether it be meditation, dreams or movement, is generally approached with a mystical experience. Thus, a mystical experience is a spiritual means for achieving a peak experience. In a sense, one is extending the self beyond the ordinary field of human consciousness. In this state, insight occurs, which a Sufi might call "touching the face of God." For Sufis, the spiritual is a mystical experience and as such is the highest state of human knowing. As a vehicle, mysticism can be approached through mediation, prayer and ascetic discipline. In addition, Sufism embraces experiences of ecstasy, levitation, dreams, visions and power to discern human hearts, to heal and to perform other unusual acts. But what happens in these transpersonal experiences? Sufis' report that experience is always immediate, overwhelming and divorced from reality. Yet the experience or the knowledge does not have to be justified, because it is highly individual and in fact does not have to be understood outside the experience itself. But when do people know how they must approach the power that is within? Idries Shah (1981), one of the most articulate exponents of Sufism in the West, uses the metaphor of the "limbless fox" to explain. In the story, a person observes a fox with no limbs in the wild and wonders how it survives. Through observing the fox, the person discovers that the fox waits for a lion to leave the leftovers from the kill. The person, seeing this as a lesson for living, tries to practice the way of the limbless fox. The person sits and waits on a street corner for the meaning of life. But instead of learning more, s/he becomes weaker and weaker. Eventually a "voice" asks the person: "why should you behave like a limbless fox? Why not be a lion and let others benefit from your leavings!" In other words, the healing must come from the power within and wisdom is not found from others. Thus, "…God provides the food, (humankind) the cooks" (Shah, 1981, p. 188).

References

Arasteh, A. & Sheikh, A. (1989). Sufism: The way to universal self. In A Sheikh & (Eds.), *Eastern & Western Approaches to Healing*. New York: John Wiley & Sons.

Arasteh, A. (1980). *Growth to Selfhood*. London, UK: Routledge & Kegan Paul.

Arberry, A.J. (1961). *Tales from the Masnavi*. London, UK: London University Press.

Deikman, A. (1979). Sufism and psychiatry. In *The World of the Sufi*, Sufi Trust, London, UK: Octagon Press.

Durant, W. (1950). *The Age of Faith*. New York: Simon & Shulster.

Gibran, K. (1933). *The Prophet.* New York: Alfred Knopf Publishers.

Khan, M. (1979). Meditation method. In *The World of the Sufi*, Sufi Trust, London, UK: Octagon Press.

Hallaji, J. (1979). Therapy and the Sufi. In *The World of the Sufi*, Sufi Trust, London, UK: Octagon Press.

Harvat, A. (2003). Sufi Psychology [on-line]. Retrieved May 1, 2003 from http://Sufi Psychology.htm.

Nicholson, R.A. (1922). *The Mystics of Islam.* Cambridge, UK: Cambridge University Press.

Shah, I. (1981). *Learning How to Learn: Psychology and Spirituality in the Sufi Way.* San Francisco, CA: Harper & Row, Publishers.

Shafii, M. (l985). *Freedom from the Self: Sufism, Meditation and the Psychotherapy,* New York: Human Science Press.

Chapter 23

Creating Compassion and Selflessness Through Naikan

M. Honoré France

Counselling practices have long been dominated by Western counselling procedures, yet many Asian psychotherapies offer creative and sophisticated strategies that are easily adapted to a variety of theoretical approaches. Naikan is one of the most simplistic, yet elegant modalities that helpers can embrace. Naikan is a Japanese psychotherapy with philosophical roots in Buddhist spiritual practices and emphasizes reflection on past relationships. Like many Asian psychotherapies, Naikan focuses "...primarily on existential and transpersonal levels and little on the pathological" (Walsh, 1989, p. 547). The essence of Naikan is revealed in the meaning from the Japanese words "nai" meaning inner and "kan" meaning observation or introspection. Personal problems and dissatisfactions are often the result of the discrepancy between the actual self and the ideal self or what is and what should be. Buddhism teaches that experience of living is far more valuable than metaphysical speculations. To philosophize too much about existence is a waste of energy, just as is preoccupation with one's condition. Even to focus too much on a problem can lead to attachment. Yet Buddha taught that life should not be seen as a mystery to be figured out. No, life should be lived, simply and practically, accepting events and circumstances as they occur. To emphasize these ideas, consider the wisdom in the words of the poet Chao-chou: "I have come empty-handed," said the student. "Lay it down then!" said the teacher. "But I have brought nothing with me: what can I lay down?" "Then keep on carrying it." Thus what is natural is lost as people use artificial means to deal with their anxieties and fears. If people will allow themselves to be like "water," then they can regain their naturalness and live a more constructive life. Essentially, there is no pretending for "...water reflects whatever reality brings it" (Reynolds, 1989, p. 181). When people deny reality, whether it is joy or sadness, they fight against the truth of their feelings. "Shoulds" block them and prevent them from making changes to co-exist with the changing context in the environment. Like water, which always flows around objects and doesn't try to fight rocks or other obstacles, people can learn to be more flexible and move at a pace that is in keeping with the circumstances of existence.

Historical Background of Naikan Therapy

Naikan began as a form of spiritual training for priests of the Jodo Shinshu sect of Buddhism. Jodo Shinshu emphasized the love and self sacrifice of Buddha and how this was used to help others achieve enlightenment. Through acceptance of life the way it is and giving joyously to others, followers were promised relief from the cycle of birth and death. The early spiritual training consisted of introspective meditation and fasting. In some circumstances, these priests would go without food, water, sleep and engage in other forms of self-deprivation. The modern practice of Naikan was modified 50 years ago for lay people by Yoshimoto Ishin. "Nowadays the goal need not be a religious one of an existential confrontation with death; the aim of self-understanding is acceptable" (Reynolds, 1982, p. 50). As the practice of Naikan has become more popularized, it has become more of a rational and scientific method of therapy, yet it has also retained many of the spiritual constructs of Buddhism. Interestingly, it is in the prisons of Japan where Naikan has had its greatest impact. In fact, 60% of the prison facilities in Japan have used Naikan at one time or another. Prison officials reported reduced rates of recidivism among *naikansha* prisoners compared to those who are not following the Naikan approach (Reynolds, 1982). Naikan's popularity is increasing, particularly with those working with juvenile delinquents and alcoholics, in part because Naikan can be combined with a short prison sentence and training during probationary periods.

Theoretical Basis of Naikan

In order to enhance well-being, Buddhism emphasizes self discipline or self control, particularly the power to control or modify physical aspects of the body: "Meditation, the principal psycho- therapeutic tool of Buddhism, also can enrich traditional Western psychotherapy in several ways: 1) by offering insight into self-defeating behaviors by focusing on them and exaggerating them; 2) by severing the tight grip of thinking on behavior by retraining attention; and 3) by producing an integrated hypothalamic response that decreases sympathetic activity" (Ramaswami & Sheikh, 1989, p. 109). Through exploring early experiences and present actions, clients using the Naikan approach are helped to let go of selfish attachments and guilt associated with living a self absorbed life. While the introspection is carefully guided by the therapist, clients share their recollections on: 1) what was received from significant others in terms of services, kindness, objects and other important gifts; 2) what has been returned to significant others in life; 3) what troubles, inconveniences, deceits, pettiness and the other selfish acts occurred with these people. The rationale is to focus clients on personal actions, past and present, that influenced their present situation. An important goal of Naikan therapy is to assist clients in accepting responsibility for "...their selfish and irrational behavior" (Ramaswami & Sheikh, 1989, p. 108). Responsibility extends not only to significant others in clients' lives, but also to the objects in the environment around the clients. Clients not only have to consider how they have polluted their bodies and relationships, but also how they have polluted their environment.

The Naikan Therapeutic Process

Traditional Naikan therapy consists of two parts: immersion and counselling. The immersion will take place either in a temple or place where the client can be isolated. Clients are isolated, sleeping and taking meals alone and required to undergo meditation training. Meditation, as the primary helping strategy, may last from 4:30 am until 7 pm. Therapists visit clients, at intervals of one to two hours during the day, to instruct them on meditation and engage them in dialogue. In addition, therapists will also guide clients in introspection and dialogue by focusing on recurring life themes. For example, clients may explore desires that block constructive living, such as dishonesty, negativity or blaming. In a sense, therapists are "fellow travelers," but with some experience in life. Despite being guides, therapists must show honor to clients and continually reinforce their ability to solve personal problems. To empower the client, the therapist will bow his or her "...head to the floor, open the folding screen, bow again and ask clients the topic of [the] current meditation. This ritualized format symbolizes the therapist's humility as he [or she] prepares to listen to the client's confession. The client's response is similarity in ritual form. He [or she] reports the person and time period of his [or her] recollections" (Reynolds, l982, p. 47).

About 20 percent of clients' meditation is spent on significant people who have given and what they have returned to them. Sixty percent of clients' meditation is spent on the trouble or inconveniences that clients have caused significant others. Interestingly, one of the common themes during meditation are clients' relationship with their parents. Since relationships are strongly influenced by parents, this topic is often discussed early on in therapy. One of the assumptions is that people develop a distorted self or destructive patterns in the process of growing up. While the traumas or failures of the past cannot be undone, clients' attitudes can be changed. The Naikan therapy process attempts to restructure clients' thinking and provide a moral structure for living life based on the Buddha's ideal of "giving." Clients share their idea of past events working from the past to the present. In the first week of reflection, clients share their remembrances about the themes in their relationships, while therapists listen without interpretation or comment. Besides instruction in meditation, the therapeutic process involves rephrasing, recasting and reflecting clients' statements. Once therapists have a solid understanding of clients' issues, they will engage in interpreting and then guiding clients actions. According to Reynolds (l982) the therapist "...directs the client away from abstract or vague descriptions of past events and personal suffering. The goal is [for clients to use] concrete statements about specific personal experiences" (p. 48).

In the second phase, counselling consists of weekly or monthly visits to therapists in which clients report on their activities and the progress of their meditation. A journal is often used as a means for structuring client-therapist interactions. Homework assignments are also given to clients, which can consist of summaries of "good works" (helping others) and saying things that show appreciation to others (i.e., "saying thank you at least ten times during the day"). Reynolds (1989) describes how a client must also consider how he or she is served not only by people, but also by the energy of objects. A client can be asked to remove objects from a place where they keep personal items, such as a drawer: "as the items are returned to the drawer one by one, each item is thanked for some specific service it performed for the [client]...conservation of the resources in our world becomes a natural consequence of the grateful recognition of their services they perform for us" (p. 191). Since obtaining a higher state of consciousness and becoming more aware are important goals in living constructively, clients must practice daily meditation at a certain place and time. As an active strategy, meditation is invaluable. The research in meditation has solidly demonstrated benefits in increasing perceptual and empathic sensitivity (Walsh, 1989). Usually, clients are instructed to meditate on how someone has given to them, visualizing him or her, letting whatever feelings and thoughts develop. However, in the dialoguing with therapists, clients share how they can live life by giving back. Clients must develop strategies that do not see others as tools for satisfying personal desires, but develop relationships that are open and giving.

An Example of Using Naikan in a Western Context

To illustrate how Naikan therapy is used in a Western context, the following case of a 35-year-old man trying to come to grips with a relationship breakup is discussed. "M" came to therapy with the desire to reduce stress and overcome a generally "blue" feeling. "M" reported that he felt a great deal of anger, yet even after expressing his anger, he felt "stuck." After explaining the Naikan form of therapeutic intervention, "M" was invited by the therapist to share his feelings. He talked for over an hour about his state of mind and how he thought he had been coping. The therapist listened and asked only clarifying questions. The therapist's sense of "M's" condition is personified in "M's" imagery of how he saw his life. "M" described his existence as: "Going down the road of life, minding my own business and being attacked by colleagues who disagreed with me. The viciousness of their attacks was a real surprise and I felt myself being knocked down in the mud. The sorrow of their attacks seems to have somehow paralyzed me...I don't feel that I can get up, yet I see the uselessness of staying and wallowing in the mud."

After mastering the skill of meditation and practicing it for some time, the therapist focused on significant relationships, positive and negative, in his life. Of the many people he felt were significant in his life, he chose to "work" on a relationship involving a colleague who he felt had treated him in a unfair way. Rather than focusing on the negative aspects of his relationship with the person, he was asked to focus on what he had learned in the encounter with that person. While finding it difficult to explore the positive parts, he did list of number of things he had learned about himself and how the experience had changed his life. After considerable time exploring this experience (two sessions consisting of one-hour each), he was surprised at what he had learned. Of these, what predominated was the "little kindnesses" of acquaintances and how much "closer" he had been drawn to his family. The method used to explore these themes was as follows: instruction from the therapist on the topic to focus on; meditation for one hour on the topic; dialoguing the messages in the meditation in a journal; and sharing of the messages with the therapist. Generally, the therapist focused on actions and meaning. In every case "M" was asked to make sense of what was given and what he did to repay others. While the emphasis was on the positive, "M" feelings were honored. However, rather than staying with those feelings, the therapist refocused him towards the positive. Over the next two sessions, "M" explored a number of other relationships from the past, including the relationship with his parents, siblings and ex-spouse. In each case, he was asked to meditate on how these people had influenced and given "something" to him. This was followed by an exploration of how he had given back to others. After tying all these themes together, "M" was asked to write out how, when, where and with who he would return the "gifts" that he had been given. In addition to the dialoguing, meditation and journaling, "M" was asked to consider how he treated pets (cats), plants and objects in his daily life. A clear theme was his pleasure at "taking care" of his pets and house plants. In fact, he learned that he was happier in "nurturing" than in controlling his relationships.

The basic Naikan approach was followed by the therapist in counselling "M," with the philosophy and basic strategies remaining constant. However, in adapting the approach to "M's" cultural milieu, the therapist structured the intervention by teaching meditation skills and encouraging him to focus on the meaning in his actions. The therapist did not engage in interpreting his actions, but in encouraging him to arrive at his own meanings. Finally, the therapist focused on moving "M" towards active and positive strategies for living in harmony with himself and his environment. Specific living strategies that gave back were discussed and clarified so "M" had a clearer idea of what he could do. The two follow-up sessions evaluated how well the strategies were working for him. It was not surprising that a motto he developed and promised to repeat everyday consisted of this thought: "the best way to receive is to give."

Conclusion

The "spiritual" aspects of Buddhism are reflected in the human condition; moreover, Naikan reinforces a positive method for living life in a practical manner. As "M" discovered, there are some things that occur in life that cannot be changed or explained. What "M" learned to do was "let go" of his anger and hopelessness about regaining what he had before.

However, it was not just a "letting go," but a development of a more constructive way of living in the world. "M" learned that he had been given a great deal in life, in fact he said many times he had been fortunate, but he also discovered that he had given very little back. In fact, he discovered that in "giving" he had a great sense of satisfaction and an outlet for his sadness about the breakup of his marriage. In the process, he learned how to use meditation and "good works" to gain more control over his anxieties and fears. The most difficult strategy was learning how to "let go" of his anger and disappointments, but he realized that survival depended on being more flexible (just like water). While much can be made of how different Naikan is to many Western forms of therapy, in fact, the differences are not as great as first seen. Take for example, Behavioralism, a very Western approach and one can see many similarities. Both emphasize self-control and both avow the intention of helping to modify bodily process to enhance well-being. Both have the same objective of teaching clients new behaviors and reducing the gap between the real self and the ideal self. However, they differ in that behaviorism stresses the value of counter-conditioning in undoing neurotic behavior, while Naikan stresses insight. Naikan views insight and training as the best means for developing a constructive life style. My experience with "M" and other clients who opt for the Naikan approach reinforces my belief that Naikan is easily adapted into a Western cultural mode. I continue to believe that meditation is one of the best coping strategies to empower clients and provide them with the ability to be more positive. Naikan has a simplicity about it that I can only describe as eloquent and expressive. It is easily adapted to Western culture and the transpersonal therapeutic approach that I normally practice. Naikan respects the dignity of all things. In fact, the Buddhist ideal may not be all that different from the Christian ideal or any other spiritual approach that seeks harmony. I have found that the premises of Naikan, which emphasizes the connectedness of all things, the impermanence of existence, the acceptance of suffering and the giving to others has a seductive quality about it that is empowering.

References

Reynolds, D. (1982). *Quiet Therapies*. Honolulu, HA: University of Hawaii Press.

Reynolds, D. (1989). On being natural: Two Japanese approaches to healing. In A. Sheikh & S. Sheikh, (Eds.) *Eastern and Western Approaches to Healing: Ancient Wisdom & Modern Knowledge*. New York: John Wiley.

Ramaswami, S. & Sheikh, A. (1989). Buddhist psychology: Implications for healing. In A. Sheikh & S. Sheikh, *Eastern and Western Approaches to Healing: Ancient Wisdom & Modern Knowledge*. New York: John Wiley.

Walsh, R. (1989). Asian psychotherapies. In R. Corsini & D. Wedding, (Eds.), *Current Psychotherapies* (4th Edition). Itasca, NY: F.E. Peacock.

Chapter 24

Re-Connecting to Nature: Using Nature to Penhance Counselling

M. Honoré France & María del Carmen Rodríguez

Aboriginal peoples around the world have always stressed the sacredness of humanity's connection with nature, not only for spiritual well-being, but also for their physical, social and psychological well-being. Our experience in counselling reinforces these practices and suggests that human-kind's separation from nature in the modern world increases stress and leaves people with a sense of psychological, social and spiritual isolation. Along with relevant case studies, this chapter offers a rationale and description for using nature in counselling to help clients clarify their values, increase personal awareness and self-esteem and reduce stress in everyday life and thus tap into the "higher power" wisdom inherent in each individual.

In *Walden, or Life in the Woods,* Thoreau showed that connecting with nature could heal the mind and provide people with a sense of meaning, because by going out into nature, one could "...live deliberately, to feel only the essential facts of life, to see if...[one]...could not learn what it had to teach and not when...[one]...came to die, discover that...[one]...had not lived" (1970, p. 25). From earliest time, going out and experiencing nature, particularly through what Aboriginal people call the Vision Quest, has been a common feature of humans. According to Matheson (l996), what happens is that "ordinary boundaries between entities that are defined without question in the Euro-American world suddenly become fluid, interactive and blurred" (p. 53). However, interest in nature and its healing effects continues to grow among all people in the world as people see that the well-being of the planet is directly linked to the well-being of humankind.

There seems to be an estrangement now between humans and nature, giving rise to some speculation that nature is finally rebelling against the pollution and maltreatment of humans and the environment. Could it be that the benign aspect attributed by some is not so benign after all? Could it be that nature is a force in the universe that humankind will "fight" as the effects of human endeavors such as development of the land continue? Examples are global warming or the floods in Europe, Asia and North America. Cultural values coming out of the attempt to "conquer" the land have affected North American views on a variety of cultural value preferences. Sue and Sue (l999) suggest that in regards to nature, aboriginal people's value preference is one of living in harmony versus the majority value preference of control of nature. Berkes (2003) found that Aboriginal peoples' traditional knowledge of nature is in fact ecologically sound and therefore contributes to environmental sustainability. The relationship between the Cree people in the Hudson Bay area and the environment in which they live has a mutuality to it and benefits their traditional way of life and is ecologically healthy. Perhaps the notion of controlling nature objectifies it rather than seeing nature as an extension of life. Taken one step further, people with this attitude also have to control those urges that they feel within themselves. Thus, control becomes a major issue for society and the individual. The way to control nature, it is thought, is not to leave it to its natural cycle, but to "bend" it to the will of humanity.

The Connection with Nature Enhances Well-being

There are a number of positive results observed in our clients when using nature either as a background, metaphor to express values, or a place to go and experience something beyond themselves. The latter is particularly powerful in that it immerses the person in nature and helps them to move beyond themselves (i.e., moving away from self-centered attitude). The anecdotal findings in this paper reinforce what Cammack (1996) found in a study of wilderness guides: "the results suggest that there appears to be a movement from egocentrism towards ecocentrism; that is an expansive process that occurs with most persons over a period of time" (p. 80). The following case studies provide a rationale for our belief that nature can enhance well-being. Glendinning (1994) states that democracy is encouraged by one's contact with the environment. Perhaps love and a sense of belonging can be reinforced as a means to overcoming evil and mean spiritedness by humankind.

Two Case Studies of Using Nature with Counselling

Case Study # 1: TR is a young adult female exploring new directions in her life. She is examining her values and experimenting with what she calls "a new way of being." When offered an opportunity to use nature as a means for clarifying her values, she readily agreed. She described the idea as a chance to get "out of her head." At the conclusion of the counselling, TR shared the following from her journal: "I was going through a rough period in my marriage and felt the urge to run. It just seemed like all the talk in therapy didn't seem to help...Although the change of environment and meeting new people and all the physical activities were pleasant, nothing changed for me internally until a solo two-day wilderness survival trip. It was then that the extraneous and unimportant parts of my life that were obscuring the problem disappeared and allowed me to focus on my true feelings, followed by a vision of alternatives and possible solutions. When "survival," or aloneness in the wilderness became my social and physical focus, the mental/emotional aspects took on a greater clarity. Now when I feel the need to re-focus or re-charge, I spend some time with nature in a wilderness situation."

Case Study # 2: RG is a professional male who came to counselling reporting extreme stress related to his work. According to RG, the stress of a changing workplace put stress on his professional life and work life. In discussing his issues, RG reported dissatisfaction with the verbal interaction between himself and the therapist. Because of RG's interest in the out of doors, he was encouraged to go out into nature, but to keep a journal and undertake a series of structured activities during his hike. Afterwards, he returned to face-to-face counselling with the therapist where the experience was processed using his journal. The following are some excerpts from his journal that the therapist used to focus the face-to-face encounters. "I want to become more authentic and natural and that means moving away from what is polite and ritualistic. Again, I drank greedily from the pristine stream. The water has such a sparkle and clearness that, when I drank from it, it became like "champagne." My taste buds are used to chlorinated water and were surprised by fresh, natural water...The message is clear, I want to live life in a respectful way, because that is nature's way."

Clarifying Values

Nature is full of metaphors in which people can express their values. For example, the seasons are a cycle of birth, life, dying and rebirth. Both clients (TR and RG) begin to use the vocabulary of nature to describe their views of how to live a more effective life. In essence, the fixed laws of nature offered them a constant lesson for what was important in their lives. For example, when one looks at the clouds, which are constantly changing, it is easy to see how life to changes. The effect is learning the lessons of nature and applying it to everyday life. Most of our clients, including the two cases described in this chapter, readily project their thoughts and feelings on to what they observed in nature. When TR spoke of the coming and goings of the tide, it was quite straightforward to ask her to describe what it meant to her life. Underlying everything she said was an expressed value that could easily be brought out and reflected back to her, thus allowing her to transcribe the metaphors to important values.

Increasing personal awareness

The journals of these two clients demonstrate that when their awareness was sharpened, they felt more in touch with their senses, emotions, thoughts and perceptions. The self cannot be examined without looking at the context; it is best discovered by looking at the whole, part of which is being in touch with nature. If people are to live an effective life, they must be open to experiencing things in their immediate environment. The acceptance of responsibility and the recognition of their powers occur through awareness. To this end, being aware is focusing on what is there and what is not there. What is not there is also a part of what is there. The silence occurring is just as important as our verbal and nonverbal communication. For example, as people go outside and into the forest, they can only see what is in view, yet there exists life beyond that which cannot be seen nor even sensed, yet it is there. There is nothing in nature that is empty. When using nature to increase awareness, we ask clients to experience all aspects of their environment, including all the temperature changes, smells, sounds, tactile awareness and movement around them, just to name a few. It is a discipline of being observant, immediate and open. When they are, people open all their perceptions to the sensations around them. What our clients expressed is that they can increase their ability to be aware of other aspects in their life at home and work.

Two aspects of this process of awareness assist people in understanding and putting into perspective what is happening. The first aspect is that it allows them to keep up to date with themselves, because at any given time they know how they feel and what they think. Meaning is not something that has to be processed before they can act for themselves as people who are acting as themselves – authentic. The second aspect is the interaction people have with their environment. Boundaries become clear and they react more spontaneously to their environment. They see more, experience more and are aware of more in their surroundings. If people try to split feelings and thoughts, they will find that it is difficult, if not impossible. Nature orients rhythms between awareness and the frequent interruptions that exist in day-to-day activities in the environment. In essence they start to think and analyze and cannot be completely aware of what is going on around them. To attend simultaneously to two things with the same degree of awareness is difficult, because they will always miss out on something. If people can just be aware of what is happening and let it flow, they will experience it, not in parts, but as a whole.

Increasing Self Esteem

It has been well documented both anecdotally and quantitatively that being out and involved in nature, whether passively observing it (e.g., sitting in a park) or actively involved in action-oriented activities (e.g., hiking or gardening) brings about a sense of well-being. We have found that there are two important aspects of this phenomenon, which can be described as "natural rhythms," that reflect life in general (e.g., like one's heartbeat). In addition, our clients report that they have found that being connected to something greater than themselves provides a sense of empowerment.

Part of the sense of well being is the peacefulness of nature compared to most people's stressful existence in the home and at work. Nature, to most people, seems somehow slower and thus more relaxed, producing a mirror effect in people. When people sit in a natural setting, they physically and psychologically slow down, which produces a positive sense of well-being. There is a sense of being connected to something that is greater than oneself; that one's existence is part of a "larger self," and an absence of deadlines, commitment and demands.

Stress Reduction

"As I worked in my garden, I felt a sense of relief from the stress of the day," reported RG in his journal. This response to some involvement in nature-type activities is typical of the kind of responses that are reported by a variety of people (Debring & Wilis, 1987; Cohen, 1989; Cammack, 1996). As individual homework or with the counselor, we ask clients to go for a walk, sit in a park or go camping as a means of helping them to re-focus their attention and energy away from the stress in the home and at work. It is the natural rhythm in nature that is quite the opposite of the kind of drive and energy that push people to the point of increased stress. Thus, by re-focusing on these natural rhythms, people can slow down and move at the same speed as everything around them.

In order to achieve attunement with nature and other human beings, we have suggested to our clients a variety of strategies that can be used to re-focus people, raise their level of awareness, and develop spiritual sensitivity. Re-connecting to nature can be done at different levels or stages of life; one could encourage younger children and youth to explore the outdoors and be attentive to the metaphors and the challenges that nature offers. Re-connecting is also a way of taking care of the environment by keeping it healthy and clean like one's mind, body, and spirit. The following exercise is a helpful approach to reaching these goals. It can be performed individually but in our experience it has always worked better with groups.

The Walk of Life
"There is no path; the path is made by walking"

Antonio Machado

This activity consists of taking people on a hike to a nearby mountain or hill where they can reflect on their life, its rewards, difficulties, struggles, opportunities, and so forth. Along the hike there are three "stations" or "posts" where people are asked to ponder and reflect upon some questions to later exchange views with the rest of the small group. They are all invited to look at their present life and reflect on the qualities they have developed, ponder them, and consider their spiritual growth. The definition of spirituality is an individual construction and there may or may not be any specific religious affiliations or connotations in this activity.

Being present -First Station (Increasing personal awareness and self-esteem): It is important for people to realize how they would go from the present stage of their life to what they want to achieve and thus teaching them to honour the different dimensions of their new self is one of the goals of the project. After walking for 15 or 20 minutes, we sit in a circle and take some time to answer the following questions. The answers are shared only by those who wish to do so.

- Pay attention to the sounds [and silences], sights, smells, and textures of nature.
- What do you perceive?
- Is this some how like you? In what way(s)?
- What does this mean to you?
- How can you represent such meaning?

At this time, people come up with different representations of their sense of awareness and themselves (i.e., drawings, words or phrases, movements, and so forth). Everything is recorded with their permission.

All Our Relations- Second Station (Clarifying Values): As human beings, our relation to nature develops and unfolds in diverse ways. Some people see themselves as part of the natural world; others see nature as separate from themselves and as an entity that needs to be taken care of. Others see nature as a force that subjugates humankind and therefore, it becomes something that is feared. Indigenous people around the world have always perceived the land and its creatures as part of their web of life where everyon e is interconnected and relies on each other for survival and growth. The self is not split into different dimensions but it is considered to be one (physical, emotional, psychological and spiritual) with nature. It is within this belief that this activity takes place. Participants are encouraged to "live and breathe" this exercise and relate their life to the metaphors found in nature.

The questions posed to at this time are:

- List three things that are important to you. (i.e., family, friends, education/school, car, etc.).
- Do you feel related/connected to nature? If so, how?
- If you were something in nature, what would you be? Why?

At this point the participants are asked to exchange and comment on their answers with a partner. Then each person takes some minutes to retell what his or her partner had answer. The goal of this description is to make them feel empathic and closer to understanding other people's views.

Rehearsal for the future- Third Station (The Idea of Possible Selves):

The last station requires a deeper understanding of this exploration. Here people are encouraged to imagine their immediate future by exploring their possible selves. Possible selves are thought to influence an individual's motivation process in two ways: a) they provide clear goals to strive for and offer clear images to avoid negative outcomes; and b) they energize an individual to pursue the actions necessary for attaining a possible self (Martin, 1997). The following questions are offered as a means to reach this goal:

- What personal characteristics do you admire in yourself? Why?
- Would you change them? How?
- What kind of person would you like to be in X (i.e., three) years?
- What can you do to achieve it? (Name at least five concrete ways)

At the end of the exercise participants are asked to reflect on the overall sensations, feelings, emotions, and general thoughts that this activity had brought for them. They are asked to cluster the recurring themes they find in their responses in order to share them with the large group. People may use drawings or write a poem that represent the main ideas of their small group while others may represent their outcomes in the form of a story. Once they were assembled as a large group, each group is given some minutes to share their creative representation and answer any questions that the rest of the large group may have. These final moments provide participants with an opportunity to see the common threads and themes of their life at this stage and at the same time, offer moments for them to see their emerging spirituality as an element within and not outside themselves.

Discussion and the Implications for Counselling

The research by Berkes (2003) and others shows that living in a positive relationship with nature has beneficial results for people and the ecology of a given area. The bond with nature demonstrated by those who live according to traditional ecological knowledge is not only adaptive, but is transmitted by cultural practices over time. In an age where society favors technology over culture and traditions, the relationship with nature becomes paramount to maintaining a sense of balance. Further, in the two cases presented, nature can be extremely useful not only as a metaphor for well-being and healing, but also as an arena or environment for personal change. Glendinning (1994) feels that the first step to healing using nature is very similar to that used by Alcoholics Anonymous – admitting that people are powerless and their lives are unmanageable. This creates a sense of being able to direct the next steps in re-connecting to nature, by not denying the trauma, which "...is individual...is social...is historic" (Glendinning, 1994, p. 126). Once healing begins, people must be open, focused and alert to the wealth hidden within and between themselves and the environment. This is a different and more natural way of thinking of oneself, that Cohen (1989) calls, "old brain" thinking. That is, "the tearing down of fences and the dismantling of the mechanistic ways that characterized the dissociated state" (Glendinning, 1994, p. 132). Thus, people work towards reuniting with the wildness in nature and in the unconscious self in a holistic way.

How does one reconnect to nature? As was demonstrated with both clients from their journals, they went out to become more aware of nature. This occurs by sharpening the senses, by listening to or witnessing the natural phenomena that occur in nature. As the clients became more aware, they gained a greater sense of safety and trust with their environment, which translated to them by accepting their place in the ecological process. Values in regards to life were strengthened at the same time, enabling them to vocalize important messages of living by what they observed in nature. The recounting of the hike by RG assisted him in finding a connecting and meaning in his life. When people start to tell their stories, parts of the trauma will come up while other parts will be suppressed. The task is re-defining one-self in relation to the environment, so that we can come into an alignment with the whole-ness of the universe (Drebing & Wilis, 1987). According to Glendinning (1994), people are "sitting around the fire" (p. 158) and telling their stories, while working through the pain and fragmentation (e.g., metaphorically tearing down the chain link fence and restoring the land to the wilderness).

There are many other ways in which one can establish or renew a relationship to the land, the earth, and its creatures. Some processes are:

• **Lighten one's awareness** - This occurs by sharpening the senses, by listening to or wit-nessing the natural phenomena that occur in nature. As participants become more aware, they gain a greater sense of safety and trust with their environment, which translates to them by accepting their place in the ecological process.

Reflect on personal worth- Looking at one's being- even at a tender age- might help develop a better sense of who one is and how life is unfolding. People are able to name and describe their feelings as well as to ponder and strengthen personal values by relating them to what they see in nature.

Sensing nature- by opening our senses to nature, we can begin to perceive aromas, tex-tures, flavours, and movement and relate it to our personal life. Hugging trees, learning to work with bark, tasting some roots that have never been tried before, or even trying alterna-tive ways of "seeing" nature (i.e., plating a seed, reading magazines, learning new vocabulary, etc.).

Alternative ways to relate to nature- Besides interacting directly with nature, one could also explore alternative ways of developing such connections. Some of these ideas are using metaphors to work on:

- Journal writing
- Poetry
- Writing stories
- Telling stories
- Song writing, and
- Artistic representations and creations
- Taking photographs

• Creating analogies

"Heal the earth, heal each other" (an Ojibway prayer), embodies the healing process. People need to develop an unfamiliar sense of reintegration of themselves by trying to live in harmony rather than trying to maintain a sense of control in all aspects of life. When this happens, paralysis and despair can be transformed to a sense of passion and "connectedness" to the Earth. The primal self (reflected by many aboriginal and Asian people) can be re-discovered. Healing, through active participation with nature, thus becomes possible. Connecting to nature can help people reach a state of enlightenment, which is non-discriminative, because no element is valued over any other. In the same way, there should not be a separation of self, including the physical, social, psychological and spiritual, from nature. The basic practice of nature re-connecting starts in the body, for the body epitomizes the natural process of living.

References

Berkes, F. (2003). Sacred ecology: Re-assessing traditional ecological knowledge, presentation given at the Department of Environmental Studies, University of Victoria, Victoria, BC in March.

Cammack, M. (1996). A Rite of Passage with Outward Bound: Transpersonal Perspective of the Solo from 16 Wilderness Guides. An unpublished MA thesis, University of Victoria, Victoria, BC, Canada.

Cohen, M. (1989). *Connecting with Nature: Creating Moments that let Earth Teach.* Eugene, ON: World Peace University.

Drebing, C. & Wilis, S.C. (1987). *Wilderness Stress Camping as an Adjunctive Therapeutic Modality.* An unpublished paper presented at the Western Psychological Association, Long Beach, CA.

Glendinning, C. (1994). *My Name is Chellis and I'm in Recovery from Western Civilization,* Boston, MA: Shambala Press.

Matheson, L. (1996). Valuing spirituality among Native American populations. *Counselling and Values, 41,* 51-70.

Martin, N.C. (1997). Adolescents' possible selves and the transition to adulthood. Paper presented at the meeting of the Society for Research in Child Development, Washington, DC.

Sue, D.W. & Sue, D. (1999). *Counselling the Culturally Different: Theory & Practice.* New York, NY: John Wiley and Sons.

Thoreau, H.D. (1970). *Walden.* New York, NY: Harper Collins Publishers.

Chapter 25

Cognitive Behavioral Counselling and Multiculturalism

Geoff Hett, M. Honoré France and María del Carmen Rodríguez

Central to counselling is the question, "What counselling interventions are most likely to effect change with a particular client?" Research suggests that client characteristics account for most of the outcome variance (Cormier & Nurius, 2003). This means that the characteristics a client brings to counselling (for example, cultural values) play a pivotal role in the outcome of the counselling program. According to Tanaka-Matsumi, Higginbotham and Chang (2002), multicultural counselling "…involves an integration of universal principles and culturally distinctive values" (p. 338). In Canada, most counselling intervention programs and strategies reflect the dominant culture, that is, the white, middle class, heterosexual male and female. Caution is suggested in the use of these programs for clients not in the mainstream culture. What strategies are, then, appropriate for culturally different clients? From a theoretical perspective, cognitive behavioral strategies may offer culturally sensitive approaches. Cormier and Nurius (2003) propose guidelines for identifying intervention plans for culturally different clients:

1. Intervention planning must reflect the values and world views of the client's cultural identity.

2. Intervention planning must meet the needs of the individual client and his or her social system.

3. Intervention planning must encompass the role of important subsystems and resources in the client's life, such as family structure, support systems, local community, spiritual practices and folk beliefs.

4. Intervention planning must address issues of health, recovery and ways of solving problems.

5. The client's level of acculturation and language must also be considered, as must the length of treatment.

Cognitive Behavioral Counselling to Promote Changes in Thinking and Behavior

Cognitive behavioral counselling strategies have been used successfully to help children and adults overcome a wide variety of problems. These strategies are designed to produce changes in human performance and thinking. They are problem based. That is, clients are helped to identify individual problems and then taught methods to resolve and overcome these difficulties.

Several assumptions underlie cognitive behavioral approaches. First, it is assumed that a person's thoughts, mental images, beliefs as well as one's external environment assert a profound influence on human behavior. A corollary assumption is that a specific focus on a client's cognition and environment is an effective approach to bring about change. As problem behaviors develop from internal processes and external events, both must be the focus for change.

The belief is that most problem behaviors are learned, maintained and modified in the same manner as appropriate behavior. That is, human behavior is developed and maintained by external events (antecedents and consequences) and by internal processes such as thoughts, attitudes and worldviews (antecedents and consequences). As antecedents and consequences are functionally related to behavior, a change in one or both variables is capable of changing the behavior it is related to. For example, what a parent or teacher says to a child about his or her behavior (consequence) influences how the child will behave under similar circumstances in the future. What a person says to themselves about an event or another person (antecedent) will influence how that person behaves during the event or when meeting the other person. An antecedent that precedes a "panic" attack might be the internal dialogue or self-talk a person engages in such as, "I can't handle this situation" or "I'm going to look like such a fool!" Fleeing from this uncomfortable situation might result in the reinforcing consequence of thinking, "Thank God I'm out of there" and the body sensation of reduced arousal and the feeling of relief. The functional relationship that exists between the individual's behavior and the internal and external antecedents and consequences is emphasized in cognitive behavioral assessment and counselling.

Culture, Functional Assessment and Cognitive Behavioral Counselling

It is easy to get confused with the terminology of cognitive behavioral approaches because it appears to quantify behavior, thus appearing as unfriendly and culturally insensitive. However, consider that the way in which a person learns is similar across cultures and that if people basically learn by observing and experiencing, then these are aspects of learning that are not value laden. Cognitive Behavioral counselling does not infer that a person is good or bad or what constitutes what is acceptable or not. It simply focuses on how a person reacts or learns from a given situation, not whether the stimulus is good or bad. In a sense, the environment determines this, making it a relative fact based on the cultural context in which the behavior occurs. It is the cultural milieu of a person that values whether a person is doing the right thing or wrong thing. A behavior in which one shows the bottom of the feet or sits in a way with their feet on a table in Thai society, for example, is considered insulting, while in England it is seen as sitting comfortably. Thai society ensures, through conditioning, that no one shows the soles of their feet because it is bad, while in England no such thing is done. Skinner (1953) said, "....culture is the social environment" (p. 40). In other words, people shape contingencies of reinforcement and what behavior they shape and hence what behavior they share are determinants of evolving environments or culture.

In every society, norms or rules of behavior evolve that correspond with expected social roles and behavior. In Anglo, North American society, maintaining eye contact is thought of as a positive behavior. It is normal for someone to look into the eyes of another when speaking. It is even thought of as being more honest to look a person in the eyes. However, among some aboriginal groups, such as the Navaho, looking into the eyes of another person might be intrusive, thus something negative. In fact, the Navaho go further and see intense eye contact as a stare or the "evil eye" (Trimble & Thurman 2002, p. 63). Asking a lot of questions is considered rude in some cultures, yet is seen by many European societies as a mark of interest – a positive. Consider the results of a study of differing perception of Black and White Americans (Matsumoto, 2000) evaluating:

> *....the same behavior by Caucasians as assertiveness, but aggressive for blacks. Blacks are perceived as aggressive by Whites when they express their feelings, raise questions, or are assertive in interracial situations (p. 56).*

One of the main ways in which cognitive behavioral counsellors work is helping clients see factors that influence behaviors and the consequences of the behavior. In a multicultural situation, the counsellor helps clients identify those situations and personal variables that control the current problematic behaviors. More specifically, the counsellor calls attention to the events preceding target behavior. That is, behavioral counselling does not dwell on philosophical patterns of behavior, rather it emphasizes its empirical and functional aspects. The essence is using learning techniques to bring about change in the target behavior. Consider the following example. Among some Hispanics, seeing and speaking with entities from the spirit world is part of everyday life. It is similar to experiencing auditory and visual hallucinations that can occur during religious situations. Majority society would view this same response as a sign of mental illness. The cognitive behavioral counsellor, using functional analysis, would help the client:

> *...identify specific social conditions under which hallucinations can take place and where these may be culturally appropriate, sets the stage for establishing environmental control over*

hallucinations rather than reducing them by the use of drugs or social sanctions (Matsumoto, 2000, p. 273).

One method, following cognitive behavioral principles, uses a process called functional assessment before engaging the client in actual counselling. It is based on the notion that besides the establishment of positive rapport with the clients, counsellors need to have an accurate sense of the client's cultural background and any relevant aspects of culture in regards to behavior. In addition, the counsellor's understanding and sensitivity towards culture is a preventive measure of early termination of counselling by the client. Clients need to feel that they have the power to make some progress on addressing whatever issue brought them to counselling. Finally, the functional assessment process attempts to help the client be more active in the treatment of the problem. It means continually ensuring that the perception of the client is in sync with culturally relevant ideas of the target behaviors and the counselling. The assessment process has eight steps (Tanaka-Masumi, Higgenbotham & Chang, 2002):

1. Assessment of cultural identity and acculturation: The counsellor should have a sense of what levels the client adheres to in his or her cultural norms (e.g., high acculturation vs. low acculturation);

2. Evaluation of the presenting problem: In order not to misunderstand the problem, the counsellor needs to develop a good understanding of cultural norms, levels of discomfort and idiomatic patterns of the client;

3. Causal explanatory model elicitation: The counsellor gathers information on the problem within a cultural context;

4. Functional assessment The counsellor needs to be able to identify the problem, select the target behaviors and how the target is achieved based on an accurate understanding of the problem and cultural norms of the client;

5. The causal explanatory model comparison and negotiation: The counsellor needs to explain clearly the treatment process and what the treatment is based on in order to decrease frustration and increase client satisfaction;

6. Establishment of treatment variables: The counsellor, in consultation with the client, works with acceptable treatment goals, target behaviors, counselling techniques, etc.;

7. Data collection: Clients are asked to focus on their behavior and the antecedents and consequences of that behavior. The client monitors their behavior throughout counselling, with the counsellor paying particular attention to issues around social comparison (e.g., the bind a minority culture might have because the appropriate behavior in one context might mean something different in another cultural perspective);

8. Discussion of ethical considerations and other treatment concerns: This part consists of a thorough discussion with the client and the family about issues relating to the therapy and the consequence of the counselling (i.e., confidentiality).

Thus, the counsellor helps the client identify specific social conditions (antecedents) important to them so he or she can feel free to express problem behaviors without negative evaluation (consequences) from someone of a different cultural background. One of the most effective ways of treating culture shock is helping clients first understand what is happening, then helping them learn new responses to culturally new situations. Clients can even rehearse behaviors in order to understand how they fit culturally or value wise. Finally, the cognitive behavioral approach emphasizes negotiating treatment strategies with clients rather than imposing them. In fact, the purpose of conducting functional analysis, is to give clients and counsellors a basis for negotiating plausible treatment strategies to change a target behavior.

Rarely is a problem caused by one factor and rarely does one approach overcome most human problems. Cognitive behavioral assessment and counselling approaches recognize problems as being multi-faceted. Included within this model are such strategies as problem solving, modelling, visualization, cognitive restructuring, reframing, stress inoculation, relaxation, systematic desensitization, meditation, self-management and self-guidance procedures. Several of these strategies are discussed below and the case example, which follows, describes how some of these strategies were combined to help a man with a developmental disability overcome his fears of public places.

Cognitive Behavioral Strategies

There are a number of useful strategies that can be utilized with a variety of clients from different cultures. However, counsellors need to be sensitive with these strategies in that they need to be done with culture in mind and how the strategy may be perceived by the client. Historically, counselling has been a tool by some to manipulate them into thinking in the "white way," therefore, the client needs to feel in control of the therapeutic process (Duran & Duran, l995). Being cognizant of the clashes of expectation could help defuse misunderstanding. Pfeiffer (in Tanaka-Matsumi, Higgenbotham & Chang, 2002) has identified common conflicts to be aware of:

1. direct versus indirect therapy style;
2. individual-based versus multilevel therapy involving significant others and community;
3. a hierarchical versus an egalitarian power base in therapy;
4. an intrapsychic versus a functional approach to the presenting problem; and
5. attention to somatic versus psychological expressions of distress (p. 350).

Problem Solving

Problem solving is a cognitive behavioral approach that employs several sequential steps. These steps include identifying and defining the presenting problems, generating multiple solutions, evaluating and selecting suitable solutions to resolve the problems and evaluating the success of the solutions. Problem solving strategies have shown to be successful in improving social skills, the aggressive behavior of children, parenting skills, health, stress and the performance of children and adults in a wide variety of other areas. Problem solving also has important implications for school counsellors in helping children develop education and achievement goals. Of the counselling strategies discussed in this chapter, problem solving is one of the most widely used strategies to assist people with diverse backgrounds.

Progressive Muscle Relaxation

Progressive muscle relaxation is a procedure that can help people cope with the stressful events they encounter in their lives. Although stress is a fact of life, in recent years it has become increasingly apparent that chronic and prolonged stress can contribute substantially to physical and emotional health. Stress comes from a wide variety of sources. These sources include human relationships, family problems, finances and even the time of year, the food we eat and the news we watch on TV or read in the newspaper. Stress can also come from loneliness, aging and the threat to our security and self-esteem. It also stems from our thoughts about past and present events and thoughts about the future.

Muscle relaxation involves learning to tense and relax various muscle groups in one's body. This allows people to note the difference between having a tense and a relaxed body. Normally the client is instructed to tense and relax their hand and arm muscles, then various muscle groups in their face, neck and shoulders, body and finally their legs and feet. Muscle relaxation, although not new, has become popular for helping people overcome headaches, depression, panic, hypertension and many other related problems.

Systematic Desensitization

Systematic desensitization is a widely used anxiety-reducing strategy. The premise upon which this procedure is based is that one cannot be fearful, anxious and relaxed at the same time. This counselling strategy includes identifying the source of a client's anxiety, developing a hierarchy of anxiety-evoking situations by listing situations from those that are least anxiety evoking to those that are most anxiety evoking, teaching the skill of progressive muscle relaxation and beginning with the least anxiety-evoking situation, having clients visualize each situation several times while in a state of complete relaxation. This procedure is repeated for each item on the hierarchy until the situation loses the ability to evoke anxiety. Systematic desensitization is employed when clients have the ability and skill to handle a situation, but avoid doing so or perform poorly because of stress and anxiety. This procedure has been successful in helping people reduce their anxiety and improve their performance in a wide variety of anxiety evoking situations.

Cognitive Restructuring

Cognitive restructuring is a counselling procedure that assists clients recognize how their internal dialogue, sometimes referred to as "self-talk," can profoundly influence their emotions and performance. The goal of counselling is to have people change their self-defeating thinking. This is accomplished by having clients first recognize their negative and self-defeating thoughts. Next, thought-stopping procedures are taught. Finally, clients are taught to recognize and stop their negative thinking and substitute these behaviors with self-enhancing positive self-statements.

When faced with problems and life's difficulties, people often neglect to consider how their thinking about themselves in these problem situations affects their level of stress, anxiety and performance. The level of stress and anxiety we all experience in any situation is linked to what we think and say to ourselves about the problem situation and about ourselves in these situations. When thinking or self-talk is primarily negative, stress and anxiety levels increase. High levels of stress result in poor performance. Helping clients to "clean up their thinking" can relieve stress and anxiety and enhance performance.

Research suggests that cognitive restructuring has been successful in helping people with a variety of concerns. For example, cognitive restructuring has been used in the treatment of test anxiety with school children, anger, general anxiety, depression, self-esteem, worry and improving athletic performance.

Self-Guidance

Self-guidance is a procedure in which people are taught what to say to themselves to assist in the performance of a desired task. This procedure begins with the counsellor modelling the desired self-talk. Next, the client engages in the appropriate self-talk while the counsellor coaches. Finally, the client performs the task while guiding or instructing himself or herself through the task. The purpose of this procedure is to help clients produce the kind of self-talk that demands attention to the task and minimizes distractions. This procedure helps clients concentrate on the task rather than on their fears associated with the task.

A Case Example

To illustrate the use of cognitive behavioral counselling, Thomas, a 60-year-old aboriginal (Mohawk) man with a developmental disability is used as a case example. During childhood, Thomas suffered from seizures and at the age of three he had a growth removed from his brain. He continued to have seizures and often had as many as eight seizures a day. When he was a young boy, he was removed from his rural reservation where his family resided and placed in an institution where he remained for many years. When repatriated back to the community a hundred kilometers from his reservation, he lived in a succession of group homes and apartments until finding his current basement suite where he lives relatively independently. The couple that lived upstairs helped Thomas with medical appointments, budgeting, shopping and personal living skills.

Thomas has good verbal skills, although his speech is slow and slurred. Although he did not have the opportunity to attend school past grade three, he reads at about a grade six level. He is outgoing and personable and has taken up woodcarving in which he has begun to excel. In addition, he involves himself in self-help groups, the local Native Friendship Centre and an older adult group. He exercises daily by walking around the block with his walker. During several months prior to counselling, however, he suddenly appeared disinterested in his friends and group activities. He remained in his apartment, isolating himself from others. With Thomas's permission, his caregivers referred him for counselling.

Assessment

The observations made by his caregivers were that Thomas was indeed becoming withdrawn and isolating himself from others. Sharing these concerns with Thomas, they learned that he was afraid to go out into public places for fear of having seizures. He stated that his seizures had "control over him" and that he could no longer control them. He believed that when he went out into the community his seizures increased in frequency. Because of this he grew fearful of leaving his apartment. Thomas's caregivers and caseworker believed that his increased anxiety was triggering his seizures. When Thomas was asked to recall his thoughts and feelings, he stated being "scared" and "hot." He remembered thinking that he was going to have a seizure, worrying about how others would react and feeling the need to "get out of there." Thomas's caseworker reported that recently, when Thomas was faced with a new situation, he would stop, appear confused, breathe heavily and often bolt out of the door. She recognized that by leaving the situation, Thomas would begin to feel better, and that this method of reducing his fear and anxiety served to reinforce his escape from and avoidance of these situations. Because of the absense of trained aboriginal counsellors, Thomas was paired with a "white counsellor" recommended by the Native Friendship Centre as being culturally sensitive and experienced in working with aboriginal clients. In addition, it was recommended by the director to work in conjunction with one of the elders working as a volunteer at the Friendship Centre.

Intervention

As an aboriginal becoming more and more in touch with his culture, this is where the counsellor began to work with Thomas. Thomas had spoken highly of an elder he met at the Native Friendship Centre, whom the counsellor contacted for assistance. In the first meeting, the elder came with the counsellor and together with Thomas performed a smudge. Next, they talked with Thomas about his carving, encouraging him to continue with it and even contemplate sharing his knowledge with others. The counsellor explained the four cognitive behavioral counselling strategies would be combined to assist Thomas in overcome his fear of having a seizure in public places. These strategies included progressive muscle relaxation, systematic desensitization, cognitive restructuring and self-guidance. It was hoped that by using these procedures to lower Thomas's anxiety, his seizures would also be reduced. In addition, the elder suggested that Thomas begin to use cleansing techniques, such as a smudge and the brush off with an eagle feather. The elder presented an eagle feather to Thomas, who accepted it with great ceremony. The first step in Thomas's intervention program was to teach him the skill of progressive muscle relaxation. Relaxation training for people with developmental disabilities typically involves 5 to 10 sessions of about 20 to 30 minutes in length. Due to Thomas's difficulty with short-term memory, it was decided that the relaxation training should occur three times a week for approximately three weeks.

Thomas was encouraged to wear loose, comfortable clothing to the training sessions. The sessions began with the elder brushing him and the counsellor off with the eagle feather followed by a traditional prayer in the Mohawk language. Next, the counsellor helped Thomas discriminate between having "tense" and "relaxed" muscles. Thomas found it helpful to feel the counsellor's muscles, as they were "tensed" and "relaxed," until he could replicate this procedure. Once Thomas became proficient at relaxing his body, he was encouraged to repeat the word "relax" while experiencing the sensation of having a relaxed body. This was also paired with the image of the lake on the reserve where Thomas was born. It was expected that with practice he could use the word "relax" and the image of the lake as cues to induce relaxation during times of anxiety. Thomas was also encouraged to practice relaxation at home. He was provided with an audiotape to guide him in his practice sessions with traditional native music (e.g., Carlos Nakai). His caregivers helped him develop a chart to record his home practice sessions and to rate his level of relaxation. As Thomas became more proficient at relaxing the muscles in his body, less time was spent on alternating "tensing" and "relaxing" muscles and the focus moved to rhythmic breathing and using the word "relax" as a cue to induce relaxation.

The second step in this program was to help Thomas reduce his level of anxiety during visits into the community. To do this his caseworker took pictures of the places Thomas visited and which evoked anxiety. These pictures were ranked according to the levels of anxiety they produced. Thomas was then shown each picture in succession, beginning with the situation that evoked the least anxiety, and taught to relax as he visualized himself being in that particular situation. During several counselling sessions this procedure was repeated for each picture until Thomas could visualize being in each situation while remaining relaxed.

Finally, Thomas was taught to talk himself successfully through these difficult situations, to replace the negative statements he had previously used with positive coping statements and to use the word "relax" to achieve a state of relaxation whenever physiological signs of anxiety were evident. By having Thomas engage in self-talk that is self-instructional, it was expected that he would be fully concentrating on the behavior he was engaging in and therefore not on his feeling of being "scared." It was also assumed the negative self-talk that Thomas had engaged in, such as, "I shouldn't be here," "What will people think if I have a seizure?" and "I want to get out of here" were partially responsible for his high levels of anxiety. It was expected that teaching Thomas positive coping statements to replace his negative thoughts would assist him to remain more relaxed and able to cope with these situations. For example, Thomas was encouraged to "brush off" with the eagle feather anything negative that "sticks" to him and then rehearse an internal dialogue such as:

> ...Now I am getting off of the Handi-Dart and going into the Seniors Centre and everything is okay. I am going to walk through the doors and into the cafeteria for lunch. If I meet anyone, whether I know them or not, I will say hello and smile and maybe talk to them. I feel fine; I don't feel as though I will have a seizure. These people are nice and my friends are here. I feel good being here. And if I feel tense I need to repeat the word relax several times and relax my body.

To ensure that Thomas was successful at applying these skills, the counsellor, along with the elder, accompanied Thomas initially to each location that had evoked anxiety. The elder modelled the behavior Thomas had been taught and then encouraged and prompted Thomas in their use. In addition, the elder gave Thomas a stone from his home reserve to carry with him for strength. This approach was repeated at each location until he was capable of using these skills independently. Thomas was taken to a park and instructed to enjoy the natural surroundings as a means of relaxing himself. In addition, Thomas was encouraged to attend an increasing number of events at the Friendship Centre and become more involved in cultural endeavors in the community.

An Expressive Behavioral Strategy: IMM

The Imagery in Movement Method (IMM) is a four-step process used as a tool to explore any topic or question of concern or to simply open investigation into the structure of one's consciousness. It is generally a facilitated process, but people can be trained to work alone. Because every client brings to the counseling session a very personal question or topic to work with, the facilitator or counsellor should consider the IMM a tool for working individually with clients and not in groups. The main goal is to help the client explore certain issues having to do with feelings and emotions, thus leading to an awareness and change in his/her life. The counsellor must act as a supporter and make the client feel confident and safe about the issues that will be explored throughout the four steps. The counsellor must also remember that some individuals might feel vulnerable at any of the four stages because they are dealing with private and intimate situations.

Step one: Expression

For this first step, any kind of self-created art may be used; however, drawing is a preferred technique due to the availability of the materials (paper and crayons), the outcome (a tangible product) and the ease of this form of expression. The purpose of tangible expression is to make the implicit explicit and that the non-verbal aspects of the explored issue are experienced through images; that "the feeling in my gut," "an intuition," "on the tip of my tongue" or "my sense of things" are brought into consciousness transforming the ground of being, into a view. Even when the participant thinks that there are no images in his/her mind to draw, the feeling quickly fades and everyone is able to create. Individuals must be reminded that this is not art, so all they are doing is letting their hand do whatever it wants. It is important that the facilitator does not make any suggestions to the participants about what to draw nor that he or she expresses his or her own emotional reactions to the unfolding drawing.

Step two: Mapping

Mapping is an exploration of each element of the drawing and the overall organization of the drawing itself in order to guide the client through his or her own inner landscape, revealing the dynamics of the psyche by implying the direction of growth. The facilitator asks the person to look for a particular shape, pattern or color in the drawing and the person is then asked to report on any body sensations, feelings, images or thoughts that might speak to him or her. The facilitator helps the client to explore the full sensory experience associated with the drawing, not only in terms of visual images, but also in olfactory and kinesthetic images. Sometimes, the client might be asked to "step into the drawing" and report what is happening (i.e., describe whatever the images evoke at any given time). The next step is to encourage the client to be receptive to the symbolic meaning of each element of the drawing by asking him/herself what is the symbolic meaning of a particular part of the drawing and to pay close attention to the answer. If the client should answer "I don't know," it is suggested that the facilitator gives a simple instruction to access the appropriate mode by saying something like: "That is your verbal mind and it does not know, ask your imagery mind what it means." The facilitator must comment on or interpret the associations (in the drawing) reported by the participant and must be really careful on the kinds of questions utilized to trigger ideas, thoughts or sensations.

Step three: Fantasy enactment

The purpose of fantasy enactment is self-transformation. When memory and waking dream (stepping "into the drawing") experiences have been accessed, the client understands the source of an issue, has become aware of how the body has participated in sharing that specific issue and has seen the solution to the issue within the larger context of his or her life. First, the group member or participant is asked to identify the most charged part of the drawing, then he or she is asked to step into it once again and report what is happening. One major role of the facilitator is to focus the participant's attention on the sensory details that first present themselves. Based on information given by the participant, the facilitator can ask questions such as: "What color is the floor?", "How does your body feel?", "What do you smell?" or "What do you hear?" As the scene becomes more and more vivid to the individual, it begins to unfold and evoke sensations, feelings and thoughts. It is then that the facilitator might want to begin the enactment process by asking the participant to role-play the scene as it unfolds. The facilitator acts as an aid for the participant by performing any roles that might be requested. Typically, when there is bodily engagement in the exploration process, a dramatic shift occurs in the person's experience: there is an experience of being at a frightening edge and fearing the unknown. The participant often experiences his or her body moving spontaneously and without any conscious forethought. The client becomes the process, becomes the fantasy unfolding itself; and as he or she experiences catharsis and insight that is at once intellectual, emotional and embodied, the experience finds its own path for resolution. It is not unusual that either a memory experience or a waking dream unfold in this part of the process.

A participant might find him/herself reliving a memory in very vivid detail, recalling aspects that have been long forgotten. Once one scene is retrieved in full sensory detail, the entire memory of the event(s) usually unfolds. The fantasy sequence may be a waking dream and sometimes it is a symbolic dream, where reality is remade in ways that resolve the issue expressed in a particular part of the drawing. Waking dreams that emerge when the client enters a particular color or shape of the drawing express the issue represented by that part of the drawing and attempt to resolve it. On the other hand, symbolic dreams place the issue in a larger context and provide wisdom about its resolution in terms of options, resources and/or actions. With the conclusion of the fantasy enactment work, the client moves from accessing material to utilizing the methods of verbal translation to understand the relevance of that material for use in finding a solution to the issue, or simply discovering alternatives for daily life situations.

Step four: Verbal translation

The goal in this last step is to help the client in the understanding of the experiences that have unfolded through the drawings and their explorations. Because the participant has experienced very vivid emotions through the enactment of the fantasy, he or she might be in an altered condition. At this stage, the facilitator's role is to ask general questions about the process in order to move the participant back into his or her everyday situations (e.g.,

"How was that for you?"; "How do these images relate to your reality?"; "What in your life reminds you of this memory and fantasy?"). Because some participants might be more vulnerable than others, the "bringing back" process must be subtle and must be accompanied, preferably, by a gentle and soothing voice. Typically, participants wipe their faces, adjust their clothes and straighten their body posture; all these indicate that they have returned to the "here and now" world. After this last part of the process has been completed, the participant is given a writing task as homework divided into three major parts. The first part is a section for reflecting on the graphic elements of the drawing and the emerging experiences during the mapping; the next section is dedicated to reflecting on the major events of the fantasy enactment and the last part of the assignment includes various summary sections about the impact that the overall experience has in the participant's current life.

The first two sections ask the person to divide the experience into meaningful segments, with the only difference that, for the drawing, the client is asked to identify the most significant graphic elements, while for the fantasy, the client identifies the major events and/or scenes. Next, the client notes all the sensory experiences and feelings associated with these elements, recording them below the element, scene or event that triggered them. Then, the client asks him/herself what the symbolic meaning of the event is and pays attention to his or her own answer, which is recorded under the column labeled symbolic meaning. All these components (the chunking of the drawing and the fantasy, the identification of the meaningful parts and so on) are preparatory steps to the next and most important part of the write-up: tracing the analogies. This is accomplished by using open-ended questioning. For example, the facilitator asks the client: Why did your imaginary mind choose this particular sensory experience to represent the symbolic meaning? The client is supposed to use the section of the writing form labeled analogies to write an answer for each sensory image that emerged for that element. After this exploration has concluded, the client fills out the summary part of the form; first, he or she identifies the major themes that emerged during the work and then relating them to his or her current life situation. By tracing the themes and discovering how they relate to a present situation, the client is able to see how the inner life and structure are reflected in his or her own daily world. It reveals why the client does this particular drawing at this particular time of his or her life. Finally, in the summary part of the task, the client enfolds the imagery and the fantasy material that has emanated throughout the process. The client writes an integrated summary of the insights and in this way, evokes powerful experiences of greater expansion and wholeness. The client not only witnesses and experiences him/herself in many different levels of being, but also sees his or her current life and past life through the symbolic and imagery representations that organize these experiences. Verbal translation returns the client to his or her ordinary life situations with renewed insights; there is a new and expanded sense of self.

Certain variables need to be considered when using this method to help clients find solutions to their situations. One such variable is time; depending on the depth of the problem and how immediate an option is needed, the possibility of going through all the four steps will vary. It is not mandatory to deal with all four parts of the method if the issue is a deep one or if the person needs some time to establish a relationship with the counsellor. The average time to go through the four steps is four sessions. It is not recommended that the in-depth exploration (steps one and two) takes more than two sessions, since this might weaken the emotions/feelings. The latter part of the method might be explored in a more unhurried way once the initial reactions and emotions have been laid out. Used overtime, IMM helps in the development of a "new something" that is felt and experienced differently by each person. This new something appears to be self-healing; it presents key issues, works on those issues and resolves them and then the new something moves on to present the next issue. As the drawings change, so does the behavior. Albeit the idiosyncrasies in the way in which each person's process unfolds, the process appears to move towards increasing joy, freedom and capacity.

Conclusion

With any therapy, it is vital to keep in mind that "...the models of treatment that are the most effective are those in which traditional [First Nations and other minorities] thinking and practice are utilized in conjunction with Western practices" (Duran & Duran, 1995, p. 87). Cognitive behavorial strategies have proven effective in helping children and adults who are members of our dominant culture. There is growing evidence that these strategies are also useful with people of diversity. The basic assumption this approach has about people and how people behave has the least value-laden therapeutic approach. People are not judged, but are taught to recognize how antecedents and consequences influence their behavior. Once clients recognize these influences, they are in a position to make changes in their lives.

Many factors contribute to an effective counselling program. In this chapter we focused on a number of cognitive behavioral counselling strategies for assisting a man with developmental disabilities overcome his fear of public places. By the end of a three-month program, that combined several cognitive behavioral strategies, Thomas was able to again engage in community activities. Although his seizures continued, they did appear to be fewer in number. Thomas had learned to recognize the physiological cues to anxiety and continued to use these cues to remind himself to apply the new skills he learned. Thomas stated that he continues to feel "a bit scared" on some occasions when he is in public places, but he no longer isolates himself from others or avoids social situations. With encouragement from his caregivers, Thomas continues to use these skills to take charge of his life and he has begun to relearn his own language. The reconnection with culture is an important element in

Thomas's recovery, particularly in that he has begin to describe himself as a "warrior," thereby empowering himself beyond just the learning of cognitive skills. In recent years, cognitive behavioral strategies have grown in popularity. Numerous books and hundreds of articles have been written which attest to their success. More recently, an increased number of articles have appeared which discuss the use and benefit of these programs with children and adults with developmental disabilities and cultural differences.

References

Cormier, C. & Nurius, P.S. (2003). *Interviewing and Change Strategies for Helpers: Fundamental Skills and Cognitive Behavioral Interventions*, 5th Edition. Thomson Learning, CA: Brooks/Cole.

Duran, E. & Duran, B. (l995). *Native American Postcolonial Psychology*. Albany, NY: SUNY Press.

Matsumoto. (2000). *Culture and Psychology: People Around the World*, 2nd Edition. Belmont, CA: Wadsworth.

Skinner, B.F. (1953). *Science and Human Behavior*. New York: Macmillan.

Tanaka-Matsumi, J., Higginbotham, H.N. & Chang, R. (2002). Cognitive-behavioral approaches to counseling across cultures: A functional analytic approach for clinical applications. In P. Pedersen, J. Draguns, W. Lonner & J. Trimble, *Counseling Across Cultures*, 5th Edition. Thousand Oaks, CA: Sage, pp. 337-354.

Trimble, J. & Thurman, P. (2002). Ethnocultural considerations and strategies for providing counseling services to Native American Indians. In P. Pedersen, J. Draguns, W. Lonner & J. Trimble, *Counseling Across Cultures*, 5th Edition. Thousand Oaks, CA: Sage, pp. 52-92.

Chapter 26

Transpersonal Theory of Counselling: A Multicultural Approach

Honoré France

Scientism is what has removed the Western psyche from the ability to have that close relationship with creation. Sensation or perception used in the constructing of a quantifiable world can make sense only in the logical positivistic paradigm (Duran & Duran, l995, p. 78).

The Transpersonal Counselling approach has been called the fourth force in counselling, because it significantly moved the theory away from cultural bound Euro-centric values to a more multicultural philosophy. In essence, the Transpersonal theory moved away from the subject or object split, by substituting the word "or" for the word "and." Now there is inclusion, more choices and a radical move away the logic of Rene Descartes, which is embedded in European thinking, to a more holistic thought embracing a variety of worldviews. The idea is that all things are interrelated in the world and making separations, such as subject-object, makes little sense in a world where a "…butterfly in Beijing that flaps its wings and causes a storm in the other side of the world has become a reality" (Coxe, 2003, p. 36). There are contradictions in our institutions, which affect who and what one is and in essence is a creation of what goes on in the world. Thus on one hand, humanity cannot escape the contradictions in the world, just as one cannot escape cultural upheavals that occur a continent away.

Humanity is left with the duality to life that produces energy, yet creates problems. There are solutions in the "game of life," but how does one play the "game" when the fixed order of the world is constantly changing? On an individual level, people are faced with a dilemma of the duality in the order of the universe. In nature there are always opposites, but never good or evil or forces that push and pull. As counsellors we live with the contradictions in our lives and grope for answers and solutions, which challenges us to go beyond what we have done before. Culture plays a major role in what we are and in how we help others cope with the new challenges that face everyone in a world growing "smaller and smaller." Approaches that only utilize a Euro-centric worldview cannot explain what happens and are not comprehensive enough to embrace the human condition. Neither can counsellors separate the spirit, mind, emotions and the physical world, as is customary with previous theories of counselling. However, the Transpersonal theory does combine all of these elements with "culture friendly" strategies that can work with a variety of people. Vaughan (1991) stressed that we:

> .... have mapped transpersonal development beyond what was formerly considered the ceiling of human possibility and have found preliminary evidence of common psychological and spiritual developmental sequences across traditions (p. 94).

Transpersonal counselling has often been referred to as the "fourth force" in psychology in that it is quite different than the traditional approaches in orientation, scope and strategies (Sheikh & Sheikh, 1989). The literal definition of transpersonal is quite simple – beyond the personal. In a sense, one might say that it is beyond the constructs of traditional psychology's conception of personality. Walsh and Vaughan (1993) stress that the transpersonal is a developmental process in which one goes beyond the self limitation of the physical, psychological, social and spiritual, to a point of self-realization of unlimited potentialities. Another important consideration that reflects the holistic idea is expressed by Duran and Duran (1995) who stress that "...a postcolonial paradigm would accept knowledge from differing cosmologies as valid in their own right, without their having to adhere to a separate cultural body for legitimacy" (p. 6). Transpersonal experiences may be defined as experiences in which the sense of identity of self extends beyond the individual or personal to encompass wider aspects of humankind, life, psyche or cosmos. As a holistic process, the Transpersonal approach addresses the thinking, feeling, behavioral and spiritual aspects of humankind.

Multicultural and Theoretical Foundations of Transpersonal Thought

Unlike many of the other theories of counselling, there has not been one individual who stands out or who could be considered the original theorist of the Transpersonal approach. The following people have been cited among a large field of writers currently creating, formulating and researching strategies that follow the Transpersonal theory. They are Ken Wilber, Charles Tart, Stanislav Grof, Roger Walsh and Frances Vaughan. Wilber has introduced many Eastern forms of wisdom into Western therapy and psychology by making them more accessible and less esoteric. His writings have helped people better understand Eastern esotericism by recasting them in a logical manner. Charles Tart researched and described human consciousness and modelling/mapping human states of alternative consciousness. While Stanislav Grof researched chemically induced states of consciousness and developed a version of archtypes that is similar to Jung, Roger Walsh and Frances Vaughan have essentially made Transpersonal psychology "...scientifically respectable to assert alternatives, views of reality that are as substantial, consistent and functional as the ones that are accepted with traditional Western psychology" (Fadiman, in Leuger & Sheikh, 1989, p. 226).

The Transpersonal model features core group areas of exploration that are based on three fundamental assumptions about the nature and potential of the mind: that our usual state of mind is clouded, entranced, mostly out of our control; that this untrained mind can be trained and clarified; that this training catalyzes transpersonal consciousness and action. These areas can be grouped into ethical training, attentional training, emotional transformation, motivation, refining awareness and wisdom (Walsh & Vaughan, 1993). This proposed group model adds additional methods to explore intrapersonal and interpersonal functioning. Walsh (1989) voices the paradoxical and multicultural nature of the Transpersonal by stressing that:

Since nobody is perfect and since we can learn from each other's mistakes, it may be useful to regard those who disagree with us as potential teachers from whom we can learn about a different perception of reality. This seems to be a more rational, democratic and compassionate attitude than one which assumes others are either totally right or totally wrong. Furthermore, it enables us to understand and communicate with a wide variety of human beings who have different views of reality and nevertheless share the same human experiences of fear and the same human desire for happiness (p. 133).

The Transpersonal approach is not linear nor even necessarily new. Walsh and Vaughan (1993) stress that the Transpersonal approach brings a "…recognition of old wisdom" (p. 1). What they mean is that the basic concepts and practices are only new to the West. For example, altered states of consciousness have been a part of many ancient and traditional approaches from Asia to native peoples from the Western Hemisphere. The Transpersonal approach embraces and incorporates folk medicines and practices from a variety of traditions. Altered states of consciousness can be achieved by focusing on perceptual sensitivity, thus producing more clarity. As such, perceptual processes vary with state of consciousness in predictable ways. Functionally this made it possible to achieve specific states of awareness not known in traditional psychotherapy. For example, according to Leuger and Sheikh (1989) developed higher levels of awareness and consciousness were used in the ancient traditions of "…Hinduism, Buddhism and Sufism [expanded by transcending] in order to connect with the real or cosmic self and to establish a genuine sense of unity with nature" (p. 226). Ordinarily, the usual state of consciousness is less than optimal, thus by increasing one's ability to expand the consciousness beyond increases one's knowledge about the forces in the self and the environment. In a sense, one achieves understanding and insight or perhaps "*satori*" (enlightenment), when one's alienated or phony self (*maya*) is discarded. One might even refer to a neurosis as the illusory distortion of perception, which when one becomes more balanced, is not needed and discarded. Awakening from maya (illusion) and experiencing liberation is the aim of the Transpersonal approach to counselling. Thus, by psychological healing, one can become enlightened. In that sense, the Transpersonal approach, "…is not seen as successful adjustments to the prevailing culture, but rather the daily experience of that state called liberation, enlightenment, individuation, certainty or gnosis according to various traditions" (Fadiman, in Leuger & Sheikh, 1989, p. 227).

The mechanism for achieving higher levels of consciousness is to become more aware of the self and one's surroundings. In addition, meditation helps one recognize the flow of thoughts and fantasies for what they are (this is called dehypnosis). There is an insight into how one's behavior has been shaped by societal forces and so one can "let go" of any illusions that here-to-for have conditioned one to act and believe in a certain way. Consequently, the goal is a release of the conscious self and a new knowledge that might be called "enlightenment." There are seven factors of enlightenment:

mindfulness: precise conscious awareness of the stimulus;

effort = energy + arousal;

investigation: active exploration of experience;

rapture: delight in the awareness and exploration of experiences;

concentration: ability to maintain attention on the specific object;

calm: tranquility and freedom from anxiety and agitation;

equanimity: the capacity to experience stimuli without agitation.

Elements for Achieving Wellness

There have never been any secrets to wellness or even enlightenment, because these conditions occur by just "living" in a harmonious and spontaneous state that exists in nature. In surveying many healing traditions, Walsh and Vaughan (l993) put forth a number of elements that they called "…the heart of the art of transcendence: ethical training, concentration, emotional transformation, redirection of motivation, refinement of awareness and the cultivation of wisdom" (p. 2). The following are descriptions of how these elements intertwine with well-being, along with several that I feel augment or expand on their ideas: awareness, compassion, emotional transformation, ethical training, meditation and re-focusing, motivation and wisdom.

Developing Awareness

As a process, awareness sounds like it is similar to introspection, but it is different. The difference is that introspection is a way of looking inward to learn something. It is a process whereby one tries to figure out something or to make sense of it. In doing this, there is a review and analysis of behavior. In the end, perhaps one is, as Polster (1966) suggests, distracted:

> …by expectations of failure or success. We are so prejudiced in favor of one behavior over another. We are prejudiced…in favor of taking over other behavior, so we are prejudiced in

favor of relevance over irrelevance…and given these prejudices, we might not be fascinated with people who don't fit those prejudices (p. 9).

This does not mean that people detach themselves from what is going on around them and become introspective. While detachment from time to time is comfortable and even protective, in the end it is very destructive. Awareness is a process of noticing and observing what one does, how one feels it, what one's thoughts are and what one's body sensations are. These thoughts and body sensations are like a passing scenery, which unfurls like a panorama that people experience as it occurs. Consider the following perspectives on what it means to become aware:

In Freud's narrow view, it meant calling into awareness repressed impulses and instinctual desires. In Fromm's view, the average individual is only half awake; he or she is conscious of fictions but has the potential to become conscious of the reality behind the fiction. Consequently, to make the unconscious conscious means to wake up, to know reality (Sheikh & Sheikh, 1989, p. 115).

In the ordinary movement of life around, it is possible to observe the silences, which allows one to hear what is not said, and to feel the energy flow around unseen. It is all a pattern or process. In the same way as people listen to what others say to them, they will notice how they say it and experience all the sensations, feelings, thoughts and physical reactions. When this happens, there is total contact which allows one to be open to all kinds of possibilities. This contact is the process of awareness.

Two aspects of this process of awareness that assist in understanding and putting into perspective what is happening are meaning and boundary awareness. The first aspect is that it allows people to keep up to date with themselves. At any given time they know how they feel and what they think. Meaning is not something that has to be processed before they can act. People are people and they act as themselves. The second aspect is the interaction people have with their environment. Boundaries become clear and they react more spontaneously to their environment. They see more, experience more and are aware of more in their surroundings. If people try to split feelings and thoughts, they will find that it is difficult, if not impossible. The focus of the Transpersonal approach is to help people to re-awaken to the natural rhythm between awareness and the frequent interruptions that exist in day-to-day activities in the environment. When one starts to think and analyze, it is impossible to be aware of what is going on. To attend simultaneously to two things with the same degree of awareness is very difficult, because there will always be something missed. If one can just be aware of what is happening and let it flow, one will experience it, not in parts, but as a whole. Arasteh and Sheikh (1989) emphasized that, in the healthy person:

…experience and behavior overlap and inner and outer expression are the same; but in many cases, behavior is the rationalization or inhibitor of experience — it is a cover. Experience has an organic and illuminary nature, whereas, behavior is characterized by conditioning. It is

experience, not behavior, that produces change and, at the same time, strengthens one's sensitivity. (p. 150)

This means that, if people are more aware, they can learn to trust their natural processes. If they ignore it or abuse their body, they know that they will destroy it; but if they work with it and not against it, it will give back to them and help them. As they grow in awareness, they will sense more of the wisdom of their whole being. For example, when people jog they know that once they overcome limitations they put on themselves, their running takes on a natural rhythm. They seem to glide as they run. Their mind is not telling their body what to do, for if they let their mind take over, they will feel tired. They will think about finishing. Their rhythm will falter and finally they will want to rest; but when they run without thoughts, they will become aware of all the things around them. They are now in a state of awareness where they have become open to new insights, experiences and understandings. In the Sufi tradition, awareness is a final rebirth that starts people on the road to living in a new light.

Awareness may come to a person suddenly, or it may develop gradually. Yet awareness is not enough. The seeker must cease unsuitable past behavior: he or she must experience repentance, decide to reform and finally cleanse the self of enmity and cruelty (Arasteh & Sheikh, 1989, p. 157).

Becoming Compassionate

To have an open heart that lets the waters of compassion, of understanding and of forgiveness flow forth is a sign of a mature person....Then we...will walk towards greater freedom and let waters flow onto others, healing them and finding healing through them (Vanier, 1998, p. 102).

From a transpersonal perspective, compassion for others is one of the most empowering characteristics that we can wish for. To be compassionate means to wish others not to suffer the indignities of pain and sorrow, socially, intellectually, psychologically and spiritually. However, compassion that emanates from the heart and embraces all of nature's creatures is the transcendental sense that unites us with everything in existence. When we empathize we are separate, but when we feel compassion that goes beyond ourselves, we are joined with the cosmos. That happens when we realize that we are not a separate ego or self, but part of a collective identity that unites us. Brazier (1995) says that:

Compassion is to understand the other person's subjective world without stealing anything. Stealing means taking over...In compassion one sees through the eyes of the other and feels with their heart, without any private agenda (p. 195).

In a world that is characterized by oppression, people become burdened by the lack of acceptance, thus they lose one of life's most precious gifts – love. Oppression robs one's opportunities for being compassionate and without compassion, there is no love. When one is compassionate, one gains meaning, lives with purpose and has understanding for the welfare of other living things. This is the ability to see one's self in a context of all living things and to understand that one is related to all of creation. When one is compassionate, every experience is full of meaning, reminding us that even bad experiences help us along the "road" to greater awareness. That is, that one is a part of a great family that loves every member, no matter how small. This is living with the humility that one has survived because another has given to us; it means that to be humble is to receive a reminder of one's humanness. Even disappointments become opportunities for growth. Brazier (1995) goes on to say that compassion:

...may begin as a set of observational, empathic and caring skills — thoughtfulness, giving time and attention, listening, helping and generous in action — which we can all improve with good effects upon both our professional work and our private lives. As it grows it becomes, inexorably, a challenge to us to overcome the obstacles to life within ourselves and to flow with the boundless Tao in which we lose our attachment to separateness. The world needs kindness (p. 200).

Emotional Transformation

Consider Dass' (1970) idea on the nature of truth:

The truth is everywhere. Wherever you are, it's right where you are, when you can't see it. And you can see it through whatever vehicle you are working with, you can free yourself from certain attachments that keep you from seeing it. The scientist doesn't stop being a scientist, nor anybody stops being anything. You find how to do the things to yourself, which allow you to find truth where you are at that moment (p. 2).

The purpose of truth is to sharpen awareness by focusing on senses, emotions, thoughts and perceptions. People are not their different parts but the sum total of all of them and by being more aware of the whole, they can become more responsible and integrated. Thus, the self cannot be examined without looking at the context; it is best discovered by looking at the whole, that is, the individual, the group, the environment in which the group lives and the relationship these people have with the cosmos. This is the essence of emotional transformation or to "...nurture those aspects that permit a person to dis-identify from the restrictions of the personality and to recognize his or her identity with the total self" (Leuger & Sheikh, 1989, p. 228). Furthermore, if people are to live an effective life, they must reduce "destructive emotions such as fear and anger" (Walsh & Vaughan, 1993, p. 4). However, it is not just the reduction of the negative, but the enhancement of positive emotions and the development of optimism. Thus, being accepting, compassionate, forgiving, generous, just to name a few, is not enough. One has to learn to transform one's being to reflect the equilibrium of water and fostering a calm demeanor. In other words, one must be open to experiencing things as they are and not what is desirable for them to be. Rumi's (1995) eloquent poem describes this attitude as:

Keep walking, though there's no place to get to

Don't try to see through the distances.

That's not for human beings. Move within,

But don't move, the way fear makes you move.

(p. 278)

Along with this equanimity, individuals should learn not to put themselves first and they must begin to unattach themselves from gross materialism; for only then can they strive to be more humane. Attachment is considered those conditionings that keep the human spirit down and create petty emotional reactions. Unconsciously, people attach themselves to "things" without realizing that "holding on" is the cause of suffering (i.e., identification with external objects). Once this is accepted, then the potential that exists within everyone can be released. In essence, each human being is a miniature universe. And so practicing generosity and forgiveness helps transform each person beyond their material existence. And along with this, there has to be an acceptance of responsibility and the recognition of their interconnectedness. One way to achieve this is building a great sense of awareness of that which is inside the self and outside the self.

Ethical Training

The focus on ethical training arises from the observation that unethical behavior both stems from and reinforces destructive mental factors (e.g., greed, fear, anger). Ethical behavior undermines these and promotes factors of kindness, compassion and calm. As transpersonal maturation occurs, ethical behavior is said to flow naturally from one's identification with all people and life. The simplest technique in a group is to advocate such behavior by the leader and members, to point out that it is both a group ground rule and a method of development for all and to discuss when it does or does not occur. Ethical conduct in a group helps create a climate of trust, which enhances risk taking and sincere participation. All of this fosters the transpersonal group community itself and imbeds values and standards that enhance the participants' behavior in the surrounding community.

Initial ethical training for a group member involves turning his or her attention inward. In the Sufi tradition, this is considered part of the process of repentance, the first step on the path of integration. This is the recognition of one's lack of fulfillment in life; the observing of one's impulses, wishes and deeds; and the cleansing of oneself from injustice and animosities. To explore this, a counsellor might create situations in which clients see themselves and are shocked with insight into their true conditions, then would offer a variety of practices that move them along a specific line of development. For example, a counsellor changes the meeting time at the last minute. Perhaps clients would arrive complaining about the abrupt change and the lack of respect it offers them. The counsellor then explains that the change was intentional and describes the difference between seeking respect and seeking knowledge. The counsellor notes that when seeking respect, one often behaves in a manipulative way, acting pious or knowledgeable or with a sense of entitlement. This is a very different posture than that which is effective for seeking knowledge, a posture that demands humility and openness and an absence of manipulations. Real-world changes in one's surrounding community would also produce such reactions in group members. A distinction could be made between personal impulsive reactions (apathy, anger) and deliberate transpersonal responses (i.e., attention, collaboration, secret generous acts). The point is that individuals can observe when they are seeking respect from others. If they are at the stage of ego strengthening, this is important. If at the stage of ego transcendence, this gets in the way.

Meditation and Re-focusing

Walsh and Vaughan (1993) used the term "attentional training" to describe one of the important elements of the Transpersonal approach. Attentional training was the process of cultivating or focusing one's mind on mind, keeping it from wandering. Meditation is often misunderstood in the west. It is often exaggerated as something that either has miraculous properties or as a means for withdrawal from life. But there are different kinds of meditation that have the properties of mystical experiences or the heightened skill of awareness. In some ways, forms of meditation are culturally derived. Yet despite these cultural differences there is a philosophical similarity in the process that goes beyond culture and ends in similar experiences. For example, meditation takes different forms. In Sufism dancing in circles, called a dervish, is a form of meditation, and in Yoga the constant repetition of a mantra is yet another form of meditation. In Buddhism being attentive to one's breathing or contemplating the message in a *koan* (riddle) is another form of meditation. In all of these examples, the end result leads to emptiness or a dulling of one's self and an insight that is quite literally beyond the self. In Buddhism it culminates in Nirvana or a union with the cosmic all. In Sufism and Christianity, this might be a mystical union with God. The idea is indescribable. Perhaps it is T.S. Elliot (1944) who said it best: "words strain, crack and sometimes break under the burden, under the tension slip, slide, perish, decay with imprecision, will not stay in place, will not stay in play" (p. 12).

Meditation is a natural process where the aim is to develop awareness. What happens when someone meditates is an altering of his or her consciousness. In fact, the aim in developing concentration, just as in meditation, is to increase understanding, by realizing and perfecting one's own mind. Yet, paradoxically, meditation strives to release one from the domination of the intellect. According to Humphrey's (1968), no person "should go further into meditation who has not found within. . .a faculty superior to the thinking mind" (p.

154). Thinking is important, but must be abandoned if enlightenment is to occur and truth is to be revealed. In the Sutra of Hui Neng, there is no difference between the enlightened and ignorant person, but what makes these two different is that one realizes it and the other one does not. Thus, one can become a new person by acting in a natural, mindful and skillful manner. According to Ma-tsu (Hoover, 1980):

> *Grasping of the truth is the function of everyday-mindedness. Everyday-mindedness is free from intentional action, free from concepts of right and wrong, taking and giving, the finite or the infinite...All our daily activities – walking standing, sitting, lying down – all response to situations, our dealings with circumstances as they arise (pp. 77-78).*

The message in meditation is as old as humanity itself. The process of the meditation experience in the East and West is the openness of the soul or self to god or the divine. Depending on one's culture or perspective, this could be identified in different ways. For example, Saint Catherine of Genoa described it as: "Me as god nor do I recognize any other me except my god himself." While Jallal-Uddin Rumi described it as "the beloved is all in all, the lover merely veils him; the beloved is all that lives, the lover a dead thing" (Rumi, l995, p. 27). What is inherent in these ideas is that there is an inner knowledge that exists in everyone. The inner knowledge can only be revealed when one achieves oneness with all things or the total illumination of the self with god. Yet knowledge is not the goal, but salvation. Thus, the Christian and Islamic mystics suggest that there is a deliverance from a separate self towards a unity with God. Freedom is the key, for:

> *. . .only one who is ever free of desire can apprehend its spiritual essence; he [or she] who is ever a slave to desire can see no more than its outer fringe...all things depend on it for life and it rejects them not...it lives and nourishes all things...all things return to it (Happold, l963, p. 152).*

Notice the themes of humility and love. It seems these elements are required to be receptive along with a degree of mortification. It is denial of the self by eliminating all attachments, craving, pleasures and self-interests. In other words, the divine within the self can only be gained by losing egocentric impulses and wishing, thinking and feeling. Chuang Tzu (Ramaswami & Sheikh, l989) emphasizes that a person "...without passions...does not permit good or evil to disturb his [her] inward economy but rather falls in with what happens and does not add to the sum of his mortality" (p. 447). Thus, meditation is a process of hearing the music of the inner life, which is mystical and creative. The inner holds the knowledge of the cosmos, waiting to be revealed to us in an entirely new order. Our spiritual world, which is full of symbols, ideas and images, can lead us to enlightenment. The Buddhist mystical experience is correlated with the Christian, Islamic and Hindu path. In the Bhagavad-Gita (Happold, 1963), Krishna said:

> *Resign all your actions to me. Regard me, as your dearest loved one. Know me to be your only refuge. Be united always in heart and consciousness to me. United with me, you shall over-*

come all difficulties by my grace…for the Lord lives in the heart of every creature (Happold, 1963, p. 158).

Understanding Motivation

In order to create a balanced self that is free from distractions and meditation, one must be motivated to be healthier. To do this, Walsh and Vaughan (1993) noted that, "desires gradually become less self-centered and more self-transcendent with less emphasis on getting and more on giving" (p. 5). But how does one free the self from self-centered urges? Social conditions do affect how one performs, thus getting beyond this phenomena may go against one's nature. In fact, this is widespread across the animal world. In an early experiment with cockroaches, researchers found that they went faster if there were other cockroaches present (Zajonc, Heingartner & Herman, 1969). This study compared cockroaches running with an audience of other cockroaches and without an audience down a runway away from a light. Among rats, sexual behavior occurs more often when other rats are present (Baron, Kerr & Miller, 1992). Social psychologists call it "social facilitation," which Forsyth (1999) defines as "improvement in task performance that occurs when people work in the presence of other people" (p. 269).

The social awareness theory is based on the idea of the heightened awareness one has in social situations. When others watch, the performers will become more self-conscious of their actions. In turn, they will become aware of the discrepancies between an ideal and their own performance. This causes them to do better or work harder. Mirrors are often used in physical training to increase personal awareness, thus producing better results. Social awareness can also cause people to be impaired if they feel they are not doing as well as their goal and feel they cannot come close to achieving the ideal. Physically and psychologically, they withdraw from the task. Thus self-consciousness can improve performance, but more than likely, it decreases performance. But how does this translate to redirecting motivation and transcending the need to care about what others think? In Buddhism, this translates into decreasing one's desires as a means of achieving true happiness. Walsh and Vaughan (1993) stress, "the reduction of compulsive craving is…said to result in a corresponding reduction in intrapsychic conflict, a claim now supported by studies of advanced mediators" (p. 5).

Wisdom

If a person is psychologically secure, they are able to shift from a personal focus to a universal focus. This is what I believe is meant in spiritual practice when people talk about "losing one's ego". I believe that if people have a level of personal maturity and ego integration, they can make the shift from "life is happening to me" to "life is happening". It is a happy shift, a shift from an inside-out, "me-focused" view to a cosmic or universal overview (Boorstein, 1994, p. 101).

Walsh and Vaughan (l993) make a distinction between knowledge and wisdom, by stating that the former is something anyone can gain, while the latter is a state of being. Wisdom, then, is a process of "growth" that occurs as one gains personal insight into the self and the environment. From a therapeutic perspective Brazier (1997) that "...each time the therapist dies, a part of the client's prison dies with him [her]" (p. 215). The influence of others becomes less and less as one becomes wise and becomes correspondingly more at one with the self and the world around. While one can become aware of the meaninglessness of objects and material things, there is much more to having wisdom. That is, one transcends the nature of suffering in which the intuitive self becomes more focused on the cosmos or the power beyond. That what may seem solid is only an illusion and so through wisdom one is liberated from external forces that bind creativity, joy and spontaneity. Brazier (l997) goes on to say that "...a deluded person is attracted, repulsed or confused by everything. An enlightened person is enlightened by everything" (p. 222). Walsh and Vaughan (l993) state that this liberating insight is known in many traditions "...in the East as jnana (Hinduism), prjna (Buddhism), or ma'rifah (Islam) and in the West as gnosis or scientia sacra. And with this liberation the goal of the art of transcendence is realized" (p. 7).

Psychotherapeutic Techniques

The challenge for practitioners is to practice what "they preach" or to embody what they share with their client. The same vision they have for others is what should be developed inside oneself. That is, according to Walsh (l989), "...to share and communicate it where we can; to use it to help the healing of our world; and to let it use us as willing servants for the awakening and welfare of all" (p. 136). In an empirical study, Hutton (l993) describes those variables that make a transpersonal practitioner different from other therapists (i.e., behavior-cognitive and psychoanalytic). What he found was that in comparison, the transpersonal practitioners used less verbal interactions and more action-oriented techniques (i.e., experiments and specific skills promoting action on the part of clients). In addition, transpersonal therapists utilized meditation, guided imagery (more often with a spiritual focus), dream work and specific books to read than the other groups.

Transpersonal practitioners use a variety of techniques including desensitization, dream work, drama, guided imagery, meditation, nature connecting experiments and practices that develop ethical personal conduct. That is, they use seven elements – awareness, compassion, emotional transformation, ethical training, motivation, meditation and wisdom – as dimensions for becoming a "whole person." The practitioners help clients work toward creating a sense of balance within and without, a greater sense of connectedness to the environment and a desire to be a "good" person (spiritual enhancement). As a result, to practice in the transpersonal method, practitioners must possess:

An Openness to the transpersonal dimension, including the belief that contacts with transpersonal realms may be Transformative and of greatest healing potential;

The ability to sense the presence of, or a report of numinous experience, whether it should appear in a dream, a vision, a synchronous event or a contact with a spiritual teacher;

Some knowledge of a variety of spiritual paths;

An active pursuit of his/her own spiritual development;

A degree of openness about him/herself, his/her own spiritual orientation and experience;

A firm grounding in psychotherapy (Scotton, in Hutton, l993, p. 141).

Conclusion

The most exciting aspect of all the revolutionary developments in modern Western science — astronomy, physics, biology, medicine, information and systems theory, depth psychology, parapsychology and consciousness research — is the fact that the new image of the universe and of human nature increasingly resembles that of the ancient and Eastern spiritual philosophies, such as the different systems of yoga, the Tibetan Vajrayana, Kashmir Shaivism, Zen Buddhism, Taoism, Kabbalah, Christian mysticism, or gnosticism. It seems that we are approaching a phenomenal synthesis of the ancient and the modern and a far-reaching integration of the great achievements of the East and the West that might have profound consequences for the life on this planet (Grof, 1983, p. 33).

There are some riddles in life that may never be answered or resolved. In the search to find meaning in life it is easy to despair in this chaotic world. Camus (l947) referred to this as rolling the rock up the hill after it rolls down. In other words, life is a matter of "plugging away" as a way of transcending the "dark" forces that pull one down. If nothing else, the "plugging away" serves as a means for directing energy. However, when self doubt occurs and it is inevitable that it will, answers are not easy to find. Camus, like many, dealt with this by romanticizing about the absurdity of life, but of course, the tragedy for Camus was that the absurdity of it all was too much and he drowned himself in the River Seine one rainy evening. The goal of the Transpersonal approach is help others see the impasse as a challenge and refocus one's energy away from selfishness and channel one's energy towards selflessness. Life provides each person with the opportunity to be aware, compassionate and wise. Henri-Frédéric Amiel, the Swiss philosopher and poet, said that "...it is by teaching that we teach ourselves, by relating that we observe, by affirming that we examine, by showing that we look, by writing that we think, by pumping that we draw water into the well."

It is not surprising that nature is not only used as a metaphor in Transpersonal psychology, but also as mechanism for transcendence. For one of the mysteries in nature is that it is not perfect. It is not symmetrical. Nature is something that can never be defined like the ridges of the mountains we have seen at various places in our lives. And if one contemplates the shape and beauty of the mountains, it is impossible to know exactly what it is about them that is so inspiring. And not surprisingly, it can bring similar feelings to the ones we feel for someone we love, because they always escape exact definitions. Yet when we let go of the definitions, of the attempt to try and pin down friendship, love and nature, they flow. When we try to define life in our mind, so that we understand and feel in complete control of it, we only get confused. What happens is that we go into our head, because we base our thoughts on the idea that we are different from it. When that happens, we have limited friendship, love, nature and ultimately, ourselves. Perhaps that is an indication that we are trying to master our lives. Yet, when we let go, life has about it a sense of flowing, like water. So as I close my eyes and see the reflection of the water, I stop thinking, analyzing and just accept what is there. It is the attraction of the river that provided wisdom and peace for Siddhartha; and as people move towards one polarity and back again, they must remember that there is no guarantee that there will be no pain in life or in relationships. They will experience pleasure, but also pain. And like water, they always go away, but they'll always come back. We need to remember that going away and coming back are two sides of the same thing.

References

Arasteh, A.R. & Sheikh, A. (1989). Sufism: The way to universal self. In A. Sheikh & S. Sheikh, (Eds.)*Eastern and Western Approaches to Healing: Ancient Wisdom & Modern Knowledge.* (pp. 166-179)New York: John Wiley.

Baron, R., Kerr, N. & Miller, N. (1992) *Group Process, Group Decision, Group Action.* Pacific Grove, CA: Brooks/Cole.

Brazier, R. (1995). *Zen Therapy.* Boston, MA: Allyn and Bacon.

Boorstein, S. (1994). Spiritual Issues in Psychotherapy. *Journal of Transpersonal Psychology, 26*(2), 95-106.

Camus, A. (1947). *La Peste.* London, U.K.: Penguin Books.

Coxe, D. (2003). The new infodemic age. *Maclean's,* June 9, p. 36.

Dass, B.R. (1970). Lecture at the Menninger Clinic. *Journal of Transpersonal Psychology, 2*(2), 45-98.

Duran, E. & Duran, B. (1995). *Native American Postcolonial Psychology.* Albany, NY: State University of New York Press.

Elliot, T.S. (1944). *Four Quartets.* New York: Farber and Farber.

Forsyth, D. (1999). *Group Dynamics* (Third Edition). Belmont, CA: Brooks/Cole.

Grof, S. (1983). East and West: Ancient Wisdom and Modern Science. *Journal of Transpersonal Psychology, 15*(1), 134-167.

Happold, F.C. (1963). *Mysticism.* Baltimore, MD: Penguin Books.

Hoover, T. (1980). *The Zen Experience: This Historical Evolution of Zen Through the Lives and Teachings of its Great Masters.* New York: New American Library.

Humphreys, C. (1968). *Concentration and Meditation*. Baltimore, MD: Penguin Books.

Hutton, M. (1993). How transpersonal psychotherapists differ from other practitioners: An empirical study. *Journal of Transpersonal Psychology, 26*(3), 139-174.

Leuger, L. & Sheikh, A. (1989). The four forces of psychotherapy. In A. Sheikh & S. Sheikh, (Eds.) *Eastern and Western Approaches to Healing: Ancient Wisdom & Modern Knowledge.* (pp. 197-236) New York: John Wiley.

Polster, I. (1966). Imprisoned in the present. *The Gestalt Journal, 8*(1), 5-22.

Ramaswami, S. & Sheikh, A. (1989). Buddhist psychology: Implications for healing. In A. Sheikh & S. Sheikh, *Eastern and Western Approaches to Healing: Ancient Wisdom & Modern Knowledge*. New York: John Wiley.

Rumi, J. (1995). *The Essential Rumi* [transated by C. Barks). San Francisco, CA: Harper.

Sheikh, A. & Sheikh, K. (1989). *Eastern and Western Approaches to Healing*. Toronto, ON: John Wiley & Sons.

Vanier, J. (1998). *On Being Human*. Toronto, ON: House of Anansi Press.

Vaughan, E. (1991). Spiritual issues in psychotherapy. *Journal of Transpersonal Psychology, 23*(2), 105-120.

Walsh, R. (1989). Asian psychotherapies. In R. Corsini & D. Wedding, (Eds.) *Current Psychotherapies* (4th Edition). Itasca, NY: F.E. Peacock.

Walsh, R. & Vaughan, F. (1993). On Transpersonal Definitions. *Journal of Transpersonal Psychology, 25*(2), 199-208.

Zajonc, R.B., Heingartner, A. & Herman, E.M. (1969). Social enhancement and impairment of performance in the cockroach. *Journal of Personality and Social Psychology, 13*, 83-92.

Chapter 27

Towards an Integrated Perspective: Restorative Justice, Cross-cultural Counselling and School Based Programming

Shannon A. Moore

Restorative Justice cannot be categorically defined; rather, it is a major philosophical movement and social construction in contemporary society (Clairmont, 2000). Philosophically, Restorative Justice processes are focused on accountability for one's actions, respect for all persons, cooperation, compassion, a focus on human relationships and community . These formative principles often compel individuals to have a degree of insight into their choices and self-reflection; as well as humility, an open heart and mind. Commitment to work towards changing social, economic and political injustices are also germane to restorative practices.

> *Whenever I am asked to explain Restorative Justice, or how it differs from the current criminal justice system, I am always torn between the simple and the complex. Restorative justice is simple yet it is complex. It is not a formula or a method but a process by which we view ourselves, others and the world around us. It is grounded in the spiritual being. Simply stated, it's how we choose to live our lives.…The restorative justice approach is positive and future oriented. It offers a process that empowers people to search for healing and constructive solutions, as there is a need for victims and offenders to focus on healing and restoring. It is not surprising that victims and offenders begin to explore issues of compassion, forgiveness and reconciliation when dialogue for healing begins (E. Evans cited in Restorative Justice and Dispute Resolution Unit, 2000, p. 7)*

Restorative Justice implies both process and outcome (Umbreit & Coates, 1999) and provides a lens through which we can understand interpersonal encounters as we transform conflicts, hurt and the impact of crime (Zehr, 1995). The most recognizable Restorative Justice movements include reparative parole, family group conferencing, circle sentencing and victim-offender mediation. Several principles are foundational for Restorative Justice and facilitate movement towards healing harm. The following are the principles and practices connecting the movements mentioned above:

1. Harm inflicted and crimes committed create hurt that is fundamentally the violation of a human being or human relationships, not merely an act of lawbreaking: it tears the social and community fabric.

2. The goal is to repair the harm done and restore relationships among individuals and community.

3. Those who are the victims of hurt or crime must have free choice to participate in a restorative process.

4. Those who are the perpetrators of hurt or crime must have the opportunity to accept responsibility for their crimes, the harm they have caused and choose to participate in a restorative process.

5. Victims must be of central concern in all Restorative Justice processes (adapted from Umbreit and Coates, 1999).

It is imperative that victims remain at the centre of Restorative Justice. Engagement and participation in Restorative Justice initiatives also must be non-coercive and completely voluntary for all involved. The process can be simple or complex and may include information, dialogue between impacted parties, mutual resolution of conflict between victim and offender, restitution, reduction of fear, heightened sense of safety, acceptance of responsibility and/or renewal of hope (Van Ness & Heetderks Strong, 1997).

Historical Roots of Restorative Justice

Restorative Justice is not a 'new wave' movement: it is a return to traditional Western and non-Western patterns of coping with conflict and crime that have been present throughout human history (Llewllyn & Howse, 1999). The retributive system that dominates our Western judicial system has in fact only governed our understanding of crime and justice for a few centuries. Howard Zehr (1995) contrasts the retributive and restorative system as follows:

> *[In the retributive system] crime is a violation of the state, defined by lawbreaking and guilt. Justice determines blame and administers pain in a contest between the offender and the state directed by systematic rules... [In contrast, for Restorative Justice] crime is a violation of people and relationships. It creates obligations to make things right. Justice involves the victim, the offender and the community in a search for solutions which promote repair, reconciliation and reassurance (p. 181).*

The period of justice that predates our current retributive system has been described as an era of Community Justice (1995) and reflects customary or indigenous approaches to justice (Van Ness & Heetderks Strong, 1997). Analogies between a community justice process of dispute resolution and traditional healing practices have been made. For example, traditionally, doctors and healers were charged with keeping the human body in healthy balance and law was to keep the social body in good health by bringing relationships back into balance (Llewellyn & Howse, 1999). Survival of the community at large was dependent on the effectiveness of both of these processes. In the contemporary sense, Restorative Justice emerged from several earlier movements that contributed to its theory over the past three decades. These include the Informal Justice Movement; Restitution; the Victims' Movement; Reconciliation and Conferencing; and the Social Justice Movement.

Informal Justice

Legal anthropologists distinguished between informal and formal justice movements, since virtually all societies facilitate both these forms of proceedings. During the 1970s the Western formal legal system was criticized for its legitimacy, which in turn created the possibility of a stronger role for the informal legal structures. These emphasized increased participation, increased access, deprofessionalization, deregulation and the minimization of stigmatization and coercion. In particular, North American Native views of justice, African Customary Law and approaches found in the Pacific Islands have provided rich insights for Western informal and alternative justice processes (N. Christie, personal communication, October 27, 2000; Van Ness & Heetderks Strong, 1997).

Restitution.

The restitution movement emerged from the dawning awareness in the 1960s that compensating victims for the impact of crime was sensible. The rationale for this process of restitution include the following:

1. The rediscovery of the victim as the party harmed by criminal behavior;

2. The search for alternatives to more restrictive or intrusive sanctions such as imprisonment;

3. The expected rehabilitative value of paying the victim for the offender;

4. The relative ease of implementation; and,

5. The anticipated reduction in vengeful and retributive sanctions that would come when the public observed the offender actively repairing the harm done (Van Ness & Heetderks Strong, 1997, p. 18).

The rights of the victim are of central concern in restorative justice processes; this is in sharp contrast to justice motivated solely by the examination of the offenders' behavior.

The Victims' Movement

The 'rediscovery of the victim' and the establishment of a centralized role for victims rights was the result of accumulated effort from several individuals and groups. This movement continues to be motivated by the following tenets:

1. Increasing services to victims in the aftermath of crime;

2. Increasing the likelihood of financial reimbursement for the harm done; and,

3. Expanding victims' opportunities to intervene during the course of the criminal justice process (Van Ness & Heetderks Strong, 1997, p. 20).

At best, the current formal Western system has been described as alienating to victims. In contrast, the victims' movement demands that the complexities of victimization and the process of traumatization be accounted for and ultimately compensated for by our judicial processes.

Reconciliation and Conferencing

Reconciliation and Conferencing is composed of two major activities: 1) victim-offender mediation and 2) a decision for a future action that will help bring restitution and heal the harm done (Van Ness & Heetderks Strong, 1997). Mark Umbreit has written extensively on the subject of victim-offender mediation as a way to improve the current delivery of justice in North America. For the past three decades, victim-offender mediation has been active in North America and has spread to South Africa, England, Germany and other European countries. Victim-offender mediation has moved from the margins to find a place in mainstream Western justice, clearly indicating international interest in Restorative Justice (Umbreit, Coates & Warner Roberts, 2000).

Critical social theorists Howard Zehr and Ron Claasen have also contributed to the establishment of victim-offender mediation as an integral part of conflict resolution and judicial proceedings in North America. The roots of Zehr and Claasen's practice emerge from their participation in the Mennonite faith. Both Zehr and Claasen stress the importance of community-driven and funded victim-offender mediation programs in contrast to programs funded by the criminal justice system (Claasen, 1996; Van Ness & Heetderks Strong, 1997; Zehr, 1995). In 1989 New Zealand and Australia introduced another branch of Victim-Offender Mediation called Family Group Conferencing (Morris & Maxwell, 1998). This form of conferencing is founded on Maori traditional practices and is characterized by the key principles found in Restorative Justice. What differentiates Family Group Conferencing from Victim-Offender Mediation is essentially the number of parties involved in the conflict resolution process. In Family Group Conferencing, organizers strive to include all persons impacted by crime in the community, rather than solely focussing on primary victims (Van Ness & Heetderks Strong, 1997).

Social Justice

Together, members of a variety of religious communities and supporters of the feminist movement have shared a common cause: to critique and pressure the retributive judicial system to adopt fundamental changes. During the past four decades, Quakers advocated for significantly reduced use of prisons and for the complete abolition of the prison system. Largely, this standpoint is based on the conviction that criminal justice simply cannot be achieved in an unjust society, nor can it be manifest in judicial and prison systems overrun with abuse and human rights violations (R. Morris, personal communication, October 26, 2000; Van Ness & Heetderks Strong, 1997). Other researchers have argued that the current model of retributive justice emerged from the Medieval Christian view of sin and punishment, although this particular viewpoint of Christianity is narrowly framed in place and time. Interpretations of Christian doctrine also proclaim values of relationship, restoration, forgiveness, reconciliation and hope. These latter characteristics are the same principles that form the foundation of Restorative Justice and are promoted by other faith communities, including the Mennonites and Quakers (Hadley, in press; Van Ness & Heetderks Strong, 1997).

Likewise, feminist theory asserts "that all people have equal value as human beings, that harmony and felicity are more important than power and possession and that the personal is political" (M. Kay Harris cited in Van Ness & Heetderks Strong, 1997, pp. 23-24). These assertions are fundamentally opposed to the formal retributive judicial system that is founded on principles of power, control and punishment. In this way feminist theorists continue to be vocal opponents to the dominant Western judicial system.

Cross-Cultural Counselling Implications

All interpersonal exchanges, particularly in the context of helping professions, are potentially cross-cultural in nature. These boundaries where people meet are filled with tensions among values, beliefs, worldviews and other cultural and personal artifacts – including aspects of Being and consciousness. All of us are challenged to navigate through this diversity with knowledge of self and openness to others. It is also important that we have an awareness of our own cultural heritage at the same time as being open to the perspectives of others: centered in a personal sense of truth yet open to other ways of knowing. In this way I understand culture as a shared reservoir of knowledge that is both tacitly and overtly known while informing multiple aspects of being. Cross-cultural counselling is complex as a result of the multiple dimensions of self and environment that influence interpersonal exchanges. The following include principles that may assist counsellors to navigate through cross-cultural exchanges and the complexities of diversity:

1. Self-awareness and self-knowledge: including understanding about one's own values, beliefs, worldviews and prejudices.

2. Understanding the basic worldview and value system of client's culture: suspend disbelief and listen without judgment.

3. Listen to the client's history, belief system and spirituality.

4. Exude respect, genuineness, availability, congruence and humility.

5. Focus on how you are similar as well as different.

6. Create psychological space for the client's individuality and diversity.

7. Allowing the client to lead/celebrate mutuality experiences of meaning and a sense of spirituality (Matheson, 1996; Pedersen, Draguns, Lonner & Trimble, 1996).

With the above points in as a template, it becomes possible to facilitate sensitive and effective cross-cultural counselling practice in any context. The next section will specifically integrate principles of cross-cultural counselling within the context of Restorative Justice practice.

Cross-Cultural Restorative Justice Processes and School Based Interventions

It is vital that persons involved with Restorative Justice practices have awareness of the impact of divergent cross-cultural perspectives on conflict resolution as well as having the self-knowledge to sensitively negotiate diversity (Umbriet & Coates, 1999). This is important in any context and may enhance facilitation and mediation within schools where beyond traditional bounds of geographic culture, the world of children and youth today is often viscerally different than the experiences of adult facilitators and school administrators. The following are key aspects of cross-cultural counselling important to consider in Restorative Justice within school programming (adapted from, Minister Public Works and Government Services Canada, 1998; Pedersen, Draguns, Lonner & Trimble, 1996; Sue & Sue, 1990; Umbreit & Coates, 1999):

Proximity:

Distance between victims, offenders and other persons engaged in Restorative Justice processes.

Degree of face to face interactions.

Sitting side by side without desks or other pieces of furniture between individuals.

Sitting in a circle demonstrating equality between persons present.

Body Movements:

It is often suggested that the facilitator of restorative justice process retain a neutral stance so that resolution is negotiated between those impacted by whatever harm was committed.

It is important to be conscious of eye contact, gestures of approval or disapproval such as smiling or frowning.

Also, Offenders may not show remorse through demonstrations of emotions such as tears.

Lack of eye-contact on behalf of offender or victim does not necessarily indicate avoidance of an issue, lack of attentiveness, submissiveness, guilt or shame.

Paralanguage:

Be conscious of forms of vocal cues such as hesitations, inflections, silences, intonation, cadence and projection of one's voice.

It is importance for the Restorative Justice facilitator to become comfortable with silence so that the emotive aspects of the Restorative Justice process may have space to manifest.

Density of Language:

Persons from differing cultural backgrounds vary in the verbal delivery of ideas.

Some people are concise and sparse with their verbiage, which should not necessarily be taken as a terse or uninterested tone.

Others may use many words to express ideas: "The poetry of the story may be more important than the content of the story and may actually be the point of the story" (Umbreit & Coates, 1999, p. 46).

The style of communication between people may range from low-key indirect to objective and task oriented.

Values and Ideology:

It is essential that one is aware of differences in cross-cultural ideologies of collectivism and individualism as well as religious and faith perspectives, as these will likely impact the process of conflict resolution and individuals' definitions of justice.

This difference in ideology may also impact the identification of primary and secondary victims in facilitation processes.

Across Canada and throughout British Columbia, Restorative Justice is becoming increasing acknowledged as an important alternative to traditional systems of discipline within our schools. In Greater Victoria, community-based initiatives have emerged in conjunction with several community partners including school districts, Royal Canadian Mounted Police and the Ministry of the Attorney General. Individual elementary, middle and secondary school, have also begun to explore the use of Restorative Justice initiatives founded on the core principles discussed above. The following describes such a program in Greater Vancouver, Canada:

> *Students at the Canada Way education centre, a last-chance alternative school for kids with problems, have experienced what is know as restorative justice, a process that has been used in criminal matters for many years but is just now being tested by BC schools anxious to tame schoolyard bullying and violence. While it's too early to predict its overall success, it's not too early for rave reviews. Restorative justice, also called transformative justice, aims to heal relationships rather than punish wrongdoers by bringing feuding parties together to talk about*

their dispute. Sometimes that meeting is expanded into a "conference" of everyone affected by the row – which in schools could include a sizeable group of students, participants and bystanders, teachers, patents and support staff. They come on equal footing – as people touched by a conflict – not as authority figures ready to make judgments about who is right and who is wrong. They talk about what they believe happened, how it affected them and what might be done to prevent it from occurring again. It's an emotional process that proponents say is much more of a deterrent than traditional punishments such as suspension or expulsion (Steffenhagen, 2001).

Victims must be at the centre of any Restorative Justice initiative within a context of accountability, respect, safety and honesty on behalf of all. These principles may be integrated within a school system to reduce and prevent conflicts, ultimately fostering an atmosphere of non-violence. In this way, detentions and suspensions administered by school officials may be avoided as accountability and responsibility is restored to students. Students are supported to resolve their own conflicts without escalating violence and bullying. The following description of a school based Restorative Justice program was adapted from the work of Vincent Stancato (2000) of the Community Justice Branch of the Ministry of the Attorney General:

What is a School Based Restorative Justice?

Bringing together the affected community – those most directly involved in the incident or pattern of behavior that has caused harm within the school community.

Provides an opportunity for the affected community to gain insight into the extent of harm caused to themselves, others and the broader school community.

Provides an opportunity to determine how to best repair the harm, learn from the experience and prevent further harmful behavior.

Who participates?

Victim(s) of the harm caused

Support people for the victim(s), e.g., family, friends and/or mentors

Perpetrator(s) of the harm caused

Support people for the perpetrator(s), e.g., family, friends and/or mentors

Facilitator for the Restorative Justice process

Anyone else involved or investigating the incident

Reflections

It is imperative that all parties participate as volunteers and offenders of hurt express accountability for the harm done prior to engagement in restorative processes. Through